Organizations

seventh edition

Organizations

Structures, Processes, and Outcomes

Richard H. Hall

Distinguished Service Professor
University at Albany
State University of New York

Prentice Hall, Upper Saddle River, New Jersey 07458

Library of Congress Cataloging-in-Publication Data

Hall, Richard H., (date)
   Organizations : structures, processes, and outcomes / Richard H.
Hall, — 7th ed.
    p.   cm.
   Includes bibliographical references and indexes.
   ISBN 0-13-903394-7
   1. Organizational sociology. 2. Organizational change.
  I. Title.
HM131.H237 1998
302.3'5—DC21   98-16393
                               CIP

Editorial director: Charlyce Jones Owen
Editor in chief: Nancy Roberts
Acquisitions editor: John Chillingworth
Managing editor: Sharon Chambliss
Project manager: Merrill Peterson
Prepress and manufacturing buyer: Mary Ann Gloriande
Marketing manager: Christopher DeJohn
Cover art director: Jayne Conte

This book was set in 10.5/12 Times Roman by
Pub-Set, Inc., and was printed and bound by Courier
Companies, Inc. The cover was printed by
Phoenix Color Corp.

Printed in the United States of America

10 9 8 7 6 5 4 3 2 1

ISBN 0-13-903394-7

PRENTICE-HALL INTERNATIONAL (UK) LIMITED, *London*
PRENTICE-HALL OF AUSTRALIA PTY. LIMITED, *Sydney*
PRENTICE-HALL CANADA INC., *Toronto*
PRENTICE-HALL HISPANOAMERICANA, S.A., *Mexico*
PRENTICE-HALL OF INDIA PRIVATE LIMITED, *New Delhi*
PRENTICE-HALL OF JAPAN, INC., *Tokyo*
SIMON & SCHUSTER ASIA PTE. LTD., *Singapore*
EDITORA PRENTICE-HALL DO BRASIL, LTDA., *Rio de Janeiro*

for Sherry

Contents

Preface

This seventh edition of *Organizations: Structures, Processes, and Outcomes* contains some important differences from previous versions of the book. The most important difference is that I have tried to link the entire book to the idea of organizational effectiveness. After all, that is why we have all the organizations that we have. We do not form organizations to be ineffective. No, we want them to succeed at whatever it is they are doing. Thus, organizational structures are modified, power and leadership are exercised, decisions are made, and linkages to environments are maintained, all in the name of effectiveness.

This linkage to effectiveness is not meant to be simplistic. Indeed, the idea that contradictions and paradoxes are an essential part of all but the smallest organizations is explicitly addressed throughout the book. At the same time, it is mindless, in my opinion, to treat organizations as neutral entities. They have positive and negative outcomes, as I have repeatedly stressed.

Organizations can also do things that are silly and even stupid—everyone can supply his or her own examples here—but in some people's minds the actions have a purpose. I thus base the arguments on a loosely rational model, and do so without shame.

This edition also contains some reorganization of materials. The most important reorganization is the combination of the chapters on organizational environments and interorganizational relationships. Several recent articles, which are noted in the text of the book, have emphasized that interorganizational relationships are the mechanisms by which "the environment" has an impact on organizations. All of the previous writing on organizational environments, including my own work, has missed this rather obvious point.

Another small reorganization is the combination of the chapters on power and the outcomes of power. This is a small change that was probably overdue.

Reviewers of earlier editions of this book have complained about the long quotations found in some chapters. I have tried to remedy this wherever possible. I have also tried to make all of the writing clearer and simpler, without "dumbing down" the complex ideas that are necessary in understanding organizations. I wish to thank the reviewers of this edition for their helpful comments: Cheryl Childers, Washburn University; John Mitrano, Central Connecticut State University; Harry Perlstadt, Michigan State University; and Lisa Troyer, University of Iowa.

Finally, I have tried to listen to my own undergraduate and graduate students who have used this book. They have not been shy in pointing out confusing sections. Undoubtedly, some of these remain.

I give my thanks to Sharon Chambliss of Prentice Hall for her continuing support and help. And, of course, another Sharon—my Sherry—gives continuing love and support.

chapter 1

The Outcomes
of Organizations

WHY STUDY ORGANIZATIONS?

There are two answers to this question. The first answer is obvious: Organizations are a dominant component of contemporary society. They surround us. We are born in them and usually die in them. Our life space in between is filled with them. They are just about impossible to escape. They are as inevitable as death and taxes.

A simple exercise will illustrate the pervasiveness of organizations in our lives. Think of all the activities that we engage in during a day. Which, if any, are not influenced by an organization in one way or another? If you are reading this book by yourself, it may seem to be an individual matter; however, the book was prepared and published by an organization—Prentice-Hall, Inc.—and you are reading probably because of some kind of organizational demand from your college or university. I wrote the book in an organizational context—the University at Albany. Our tastes in food and drink (and the amounts we consume) are shaped by marketing organizations. The food and drinks themselves are processed and distributed by organizations. The products we come into contact with, such as automobiles and desks, are made in organizational settings. The services we rely upon, such as police, banking, and insurance, are clearly organizational. We work in organizations. Even our leisure activities typically take place in some sort of organizational setting. My favorite leisure activity is alpine skiing. I cannot imagine how I could pursue this sport without a "ski area," which, after all, is just another organization.

The great social transformations in history have been essentially organizationally based. The rise of the Roman Empire, the spread of Christianity, and the growth and development of, and the changes in, capitalism and socialism have been accomplished through organizations. Toxic-waste disposal, nuclear energy, terrorism, unemployment, abortion, and all the issues facing contemporary society cannot be understood without a consideration and an understanding of their organizational contexts.

These simple examples were intended to suggest that the careful analysis of organizations is a serious and important matter. It is not just an academic exercise. Organizations are continually analyzed from a variety of perspectives. The stock market, for example, is an ongoing organizational analysis. Investors constantly assess how business firms are doing and buy and sell stocks accordingly. The major investment decisions are actually made by other organizations. Like other forms of organizational analysis, stock market analysis is not an exact science.

If we have the opportunity to choose between potential employers, we are making an organizational analysis—we are attempting to decide which would be a better place to work. To a surprising extent, the election of the president of the United States is an assessment of an organization. A large organization has handled the campaign, and the voters estimate what kind of organization the individual will bring to office.

Organizational analysis also occurs at other levels. The job of organizational management is to assess the state of the organization. Labor unions, themselves organizations, analyze the operations of the companies with which they have contracts. Customers assess the quality of stores and their merchandise. A car buyer wants to be sure that the manufacturer has a reputation for producing high-quality cars and is likely to be in business for a long time, and that the dealer can handle any problems that might arise. The selection of an organization such as a health provider is of even greater concern to each client.

Organizations have the capacity to do great good or great evil. Most are somewhere in between, and that brings us to the *second* answer to our opening question: We study organizations because organizations have outcomes. They are not benign objects. They can spread hate but also save lives and maybe souls. They can wage war but also bring peace. These outcomes can be intentional or unintentional, recognized or not recognized (Merton, 1957). They can also be surprising. For example, in states that have a large sector of private-school organizations, students in public-school organizations perform better than those in states with smaller private-school populations. The reason is that public schools are provided with more resources (Arum, 1996). The outcome of the presence of private schools is *not* harm for public schools. In this first chapter we will analyze the outcomes of organizations for individuals, for categories of individuals, for communities, and for society.

Before we examine these outcomes, however, it is important to note that *not everything* is organizational. My feelings and emotions are my own, even though they are in part shaped by my organizational experiences. My relationships with my wife and children are also not organizational. This last point becomes a little complicated, however, when I consider that my wife and I do attend university events together, do attend church together, do work at the same ski area, and share other facets of our lives that are shaped by organizations.

There are a number of paradoxes about the organizations that shape our lives. For example, the "typical U.S. employee works in an establishment with 599 full-time workers . . . and 72 part-time workers . . ." (Marsden, Cook, and Knoke, 1996: p. 49). At the same time, almost two-thirds of the business firms in the United States have fewer than 5 employees (*Dun's Census of American Business*, 1995; p. 26). The reason for this paradox is that although most business firms are small, organizations in the not-for-profit and public sectors are larger (Marsden et al., 1996: p. 50).

We will deal with the issue of organizational size more fully in Chapter 4, but two points regarding size are important here. First, goods and services once supplied by solo practitioners or small organizations are increasingly being delivered by large organizations, which are often branches of still-larger organizations (Danet, 1981: p. 382). For example, Prentice-Hall, Inc., the publisher of this book, is a subsidiary of Simon & Schuster, which in turn is part of Paramount Communications, which is owned by Viacom, Inc.

Second, this tendency toward consolidation and growth is countered by the fact that many organizations have joined the downsizing movement. It may be the case that the actual heart of the American economy is shifting from large firms to smaller ones (Ritzer, 1989). Ritzer reports that the large Fortune 500 companies laid off over 3 million workers between 1980 and 1987. During the same period, firms with fewer than 100 employees created 12 million new jobs. When these small organizations are successful, of course, there is a strong tendency for them to become larger and larger through growth or merger.

Small organizations are vitally important as incubators of ideas. They have also been identified as vitally important in developing countries in the form of the "informal economy" or "microenterprises" (Liedholm and Mead, 1993; Rakowski, 1994).

There is another interesting twist here. There are some organizations that have many employees but whose operations seem to be very small. These are "direct selling" or "multilevel" organizations such as Amway, Tupperware, and Mary Kay Cosmetics (Biggart, 1989; Johnston and Snizek, 1991). One insurance company, for example, has a sales force of 155,000 agents (Biggart, p. 117), but its home office is small and each agent acts independently.

WHY DO WE HAVE ORGANIZATIONS?

The answer here is simple: to get things done. We have organizations to do things that individuals cannot do by themselves. I will use a very simple personal example to illustrate this point. One of the organizations that I belong to is the National Ski Patrol. This organization did not exist until alpine skiing began to become popular in the United States. The founder of the National Ski Patrol, Minnie Dole, came upon an injured skier in Vermont and couldn't help the injured person by himself. He started the organization, which is now found at almost every alpine and nordic ski area in the United States.

This same process takes place when people want to make a profit, save souls, have fun, or fight drunk driving. Organizations are the answer. Economists such as Oliver Williamson (1975, 1985) have developed more sophisticated and complicated models to explain why we have organizations, but this simpler model works just as well.

Although this simple model does work well, the analysis of organizations is not simple. We now turn to a complicated set of matters—the *outcomes* of organizations. Sociologists and others have had a long-standing interest in and concern about the outcomes or impacts of organizations (Stern and Barley, 1996; Scott, 1996; Blau, 1996). We will begin our analysis of outcomes by considering the impacts of organizations on individuals.

ORGANIZATIONS AND THE INDIVIDUAL

Most analyses of the impact of organizations on individuals focus on work organizations. That is appropriate, of course, since work organizations take up so much of individuals' lives. At the same time, participation in voluntary organizations provides individuals with all kinds of possibilities for growth and development. Having noted this, we will focus here primarily on organizations in which people work. Although some analysts foresee an "end of work" (Rifkin, 1995), the end of work and work organizations has not yet taken place. We will, therefore, proceed as usual, with the awareness that work organizations may well decline in the future.

Many analyses have examined how individuals react to their lives as employees of organizations (Terkel, 1974; Rosow, 1974; Aronowitz, 1973; *Work in America,* 1973; Hall, 1994). These analyses agree that work that is highly routinized, repetitive, and dull is highly alienating for the individual. There is no evidence, of course, that work in preorganizational societies was not alienating. Subsistence farming or hunting and gathering is hardly enlightening. Romanticized imageries of preorganizational systems forget that people starved to death and froze to death. Some people were slaves. Early industrialization, with its exceedingly low pay, child labor, and absence of worker protection, was also alienating but in a truer Marxian sense than the social-psychological alienation felt by today's worker in a routine job.

The studies of individual reactions to work also reveal that work which provides challenge, potential for advancement, and the use of creative or expressive capabilities is enjoyable and even enlightening. People's reactions to their work result from the individuals' own expectations and the characteristics of the employing organization (Lorsch and Morse, 1974). Neither organizations nor individuals can be easily changed to yield consistent positive reactions.

There is another side to working in organizations. In an important study, Kohn (1971) found small but consistent tendencies for people who work in more bureaucratized organizations to be more intellectually flexible, more open to new experiences, and more self-directed than those working in non-bureaucratized settings. People's occupational conditions both affect and are affected by their psychological functioning (Kohn and Schooler, 1978, 1982). In regard to work in a bureaucratized setting, Kohn attributes the findings to the fact that bureaucratized organizations require their workforce to be better educated and also provide more job protection, higher salary, and more complex work. The implication of these studies is that work in organizations is not necessarily deadening to the individual. The work of a secretary or an executive can be challenging and have potential for advancement in one organization but not in another. Some jobs have a strong potential for idiosyncratic behavior, and others do not (Miner, 1987). Here again, organizational characteristics are critical variables as they interact with those of the individual.

Thus far, the discussion of individuals in organizations has been based on studies of full-time, permanent workers. There is a growing trend toward part-time and nonpermanent work. In 1988, for example, one-fourth of all U.S. workers were nonpermanent or part-time workers (Davis-Blake and Uzzi, 1993)—that is, temporary workers, leased workers, or independent contractors. Another growing trend is home-based work, or telecommuting, in which people work from their homes and use electronic communications to link with their employers (Lozano, 1989). Clerical work can be done this way, as can the work of some professionals, such as professors. Home workers see themselves as having more freedom than their office-bound counterparts. In some cases, home work entails a loss of employee benefits, so it cannot be seen as suitable for everyone.

People not only work in organizations but also have extensive contacts with them as customers or clients. The growth of consumer and client-advocacy organizations is testimony to the fact that those who come to organizations for products or services are not totally satisfied with what they receive. Advocacy organizations, of course, are every bit as much organizations as the ones they are advocating against.

A survey of people's reactions to their contacts with government agencies in the areas of employment, job training, workmen's compensation, unemployment compensation, welfare services, hospital and medical services, and retirement services found that the majority of the clients interviewed were satisfied with the service and treatment they received (Katz et al., 1975). Thus, widespread discontent with the "system" in this regard appears to be a myth, because common stereotypes about encounters with government bureaucracies are contradicted by the data. Nevertheless, the fact that most people are satisfied does not mean that the organizations are operating as effectively as possible. Katz and her colleagues note:

> A majority of satisfied clients may leave a sizable minority dissatisfied. Even a 75 percent level of satisfaction may be low for some programs in which 90 percent or higher is desirable and feasible. In a population of 200 million, small percentages are large numbers. (p. 115)

In a related study of the same phenomenon, this time among juveniles who have had contact with the juvenile justice system, Giordano (1974) found "something less than a seething rage against the professionals who staff the juvenile justice system." Apparently, even in this population, which is thought to have very negative encounters with the establishment, organizations are not viewed with the distaste that is generally believed to be present.

An element in the Giordano research is worth noting: If a client feels close to an individual in an organization, his or her interpretation of the total organization appears to be affected. Individuals coming to an organization do so as individuals. The person in the organization may or may not be able to respond in a personal way. Many organizations prescribe the manner in which their employees are to respond to outsiders. Even if the prescribed manner is warm and friendly, as is the case for airline cabin attendants, it is still an organizational prescription (see Hochschild, 1983). In the case of the professional staffs with which Giordano dealt, and which formed the bulk of the services studied by Katz et al. (1975), the professional is granted some latitude in interpersonal interactions. Such latitude is less likely at the clerical or retail sales level, where many individual contacts with organizations are made.

The analysis of individuals in organizations must also consider economic factors. Sociologists have a tendency to ignore the economic, but it is a mistake to do so. Focusing on factors such as morale and satisfaction deflects attention from the fact that economic factors are a major consideration for both management and workers. Hage (1980) notes that "on the one hand managerial elites and owners of capital want to drive costs down by means of policies of low wages and uniform tasks. On the other hand workers want to increase their standard of living and have interesting work. There is an inherent conflict of interest between these two perspectives" (p. 7). Hage goes on to suggest that the inherent conflict can be handled by either fighting or quitting, as suggested by Hirschman (1972). When workers neither fight nor quit, they may neglect their work (Withey and Cooper, 1989). People have an obvious economic stake in the organizations in which they work. Organizations affect the economic well-being of workers and hence also their dependents.

Organizations are the context in which people work. The performances of individuals are shaped by that context. For example, the productivity of scientists is strongly affected by their work context (Long and McGinnis, 1981; Allison and Long, 1990). These studies find that departments encourage scientific productivity through motivation, intellectual stimulation, and good facilities. If the expectations are that an individual be highly productive, behavior tends to conform to those expectations.

The most important outcome of organizations for individuals is the placement or attainment of individuals within the social stratification system. In the 1980s there was a dramatic realization that organizations are key actors in stratification. The division of labor among jobs (the internal labor market) within an organization and differentiation among organizations result in a situation in which unequal opportunities and rewards are attached to organizational positions. These are present before the arrival of any particular incumbent. Organizations also have procedures for filling their positions. Education, skill, or experience of varying levels and intensities are specified in advance. Organizations then match workers with jobs. Organizations are thus the process by which stratification is accomplished (Baron, 1984; Stolzenberg, 1978; Baron and Bielby, 1980; Kalleberg, 1983; and Pfeffer and Cohen, 1984: Kalleberg and Van Buren, 1996). This is a dynamic process. When organizations are growing, there are more promotional opportunities (Rosenbaum, 1979). When organizations are in a decline, the opportunity structure also is diminished.

CATEGORIES OF INDIVIDUALS

The topic of this section is probably best captured by the phrase "the glass ceiling," through which it is commonly believed that women can't pass. It is also captured in a conversation I had with an acquaintance who worked for a major office-equipment firm who told me that there was an informal (and probably illegal) company policy not to promote people who were older than 45. Categories of individuals are based on gender, age, race, religion, and ethnicity.

Organizations can have and have had *policies* regarding hiring and promotion aimed at specific categories of individuals. For example, "No Irish Need Apply" was frequently seen on signs outside some business firms at the height of Irish immigration to the United States.

The Civil Rights legislation of the 1960s has had an ongoing impact on organizational policies regarding categories of individuals. At the same time, categories of individuals still are differentially affected by the organizations in which they work (and study).

The situation at the end of the twentieth century is one of change. Economic restructuring is happening rapidly; manufacturing work is declining and service work is increasing. This will encourage the growth of jobs in which women and minority group members are concentrated (Reskin and Padevic, 1994: p. 166). For example, nurse's aides and orderlies and food-counter and related workers are job categories that will increase, as will the categories of registered nurses and managers and administrators. These job categories are differentially filled by women and minority group members. This is *not* an organizational outcome, except that organizations do seek out the least expensive labor that they can find, at least at lower organizational levels. At the same time, organizational hiring practices will maintain pay and promotion differentials between categories of individuals.

Another important trend that has been documented is skill upgrading and simultaneous deskilling (Reskin and Padevic, 1994: pp. 167–68). Organizational policies are important here in that work with computers can be reduced to data entry or upgraded to autonomous decision making.

In a similar manner, the contingent workforce of temporary workers, part-time workers, and independent contractors is "largely driven by employer needs, not workers' choices" (Reskin and Padevic, 1994: p. 169). Contingent workers typically receive lower pay and benefits than full-time workers and, again, the impact of this shift affects categories of individuals differentially.

A final trend noted by Reskin and Padevic is the very evident increasing diversity of the labor force. Immigration to the United States, particularly from Asia and Latin America, is fueling this diversity.

The basis of discrimination in hiring is moving away from gender and minority group membership and is shifting to educational achievements on the part of individuals. Those without educational credentials will find work in the lower-paying part of the labor force. Since there is differential access to and success in educational achievement among racial, religious, and ethnic groups, differential distributions on those bases will remain.

Reskin and Padevic (1994) are pessimistic about changes in promotional opportunities for women and minority group members in the short run, since many in these categories are exactly the ones being forced into the contingent labor force because of downsizing (p. 173). At the same time, in the longer run, employing organizations may select newly trained graduates on the basis of their credentials over gender or minority group status (Acker, 1992).

It is difficult to project what will happen in regard to the age category. There will soon be a dramatic age "bulge" as the large number of "baby boomers," born after World War II, move into late middle age. Organizational policy is yet to be developed for this group.

ORGANIZATIONS AND THE COMMUNITY

Organizations are clearly not benign in their outcomes for individuals and categories of individuals. The same is true for the communities or localities in which they operate. A college or a university can be the dominant institution in the town or city in which it is located. One only has to think of Bloomington, Indiana; Ann Arbor, Michigan; and Durham, North Carolina, the homes of large universities, or of Granville, Ohio (the home of my alma mater, Denison University), a small college town, to see this point. The Mayo Clinic dominates Rochester, Minnesota. General Electric once dominated Schenectady, New York.

In the Schenectady case, the outcome can be seen dramatically. When General Electric was running its Schenectady operations at full employment, the city prospered. As G.E. changed its product mix and downsized its Schenectady operations, the city slid downhill. The downsizing of G.E. has taken retail stores, hotels, restaurants, and a whole series of other small businesses with it.

This community impact can also be seen clearly in a study reported by Seiler and Summers (1979). They examined the consequences of a large steel manufacturing firm's decision to locate a major new plant in a small town in the middle western United States. This company did not want to be identified in the community power structure as such, but their actions clearly had a major impact on the community.

The steel company, Jones and Laughlin, engaged in unilateral actions, such as buying land for their plant through ghost buyers and hiring workers from surrounding counties rather than in the home county. The company also co-opted the local community leaders by using key bankers and lawyers as their local representatives. No Jones and Laughlin personnel were active in the community, but their operatives were. The company also directly intervened in plans for a new high school in the community, forcing the building of a less expensive and more practical school, thus reducing their tax liability.

Seiler and Summers do not suggest that all the results of the company's actions were bad for the local community. Indeed, some were recognized as positive. The important point is that this organization had a direct and dramatic impact on the local community. The impact of a single powerful organization can thus be great.

Most communities have more than a single dominant organization but that does not dilute the power of organizations in the community. Local power structures reflect interorganizational competition and thus the interests of powerful organizational actors (Perrucci and Pilisuk, 1970; Galaskiewicz, 1979). Interorganizational relationships, which will be considered in detail in Chapter 10, can have both positive and negative consequences for a community. For example, Minneapolis, Minnesota, is blessed with an extraordinarily high level of corporate philanthropy (Crittenden, 1978). Much of this is based on the interorganizational linkages among the business firms there. Most other cities are less fortunate. Some, such as Schenectady, have been literally destroyed as businesses move to other areas. Still others receive virtually nothing from their organizational inhabitants. In many ways, communities can be viewed as networks of interorganizational linkages (Galaskiewicz and Krohn, 1984).

There is a more subtle way in which organizations influence the communities in which they are located. One study found that companies vary in the degree to which they encourage their middle managers to participate in community affairs (Christenson et al., 1988). If communities were filled with organizations that encourage such participation, local life would be enriched. This same study also found that those middle managers who did get involved in community life were less likely to opt for transfers to other communities.

SOCIETAL OUTCOMES

If organizations have important outcomes for individuals and communities, it is obvious that they also have important outcomes for the wider society or environment in which they are embedded. At the very outset, it must be recognized that there is a *reciprocal* relationship between organizations and their environments. Indeed, the dominant contemporary theories regarding organizations stress the central role of environments for the operations of organizations. As we will see in the chapters that follow, the environments of organizations are viewed as a major determinant of the structure and processes of organizations. In this section I am going to turn this line of reasoning around and consider the impacts of organizations on their environment. The analysis will begin with a consideration of some specific organizational impacts and then move into more broadly based conceptualizations.

Some Specific Organizational Impacts

Organizations serve the interests of individuals or groups. These controlling interests shape the directions that organizations take, and this in turn can have an impact on the wider society. Consider the Roman Empire as an organization. The Roman administrative organization was controlled by the ruling class, whose orientation was to dominate the masses (Antonio, 1979). The emphasis on domination led to a decline in the production of goods and services and "preserved, and even intensified, conditions which contributed to the erosion and eventual destruction of the socio-economic substructure of the bureaucracy" (Antonio, p. 906). Short-term success thus contributed to long-term failure—a theme to which we will return later.

The major point of the Antonio study is that the administrative bureaucracy serves the interest of the ruling elite. This has been a point of contention for organizational analysts for some time. Some analysts believe that ownership has become diffused and that control is now in the hands of corporate managers, not specific owners, with boards of directors serving as tools of management rather than of owners and stockholders (Berle and Means, 1932).

This point of view has been severely challenged on several grounds. First, there is evidence that families such as the Mellons of Pittsburgh, who had controlling interests in Gulf Oil, Alcoa, Koppers Company, and Carborundum Company in the manufacturing sector, also had controlling interests in the First Boston Corporation, the General Reinsurance Corporation, and the Mellon National Bank and Trust Company in the financial sector (Zeitlin, 1974). The Mellon National Bank, in turn, owned almost 7 percent of Jones and Laughlin Steel. The Rockefeller family had similar points of linkage among financial institutions and insurance companies. Patterns of interlock like these have also been found outside the United States. Although there is no direct evidence that such family control has direct economic implications, family ownership has the potential for organizational control, rather than control by organizational management or diffused stockholders (Aldrich, 1979).

There is also a remarkable degree of interlock among the boards of directors of corporations. This means that members of the board of directors of one corporation are likely to serve on the boards of other corporations. Such interlocks are believed to give a corporation access to capital and to co-opt or control sources of pressure in the environment (Pennings, 1980b).

In general, the more interlocks the more effective was the organization. A specific finding of interest in the Pennings study was that firms that are well interlocked with the financial community enjoyed lower interest rates for their debts than their more poorly interlocked fellow firms. Similar relationships between interlocks and profitability have been found in analyses by Burt and his colleagues (Burt et al., 1980; Burt, 1983).

There are two basic ways to view findings such as these. One way views them as sound management. Interlocks, with or without family ties, are basically a means to achieve a competitive edge. The other view is more conspiratorial. Such interlocks permit a ruling class to maintain its power and wealth at the expense of the rest of the population. Both views undoubtedly contain grains of truth.

There are some additional interpretations of the impact of corporate power in society. According to Useem (1979), an "inner group" of business elites are selected to assist in the governance of other institutions, such as governmental advisory boards, philanthropic organizations, and colleges and universities. The same pattern of interlocking directorates is found in the noncorporate sector of society. Useem concludes that this permits the promotion of the more general interests of the entire capitalist class. This political interpretation could be challenged by the claim that these institutional interlocks are merely a means by which able people are brought to the boards of directors of organizations that provide benefits for society. Whichever interpretation is taken cannot deny the importance or presence of the interlocks.

Organizations are active participants in the development and implementation of governmental or public policy. This takes place through lobbying and other political action. I am using the generic sense of the term "organizations" here, since just about every form of organization is involved in political action. The American Symphony Orchestra League (ASOL) and the National Football League (NFL) are active political players. Organizations must be concerned with all branches of government—the legislative, the executive, and the judicial. Organizations can thus be viewed as one source of laws; they are also vital in the selection of judges (Champagne, Neef, and Nagel, 1981).

Analyses of the U.S. State Department support these conclusions. One analysis of the patterns of interests that were represented in State Department actions for the period 1886–1905 found that core financial and industrial interests became vested interests for the State Department to an increasing degree.

American foreign policy came to reflect these organizational interests (Roy, 1981, 1983; see also Carstensen and Werking, 1983).

Yet another study, in the areas of energy and health, found that corporate entities in the form of trade associations, professional societies, public-interest groups, government bureaus, and congressional committees were the key actors in these state policy domains (Laumann, Knoke, and Kim, 1985). These organizations have a stake in the policies that are enacted and implemented. Individuals, unless they act on behalf of or at the behest of the corporations, have little importance in these policy domains. It is important to note that Laumann and his colleagues also found that government bureaus and congressional committees function as important actors in these policy areas. From the frequent revelations of apparent overspending on defense contracts, it is apparent that there are common interests among defense contractors and government agencies, with some congressional organizations also having common interests.

Harmful Impacts.   Organizations can bring actual and direct physical, social and mental harm to society. For example, General Electric, discussed earlier in connection with the city of Schenectady, New York, had two factories that released harmful industrial chemicals into the Hudson River (Revkin, 1997). General Electric has stopped the flow of the chemicals, PCBs, that has crippled commercial fishing and harmed wildlife and is thought to pose a danger of cancer and learning problems. The point here is not to castigate G.E. The point is that the *poisons are in the river,* whether G.E. knew of the dangers or not. The long-term consequences of short-term decisions cannot always be anticipated (Hall, 1981).

Perrow (1984) coined the term "normal accidents" to describe actual and potential disasters involving nuclear plants, nuclear weapons systems, recombinant DNA production, ships carrying highly toxic or explosive cargoes, and chemical plants. His analysis was published before the chemical plant disaster in Bhopal, India, in which thousands of individuals were killed, and the Chernobyl nuclear disaster in Russia. Perrow's contention is that highly complex technical systems that are tightly coupled or integrated have a strong potential for catastrophe because it is not individual operator error that is the source of the accident but systemic or organizational problems. Perrow may not go far enough in his organizational analyses of technologically related disasters, since there are potential organizational solutions to these very real problems (Hirschhorn, 1985). Nonetheless, Perrow's basic point remains valid and frightening—organizational arrangements have the potential to contribute to catastrophes of immense scope. This point can be underscored by an analysis of the space shuttle *Challenger* disaster. Both organizational and technical decisions were faulted in that catastrophe (Vaughan, 1990, 1996). The decision to launch the *Challenger* was the result of organizational structure and culture that led to the making of decisions under conditions of great uncertainty. According to Vaughan, the disaster was not a product of amoral calculation.

This line of reasoning has been extended to the AIDS epidemic by the same Charles Perrow and his colleague Mauro Guillen (1990). They find that AIDS is "as much an organizational problem as a biological one" (p. 150). These researchers see the organizations that deal with AIDS as "recalcitrant tools in the service of diverse interest groups" who have "performed very poorly in coping with [AIDS]" (p. 15). If they are correct, then organizations are having a very harmful impact on the wider society.

In keeping with the theme of reciprocity that was introduced at the beginning of this analysis of organizational-societal relationships, organizations can themselves experience disasters from events outside their own control. An analysis of "corporate tragedies" describes how things happen to organizations (Mitroff and Kilmann, 1984). These tragedies include events such as product tampering, as in the case of Tylenol being laced with cyanide, and the projection in the minds of some people that the logo long used by Procter & Gamble is an occult symbol. Organizations can be affected by events far beyond their control, just as activities that are within organizational control can have effects that are not anticipated by society.

Organizations can cause accidents or can be accident victims. They can also engage in criminal acts (Sutherland, 1949; Clinard and Yeager, 1980). Criminal acts have been identified in a wide array of types of organizations, including the nursing home industry, the stock market ("insider trading" on Wall Street), and the savings and loan industry (Tonry and Reiss, 1994).

Organizations can contribute to crime in two ways. Some organizations are "crime-coercive"; that is, they force their members or customers to engage in illegal activities (Needleman and Needleman, 1979). For example, some franchised automobile dealers are forced into illegal practices such as kickbacks and unrecorded income to survive financially (Farberman, 1975). Needleman and Needleman propose that there are also "crime-facilitative" organizations. For example, fire insurance companies facilitate the "torching" of buildings by arsonists. The arsonist owns the building, which is rundown and unsalable. After it burns, the arsonist collects the insurance on the building. The insurance companies facilitate the arsonist but do not benefit themselves. More vigorous investigations of slum ownership and insurance patterns could be conducted, but apparently insurance companies believe that vigorous background investigation might offend or drive away legitimate customers. Organizations thus contribute to these property crimes. In the case of arson, of course, there is the potential for the loss of life, making it more than a simple financial matter.

The well-documented history of crimes committed by corporations can be interpreted from two basic perspectives. One is that it is simply a case of individual deviance, with people attempting to line their own pockets whether it hurts the organization or not. The alternative perspective brings the organization into the picture. Vaughan (1983), for example, uses the idea of "authority leakage" (p. 74) as a means of indicating that organizational characteristics play a role in crime. Organizational leakages involve long hierarchies and intensive specialization to the extent that subunits cannot be controlled. In Vaughan's view, corporate crimes are more likely to develop in such situations, and this indeed seems to be the case in most instances of such crimes. Seldom is the total organization involved, and seldom do the majority of personnel in organizations participate in such crimes.

Other research has come to the somewhat surprising finding that corporate illegal acts are more likely to be committed in rich or "munificent" environments (Baureus and Near, 1991). There may be less fear of surveillance in such environments, and illegal acts may be seen as less risky.

One further point regarding the harmful effects of organizations must be noted to complete the picture. Although the emphasis has been on private business firms, government or public organizations can also produce harmful outcomes. After all, it is government organizations that wage wars and commit atrocities of the right and the left. Government organizations can have harmful effects of a more subtle nature—for example, by their *inactions*. Levine's (1982) analysis of the Love Canal situation in Niagara Falls, New York, is an excellent case in point. In this case toxic wastes were placed in an unused canal, which was later covered with landfill. Homes and a school were built on and near the site. When the homeowners became aware of the situation and its consequences, which included miscarriages, birth defects, and illness, they approached local, state, and federal agencies for help. At each level, government organizations, such as departments of health, worked hard to protect their own interests and in so doing prolonged the harmful outcomes for the residents.

General Societal Outcomes

The impact of organizations on the societies in which they are embedded is great. This is a fairly recent historical development, since organizations as corporate actors are actually of relatively recent origins (Kieser, 1989). The unprecedented role of organizations in contemporary society is based on the fact that the modern organization is a legal entity, just like the individual person. In a perceptive set of essays, Coleman (1974) has indicated that organizational legality is granted by the state, itself a legal creation. Whereas the individual is given a set of rights and responsibilities by the state, rights and responsibilities are extended to organizations. These rights, coupled with the large size of many organizations, give organizations an enormous amount of power within the state. Coleman also points out that the state or government is more comfortable dealing with other organizations than with individual persons and thus tends to provide more preferential treatment to organizations in areas as diverse as taxation and rights to privacy.

The recognition of organizations as legal entities is not a trivial matter. Organizations, rather than individuals, can be held responsible for certain actions. Air New Zealand, for example, was held responsible for a crash that killed 257 people (*New York Times*, 1981). The crew had not been informed that a new flight plan had been put into effect, and the plane crashed into a volcano. The judge in the case also accused airline officials of attempting to conceal their mistakes. Swigert and Farrell (1980–81) analyzed the case of the Ford Motor Company, which was charged with homicide as a result of deaths that had occurred in crashes of its Pinto models in the 1970s. They found that the mass media shifted its orientation from the recognition of harm based on mechanical defects to an attribution of nonrepentance on the part of the offender. Swigert and Farrell concluded that a shift in public attitudes had occurred in which an organization was believed to have engaged in criminality in a form previously reserved for individuals. The fact that Ford was found not guilty does not alter the importance in the shift in public attitude.

Organizations recognize that they can be held accountable for their actions and try to redefine situations so that either their actions don't appear to be criminal or mitigating circumstances relieve them of responsibility (Waegal, Ermann, and Horowitz, 1981; Marcus and Goodman, 1991). Organizations recognize that they can be blamed and thus also recognize their legal status.

The consideration of the legal status of organizations raises an issue that will be considered directly in the next chapter: Can organizations be considered as objects or entities in their own right, apart from the individuals that compose them? This is a complex question that involves more than their legal status.

At the very broadest level, then, organizations are affected by society and affect it. Even in situations in which efforts are made to reduce the impact of organizations, organizational factors intrude. For example, bureaucratic rules and specialization were evident during the extreme periods of the Cultural Revolution in the People's Republic of China (Shenkar, 1984). Organizational outcomes were inevitable in even that totalitarian situation. The specific forms of the Chinese organizations, of course, were affected by the traditional Chinese culture and social system, a point clearly punctuated by the events in Tiananmen Square in June 1989. Organizations are thus systems within the wider social system (Abbott, 1989).

ORGANIZATIONS AND SOCIAL CHANGE

Organizations are active participants in society. This becomes abundantly clear when we consider the issue of social change. Paradoxically, organizations both foster and impede social change. In this section we will first examine the ways in which *internal* changes in organizations have social-change outcomes. We will then turn to organizations as active change agents. Finally, we will consider organizations as resisters of change.

Internal Change and the Social Structure

Internal organizational changes affect the social structure in two ways. The first is through changing membership patterns. An obvious example is the employment of women in the labor force at all levels in organizations. The social structural changes that have resulted include altered family roles for women and men, altered patterns of childbearing and child rearing, and an increase in services, such as food preparation, performed by service organizations. Restaurant food is not home-cooked food.

The second way in which internal changes affect the social structure is through altered patterns of work. Although it is unclear whether people's attitudes toward their work affect their outlooks on life, or vice versa, there certainly is such a relationship (see Hall, 1994). Thus, changes in the manner in which work is performed—through programs of participative management and quality circles or through other such mechanisms—are related to other important social relationships. The current waves of downsizing are having societal impacts that will play out for years to come, in ways that we cannot now anticipate.

The Organization as a Change Agent

Besides affecting society (intentionally or unintentionally) through their structuring of social life and impacts on members, organizations are also active participants in the social-change process. This can be most readily seen in the political arena, as organizations lobby and fight for legislation and rulings favorable to their own programs. A decision favorable to one organization leads to programs that in turn affect the society. Whenever a government agency is established to carry out a new program, it becomes a social-change agent. We will begin the analysis of change agents with this point, moving from this commonly accepted form of social change to a consideration of organizations as revolutionary agents.

A prime example of the organization as a change agent is provided by Selznick's (1966) now-classic study of the Tennessee Valley Authority (TVA) during its formative years. In addition to its pertinence to the analysis of change, this study is also very important for its contribution to the analysis of the environmental impact on organizations, serving as the forerunner of many subsequent such studies.

The TVA Act was passed by the U.S. Congress in 1933. As Selznick (1966) notes:

> A great public power project was envisioned, mobilizing the "by-product" of dams built for the purpose of flood control and navigation improvement on the Tennessee River and its tributaries. Control and operation of the nitrate properties, to be used for fertilizer production, was also authorized, although this aspect was subordinated to electricity. . . . A new regional concept—the river

basin as an integral unit—was given effect, so that a government agency was created which has a special responsibility neither national nor state-wide in scope. (pp. 4–5)

That the TVA has had an effect on the physical environment is evident. Of greater interest for our purposes is its effect on the social system into which it was placed. An important consideration in understanding the social effects of the TVA is that the organization was designed to be decentralized. Not only were decisions within the organization to be made at the lowest reasonable levels with participation by members, but local organizations and even local citizens were also to be brought into the decision-making process—the grassroots level. For example, the agricultural-extension services of the land-grant colleges were intimately involved with the TVA. This, of course, is one of the prime examples of a co-optation, or "the process of absorbing new elements into the leadership or policy-determining structure of an organization as a means of averting threats to its stability or existence" (Selznick, 1966: p. 13).

Co-optation, however, is a two-way process. The organization itself is affected by the new elements brought into its decision-making process; Selznick documents the manner in which some activities of the TVA were deflected from the original goals because of the new elements in the system. At the same time, the co-optation process affects the system from which the elements were co-opted. The presence of the agricultural-extension element from the land-grant colleges gave this part of the local system much more strength than it had had in the past. The American Farm Bureau Federation was also brought into the process at an early point. In both these cases, the inclusion of one group was associated with the exclusion of another. For example, non–Farm Bureau farm organizations either lost power or did not benefit to the degree that the co-opted organizations did. In addition, the strength of the Farm Bureau in the decision-making process led to the exclusion of other federal government farm programs. Regardless of their merits, those programs were therefore unavailable to the system. Selznick notes, "This resulted in the politically paradoxical situation that the eminently New Deal TVA failed to support agencies with which it shared a political communion, and aligned itself with the enemies of those agencies" (p. 263). This becomes a rather complex analysis when one considers that the other government programs involved were also part of the same larger organization, so that internal politics in one large organization were affected by the external relationships of some of its components. An alternative analysis of the TVA sees the entire process as dominated by New Deal intellectuals, which makes the situation even more complex (Colignon, 1997).

An organization like the TVA affects the surrounding social system. Some elements prosper while others suffer. New social relationships arise as alliances among affected individuals and organizations are formed. Thus, an organization specifically designed to be a change agent can be exactly that, but perhaps in ways that can be most *inconsistent* with the original intent of the planners. The dynamics of the interactions with the environment affect both the organization and its environment.

In a later reexamination of the same study, Selznick (1966) notes that the TVA has been attacked by conservationists for strip mining. The need for coal in the production of power and the strength of those supporting an expansion of this function within the TVA have led to a further environmental impact. Selznick attributes the current state of the TVA to the internal struggles that occurred in its early history—struggles to obtain environmental support. Since such support is selective, a strong organization such as this rearranges the world around it. If the groups in power in the TVA see the need for a greater capacity to generate electrical power as more important than soil conservation, the internal decision-making process, affected as it is by external pressures, makes a further impact on the social and physical environment.

In another analysis of organizations as change agents, Selznick (1960) studied the Bolshevik revolution in Russia. Here he analyzed the nature and the role of the "organizational weapon." In defining what he means, Selznick states:

> We shall speak of organizations and organizational practices as weapons when they are used by a power-seeking elite in a manner unrestrained by the constitutional order of the arena within which the contest takes place. In this usage, "weapon" is not meant to denote any political tool, but one torn from its normal context and unacceptable to the community as a legitimate mode of action. Thus the partisan practices used in an election campaign—insofar as they adhere to the written and unwritten rules of the context—are not weapons in this sense. On the other hand, when members who join an organization in apparent good faith are in fact the agents of an outside elite, then routine affiliation becomes "infiltration." (p. 2)

An important component of the organizational weapon is the "distinctive competence to turn members of a voluntary association into disciplined and deployable political agents" (Selznick, 1960: p. xii).

Before we turn to further elements of Selznick's analysis, it should be clear that the organizational weapon cannot be regarded as a tactic of the Bolsheviks alone. Indeed, it is the vital component of most major social changes and of change within the organization itself. In other words, *to achieve change, there must be organization.* Spontaneous demonstrations or collective emotional responses may be sincere and well intended, but longer-lasting movements toward change must come about through the organizational mode.

The scope of the organization as a weapon is determined by its aims. Even if the change sought is a limited one and one that will not upset the basic system under attack, the change agent still must be viewed as a weapon, although of lesser scope than one that seeks total organizational or societal change. The aim of Bolshevism was total societal change. The basic means of accomplishing the movement's goal was the "combat party." Cadres of dedicated people are a basic component of such parties. This dedication requires that the individuals be totally committed to the cause, insulated from other concerns, and absorbed in the movement. Once a core of dedicated personnel is available, the party must protect itself from internal dissension, banning power centers that might threaten the official leadership. The party must be capable of mobilization and manipulation; it must be protected from possible isolation from the people it hopes to convert and also from possible liquidation at the hands of the existing authorities; and it must struggle for power in every possible area of action. This struggle can take place through seeking official recognition, as well as through conspiratorial or illegal practices. And at all times, the basic ideology must be kept at the forefront of the members' minds (Selznick, 1960: pp. 72–73).

The operation of these principles can be seen in the history of the movement that Selznick carefully traces. This manifesto for an organizational weapon is potentially applicable at any point in history, in any social setting, and at either the total societal or more microcosmic levels. Contemporary terrorist groups exhibit many of the same characteristics as the Bolshevik movement, and so does the history of early Christianity. The homeowners in the Love Canal situation described earlier formed an organization as their weapon for their own good. The Holocaust can certainly be viewed as an organizational weapon for evil.

The important lesson from Selznick's analysis is simple: *to be successful, an organizational weapon must gain power and support in the society it is attempting to change.* The pages of history are filled with abortive efforts that did not gather sufficient support from the society they were trying to change. The basic set of ideas underlying the change effort must therefore be compatible— or become compatible—with the values of the population as a whole. These values of the wider community can be altered during the change process to become more congruent with those of the change agent. At the same time, the change agent itself can become altered as it seeks support from the wider community.

The importance of this form of support can be extrapolated from Joseph Gusfield's (1955, 1963) analysis of the Women's Christian Temperance Union. This organization was highly successful in its attempts to change society through the passage of legislation prohibiting the sale of alcoholic beverages. Its tactics were appropriate for the values of the times, and it succeeded in mobilizing support from a sufficiently large segment of the population. But later, as it became evident that Prohibition was not accomplishing what it was intended to do—and indeed had some unintended consequences that have lasted until the present—and as the originally supportive society changed, the WCTU was faced with a decision regarding its future. It could have altered its stance on alcohol to keep it in line with the prevailing opinions or maintained its position in favor of total abstinence. The latter course was selected as the result of decisions made within the organization. The consequences of that decision were to isolate the movement from the population, reducing it to virtual ineffectiveness as a force in the wider society.

The social system around a social-change organization thus affects it as much as it does any other form of organization. Although such organizations can appear to be revolutionary, deviant, or martyred, or to fit any other emotion-laden category, the fact remains that they are organizations. The critical aspect is the acceptance of the organization by society. This is obviously important for any organization, since to survive, it must receive support in one form or another, but for these change-oriented ones it is even more so. Unfortunately (or fortunately in some cases), because organizational analysts, decision makers, and politicians have not figured out exactly how to determine when an idea's time has come, the organization embarking on a change mission is in a precarious position at best.

There are other, more subtle ways in which organizations are change agents. As Perrow (1970b) notes:

> We tend to forget, or neglect, the fact that organizations have an enormous potential for affecting the lives of all who come into contact with them. They control or can activate a multitude of resources, not just land and machinery and employees, but police, governments, communications, art, and other areas, too. That is, an organization, as a legally constituted entity, can ask for police protection and public prosecution, can sue, and can hire a private police force with considerably wider latitude and power than an individual can command. It can ask the courts to respond to requests and make legal rulings. It can petition for changes in other areas of government—zoning laws, fair-trade laws, consumer labeling, and protection and health laws. It determines the content of advertising, the art work in its products and packages, the shape and color of its buildings. It can move out of a community, and it selects the communities in which it will build. It can invest in times of imminent recession or it can retrench; support or fight government economic policies or fair employment practices. In short, organizations generate a great deal of power that may be used in a way not directly related to producing goods and services or to survival. (pp. 170–71)

The power potential of organizations is often used to thwart change, as will be seen in the next section. Even when an organization is an active change agent, it tends to resist further changes once the desired change is accomplished. The labor union movement, which was once considered revolutionary, is now viewed by some as reactionary. National revolutions lead to established governments that, in turn, are attacked as opponents of social progress. We commonly think of the American, French, Russian, Chinese, and Cuban revolutions. Now, many people inside and outside those nations view the present regimes as highly conservative and even reactionary.

Organizations as Resisters of Change

Since our concern in this chapter is with organizational outcomes, it is important to go beyond the basic fact of organizational contributions to social change. Organizations also actively resist change. This resistance is directed toward change introduced from outside the organization.

Organizations by their very nature are conservative. An analysis of populist rural socialism in Saskatchewan, Canada, provides an ironic example of this point (Lipset, 1960). In 1944 the Cooperative Commonwealth Federation (CCF) came to power in that province. Its objective was "the social ownership of all resources and the machinery of wealth production to the end that we may establish a Cooperative Commonwealth in which the basic principle regulating production, distribution and exchange will be the supplying of human needs instead of the making of profits" (p. 130). That aim was only partially realized. One reason is that there was continued political opposition to the movement; another, consistent with the argument here, is that the movement itself apparently became more conservative as it achieved power. An additional important consideration is that the new socialist government utilized the existing government structures in attempting to carry out its program. In explanation Lipset notes:

> Trained in the traditions of a laissez-faire government and belonging to conservative social groups, the civil service contributes significantly to the social inertia which blunts the changes a new radical government can make. Delay in initiating reforms means that the new government becomes absorbed in the process of operating the old institutions. The longer a new government delays making changes, the more responsible it becomes for the old practices and the harder it is to make the changes it originally desired to institute. (pp. 272–73)

The reason for this blunting is quite simple. The new ruling cabinet had to rely on the system already in operation.

> The administratively insecure cabinet ministers were overjoyed at the friendly response they obtained from the civil servants. To avoid making administrative blunders that would injure them in the eyes of the public and the party, the ministers began to depend on the civil servants. As one cabinet minister stated in an interview, "I would have been lost if not for the old members of my staff. I'm only a beginner in this work. B_____ has been at it for twenty years. If I couldn't go to him for advice, I couldn't have done a thing. Why now (after two years in office) I am only beginning to find my legs and make my own decisions. . . . I have not done a thing for two years without advice." (p. 263)

It is important to note that the aims of a movement can be blunted without malice or intent. *It is not a personal matter but an organizational one.* Certainly, personal motivations may also be important, but the crucial factor is that the new leaders did not understand the organizations they were to head. The organization itself contained rules and procedures that had to be learned along the way, so that the organization became the instrument that deflected the party in power from its goals.

The organization trains its members to follow a system for carrying out its activities. It would require a complete resocialization before the takeover of a new party to prevent this sort of thing. That, of course, is impossible in government organizations. An alternative practice would be to purge the entire system, replacing the original members with ones of the appropriate ideology.

That would in essence mean that the organization would have to start *de novo* and that nothing would be done until the organizational roles were learned and links to the society were established. Since the organization already has clients and customers, as well as a broader constituency in the case of government organizations, the expectations of nonmembers would also have to be altered. For these reasons, the likelihood of success is slim, regardless of the technique selected. The tendency for the organization to operate as it has in the past is very strong.

Most government organizations in Western democracies operate with a civil service system. An extension of Lipset's analysis suggests, therefore, that changes in the party in power will have less impact on the operation of the government agencies than political rhetoric would suggest. In most societies, the same principles seem to hold. The potentiality for major social change through change in government is therefore modified by the organizational realities that exist. Since social systems do change, of course, the organizations must be viewed as entities that do not change overnight but will change with time. The changes that occur may not be in phase with the change in political philosophy of the government in power. A liberal or conservative party in power may over time be able to introduce more of its adherents into the civil service system. Nonetheless, in whatever political direction a state, a county, or a nation is moving, organizational conservatism will remain an important consideration.

Government organizations are not the only example of organizational conservatism. In the United States, automobile manufacturers persisted in making large, fuel-inefficient automobiles, despite several kinds of warnings that the market for those cars would soon dwindle. Much higher profits were made with the large cars in the short run, but rapidly shrinking markets soon brought financial losses and layoffs for workers. Organizations' very resistance to change is a source, desirable or not, of social stability. Social stability must thus be viewed as a major organizational outcome.

MULTINATIONAL ORGANIZATIONS

The analysis of the outcomes of organizations thus far has moved from the individual to the society. Organizations also have important outcomes across societies. This is easily seen in the myriad accounts of international spy rings and terrorist groups and in the case of extractive industries that take natural resources away from developing nations and give little in return, aside from usually low wages to workers.

There have been international organizations for longer than there have been nations. The Roman Empire and the Catholic Church exemplify this as do the imperialist organizations that were at the heart of the British Empire. Many universities have overseas branches. My own sociology department had a joint Ph.D. program with Nankai University in the People's Republic of

China in which several of us taught (in English) a cadre of Chinese students. The program officially ended in 1989, but most of the students have been able to complete their degrees in the United States. There are multinational organizations in just about every sphere of life. Most of the research focus has been on the multinational corporation.

Multinational corporations involve much more than simply having branch offices in more than one nation. In the case of the multinational firm, the total operation of things as diverse as the production and sale of automobiles and chocolate candy and banks is in the hands of a subsidiary or equal firm in another nation. German, Dutch, British, French, Swedish, Canadian, U.S., and Japanese firms are all important parts of this international scene.

There are many explanations for the emergence of the multinational corporation, all with strong elements of truth. The first explanation is imperialism, or the attempt to expand corporate markets and reduce costs by exerting economic power over a weaker nation. That nation could have lower pay scales and thus provide cheap labor; it could be politically dependent and thus give corporations of the more powerful nations tax breaks and incentives. Technology is one key to the growth of multinationals. Mass-production systems and computer information handling have pushed all societies to larger and larger units of production (Heilbroner, 1974). An inevitable consequence of this is expansion to markets and production facilities overseas.

Another explanation is that local economic independence is impossible for many nations, particularly those with weak political and economic systems. The multinational firm becomes the dominant economic and political form of organization, superseding the traditional nation-state in weaker parts of the world (Toynbee, 1974).

A more complex explanation is that the multinational corporation is a consequence of corporate choices made to implement product-market strategy: As corporations begin to produce a complex range of products, these are to be sold in different markets through multiple channels of distribution (McMillan, 1973; Egelhoff, 1982). This explanation, which, as will be seen later, is solidly within contemporary organizational theory, suggests that multinational corporations are in essence inevitable. Even in a no-growth economic situation, the desire to cut costs or maintain the share of the market would lead to international expansion.

Each of the preceding points explains part of the international growth of organizations. Each also explains why organizations in general seek to expand their influence over the environment as a means of protecting their flanks and expanding their operations. These explanations all assume that the organization acts in a rational manner, which, as we will see, is a highly questionable assumption. Interestingly, these analyses have all dealt with organizations that produce goods. Relatively little attention has been paid to multinational service organizations, such as international banking, which are of crucial importance. International hotel operations, though less important, are also very evident as one travels beyond a nation's border.

Multinational firms have several kinds of impacts on their host countries and governments. Clegg and Dunkerley (1980) claim:

> It must be recognized that multi-national organizations are different from the kind of organization traditionally studied by organizational theorists. Their size and complexity and their capacity for capital investment in countries of their choice makes them able to control their environment in hitherto unknown ways. The fact of being independent of national governments in many instances enables them to pursue their goals in a ruthless and unaccountable manner. (pp. 390–91)

Clegg and Dunkerley go on to note instances in which the Ford Motor Company influenced many governments to pass laws or to provide investment capital to attract Ford installations. One dramatic instance of multinational influence came in Chile in 1970, when the Marxist Allende government was in power. In addition to the CIA, multinational firms such as ITT and Ford played a significant part in the downfall of that government.

Clegg and Dunkerley also note several other consequences of multinational corporations. Considerations of what is best for a national economy are secondary to considerations of what is best for the corporation as a whole. Although the multinational is frequently welcomed in areas of high unemployment, its presence can create extremely high dependence on the firm. Once the local economy is dependent on such a firm, the firm itself has a great deal of power. The multinational is also often able to avoid paying taxes at the rate paid by domestic corporations through reporting profits in countries with lower tax rates and other forms of financial shifts. When a multinational moves some of its production operations overseas, of course, domestic employment is adversely affected.

There is an aura of inevitability in most discussions of multinational firms. This aura is generally warranted, but there are conditions that could drastically affect the operations of multinational firms. Changes in government policy brought about by revolutions or elections in the host country can result in the nationalization of all industries or the confiscation of all foreign investments. The case of Iran and the United States is a graphic illustration of that. Not all multinational ventures are successful. Nonetheless, the multinational corporation appears to be an increasing part of the international scene and will continue to influence international events.

WHY STUDY ORGANIZATIONS?

This chapter ends with the very question with which it began. From the standpoint of empirical research on organizations, it would appear that one answer is that organizations will continue to grow, bureaucratize, and centralize (Child, 1976). In other words, we will have more of the same, which can be a depressing conclusion.

At the same time, there are organizational theorists and social philosophers who see organizations as the *only way* by which desirable ends such as peace, prosperity, and social justice can be achieved (Etzioni, 1968, 1991, 1993). In a very real sense, we are living in an "organizational state" (Laumann and Knoke, 1987), in which the major actors in national policy events are organizations and interorganizational networks. The second answer to our question, then, is that we *must* study organizations if we are to understand our society and what is happening in and around it.

One of the major contributions that our organizational analysis can make is to point out the limitations to what is feasible for organizations themselves and for the wider social system. We will also point out that organizations contain some inherent contradictions that limit the impact that individual actors can have.

Jackall (1988) noted that business is a "social and moral terrain" (p. 3). The same point is true for all organizations. Moral and ethical issues are confronted whenever decisions are made. In a book prepared under the auspices of the Business Roundtable, an organization made up of the chief executive officers of many of the largest and most powerful American business firms, Steckmest (1982; see also Burke, 1986) urges corporate social responsibility. The argument of his book is that corporations need to "develop executives and functions (e.g., government relations and consumer affairs staffs) to effectively monitor, and responsibly interact in, an increasingly complex sociopolitical environment" (Yeager, 1982: p. 748). Again, the notion of corporations has to be expanded to all organizations, including those that are part of government itself.

Organizational theory has much to contribute to "clients" of many types, ranging from politicians and journalists in the public-at-large, to workers and managers within organizations, to opponents of organizations who operate inside and outside the organizations themselves (Lammers, 1981). The true relevance of organizational theory lies in the following conclusion: "*The more we are able to create worlds that are morally cogent and politically viable, the more we are able, as workers and as citizens, to manage or resist*" (Brown, 1978: p. 378; italics added).

SUMMARY AND CONCLUSIONS

The purpose of this chapter has been a simple one—to indicate the importance of organizations at every level of human life. Thus, we examined the manner in which organizations have outcomes for the individual, classes of individuals, the community, the society, and the international order. Organizational analysis can be dull until the crucial and central role of organizations is understood. If organizations are understood, then individuals have a tool by which they can deal with the reality that they face.

The astute reader has no doubt noticed that the subject matter of this book, organizations, has not been defined or delineated. It is to this that we now turn.

On the Nature
and Types
of Organizations

This chapter has three purposes. The first is to define organizations. The intent is to indicate that we are dealing with a single subject—all organizations have characteristics that allow them to be considered as one type of social phenomenon. We will differentiate organizations from other social forms and from individuals. This is related to the second purpose of the chapter—to indicate that organizations have a *reality* of their own. The final purpose—to *differentiate* among organizations—may seem to contradict the first two purposes. Common sense tells us that large and powerful national or multinational organizations are different from a local restaurant. We will attempt to present ways in which organizations might be typed or classified.

DEFINITIONS FROM THE PAST

Discussions of definitions can be deadly. This one may be deadly also, but it is necessary. Although some writers (for example, March and Simon, 1958: p. 1) argue that definitions of organizations do not serve much purpose, a more reasonable approach would be that definitions provide a basis for understanding what is being studied. Here I will consider the definitions developed by some classical writers in the field and then offer my own approach to the subject.

Weber. Like any other field of study, and like organizations themselves, organizational analysis has a tradition. That tradition leans heavily on Max Weber, who is known for his analyses of bureaucracy and authority, topics that will be considered later. Weber also concerned himself with the more general definitions of organizations. In his definition he first distinguishes the "corporate group" from other forms of social organization (Weber, 1947). The corporate group involves "a social relationship which is either closed or limits the admission of outsiders by rules, . . . so far as its order is enforced by the action of specific individuals whose regular function this is, of a chief or 'head' and usually also an administrative staff" (pp. 145–46).

This aspect of the definition contains a number of elements that need further discussion, since they are basic to most other such definitions. In the first place, organizations involve social relationships. That is, individuals interact within the organization. However, as the reference to closed or limited boundaries suggests, these individuals are not simply in random contact. The organization (corporate group) includes some parts of the population and excludes others. Thus, the organization itself has a boundary. A major component of this definition, the idea of order, further differentiates organizations from other social entities. Interaction patterns do not simply arise; a structuring of interaction is imposed by the organization itself. This part of the definition also suggests that organizations contain a hierarchy of authority and a division of labor in carrying out their functions. Order is enforced with specific personnel designated to perform this function.

To the idea of the corporate group, Weber adds other criteria for organizations. In organizations, interaction is "associative" rather than "communal" (1947: pp. 136–39). This differentiates the organization from other social entities, such as the family, that share the other, previously noted characteristics of the corporate group. Weber also notes that organizations carry out continuous purposive activities of a specified kind (pp. 151–52). Thus, organizations transcend the lives of their members and have goals, as "purposive activities" suggests. Organizations are designed to do something. This idea of Weber's has been retained by most organizational analysts.

Weber's definition has served as the basis for many others. His focus is basically on legitimate interaction patterns among organizational members as they pursue goals and engage in activities.

Barnard.   A different focus has been taken by Chester Barnard and his followers. Although in agreement with Weber on many points, Barnard stresses a different basis for organizations. His definition of an organization is "a system of consciously coordinated activities or forces of two or more persons" (Barnard, 1938: p. 73). Activity is accomplished through conscious, deliberate, and purposeful coordination. Organizations require communications, a willingness on the part of members to contribute, and a common purpose among them. Barnard stresses the role of the individual. It is individuals who must communicate, be motivated, and make decisions. Whereas Weber emphasizes the system, Barnard is concerned with members of the system. The relevance and implications of these contrasting approaches will be considered shortly.

Marx.   Although Karl Marx did not develop a formal definition of organizations, his analyses of the social order contain many implications about organizations. Marx's key notion is *praxis,* or human practical activity (Heydebrand, 1977). Praxis is historically situated and may refer to both individual and collective activity. It is the collective that is relevant here.

Another key component of the Marxian perspective is outcomes, which, of course, are of major interest here. Heydebrand notes that there are two types of outcomes. The first is products, artifacts, or constructs, and the second is the activities themselves. This form of outcome of organizations is the organizing process itself—the ways in which work is carried out, power arrangements, and the processes by which labor is organized.

CONTEMPORARY DEFINITIONS

The dominant view of the organizing process is that it is carried out in a *bureaucracy* (Hardy and Clegg, 1996: p. 2). We will not go into detail here about what constitutes a bureaucracy and what does not; we simply note that there are other forms of organizing, which we will point out throughout our analyses.

The analysis of organizations as a distinct subject in sociology emerged full-blown in the 1960s. In that decade Etzioni (1964) and Scott (1964) made important definitional statements. Here is Etzioni's:

> Organizations are social units (or human groupings) deliberately constructed and reconstructed to *seek specific goals.* (emphasis added)
>   Corporations, armies, schools, hospitals, churches, and prisons are included; tribes, classes, ethnic groups, and families are excluded. (p. 3)

Scott adds other elements to the definition:

> . . . organizations are defined as collectivities . . . that have been established for the pursuit of relatively specific *objectives* on a more or less continuous basis. It should be clear . . . however, that organizations have distinctive features other than goal specificity and continuity. These include relatively fixed boundaries, a normative order, authority ranks, a communication system, and an incentive system which enables various types of participants to work together in the pursuit of common *goals.* (p. 488; italics added)

The issue of goals or objectives has interested and divided organizational analysts for some time. We will examine the importance of goals at several points in our analysis. For the definitional task here, several points are important. First, many things go on in organizations that are not goal related. When people are on coffee breaks and talking about the past weekend, goals are not involved. When a business firm uses its private jet aircraft to fly a single executive around the country at a much higher cost than even first-class commercial airfare and with much higher risk, goals are not involved. When I am daydreaming about skiing, goals are not involved.

Second, goals can be considered as reifications or "having an existence and behavior independent of the behavior of its members" (Simon, 1964: p. 2). Herbert Simon, who won a Nobel Prize in economics for his work on organizations, does not believe that goals should be considered apart from individual actors, even though he does refer to goals as constraints on "organizational decision making" (p. 7). In the present analysis, I will consider goals in the reified manner—they do, in fact, exist apart from individual organizational members.

Third, we are using the term "goals" in the true plural sense. Organizations have multiple goals. For the most part, these multiple goals are also contradictory. Thus, issues such as short-term versus long-term profit, quality versus quantity, and teaching versus research are part of the very fabric of organizations. A simple example illustrates this: A study of feminist health centers found that they tried to serve their client populations but at the same time tried to promote social change (Hyde, 1992). Time and effort spent working for change means time and effort not spent on client populations. This multiple and conflicting goal situation is a dilemma for all but the simplest of organizations.

Finally, goals are at the *heart of our entire analysis*. As noted in Chapter 1, one of the reasons we have organizations is to get things done. Thus, ideas such as leadership and decision making, communication procedures, and the entire subject of organizational analysis cannot be understood apart from goals.

Scott (1964) included the idea of organizational boundaries in his original definition, and it has become an important component of his more fully developed conceptualization of organizations (1991). In some situations, the issue of boundaries is very clear. For example, I put on the uniform of the National Ski Patrol when I go skiing. I am a member of that organization, and we wear uniforms to make us visible to the skiing public. Only ski patrol members may wear them—the boundary is clear. The boundary issue becomes cloudy when another example is considered. Local political parties have small paid staffs to answer mail, answer phones, and so on. The membership swells, however, at election time; the headquarters are filled with activities and people, and the organizational boundary is indistinct. Both the ski patrol and the political party are voluntary organizations, but that does not account for ambiguity in the conceptualization of boundaries. Undercover police detectives intentionally disguise their organizational boundaries.

The idea of boundaries suggests that there is something outside the organization—its environment. Contemporary organizational theory has a strong focus on the environment. Organizations have both physical and social environments. The physical environment, which is often overlooked by organizational analysts, cannot be ignored. The University at Albany usually gets heavy snow in the winter, and snow-removal costs are not an incidental part of its budget. Snow removal is not a major budget consideration at the University of California at Los Angeles, but earthquakes are.

The social environment has been the primary focus of research and theory, since it contains competitors, regulators, and other sources of pressure and opportunities for organizations. The environment is also the source of inputs for the organizations and is the recipient of organizational outcomes.

With those considerations in mind, we can now present the definition of organizations to be used here: *An organization is a collectivity with a relatively identifiable boundary, a normative order (rules), ranks of authority (hierarchy), communications systems, and membership coordinating systems (procedures); this collectivity exists on a relatively continuous basis exists, in an environment, and engages in activities that are usually related to a set of goals; the activities have outcomes for organizational members, for the organization itself, and for society.*

This is a cumbersome and perhaps unwieldy definition, but then so is the subject matter.

Some Additional Definitional Issues

There are two additional points to be made in regard to the definitional issue. First, organizations are characterized by internal differentiation. Indeed, much of the research on organizational structure has been focused on such differentiation. Organizations are political entities, with various parties, both individuals and units, struggling for control (Benson, 1977; Heydebrand, 1977). These can be called contradictions within organizations. Some writers focus on class interests in the contradiction process, but the class emphasis is not necessary for inclusion of the notion of contradiction. Organizations do contain oppositional forces, which vie for control. The nature of organizations is such that those in power tend to remain in power, but the fact that organizations contain internal oppositional forces is an important consideration. The definition just given should not blind us to the fact that organizations have internal differentiation and thus the seeds of possible dissensus.

Second, it is frequently useful and necessary to consider parts or units of organizations as organizations in their own right. There are many "multi" organizations (Hage, 1980). They are of such scope that it is wise to consider their components separate organizations. Large government agencies, corporate conglomerates, and many multidivisional organizations have units that can and should be considered separate organizations. The same is true for the University of California or the State University of New York. For our purposes here, it is sufficient to note that an *autonomous* unit of a larger organization can be considered an organization in its own right (Warriner, 1980). If the unit can provide its own input and throughput and can distribute its outputs, it can be considered an organization. This is a tricky distinction, of course, since branches of clothing stores like The Gap, toy stores such as Toys

R Us, and restaurants such as Burger King cannot set prices or make product innovations. They can, of course, hire their own personnel and make other internal personnel decisions and can be treated as organizations, as can the parent company.

The question of whether or not a subunit of a larger organization can be thought of as an autonomous organization in its own right is an important analytical distinction in comparing organizations in research settings. It is also important in legal and accounting determinations. It is probably less important in our everyday lives.

ARE ORGANIZATIONS REAL?

That question may seem inane. From the outset we have been considering the organizations that surround us and of which we are a part. We have examined some of the outcomes of organizations for individuals and society. A careful consideration of the question, however, reveals one of the basic dilemmas in sociology and in philosophy.

Most theorists have addressed this question one way or another. Simon (1964), for example, argues against reifying the concept of organization or treating it as something more than a system of interacting individuals. In his important treatise on exchange theory, Blau (1964) notes that individual behavior within organizations is based on direct or indirect exchanges among individuals, even when the exchanges are asymmetrical. Other analysts, such as Benson (1977), are even more individualistic, claiming that reality is a social construction in the minds of organizational actors. My position is that these individualistic approaches are incomplete in two ways.

Organizations and the Individual.   In the first place, individuals in organizations frequently behave without engaging in direct or indirect exchange. Many routine behaviors are learned in an exchange situation but are then carried out without mental reference to the interaction process. The behavior becomes a type of learned stimulus-response mechanism, with the intervening interaction variable deleted as a consideration. Even with the advent of ATMs, bank tellers still routinely check the status of a customer's account when transactions are done in person. As ATMs make decisions about the status of our accounts, they essentially have taken over the routine activities that were previously carried out by individuals.

The organization trains, indoctrinates, and persuades its members to respond on the basis of the requirements of their position. Responses become quite regularized and routinized and do not involve the interaction frame of reference. In some situations even the emotions and feelings of the people involved can have an organizational basis. Research on airline flight attendants demonstrates that at least some flight attendants learn to feel the friendly external demeanor that they portray (Hochschild, 1983). Their inner feelings, as well as their outward behavior, are based on organizational training.

The argument that behavior in organizations is organizationally, rather than individually or interactionally, based is not intended to mean that all behavior in organizations is so determined. There clearly are many times when individual discretion is called for, times when the individual is crucial for organizational survival. The point is that the organization can be the major determinant of individual actions in some situations and an important determinant in others. In discussing the factors that contribute to the kinds of role expectations one organizational member holds toward another (role expectations are of vital importance in any interaction situation), Kahn et al. (1964) note:

> To a considerable extent, the role expectations held by the members of a role set—the prescriptions and proscriptions associated with a particular position—are determined by the broader organizational context. The organizational structure, the functional specialization and division of labor, and the formal reward system dictate the major content of a given office. What the occupant of that office is supposed to do, with and for whom, is given by these and other properties of the organization itself. Although other human beings are doing the "supposing" and rewarding, *the structural properties of organization are sufficiently stable so that they can be treated as independent of the particular persons in the role set.* (p. 31; italics added)

Others approach this issue from a power perspective and suggest that the "capacity of management to impose its hegemony on the members of the organization" means that organizations assume a real existence for the people who are oriented to the organization. If an organization has power over the individual, then it is real (Clegg and Dunkerley, 1980: pp. 209–10).

My perspective is that organizations are real to the extent that strictly organizational factors account for part of the behavior of individuals at all times in organizations. The exact proportion of the variation in individual behavior accounted for by organizational factors, as opposed to interactional or individual factors, cannot be exactly specified at the present time. The position taken here is that organizational factors can account for most if not all of the variation in behavior in some circumstances (this is the purpose of training and indoctrination programs in many kinds of organizations). In others, organizational factors interact with other behavioral determinants.

Organizations are realities for individuals in another crucial way. Some people spend their entire careers in the same organization and move through firm internal labor markets (FILMs). These are the job structures in which people move in the course of their careers (Kalleberg and Berg, 1987; Kalleberg and Van Buren, 1996). The jobs exist *before* the individuals involved. The idea of "vacancy chains" can also be used to describe this phenomenon (White, 1971). As first one and then more positions become vacant in an organization, a chain of vacancies is created. In large organizations, there are multiple chains in the various departments of the organization.

There is an interesting historical twist in these considerations. In the Middle Ages organizations as we know them did not exist (Coleman, 1974). The concept of a "corporate actor, independent of persons and the concept of individuals, independent of corporate bodies surrounding them had not arrived" (p. 3). This distinction has arrived now.

Organizations as Actors.   The treatment of organizations as realities thus far has been concerned with the behavior of individuals. An even more basic issue is whether organizations have an existence of their own, above and beyond the behavior and performance of individuals within them. The question becomes, Do organizations act? The answer again is in the affirmative, and this is the second reason that viewing organizations just as interacting or reality-constructing individuals is too narrow a conceptualization.

Some characteristics of the definitions we discussed earlier provide indications of the existence of organizations. The fact that organizations persist over time and replace members suggests that they are not dependent upon particular individuals. Universities outlive the generations of students and faculty that pass through their gates. The General Motors Corporation has been in existence for a long time. The Roman Catholic Church is an even more striking example, since its existence can be traced back about two thousand years.

Organizations may indeed have a life cycle that includes decline and death (Kimberly and Miles, 1980), but the fact is that many of our dominant organizations persist across generations of members. Even when the life-cycle metaphor is used, it must be remembered that organizations can take actions that extend their lives, such as getting government loans, having favorable legislation passed, starting new advertising campaigns, or opening new markets. We humans can extend our life expectancies by good diet and exercise, but only up to a point.

When members enter an organization for the first time, they are confronted with a social structure, which includes the interaction patterns among organizational members and those members' expectations toward them, and a set of organizational expectations for their own behavior. It does not matter who the individuals are; the organization has established a system of norms and expectations to be followed regardless of who its personnel happen to be, and it continues to exist regardless of personnel turnover. Individuals establish the norms and expectations, to be sure, but they persist long after the persons who established the policies in the first place are gone.

When we hear statements such as "It is company policy," "The White House today announced . . . ," or "Z State University does not condone cheating," we understand that they are about organizations. Organizations have policies, make announcements, and may or may not condone cheating. They also manufacture goods, administer policies, and protect the citizenry. These are organizational actions and involve properties of organizations, not individuals.

The real heart of the matter is that organizations have outcomes of the sort that were considered in Chapter 1.

The argument being made here has certain philosophical assumptions that should be considered. Following Burrell and Morgan (1979: pp. 4–7), it can be noted that ontologically, we are taking a realist as opposed to a nominalist position. The nominalist position is that reality is constructed through individual cognition, with the external world made up of artificial creations formed in people's minds. The realist position claims that the world external to individual cognition is a real world made up of hard, tangible, and relatively immutable structures. Warriner (1956) has taken the realist position toward groups, and we are taking it toward organizations. In essence, the realist position is that individuals, groups, and organizations can all be legitimately viewed as having a reality of their own. Over ninety-five years ago Simmel (1902) wrote:

> The question now arises, however, whether traits of character in the total group are not derived from definite numbers of members, in which case, of course, the reactions between individuals constitute the real and observable event. The question merely assumes, however, that not the members in their individuality, but their assemblage in a *picture of the whole,* now constitutes the object of inquiry. (p. 193; italics added)

Our "picture of the whole" is the organization.

Epistemologically, we take the positivist position in that we seek to explain and predict what happens in the organizational world by searching for regularities and causal relationships among the elements related to organizations. Antipositivists suggest that the world is relativistic and can be understood only from the points of view of the actors in a particular situation.

Burrell and Morgan (1979) also suggest that assumptions about human nature must be considered in organizational analyses. They contrast the voluntarist position with the determinist perspective. Voluntarism sees humans as totally autonomous and free willed, whereas determinism sees people as totally controlled by their situation or environment. I lean toward the determinist perspective without embracing it totally.

There is, finally, the methodological issue. On the one hand, the ideographic approach stresses detailed analyses of the meanings that social actors attach to situations and emphasizes that social actors' meanings should be stated in their own terms. On the other hand, the nomothetic approach emphasizes the testing of hypotheses with scientific rigor and the use of systematic research protocols. The nomothetic approach will be stressed in this analysis, with the realization that ideographic studies can provide useful insights and contribute to the development of rigorous tests of the insights.

Part of the difficulty surrounding the issue of organizational reality comes from the methodologies that have been employed. There is a long tradition of obtaining information about organizations from respondents in organizations.

This is done through data collected from "key informants" or from samples of personnel in the organizations. It is possible to construct organizational properties from data gathered from individuals, through the use of averages, standard deviations, correlation coefficients, and other such figures (Lazarsfeld and Menzel, 1961; Barton, 1961). It is also possible to obtain data from individuals about organizations. There are techniques by which data from individuals can be aggregated to the organizational level with strong explanatory power (Lincoln and Zeitz, 1980). It is also very possible to obtain data about organizations from members of other organizations, as research by Blau and Rabrenovic (1989) reveals. In their research they asked directors of nonprofit organizations in New York State to describe how frequently they interacted with other such agencies and whether or not there was any duplication of services. The directors apparently had no difficulty in identifying the other organizations and simply treated them as real. They were in their picture of the whole.

This rather lengthy expedition into the issue of organizational reality was conducted for the purpose of specifying the perspective that the analysis in this book takes. Social scientists vary in their interests; some are concerned with individual phenomena, some with group phenomena, and some with organizational phenomena (Roberts, Hulin, and Rousseau, 1978). Each is a legitimate interest, and each can be an interesting picture. The distinction between structuralist and individualist pervades organizational theory (Pfeffer, 1982). The present analysis is intentionally eclectic, with a strong structural lean.

TYPES OF ORGANIZATIONS

Thus far, this chapter has done two things: It has defined organizations and distinguished them from other collectivities, and it has taken the position that organizations are real. In essence, the point has been that organizations have a set of commonalities that make them a distinct subject.

The importance of commonalities, of course, must not blind us to differences. The marvelous distinction between men and women is tremendously useful. This important difference is given a great deal of social meaning. Most of the distinctions that we develop about people, such as age, attractiveness, or abilities, are based on socially developed meanings. When we think about people, we tend to make typologies—they are our social constructions of reality.

This same point is true in regard to typologies of organizations. The distinctions that we commonly make between organizations, such as profit and not-for-profit, are social constructions. At times these social constructions are helpful; at other times they are not. Just as the distinction between men and women is very helpful in some circumstances, that distinction becomes irrelevant in other circumstances, such as in the selection of a new faculty member or the acceptance of new students. Irrelevant, too, are the distinctions between profit and not-for-profit when we examine an issue such as the relationship between organizational complexity and decision-making patterns. In this section we will consider a number of efforts that have been made to develop typologies, classifications, and even taxonomies of organizations.

Before beginning this task, however, let's consider some differences between organizations that might seem at first to be within a single type. I will start with large retail sales organizations. When we think of large retail sales organizations, what do we think of? Kmart? Wal-Mart? Sears? Well, what about Mary Kay Cosmetics or Tupperware? Their cosmetics and cookware are retailed by individuals who are door-to-door representatives of their parent companies (Biggart, 1989). These "direct-selling" or "multilevel" organizations can have thousands of members, but without the usual buildings and hierarchies that we imagine when we think of large retail operations.

Take another example—law firms. Our image is probably shaped by TV, so we envision polished-wood-paneled offices occupied by men and women wearing power suits and making huge salaries. Well, what about a law firm operating out of a storefront office with lawyers, clerks, and secretaries all earning the same low wage and all sharing equally in all phases of the work? This is a "law collective" (Rothschild and Whitt, 1986) and is admittedly a rare form, but it is a law firm, just like what we see on TV.

The point of these examples is that commonsense distinctions—retail organizations and law firms—do not tell us very much about the organizations involved. That is why organizational researchers have paid attention to typologies to help them think about organizations.

Although organizational analysts are well aware of the need for typologies, they are convinced that relatively simple, prima facie typologies probably add more confusion than clarity. Perrow (1967), for example, notes that

> types of organizations—in terms of their functions in society—will vary as much within each type as between types. Thus, some schools, hospitals, banks, and steel companies may have more in common, because of their routine character, than routine and nonroutine schools, routine and nonroutine hospitals, and so forth. To assume that you are holding constant the major variable by comparing several schools or several steel mills is unwarranted until one looks at the technologies employed by the various schools or steel mills. (p. 203)

Although we might argue with Perrow and his emphasis on technology as the key variable, his point is very important. It is organizational characteristics that should serve as the classificatory basis of organizations. The great danger in most classificatory schemes is oversimplification; they are based on a single characteristic. Typologies thus derived "can be expanded indefinitely as some new factor is seized upon to indicate an additional class" (Katz and Kahn, 1966: p. 111). Such problems with typologies are not limited just to the study of organizations. "The history of sociology, from Montesquieu through Spencer, Marx, and up to Weber himself, is littered with the debris of ruined typologies that serve only as the battleground for that academic street-fighting that so often passes for theoretical discussion" (Burns, 1967: p. 119).

Typologies that end in debris did not stop with Weber. As McKelvey (1982) has commented, "Organizational science will remain wallowing in a swampy scientific tidal basin until significant progress in systematics is forthcoming" (p. 8). By systematics, McKelvey is referring to his own approach to classification, which will be considered shortly. Despite all these pleas and the recognized need, *we still do not have an adequate organizational typology.*

Although some simple typologies can be used for limited analyses, such as comparing organizations in their turnover rates, growth rates, or rates of investment in research and development, classifications of this sort have only a limited usefulness. We end up knowing only one thing about organizations, not understanding them in their rich complexity.

The essence of any typological effort really lies in the determination of the critical variables for differentiating the phenomena under investigation. Since organizations are highly complex entities, classificatory schemes must represent that complexity. An adequate overall classification would have to take into account the array of external conditions, the total spectrum of actions and interactions within an organization, and the outcomes of organizational behaviors. A brief review of some of the efforts that have been made to classify organizations will indicate the diversity of variables that have been considered, the relative fruitlessness of the schemes, and some possible future directions for typological efforts.

Some Typologies

For the purposes of the present analysis, we will use the terms "classification," "typology," and "taxonomy" interchangeably, although in a strict sense each term has a distinct meaning (Burns, 1967: p. 119; McKelvey, 1982). The most common forms of typology are what have been labeled the traditional, folk, or commonsense typologies (Warriner, 1980). Thus, organizations can be classified as profit or nonprofit. This is clearly an important distinction in some cases but not in others, as we will see.

Another form of commonsense typology would be to classify organizations by their societal "sector"—educational, agricultural, health and medical, and so on. Like the profit-nonprofit distinction, such classifications can obscure more than they illuminate, since such typologies contain dimensions that overlap in unpredictable ways (Warriner, 1980). They are also unscientific in that the categories are not related to one another in any systematic way. The major problem with such commonsense typologies is that they simply do not classify. The State University of New York, for example, contains two-year colleges, four-year colleges, graduate university centers, medical colleges and their attendant hospitals, and specialized colleges in ceramics and forestry, plus an entirely noncampus-based administrative headquarters with no students. In addition, there is a semiautonomous research foundation that does not conduct research but, rather, seeks funds—an entrepreneurial role—and administers grants and contracts—an administrative role. In a similar manner, General Motors and the United States Army maintain college-degree-granting facilities. Are General Motors, the United States Army, and the State University of New York the same type of organization? Of course not. The realization of this type of difficulty has led organizational analysis to try to develop other forms of classification. The first forms to be discussed are "intentional" (Warriner, 1980) or "special" classifications (McKelvey, 1978) which have focused on limited aspects of the organizations.

We will move from some relatively simple schemes to more elaborate formulations. Typical of the simple schemes is that of Parsons (1960: pp. 45–46), based on the type of function or goal served by the organization. In this analysis, Parsons is concerned with the linkages between organizations and the wider society. He distinguishes four types of organizations, according to what they contribute to the society.

The first type is the production organization, which makes things that are consumed by the society. The second type is that oriented toward political goals; it seeks to ensure that society attains its valued goals, and it generates and allocates power within the society. The third type is the integrative organization, whose purposes are settling conflicts, directing motivations toward the fulfillment of institutionalized expectations, and ensuring that the parts of society work together. The final form is the pattern-maintenance organization, which attempts to provide societal continuity through educational, cultural, and expressive activities.

Although each of these activities is clearly important for society, this type of classificatory scheme does not really say much about the organizations involved. In the first place, some organizations can be placed in more than one category. A large corporation, such as IBM, is clearly a production organization. But it is also important in the allocation of power and is an important part of the research community. Through public relations, corporate contributions to foundations and colleges, and attempts at working with disadvantaged youths, the same corporation falls into the other categories. Its prime effort is production, but its subsidiary concerns make classificatory schemes such as Parsons's less than totally useful. In addition, such a typology does not differentiate among the characteristics of organizations themselves. As Perrow noted earlier, there can be as much—or more—organizational variation within such categories as between them.

The most serious limitation of this typology is that it misses an entire "category" of organizations—human-service organizations. Where do hospitals, charitable foundations, labor unions, or performing arts organizations fall in such a formulation? These organizations perform a large proportion of all human services (Gronbjerg, 1992; Powell, 1987). They could probably be squeezed into one of Parsons's categories, but it would be too much of a reach to be useful.

Another approach to developing intentional typologies is exemplified by the works of Etzioni (1961) and Blau and Scott (1962). Both attempted to classify organizations on the basis of a single principle. Their prominence in the literature deserves continued attention.

Etzioni uses compliance as the basis of his system. Compliance is the manner in which lower participants in an organization respond to the authority system of the organization. Compliance is expressed through the nature of the lower participants' involvement in the organization. According to Etzioni, there are three types of authority—coercive, remunerative, and normative. There are also three types of compliance—alienative, instrumental or calculative, and moral. The resulting three-by-three classificatory scheme yields nine possible types of organizations, with most falling into "congruent" types. These include coercive-alienative, remunerative-calculative, and normative-moral. Incongruent types, such as coercive-utilitarian, would tend to move toward congruency.

Etzioni's approach has been criticized from several standpoints. The most important is that it is difficult to place some organizations into Etzioni's categories (Hall, Haas, and Johnson, 1967a). Public schools, for example, can yield alienative, calculative, and moral compliance on the part of various students. Similarly, some people are in the army because they believe in it, whereas others join for purely calculative reasons. The distinctions do not work as well as Etzioni proposes that they will.

Lest this discussion lead to the conclusion that Etzioni's work makes little or no contribution, it should be noted that Etzioni (1975) followed up his original work by compiling the results of some sixty studies that used his typology. He found that the compliance patterns predicted by the typology generally were found. The compliance typology thus does appear to differentiate organizations according to the compliance patterns of its members, but it is not an inclusive typology. It is useful for studying compliance patterns but not for other purposes.

Blau and Scott base their classification on who benefits, or "cui bono?" The prime organizational beneficiary serves as the basis for their fourfold classification. The types are mutual-benefit organizations, in which the members themselves are the prime beneficiaries; businesses, whose owners are the beneficiaries; service organizations, in which clients are the beneficiaries; and commonweal organizations, in which the public at large benefits.

Unfortunately, it is difficult to isolate a single explicit, stable, and coherent group served by an organization. The beneficiaries themselves have factions, disagree, and engage in power struggles (Burns, 1967). In addition, this approach does not deal with the critical issue of who actually controls the organization or of who does not benefit from its activities (Clegg and Dunkerley, 1980). It is also difficult to place some organizations, such as schools, into a single category, as was the case with the Etzioni approach (Hall, Haas, and Johnson, 1967a). It must be recognized, of course, that Blau and Scott's concern with who benefits is the indirect forerunner of this volume's concern with organizational outcomes—who benefits and who is harmed.

As a final example of this form of building intentional typologies, we turn to the work of Mintzberg (1979). This is a multifaceted approach, based largely on the ways in which organizations are structured to meet the various contingencies they face. The first type or organization is the simple structure, as exemplified by the automobile dealership with a flamboyant owner, a small college headed by an aggressive president, or a new government headed by an autocrat. Supervision is direct. The organizations are small and exist in dynamic environments. Their technologies are not sophisticated.

The second type is the machine bureaucracy, such as a postal system, a steel manufacturing firm, an airline, or a custodial prison. These share the characteristics of standardized work, large size, stable environments, and control by some external body.

The third type is the professional bureaucracy, such as a university, a law firm, a social welfare agency, a craft-production firm, or a medical center. Work is standardized through professional or craft training, and the environment is stable but does not contain external controls on the organization. The key factor here is the skills and knowledge of the operating workers, who are professionals or highly skilled craft workers.

The fourth type is the divisionalized form, as exemplified by the large corporation, a multicampus university, or a socialist economy. Each division has its own structure, which may take one of the other forms already listed in this typology.

The final type is the adhocracy. This is a complex form and is exemplified by many software firms, new artistic organizations, and research and development laboratories at the frontiers of science. Their environment is dynamic and unknown, and their structure can change rapidly as events demand adjustment.

Mintzberg has a complex scheme from which these types of organizations are developed. The important point here is that the groupings shatter commonsense notions of how and why organizations differ. Mintzberg is suggesting that we look at organizational characteristics themselves as the basis for our classification schemes. This is exactly what those who advocate empirical taxonomies propose.

Organizational Taxonomy

A very different approach to the classification issue has been taken by those who have advocated and tried to develop organizational taxonomies (Haas, Hall, and Johnson, 1966; Pugh, Hickson, and Hinings, 1969; McKelvey, 1975, 1978, 1982; Pinder and Moore, 1979; Warriner, 1980; Carper and Snizek, 1980; Miller and Friesen, 1984; Rich, 1992; Sanchez, 1993). Taxonomy refers to the theory and practice of classification (McKelvey, 1982: p. 462).

The Haas, Hall, and Johnson effort was designed to be a taxonomy of organizations, similar to that used in zoology to differentiate vertebrata and phyla level (amphibia, mammalia, aves, and reptilia), at the class level, and so on. Using data from seventy-five organizations and some one hundred organizational variables, this study was able to generate nine major classes of organizations. Unfortunately, the bases of differentiation among the classes were seemingly trivial as organizational properties. The reason for the mostly unusable findings may have been the type of measurement used, or it may have been that certain key variables were not included in the analysis. In any event, this initial effort at developing a classification scheme from empirically based characteristics did not produce usable classifications.

The Pugh, Hickson, and Hinings classification effort is an attempt to type organizations according to important structural characteristics. It is also empirically based and uses the following structural dimensions: (1) the structuring of activities, or the degree of standardization of routines, formalization of procedures, specialization of roles, and stipulation of specific behavior by the organization; (2) the concentration of authority, or the centralization of authority at the upper levels of the hierarchy and in controlling units outside the organization; and (3) the line control of workflow, or the degree to which control is exercised by line personnel rather than through impersonal procedures. Using a sample of fifty-two English organizations and the three bases of classification, Pugh, Hickson, and Hinings developed a taxonomy that had seven basic types.

McKelvey (1975) criticized the Haas et al. and the Pugh et al. efforts on several grounds, and his criticisms illustrate the difficulties and complexities in taxonomic efforts. He notes that (1) broad populations of organizations should be included, and if this is not possible, a significant cultural unit, such as a nation-state, should be used; (2) a probability sample of organizations should be employed; (3) the organizational attributes should be as inclusive as possible; (4) given the large array of possible organizational attributes that could be used, a probability sampling of those attributes should be used; (5) the observers (measures) or organizational characteristics should be as inclusive as possible; (6) where necessary, a stratified probability sampling plan for selecting observers (measures) should be used. McKelvey has four additional criticisms of a technical-statistical analytical nature that will not concern us here, but McKelvey's work in general makes a seminal contribution.

Advocates of the taxonomic approach (Warriner, 1979, 1980; McKelvey, 1978, 1982; Pinder and Moore, 1979; Carper and Snizek, 1980; Warriner, Hall, and McKelvey, 1981) argue that a sound taxonomy is the only way in which theoretical advances in organizational analysis can be made. The argument is that unless there is an adequate taxonomy or classification system, both theorists and practitioners have little guide for action. Practitioners have no way of knowing if what works in one organization will work in another, since they have no basis for knowing if the organizations are of the same type. The theorist cannot theorize in the absence of an adequate system.

McKelvey's (1982) work is a major step in the taxonomic direction. Basing his approach on systematics or the science or study of diversity, McKelvey has developed a complex and comprehensive scheme by which an ultimate organizational classification might be possible. The details of McKelvey's suggestions are beyond the scope of the present analysis but include the kinds of issues that have been discussed in this section. McKelvey's approach comes from an evolutionary, population-based perspective.

For our purpose here, two points from McKelvey's work are most relevant. First is the emphasis on populations of organizations. This is equivalent to species of biological creatures. In simple terms, populations of organizations are organizations of the same type. Fast-food restaurants or computer-chip manufacturers could be thought of as populations of organizations. The process of identifying distinct populations, of course, is what the taxonomic effort is all about. The second important point is McKelvey's notion of dominant competence. This refers to the technical and managerial knowledge and skills that enable an organization to survive. McKelvey believes that dominant competencies are probably the key basis on which organizations can be differentiated. A concrete example here would be that small liberal arts colleges can be differentiated from large research universities on the bases of the competencies needed by the administrators in the two different populations of organizations of higher education. What works in one setting would not work in the other. Unfortunately, as promising as this approach seems, it has not been further developed.

On What Variables Should We Classify?

There is a set of variables that appear to be important in any classificatory or taxonomic effort. At the commonsense level is the size variable. As we will see, this is more complex than it appears on its face. At the same time, it would be foolish to develop any typology that does not include size. The size variable is important in relation to all the other factors to be considered.

A more complex variable is the publicness of the organization (Bozeman, 1987). This interesting variable refers to "the degree to which the organization is affected by political authority" (p. xi). In his analysis, Bozeman makes the interesting point that "an organization is public to the extent that it exercises or is constrained by political authority . . . and it is private to the extent that it exercises or is constrained by economic authority" (p. 84). The key point here is that publicness is a variable, as is privateness. Public wars on drugs or AIDS are differentially constrained by economic authority. Private ventures in banking or airlines are differentially constrained by publicness.

The variable of publicness brings us back to the issue of profit versus nonprofit organizations. There are public and private nonprofit organizations. The public organizations are government agencies, whereas the private nonprofit organizations are represented by organizations such as the Red Cross or the Metropolitan Museum of Art. At the same time, there are also for-profit and not-for-profit hospitals and schools.

Economists believe that nonprofit organizations behave in different ways from for-profit organizations in risk taking and engaging in antisocial behavior (Weisbrod, 1989). Sociologists have tended to focus on the social and political origins of nonprofit organizations (DiMaggio and Anheiser, 1990).

Another variable that is interesting to consider in a typology is the extent to which an organization is democratic. Rothschild and Whitt (1986) argue that democratic organizations, in which "control rests ultimately and overwhelmingly with the members" (p. 2) can be found in all sectors of the organizational world. Thus, employee-owned business firms and cooperative day care centers would share space on the democratic end of the continuum.

There is a final element that must be included in any comprehensive taxonomic or classification effort. This is the degree of market power or environmental dominance that an organization possesses (Baron and Bielby, 1984). The proponents of the taxonomic approach seldom consider this issue, but it appears to be of critical importance in understanding organizations.

After all of this discussion, I do not propose a typology or taxonomy, since I believe that a meaningful effort in this area requires empirical verification. In the last few paragraphs, I have suggested a set of variables that appear to be of crucial importance. They are a set of overlapping and intertwining dimensions along which organizations might be classified. They also are complex, but so is our subject matter.

THE VOLUNTARY ORGANIZATION

Our focus thus far has been primarily on organizations with paid employees or members. Another set of organizations—voluntary organizations—confuses typological and general theoretical concerns. According to Knoke and Prensky (1984):

> Voluntary associations are formally organized named groups, most of whose participants do not derive their livelihoods from the organizations' activities, although a few positions may receive pay as staff or leaders. A substantial proportion of associations consist of organizations or persons with economic interests, such as trade associations, professional societies, and labor unions, while many others promote the noneconomic concerns of their members. Association boundaries are often fuzzy and porous (Aldrich, 1971), since many involve episodic supporters and passively interested constituents who can be mobilized under exceptional circumstances to provide financial or political sustenance. (pp. 3–4)

The issue is more complex than Knoke and Prensky portray. The Roman Catholic Church has long been viewed as one of the more complex and comprehensive bureaucratic organizations in the world, with thousands of paid employees. Local parishes, on the other hand, are exactly like the voluntary organizations Knoke and Prensky describe. Professional associations, such as the American Medical Association or the American Nurses' Association, have extensive professional staffs. Of course, there are organizations that are strictly voluntary, such as the Greater Loudonville Association or the Willard Mountain Ski Patrol (I am a member of both). The Greater Loudonville Association is an association of homeowners concerned primarily with community beautification. This can be contrasted with the Love Canal Homeowners Association, which was concerned with matters of life and death (Levine, 1982).

Knoke and Prensky believe that traditional organizational theory has limited usefulness for voluntary organizations. They base their conclusion on analyses of incentive systems and participant commitment, formal structures, leadership and authority, environmental conditions, and organizational effectiveness issues.

From a taxonomic perspective, voluntary organizations probably form several separate classes of organizations. At the same time, to make matters more complicated, there are forms of work organizations that share the characteristics of the voluntary associations that Knoke and Prensky describe. Many new, small business firms and some employee-owned firms are very collectivist (Rothschild-Whitt, 1979; Rothschild and Whitt, 1986) in their membership orientations, leadership patterns, and so on. For the analysis here, voluntary organizations will be treated as a separate category, with most of the focus on organizations with employees, fairly clear boundaries, and the other characteristics given in the earlier definition.

SUMMARY AND CONCLUSIONS

This chapter may have raised more questions than it resolved. After developing an inclusive definition, we considered the thorny and unresolved issues of the reality of organizations and their classification, and stated that the position taken in this book is that organizations are real and that they do act. We also took the position that an empirically based taxonomy would be the best basis for classifying organizations, and we offered some suggestions about the dimensions on which a taxonomic effort might be begun.

My intent in raising these issues and taking a stand on them has been to help in the understanding of organizations. Now that the definitional, reality, and classification issues have been raised and confronted, we can turn to the actual analysis of organizations by beginning to examine organizational structure.

Organizational Structure: Forms and Outcomes

Organizational structure is very easy to understand. Just think about your undergraduate college or university. How did all students enter? Through the admissions office. Where do professors send your grades, and from what office are those grades sent at the end of the term? The registrar's office. Both offices are part of the structure of colleges and universities. They can be thought of as "parts" of those organizations. Organizational structure can be considered the arrangement of organizational parts.

In some ways, organizational structures are analogous to building structures. Buildings have doors through which we enter. Organizations have "ports of entry" as well, such as the admissions office. Hallways and corridors govern our movements. Organizations have rules and procedures, which serve this purpose for their members. Some buildings are small and simple, like my garage; others are complex and multilayered, with intricate linkages and passageways to other buildings. Organizations vary in their degree of complexity. In some buildings the heating and air conditioning are centrally controlled; in others each room is essentially autonomous and its heating and cooling destiny can be controlled by the occupants. Organizations vary in the degree to which people and units are given autonomy in decision making.

This chapter describes the nature of structure. The next chapter considers the reasons structural forms take the shape that they do. At the outset, it should be noted that the building analogy is not perfect. The structure of my house has not changed a bit since it was built some thirty years ago. Organizational structures, however, are continually changing as they are influenced by successive waves of members, interactions among the members, and incessant environmental changes. At the same time, the emergent nature of structure should not blind us to the fact that organizational structures have a strong tendency toward inertia.

What is structure? A formal definition will be given later. Here, some examples are presented to begin to indicate the nature of the topic. The examples are drawn from my own university, the State University of New York (SUNY). My campus is the University at Albany.

SUNY is quite complex. It has units scattered throughout the state of New York and an office in Washington, D.C. My own sociology department even had a degree program in the People's Republic of China for a little while. It has a myriad of divisions and departments, both by academic specialty and by administrative division. It has a tall hierarchy, with a chancellor, vice-chancellors, assistant vice-chancellors, and other ranks at the central office and presidents, vice presidents, associate and assistant vice presidents, deans, associate and assistant deans, faculty members of various ranks, and clerical and service personnel arranged along an array of civil service rankings. By almost any standard, it is a very complex organization. Very complex organizations face very complex coordination and control problems, and SUNY is no different. One way in which coordination and control can be achieved is through effective communication among units. Such communication can be facilitated by the use of a computerized management information systems (MIS). This strategy is not always successful, of course, and the system can be plagued with missing information. We will deal with organizational communication in a later chapter.

SUNY is formalized to varying degrees. In some areas rules and procedures are spelled out in minute detail; in other areas low formalization exists. High formalization at Albany can be seen in the faculty promotion process. The procedures for documenting faculty members' accomplishments in teaching, research, and service are spelled out in excruciating detail. If the details are not followed to the letter, the promotion can well fail. Low formalization, on the other hand, can be seen in the classroom. Individual faculty are almost totally free to select their texts and their methods of classroom presentation. Only in truly extreme cases would the organization intervene in the classroom.

For students, the registration process is highly formalized, with specific dates and times to register, steps to be taken in the process, and forms to be completed. Again, the classroom is at the opposite extreme, except in the case of laboratories, with no official rules on attendance, methods of taking notes, or hours required for studying for exams.

SUNY is also centralized to varying degrees. Low centralization can be seen in an academic department that is almost totally free to select graduate students and faculty members on the basis of the department's own judgment. There is a minimal amount of power utilized at the campus or central administrative levels, except when senior-level professors are being hired. The potential for the exercise of power is there, but it is seldom invoked. High centralization occurs when decision-making power is retained at or near the top of the organization. When new academic programs are developed, particularly when they involve scarce resources, the central administration is heavily involved in the decision-making process. As a general rule, the higher the quality of the higher educational organization, the lower the level of centralization (Blau, 1973), but that is not the issue here. The important conclusion is that complexity, formalization, and centralization can vary within a single organization. They are multidimensional phenomena.

Almost all of the research to be considered in the next two chapters is comparative in the sense that data are collected from more than one organization (Heydebrand, 1973). Some of the research is comparative in the sense that there is an attempt to compare organizations in different settings or societies. Comparative research is emphasized in the belief that it permits generalizations beyond a single research setting. As the discussion of typologies suggests, of course, in the absence of a sound typology such generalizations are risky. Most analysts try to make their findings as widely usable as possible, but the problem of crossing "types" should continue to be recognized. Indeed, as will be evident in the discussion, some of the major research projects have included such a limited range of organizations that generalization becomes difficult.

There is an additional problem in the studies to be considered, and this involves measurement (Price and Mueller, 1986). Data can come from organizational documents and records, key organizational informants, samples of members from the whole organization, or published data sets. (See Pennings, 1973; Azumi and McMillan, 1974; Dewar, Whetten, and Boje, 1980; Lincoln and Zeitz, 1980 and Kalleberg and Van Buren, 1996 for more detailed discussions of some of the methodological issues.) The problem has been that measures of different types, which are designed to measure the same phenomena, such as formalization, do not correlate well. Documents may tell us one thing, but informants another. Research is beginning to show us that there are measures that can be used across diverse sets of organizations (Leicht, Parcel, and Kaufman, 1992, Kalleberg et al., 1996), but as yet we do not have universal measures. These problems of typologies and measurement cannot be resolved here. The problems are raised simply to indicate that the analyses to be considered are themselves in process as researchers seek to develop a cumulative and integrated set of findings.

DEFINING ORGANIZATIONAL STRUCTURE

By organizational structure we mean *"the distributions, along various lines, of people among social positions that influence the role relations among these people"* (Blau, 1974: p. 12; italics added). This simple definition requires amplification. One implication of the definition is the division of labor; people are given different tasks or jobs within organizations. Another implication is that organizations contain ranks, or a hierarchy; the positions that people fill have rules and regulations that specify, in varying degrees, how incumbents are to behave in those positions.

Other definitions stress the importance of human interactions in the formation of structures as "structures shape people's practices, but it is also people's practices that constitute (and reproduce) structure" (Sewell, 1992: p. 4). In a similar vein, structure is seen as *a complex medium of control which is continually produced and recreated in interaction and yet shapes that interaction: structures are constituted and constitutive"* (Ranson, Hinings, and Greenwood: 1980, p. 3; italics added). These approaches emphasize that an organization's structure is not fixed for all time. Rather, it shapes what goes on in an organization and is in turn shaped by what goes on in an organization. This point highlights the fact that organizations are by nature conservative. Their structures "constitute" the interactions that take place within them. Structure does not yield total conformity, but it is intended to prevent random behavior.

A very similar conceptualization of structure is that there is a juxtaposition of technological solutions, political exchanges, and social interpretations in and around organizations, which results in modes of structuring, and that there is a dialectical unfolding of relations among organizational actors. This results in consequences for organizational forms (Fombrun, 1986). Structure is thus continually emergent.

Organizational structures serve three basic functions. First and foremost, structures are intended to produce organizational outputs and to achieve organizational goals—in other words, to be effective. Second, structures are designed to minimize or at least regulate the influence of individual variations on the organization. Structures are imposed to ensure that individuals conform to requirements of organizations and not vice versa. Third, structures are the settings in which power is exercised (structures also set or determine which positions have power in the first place), in which decisions are made (the flow of information into a decision is largely determined by structure), and in which organizations' activities are carried out (structure is the arena for organizational actions).

Multiple Structures

In the discussion that follows, there is an unfortunate problem with much of the literature. The overwhelming majority of studies of organizational structures wittingly or unwittingly make the assumption that there is *one* structure in an organization, but there is ample evidence that this is just not the case (Litwak, 1961; Hall, 1962; Heydebrand, 1990; Stinchcombe, 1990). There are structural differences between work units, departments, and divisions. There are also structural differences according to the level in the hierarchy. For example, a hospital admissions unit has explicit rules and procedures so that all persons who are admitted are treated the same way and so that employees are guided by a clear set of organizationally prescribed expectations. The physical rehabilitation unit of the same hospital has many fewer specific guidelines concerning what it is to do. Similarly, the behavior of lower-level workers, such as orderlies and kitchen workers, is prescribed to a much higher degree than is that of nurses and physicians. There is *intraorganizational variation,* both across organizational units and up and down the hierarchy.

This intraorganizational variation is a crucial factor, of course, when multinational organizations are considered. Not only are there variations within an organization in one national location, but also there can be even greater variations within the same organization across national boundaries (Gupta and Govindarajan, 1991).

Structural Forms

Organizational structures take many forms. A brief review of some of the "classic" literature in the area will demonstrate the manner in which variations occur. The seminal work on structure is Weber's (1947) description of the ideal type of bureaucracy. He states that a bureaucracy has a hierarchy of authority, limited authority, division of labor, technically competent participants, procedures for work, rules for incumbents, and differential rewards. If all these components are present to a high degree in a bureaucracy, it is the ideal type. The important implication, of course, is that organizations in practice will vary from this ideal type, as has been demonstrated (Hall, 1963). A bureaucratic organization is designed for efficiency and reliability (Hage, 1980; Perrow, 1979). This point may seem odd, since for many people, the terms "bureaucracy" and "bureaucrat" have negative connotations. Bureaucracies are actually designed to work well.

Burns and Stalker (1961) took a major step forward with their development of a model of multiple organizational forms. They identified the "mechanical" form, which is very close to Weber's ideal type of bureaucracy, and the "organic" form, which is almost a logical opposite. Thus, instead of having hierarchical authority, organic organizations have a network structure of control; instead of task specialization, a continual adjustment and redefinition of tasks; instead of hierarchical supervision, a communication context involving information and advice; and so on. The authors see organizational forms as being closely linked to the environment in which organizations are embedded, particularly in regard to the technology being employed by the organization, a point later emphasized by Lawrence and Lorsch's (1967) classical research.

The analysis of organizational forms moved forward again when Hage (1965) noted that structural characteristics, such as complexity, formalization, and centralization, vary in their presence from high to low. This formulation serves as the basis for the analysis that follows.

COMPLEXITY

The term "complex organizations" describes the subject matter of this entire book—and indeed is the title of several important works. In this section we will look carefully at the concept of complexity, noting what it is and what are its sources and its consequences. From this examination it should become clear that the complexity of an organization has major effects on the behavior of its members, on other structural conditions, on processes within the organization, and on relationships between the organization and its environment. It has particular importance for communication.

Complexity is one of the first things that hits a person entering any organization except the simplest: Division of labor, job titles, multiple divisions, and hierarchical levels are usually immediately evident. Any familiarity with large corporations (and many small ones), the government, the military, or a school system verifies this. Even organizations that seem very simple at first may exhibit interesting forms of complexity. Local voluntary organizations, such as the Rotary Club, labor union locals, and garden clubs usually have committees for programs, publicity, membership, community service, education, finance, and other matters, all with their attendant structures. These kinds of organizations must make provisions for the control and coordination of activities just as their more complex counterparts must.

The issue is itself made more complex by the fact that individual parts of an organization can vary in their degree of complexity. In a study of the regional office of a major oil company, for example, it was found that there were six divisions, as shown on the organization chart, Figure 3–1. The heads of the divisions had equal rank in the organization, and each was thought to be equally important to the overall success of the organization. When the divisions themselves were examined, it was found that they varied not only in size—from three·to one hundred members—but also in complexity. The largest division, distribution, had five hierarchical levels and three important subdivisions, each of which was further specialized by tasks performed by specific work groups. The smallest division, which performed legal services associated with land acquisition and other problems of service station development, was composed of a lawyer and two secretaries.

These intraorganizational variations in complexity can also be seen in manufacturing firms with research and development departments. These departments are likely to be characterized by a shallower hierarchy than that found in other divisions of the organization. Although there may be several levels above them, the research and development workers will be rather loosely supervised and have a wide span of control. In manufacturing departments, the span of control for each supervisor is shorter, and the whole unit looks more like a pyramid. (See Figure 3–2.)

These examples indicate the obvious—complexity is not a simple issue. It has several components, which do not necessarily vary together. At the same

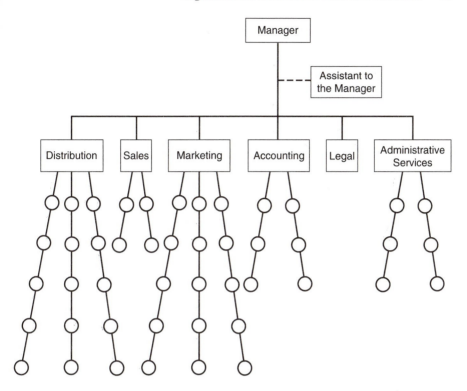

FIGURE 3–1 Regional Office Organization

FIGURE 3–2 The Shape of Two Departments in the Same Organization

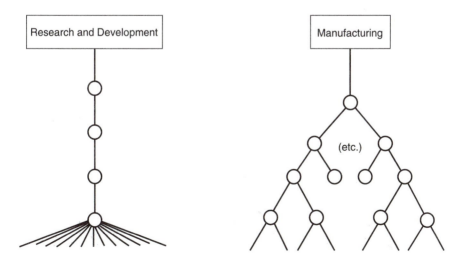

time, the concept itself conveys a meaning in organizational literature: Complex organizations contain many subparts requiring coordination and control, and the more complex an organization is, coordination and control become more difficult to achieve. Since organizations vary widely in their degree of complexity, regardless of the specific component of complexity used, and since wide variations are found within specific organizations, an understanding of complexity is important for the overall understanding of organizations.

To make sense out of the literature on complexity, we must examine the components of the concept. The three elements of complexity most commonly identified are horizontal differentiation; vertical, or hierarchical, differentiation; and geographical dispersion.

Horizontal Differentiation. Horizontal differentiation refers to the ways the tasks performed by the organization are subdivided. Unfortunately for conceptual clarity, there are two basic ways in which such tasks can be subdivided and two ways by which complexity can be measured.

The first way tasks can be subdivided is to give highly trained specialists a comprehensive range of activities to perform; the second is to minutely subdivide the tasks so that nonspecialists can perform them. The first approach is exemplified by professionals or craft workers in the organizational setting who are solely responsible for complete operations. (For a discussion of craft-organized work, see Stinchcombe, 1959. For a comprehensive discussion of the nature of professionally controlled work, see Ritzer and Walczak, 1986.) They are given the responsibility and the authority to carry out the task to its completion.

The second form of horizontal differentiation is most plainly seen on the assembly line, where each worker performs only one or a few repetitive tasks. The nature of the task itself is important here, since it is the routine and uniform task that is most amenable to the second type of differentiation; nonroutine and quite varied tasks are more commonly subdivided according to the first type.

Several writers have elaborated on the first form of horizontal complexity. Hage (1965) defines complexity as the "specialization in an organization . . . measured by the number of occupational specialties and the length of training required by each. The greater the number of occupations and the longer the period of training required, the more complex the organization" (p. 294). Hage's assumption is that the more training people have, the more they are differentiated from people who might have similar amounts of training but in different specialties. This definition is almost identical in its implications to that of Price (1968), who states: "Complexity may be defined as the degree of knowledge required to produce the output of a system. The degree of complexity of an organization can be measured by the degree of education of its members. The higher the education, the higher the complexity" (p. 26).

In some later research, Hage and Aiken (1967a) develop this approach further:

> We interpret complexity to mean at least three things: the number of occupational specialties, the professional activity, and the professional training. Organizations vary in the number of occupational specialties that they utilize in achieving their goals. This variable was measured by asking respondents to report their major duties; each respondent was then classified according to the type of occupational specialty, e.g., psychiatrist, rehabilitation, counselor, teacher, nurse, social worker, and so on. The variable, degree of professional activity, reflects the number of professional associations in which the respondents were involved, the number of meetings attended, and the number of offices held or number of papers given at professional meetings. The amount of professional training was based on the amount of college training as well as other professional training. (pp. 79–80)

Hage and Aiken's research was carried out in health and welfare organizations, where the emphasis on professional backgrounds was very appropriate. The first form of horizontal complexity, then, is based on the number of occupational and professional specialties in the organization.

This form of horizontal differentiation introduces additional complications for the organization, in that a high level of specialization requires coordination of the specialists. In many cases, personnel specifically designated as coordinating personnel have to be assigned to ensure that the various efforts do not work at cross-purposes and that the overall organizational tasks are accomplished.

The second form of horizontal complexity is typically based on counts of job titles within an organization. In large offices, for example, one can find a number of job titles for clerical personnel, such as Typist-1, Typist-2, Typist-3. These distinctions frequently are based on salary or seniority, but they also are usually based on the way labor is divided in the organization. The greater the division of labor, the higher the level of horizontal complexity. The division of labor here is into highly specialized work that is repetitive and routine.

There is greater proliferation of job titles when an organization's racial and sexual composition is heterogeneous (Strang and Baron, 1990). This study found that newer and larger organizations are lowering their number of job titles as they attempt to "streamline" their operations. It is probable, also, that job distinctions based on race and sex are declining in larger, more bureaucratic organizations.

These two approaches to horizontal differentiation appear to have very similar roots, since both are concerned with the division of labor of people within the organization. The critical difference between these forms of horizontal differentiation appears to be the scope of the ultimate tasks of organizations (Dewar and Hage, 1978). Organizations that attempt to carry out a wide variety of activities and that have clients or customers who require a variety of services divide the labor into work performed by specialists. Probably the clearest examples are hospitals, with their medical, dietary, and other specialties. The more minute division of labor occurs when the organization's tasks are not so diffuse and when the organization has grown in size, since such a division of labor provides an economy of scale. Examples are automobile manufacturing firms or a state bureau of motor vehicles. These two forms of complexity are *not* alternative ways to organize for the same task.

The last two paragraphs contain an apparent contradiction that must be addressed. The Strang and Baron (1990) research found that larger and newer organizations have fewer job titles, whereas Dewar and Hage (1978) found that large organizations have more minute division of labor, which means more job titles. There are two probable explanations for the contradiction. One is that large organizations—either by choice or by force—have eliminated job title distinctions based on race and gender since the 1970s and thus have fewer job titles. The second explanation is that Hage and Dewar might have studied organizations that engaged in more routine work than those studied by Strang and Baron. As the next chapter will show, these explanations are consistent with organizational theorists who emphasize the importance of the environment of organizations and technology, respectively. Finally, there is a generally positive relationship between complexity and size, the Strang and Baron findings notwithstanding.

Horizontal complexity can be measured by the number of different jobs that people have, whether the jobs are in specialized professions or crafts or in routine specialized work, through counting job titles.

Horizontal complexity can also be measured by counting the number of divisions, departments, or units within an organization. This is a completely different unit of analysis, which can be found in the research of Blau and Schoenherr (1971), Hall, Haas, and Johnson (1967b), and Pugh et al. (1968). Using measures of this sort, we would find the U.S. Army to be very complex, with its vast array of commands, battalions, brigades, companies, and so on. Organizations low on the complexity scale would be a local church or an auto dealership.

Even though the unit of analysis is very different, the control and coordination issues would be the same whichever measure is used. At the present time, there have not been sufficient attempts to integrate the measurement levels to permit us to determine whether or not the measures really are alternative approaches to the same phenomena.

Vertical Differentiation.   Vertical, or hierarchical, differentiation is less complicated than horizontal differentiation. Research into the vertical dimension has used straightforward indicators of the depth of the hierarchy. Meyer (1968a) uses the "proliferation of supervisory levels" as his measures of the depth of an organization. Pugh et al. (1968) suggest that the vertical dimension can be measured by a "count of the number of job positions between the chief executive and the employees working on the output" (p. 78). Hall, Haas, and Johnson (1967b) use the "number of levels in the deepest single division" and the "mean number of levels for the organization as a whole" (total number of levels in all divisions/number of divisions) as their indicators (p. 906).

These direct indicators of vertical differentiation assume that authority is distributed in accordance with the level in the hierarchy; that is, the higher the level, the greater the authority. Although in the vast majority of cases that would be a valid assumption, there are situations in which proliferation of levels can represent phenomena other than the distribution of authority. For example, in organizations that utilize professional personnel, arrangements may not have been made to allow advancement within the same job title. Physicists may be hired as physicists, but if the organization's policies do not allow much of a salary range for that job title, some physicists may be "promoted" to a higher position without an actual change in their work or an increase in authority. This is known as the "dual ladder."

Both horizontal and vertical differentiation present organizations with problems of communication, control, and coordination. Subunits along either axis (this would include both aspects of horizontal differentiation) are nuclei that are differentiated from adjacent units and the total organization according to horizontal or vertical factors. The greater the differentiation, the greater the potentiality for difficulties in control, coordination, and communication. Informal social networks are also differentiated vertically (Stevenson, 1990).

Geographical Dispersion.   The final element in complexity, geographical dispersion, can actually be a form of horizontal or vertical differentiation. That is, activities and personnel can be geographically dispersed, according to either horizontal or vertical functions, by the separation of power centers or tasks. Field offices of sales or welfare organizations exemplify horizontal dispersion: The tasks performed by the various field offices are essentially identical (low complexity on the horizontal axis) and the power in the organization is differentiated between the central office and the field offices. Local plants of a manufacturing concern exemplify vertical dispersion: Each plant is specialized by product and technology.

Geographical dispersion becomes a separate element in the complexity concept when it is realized that an organization can perform the same functions with the same division of labor and hierarchical arrangements in multiple locations. A business firm, for example, can have a complex set of sales procedures requiring highly specialized sales personnel in the field. These sales personnel can be dispersed from a central office or through regional or state or local offices, with essentially the same hierarchical arrangements. Complexity is thus increased with the development of geographically dispersed activities, even if the horizontal and vertical differentiation remains the same across the spatially separated units.

Geographical dispersion is relatively simple to measure. One can simply count the number of locations in which an organization has offices or plants.

Alternatively, one could simply count the proportion of an organization's personnel who work away from a home headquarters (Raphael, 1967; Hall, Haas, and Johnson, 1967b).

Variance of Complexity Elements

The discussion thus far has suggested that the three major elements of complexity vary, often independently of each other. Before we discuss such independent variance further, we should note that these elements can vary together. Organizations with little horizontal, vertical, or geographical complexity can easily be identified—the small business firm with a single product or service and a single location comes most readily to mind. The same phenomena can occur, however, in large organizations. Crozier's (1964) analysis of two separate government organizations in France graphically demonstrates this.

The first organization, a clerical agency, was characterized by a very simple division of labor; although tasks were highly routine and repetitious, there was little differentiation among them. In addition, considering the size of the organization, there was a very shallow hierarchy. The organization was not complex on the horizontal and vertical axes.

The third axis, spatial dispersion, appeared in Crozier's analysis of a French tobacco company (the "Industrial Monopoly"). The system comprised thirty geographically dispersed plants. The plants were fairly large, with 350 to 400 employees on the average, but there were only six categories of workers in each plant. Production workers, who were paid equal wages throughout the system, made up the bulk of the labor force, and there was little differentiation among their tasks. Maintenance workers (electricians, boilermakers, and metalworkers) were more specialized. Shop foremen held supervisory positions in both plant and white-collar office operations. Even there, the tasks performed were quite similar. Administrative jobs, such as personnel, purchasing, or accounting, were few in number and minimally professionalized. There was one technical engineer per plant. The top position was that of the plant director, who usually had an assistant.

This relatively large dispersed organization was structurally very simple. That simplicity did not eliminate severe problems—Crozier documented these in great detail—but the problems were based on external and internal conditions that were not related to its structure. The imposition of civil service personnel regulations, the power of the maintenance personnel—who could actually control the output of the plants by the speed at which they maintained the equipment—and certain characteristics of the French society combined to make these organizations much less efficient and effective than they might have been. It seems clear that increased complexity on the vertical and horizontal axes would do little to improve the performance of these plants. These noncomplex organizations are enormous systems designed to perform simple and unchanging tasks. It can be hypothesized that if the tasks and technology were altered to develop a more effective system, the organizations would become more complex.

In direct contrast to the simple organizations just described, the diversified industrial or government organization serves as an example of the organization that is complex on all three axes. Huge businesses such as IBM or Chase Bank are characterized by extreme complexity. The same is true for operations of national, state, and some local governments, as well as such diverse organizations as the Roman Catholic Church, the New York City school system, the University of California, and my own SUNY.

These extreme cases serve as a reminder that organizations can be highly or minimally complex in all facets of complexity. Other commonsense examples suggest that such covariance is not the necessary pattern. A liberal arts college, for example, usually has a low degree of vertical differentiation and usually no geographical dispersion but a high degree of horizontal differentiation. Most manufacturing plants have a greater division of labor along the horizontal axis than those studied by Crozier, although the hierarchical levels may be the same. The offensive unit of a football team is highly specialized but essentially has only two ranks. High vertical differentiation with little horizontal differentiation is exemplified by the army battalion.

An assumption throughout this discussion is that most organizations are complex in one of the various configurations discussed. Another assumption, verifiable from a variety of forms of evidence, is that there is a strong tendency for organizations to become more complex as their own activities and the environment around them become more complex. Organizations that survive tend to grow in size, and size and complexity are related. Increased complexity leads to greater problems of coordination and control. We now turn to this outcome of complexity for organizations.

Coordination and Control

In their landmark study, *Organization and Environment,* Lawrence and Lorsch (1967) examined the sources and consequences of complexity. (They used the term "differentiation" instead of "complexity.") They found major differences between departments in the same organization. They also found that structural differentiation contributes to differences in attitudes and behaviors on the part of members of the differentiated departments. These differences include orientations toward the particular goals of the department, emphases on interpersonal skills, and time perspectives. Departments, therefore, vary not only in the specific tasks they perform but also in the underlying behavior and outlooks of their members.

The data for the analysis of differentiation came from firms in three industries in the United States. The first set of industries comprised firms making and selling plastics in the form of powder, pellets, and sheets.

Their products went to industrial customers of all sizes, from the large auto-mobile, appliance, furniture, paint, textile, and paper companies to the smaller firms making toys, containers, and household items. The organizations studied emphasized specialty plastics tailored to specific uses rather than standardized commodity plastics. They all built their product-development work on the science of polymer chemistry. Production was continuous, with relatively few workers needed to monitor the automatic and semiautomatic processing equipment. (p. 24)

These organizations were in a highly competitive market. According to the executives interviewed, the primary competitive issue was the development of new and revised products and processes. The life cycle of any product was likely to be short, since competitors were all engaged in intensive research and could make even a very successful product quickly obsolete. The executives noted that "the most hazardous aspect of the industrial environment revolved around the relevant scientific knowledge" (p. 25). These organizations were in a changing and "turbulent" environment, with both input—in the form of sci-entific knowledge—and the consumption of output—in the form of customer satisfaction after purchasing the product—highly uncertain. On the other hand, the production process itself was characterized by its certainty. Once the orig-inal technical specifications for a particular product were developed, the pro-duction process could proceed automatically, since the mix between such production variables as pressure, temperature, and chemical composition could be easily measured, and monitoring was a part of the production process itself.

The six organizations studied within the plastics industry each had four basic functional departments—sales, production, applied research, and funda-mental research—that differed in their own structures. The production de-partments were the most formalized, the fundamental research units the least. Sales department personnel were the most concerned with interpersonal rela-tionships, and production departments were the least, with the two research units falling in between. The interesting dimension of the time perspective taken by the personnel shows the departments falling into a predictable pat-tern—from shortest to longest time perspective, with sales, production, ap-plied research, and fundamental research fitting the time perspective framework in that order. In practice, this means that sales personnel wanted to have orders filled immediately, whereas the scientists in the fundamental research department were looking two or three years down the road in their time frame. The members of the various departments also differed in personal goals; sales personnel were concerned with customer problems and the mar-ketplace, production personnel with cost reduction and efficiency, and re-search personnel with scientific matters, as well as the more immediate practical issues of process improvement and modification. The scientific per-sonnel were not as concerned with purely scientific matters as the authors had anticipated, but they did have clearly different goals from those of the mem-bers of other departments.

These differences in task, behavior, and attitude are directly related to the kind of environment that various departments must work with in their short- and long-run activities. A high degree of differentiation (complexity) is, therefore, related to a highly complex and differentiated environment (Burns and Stalker, 1961). In this case the complexity refers to the competitive situation in which the organizations find themselves (this degree of competition is not limited to profit-making organizations) and to the rapidly changing and complicated technological world in which they must survive.

To provide contrasts to the plastics firms, Lawrence and Lorsch (1967) studied two other industries; the primary factor in their selection was the rate of environmental change. The second industry they chose was the standardized container industry. The standardized containers were beer bottles. The rate of sales increase in this industry was at about the level of the rate of population growth and the growth of the gross national product, so the organizations in the industry were approximately keeping even with the environment in these respects. More important for the purposes of the study, no significant new products had been introduced in two decades—in the 1960s beer bottles were almost all brown and held 12 ounces. The major competitive factors were "operational issues of maintaining customer service through prompt delivery and consistent product quality while minimizing operating costs" (p. 86). Although these are not easy or simple tasks to perform, they are stable; and the problems and prospects for the future are much more certain than in the plastics field.

The third set of organizations studied was in the packaged foods industry. The environmental conditions of these organizations were in between those of the plastics and container firms. Although the organizations engaged heavily in innovations, the rate of new-product introduction and the growth of sales were less than in the plastics industry but more than in the container field.

When the differentiation within the organizations in these three industries was examined, the findings were as predicted—the plastics firms were the most differentiated, followed by the food firms, and then by the container firms. Lawrence and Lorsch did not stop their analysis with differentiation, however.

They extended their analysis to the concept of integration, which they define as "the quality of the state of collaboration that exists among departments that are required to achieve unity of effort by the demands of the environment" (p. 47). The authors were also concerned with the effectiveness of the organizations. Here they used standard and appropriate market and economic measures, such as profit. Organizations are also more effective when they meet environmental pressures and when they allow their members to achieve their individual goals.

The results of the analysis of integration and effectiveness are in some ways surprising. In the plastics industry, the most effective organizations were those with the greatest degree of differentiation, and they also faced the most severe integration problems. Their effectiveness in the face of high differentiation was explained by their successful conflict resolution. It is not the idea of successful conflict resolution that is surprising; it is the fact that the effective organizations were characterized by a high degree of conflict in the first place—that they were not totally harmonious, with all personnel working as members of one happy team. From the data discussed earlier, it is apparent that the differentiation in departmental and individual attitudes and behavior would lead inevitably to conflict. In these organizations, such conflict contributed to effectiveness.

Conflict per se, of course, would be detrimental to the organization if it were not resolved. So another important contribution of this research is its analysis of conflict resolution. The authors do not suggest that there is one best form of such resolution. Rather, they provide evidence that conflict-resolution processes varied according to the specific conflict situations in a particular form of organization. In the case of the highly differentiated plastics organizations, integration was achieved by departments or individuals who were in a position, and had the knowledge available, to work with the departments involved in conflict situations. In this case, the position was relatively low in the managerial hierarchy rather than at the top. The lower position was necessary because of the specific knowledge required to deal with the departments and issues involved. The highly differentiated and effective organization thus anticipated conflict and established integrating (conflict-resolving) departments and individuals whose primary purpose was to work with the departments in (inherent) conflict. Another important consideration was that the integrating departments or individuals were equidistant between the conflicting departments in their time, goal, interpersonal, and structural orientations. This middle position led to effective resolution not through simple compromise but through direct confrontations between the conflicting parties. Conflict resolution in this setting thus became a process whereby the parties thrashed out their differences in the open with the assistance of integrators who understood both positions.

In the container corporations, with their lesser degree of differentiation, conflicts also arose, but not to the extent found in the plastics firms, owing to less differentiation. In the container industry, conflicts were resolved at the top of the organization, because those at the top had greater knowledge, made possible by the stable environment and the lack of differentiation between organizational segments. With less differentiation, knowledge was not as specialized, and a top executive could have a good grasp of what was going on in all the major divisions. Lawrence and Lorsch suggest that in this case, and in others like it, decentralization of influence would be harmful. The food-processing firms generally fell between the plastics and the container firms in the extent of their differentiation and in the integration problems faced.

A major conclusion from this analysis is that effectiveness is not achieved by following one organizational model. This conclusion is vitally important for understanding organizations. In other words, there is no one best way to organize for the purpose of achieving the highly varied goals of organizations within highly varied environments. This is a *contingency* approach to organizational structure, which says that under some conditions one form of structure is more effective or efficient, whereas under other conditions alternative forms are more effective or efficient. The contingency model continues to be a dominant force in organizational theory.

Research in a very different setting—hospital emergency units—reached a very similar sort of conclusion (Argote, 1982). Argote found that in situations of low uncertainty, programmed coordination contributed to greater effectiveness, whereas in situations of high uncertainty, nonprogrammed modes of coordination were more effective. The structural arrangements are contingent upon the situation being faced.

This conclusion is further strengthened by a consideration of Blau and Schoenherr's (1971) findings, which were based on research into government finance and public personnel agencies. Blau and Schoenherr also found that increased complexity engenders problems of communication and coordination. Personnel in the managerial hierarchy spend more time in dealing with these problems than in direct supervision in a highly complex organization. There is also pressure in complex organizations to add personnel to handle the increased difficulties with control and coordination, increasing the proportion of the total personnel devoted to such activities. This is known as administrative intensity.

This last finding introduces an interesting paradox into the analysis of organizations. Although large organizations can experience savings through economies of large size, the complexity that is related to large size creates cross-pressures to add managerial personnel to reduce the problems associated with control, coordination, and conflict. Decisions to physically disperse, add divisions, or add hierarchical levels may be made in the interests of economy. Paradoxically, the economies realized may be counterbalanced by the added burdens of keeping the organization together. There is yet another paradox. Although there is a positive relationship between technical and structural complexity and administrative intensity when an organization is growing, the relationship weakens when organizations are in a period of decline (McKinley, 1987).

Complex organizations are thus complex in more ways than just their structure. The processes within such organizations are also complex. The techniques that are effective and efficient within a simple structure just may not be effective or efficient in a more complex one. Also, within a complex organization, different departments deal with different degrees of uncertainty and are structured differently, as Lawrence and Lorsch's research so strongly demonstrated and Stinchcombe's recent (1990) work confirms.

Some Additional Correlates of Complexity

Complexity is related to additional characteristics of organizations. An analysis of program change in sixteen welfare organizations illustrates this point well. Program change in these agencies involves the adoption of new services and techniques designed to increase the quality of the services rendered. When this study was being conducted, a great number of new social programs were being introduced (Hage and Aiken, 1967b).

This study found that both vertical and horizontal differentiation are related to higher rates of program change. This finding suggests that when such forms of differentiation are present, much information will be flowing in the system—information that contains conflicting ideas and proposals. Organizations that are complex in this way face the problem of integrating the diverse occupations and ideas deriving from the different organizational members. Later studies confirm that such conflict is present and must be dealt with by the organization. The proper method of handling such conflict is not by suppression; we have already seen that that would represent the exact opposite of the effective utilization of highly trained personnel. We will see later that such conflicts actually work to the organization's advantage.

Hage and Aiken's work on program change implies that organizational change is related to organizational characteristics. This implication is supported in later research, which compared the effects of structural characteristics (such as size and complexity), together with environmental conditions (changing or heterogeneous), with individual characteristics (age, attitudes, and education) on organizational innovation (Baldridge and Burnham, 1975). Organizational characteristics were more strongly related to innovation in organizations than the other factors. This does not negate the role of the individual but suggests that factors such as complexity are crucial in understanding how and why processes such as innovation occur.

Aiken and Hage (1968) continued their investigation of the sixteen welfare agencies three years after their initial study. The dependent variable in their second study was organizational interdependence, as indicated by the number of joint programs in which the agencies participated. The findings from this analysis are not surprising in light of the earlier findings and discussion. *"Organizations with many joint programs are more complex organizations, that is they are more highly professionalized and have more diverse occupational structure"* (p. 920; italics in original). The interpretation given to these findings is that a decision to engage in joint programs leads to the importation of new specialties into the organization, since joint programs are likely to be highly specialized and the personnel in the agency would not have the skills necessary for participation.

These findings have interesting implications for organizations and for the society of which they are a part. Aiken and Hage note that there is a tendency for organizations to become more complex because of internal and external pressures. These findings imply that joint programs and other interorganizational relationships will continue to develop, probably at an increasing rate. In the long run, this would lead to a society in which the web of interrelationships between organizations would become extremely intricate and the total society more organizationally "dense." This in turn implies a condition in which both individuals and the society as a whole are dependent upon fewer and more complex organizations. The nature of these organizations and their orientation toward the good of the few or of the many present the society with the question of the source of control of the organizations. If this trend is realized, decisions regarding organizational futures become decisions about society.

The short-run implication of these findings seems to be that the more complex an organization is, the more complex it will become, since the development of new programs and interorganizational relationships both lead to additional complexity. These relationships remain true, but in the thirty years since the Hage and Aiken studies, there have been changes that have altered considerations of complexity. Both downsizing and the improvement of management information systems have contributed to the potential for less complexity in many organizations. Organizations thus contain cross-pressures that push toward both greater and lesser complexity.

There is one more twist to the complexity issue that is interesting. Vaughan (1983) found that corporate crimes are related to complexity. In this formulation, organizations may become so diversified and complex that top management may not be able to control subunits. The same argument is frequently made in regard to intercollegiate athletics and the illegal recruitment and payment of college athletes.

Complexity is a basic structural characteristic. It is linked to the fate of the organization and to the fates of individuals within the organization. There appears to be strong evidence that particular degrees of vertical, horizontal, or spatial complexity are related to organizational survival and continuity in particular situations. If an organization chooses an inappropriate form or is unable for whatever reason—economic, personnel, tradition, leadership—to adapt its structure to changed situations, it will likely soon be in trouble.

FORMALIZATION

We have already alluded to formalization several times. In this section the exact nature of this important aspect of organizational structure will be explicitly defined. The antecedents and outcomes of formalization will also be spelled out. In addition, the reactions of individuals to the degree of formalization will be analyzed. In many ways, formalization is the *key* structural variable for the individual, because a person's behavior is vitally affected by the degree of such formalization. The amount of individual discretion is inversely related to the amount of preprogramming of behavior by the organization.

Formalization is not a just an abstract concept. Indeed, the degree to which an organization is formalized is an indication of the perspectives of its decision makers in regard to organizational members. If the members are thought to be capable of exercising excellent judgment and self-control, formalization will be low; if they are viewed as being incapable of making their own decisions and requiring a large number of rules to guide their behavior, formalization will be high. Formalization involves organizational control over the individual (Clegg and Dunkerley, 1980) and thus has an ethical and a political meaning in addition to being a structural component.

The introduction of the individual does not mean a shift away from the organizational level of analysis. Formalization has important consequences for the organization and its subunits in regard to such processes as communications and innovation.

The rules and procedures designed to handle contingencies faced by the organization are part of what is called formalization. The extent of rules and procedures varies. The simple matter of when people get to work can vary widely among and within organizations in regard to the degree to which this act is formally specified. At the high end of the formalization continuum are organizations that specify that people must be at their desks or workstations at 8 A.M. or they will be "docked" a half-hour's pay. At the other end of the continuum are organizations that have no rules about being in the office or shop at a particular time, just as long as the work gets done. This is typified by many academic institutions and by telecommuting.

Formalization can also be enabling for individuals, since formalized procedures assist people in accomplishing their work. At the same time, it is also coercive as people are forced into compliance (Adler and Borys, 1996). It is hardly a neutral concept.

Maximal Formalization.   Rules and procedures can vary from highly stringent to extremely lax. These variations exist on the whole range of behaviors covered by organizational rules. An example of highly formalized procedures is the assembly line, where a piece of material is always passed in the same direction and the same work is always performed on it. Similarly, in an office, letters requesting a certain type of information are always processed in the same way, and the same type of information is returned to the requester. Much telemarketing also represents a high level of formalization, since telemarketers have a script from which they cannot deviate.

Minimal Formalization.   At the other end of the formalization-of-procedures continuum are unique cases, for which no procedures have been developed. In these cases, members of the organization must use their own discretion in deciding what to do. At the extreme are situations that call for intuition, and even perhaps inspiration, to be solved—unique situations with no preprogrammed answers (Perrow, 1967). Organizations that have low formalization are those that deal constantly with new situations for which precedents do not exist—for example, organizations engaging in frontier areas of scientific research. Organizations dealing with human problems, such as mental health clinics, are in a similar situation.

Most organizations are somewhere between the extremes of the continuum of formalization, as research on measuring formalization has found.

Measuring Formalization.   It usually doesn't matter whether procedures or rules are formalized in writing, since unwritten norms and standards can frequently be just as binding as written ones. Nevertheless, most research utilizes the written systems of rules and procedures as the basis for assessment and analysis.

In some familiar research, Hage and Aiken (1967a) provide the following definition of formalization:

> Formalization represents the use of rules in an organization. Job codification is a measure of how many rules define what the occupants of positions are to do, while rule observation is a measure of whether or not the rules are employed. In other words, the variable of job codification represents the degree to which the job descriptions are specified, and the variable, rule observation, refers to the degree to which job occupants are supervised in conforming to the standards established by job codification. Job codification represents the degree of work standardization while rule observation is a measure of the latitude of behavior that is tolerated from standards. (p. 79)

These variables are measured by asking the members of organizations to respond to a series of questions bearing directly on these issues. Measures of their perceptions of their own organization are thus used to determine the extent to which the organizations are formalized.

The British Aston Group (Pugh et al., 1968), working in the same era, used essentially the same conceptualization of formalization but based their measurement on official written records and documents from the organizations they studied. For example, if workers were provided with an official handbook describing their tasks and duties, the organization got a high score on formalization. In highly formalized situations, there is very little discretion available for members to operate on their own.

The similarities between these definitions point up the general consensus about the meaning of formalization. Even when quite different measures of this variable are used in research, the same meaning is utilized, an all-too-rare occurrence in organizational analysis. Unfortunately, research (Pennings, 1973; Dewar, Whetten, and Boje, 1980) has indicated that these different measures are themselves only weakly related. Thus, although there is conceptual closure in regard to formalization, measurement problems are not fully resolved.

Formalization and Other Organizational Properties

Centralization of Power.   Power is an important component of all organizations. The distribution of power in organizations is conceptualized as the degree of centralization, which is the topic of the last major section of this chapter. Here we consider the relationships between formalization and centralization.

In their study of the social welfare agencies, Hage and Aiken (1967a) found that formalization was weakly associated with a centralized decision-making system. Organizations in which the decisions were made by only a few people at the top relied on rules and close supervision as a means of ensuring consistent performance by the workers. These organizations were also characterized by a less professionalized staff. Thus, the presence of a well-trained staff is related to a reduced need for extensive rules and policies.

This interpretation is supported in an analysis of public personnel agencies (Blau, 1970). In organizations with highly formalized personnel procedures and rigid conformity to those procedures, there was decentralization of authority. At first glance this is contradictory, since the evidence seems to say that formalization and decentralization are related. A closer examination reveals strong compatibility with the Hage and Aiken findings. In this case, adherence to merit-based personnel procedures ensures the presence of highly qualified personnel at the local (decentralized) level. These people are then entrusted with more power than are personnel with fewer qualifications. Formalization in one area of operations may thus be associated with flexibility in another.

On this point Blau states:

> Rigidity in some respects may breed flexibility in others. Not all aspects of bureaucratization are concomitant. The bureaucratic elaboration of formalized personnel procedures and rigid conformity with these personnel standards do not necessarily occur together, and neither aspect of bureaucratization of procedures gives rise to a more rigid authority structure, at least not in employment security agencies. Indeed, both strict conformity with civil service standards and the elaboration of these formalized standards have the opposite effect of fostering decentralization, which permits greater flexibility. (p. 160)

This relatively simple set of findings reinforces a notion expressed earlier: Complex organizations are complex. Formalization in one area brings pressure to decrease formalization in another area. Organizations are thus constantly in conflict, not only between individuals or subunits, but also between and within the processes and structures that make up the organization. Formalization is not just a matter of internal adjustment.

It is important to note that the research of Hage and Aiken and of Blau deals with relatively professionalized workforces. One of the hallmarks of professionalization is the ability and willingness to make decisions based upon professional training and experience. It is not surprising to find lower levels of formalization in such situations. When the workforce under consideration does not or is assumed not to have this decision-making capacity, the implications of the Blau findings have to be reexamined. In that case, formalized personnel procedures would probably be associated with a more centralized decision-making system, with the formalization level probably more consistent in all phases of the operation. The organization retains control over the individual in both cases. By selecting highly qualified or indoctrinated individuals, it assures itself that the individuals will act according to organizational demands (Blau and Schoenherr, 1971: pp. 347–67).

Program Change.   Further research by Hage and Aiken (1967b) into the rate of program change in the agencies reveals that formalization is also related to the number of new programs added in the organizations. In this case, formalization is negatively associated with the adoption of new programs. The reduction of individual initiative in the more formalized setting is suggested as the primary reason for this relationship. In organizations that establish highly specific routines for the members to follow, there is likely to be little time, support, or reward for involvement in new ideas and new programs.

Technology.   In their continuing research in these sixteen agencies, Hage and Aiken (1969) divide the organizations into "routine" and "nonroutine" categories of technology. Even though these are all social agencies, there is a marked difference in the degree of routineness.

> The highest on routineness is a family agency in which the case-workers use a standard client interview that takes less than fifteen minutes. The purpose of the interview is to ascertain the eligibility of clients for county, federal, or state medical aid. An interviewee said:
>   ". . . somewhat routine—even though each patient is individual, the type of thing you do with them is the same. . . ." The organization at the other extreme is an elite psychiatric family agency in which each member is an experienced therapist and allowed to work with no supervision at all. (Hage and Aiken, 1969: p. 369)

The relationship between routinization and formalization is in the expected direction. *"Organizations with routine work are more likely to have greater formalization of organizational roles"* (Hage and Aiken, 1969: p. 371; italics in original). Since these organizations tend to be on the nonroutine end of an overall continuum of routineness, the findings are even more striking. Had organizations more toward the routine end of the continuum been included, the differences observed would probably have been greater.

Hage and Aiken's research, one of the most thorough and systematic programs of research available in the literature, is based on data from a limited number of organizations of relatively similar characteristics. The limitations inherent in using this type of database are difficult to avoid, given the intrinsic difficulties in organizational research. But despite these limitations, the findings are generally consistent with those of the Aston Group (Pugh's research team), which proceeded independently and with very different measures.

It will be remembered that the Pugh research was carried out on a sample of English work organizations. These researchers were interested in obtaining indicators of the organizations and the contexts in which they operated. Their major indicator of technology was workflow integration.

> Among organizations scoring high, with very integrated, automated, and rather rigid technologies, were an automobile factory, a food manufacturer, and a swimming baths department. Among those scoring low, with diverse, nonautomated, flexible technologies, were retail stores, an education department, and a building firm. (Pugh et al., 1968: p. 103)

Although they contain more diversity than those in the Aiken and Hage study, these organizations are clustered toward the routine end of the routine–nonroutine continuum. As would be expected from the previous discussion, technology emerges as an important predictor of the degree to which activities are structured in these organizations.

Another study that examined the technology linkage found strong evidence in favor of the high routinization—high formalization conclusion. Dornbusch and Scott (1975) studied an electronics assembly line, a physics research team, a university faculty, a major teaching hospital, a football team, schools, a student newspaper, and a Roman Catholic archdiocese. Their evidence, from that diverse set of organizations, is consistent with the technological argument that has been presented.

Lest it appear that the relationship between technology and formalization is settled because of the weight of the evidence presented, it should be noted that Glisson (1978) essentially reverses the causal ordering. He finds that procedural specifications (formalization) determine the degree of routinization in service delivery. In the Glisson study, a decision made in regard to how to structure the organization led to the utilization of a particular service delivery technology. Although the high correlation between routinization and formalization remains, the reason for the correlation is reversed in this case.

Tradition and Culture.   One more component should be added to these considerations. Organizations emerge in different historical eras (Meyer and Brown, 1977), face varying contingencies, and develop different traditions. These differences in turn influence how factors such as technology affect the degree of formalization. For example, if for some reason—such as the belief system of an important early top executive—an organization became highly formalized in its codification of job descriptions in writing, it would probably continue to be more formalized over time than other factors would predict. Organizations develop characteristics that are embedded in the formal and informal systems of the organization. They are constrained by the structure and knowledge that are built up in their history (Zhou, 1993). This point is well recognized by scholars who study organizational culture (see Frost et al., 1985). Organizational culture will be considered in more detail in the next chapter.

By its very nature, formalization is central to the life of and in organizations. The specification of rules, procedures, penalties, and so on predetermines much of what goes on in an organization. Indeed, formalization is a major defining characteristic of organizations, since behavior is not random and is directed by some degree of formalization toward a goal.

We have examined the relationships between formalization and other organizational properties. We now shift the focus to the individual in the organization. Like formalization, individuals must be treated as variables, since they bring different abilities and habits and other behaviors with them into the organization. Formalization is designed to be a control mechanism over individuals (Clegg and Dunkerley, 1980).

FORMALIZATION AND OUTCOMES FOR INDIVIDUALS

An extreme example of formalization can be found in Crozier's (1964) analysis of the two French organizations. He notes: "Impersonal rules delimit, in great detail, all the functions of every individual within the organization. They prescribe the behavior to be followed in all possible events. Equally impersonal rules determine who shall be chosen for each job and the career patterns that can be followed" (pp. 187–88). This extremely high degree of formalization, plus several other characteristics of the organizations, create a "vicious circle" in which the workers follow the rules for the sake of the rules themselves, since that is the basis on which they are evaluated. The rules become more important than the goals they were designed to help accomplish. The organization becomes very rigid and has difficulties dealing with customers and other aspects of the environment. Since the rules prescribe the kinds of decisions to be made, those in decision-making positions tend to create more rules when situations arise for which there are no precedents. Rules become security for the employee. There is no drive for greater autonomy, since that would be threatening. There is a strong desire to build safeguards through increased rigidity. The personnel in such a system become increasingly unable to operate on their own initiative and, in fact, seek to reduce the amount of freedom to which they are subject. To one who values individual freedom, this is a tragedy. It would be presumptuous to say that it is such for the individuals involved, even though the argument could be made that the long-run consequences for them and for the total social system may indeed be tragic from several moral and ethical perspectives. For the organization, the consequences are clear; it becomes maladaptive to changes of any sort.

These personal and organizational dysfunctions were recognized in Robert Merton's (1957) seminal discussion of the "bureaucratic personality." Merton notes that a trained incapacity can develop in the kind of situation under discussion. Actions and decisions based on past training and experience may be very inappropriate under new or different conditions. Merton suggests that the process whereby these conditions develop is part of the system itself.

> The bureaucrat's official life is planned for him in terms of a graded career, through the organization devices of promotion by seniority, pensions, incremental salaries, etc., all of which are designed to provide incentives for disciplined action and conformity to the official regulations. The official is tacitly expected

to and largely does adapt his thoughts, feelings, and actions to the prospect of this career. But *these very devices* which increase the probability of conformance also lead to an over-concern with strict adherence to regulations which induces timidity, conservatism, and technicism. Displacement of sentiments from goals onto means is fostered by the tremendous symbolic significance of the means (rules). (pp. 200–201; italics in original)

Organizations are concerned primarily with the work behavior of their members. They also can extend their control into other areas of life. Even though it is politically incorrect to discuss sexual attraction, it does take place, even in organizations, and organizations actually do attempt to control romance in the workplace (Quinn, 1977). Although Quinn does not claim that organizations are hotbeds of romance, he documents the obvious point that sexual intimacy does occur. When a romance develops, actions are taken to terminate the relationship, since it is typically seen as disruptive for the organization. Punitive actions, such as dismissals, are one course of action and are much more likely be taken against the women involved than against the men. Less drastic measures, such as transfers, reprimands, or simple efforts to persuade people to stop the romance, were also found. The point is that even in areas of intimacy, organizations attempt to control behavior.

Reactions to Formalization

Formalization is frequently seen as some form of evil, leading to such reactions as "bureaupathic" or "bureautic" (Thompson, 1961) in which people are consumed by organizational rules and regulations. There is another side to the issue, of course. In Chapter 1, we noted that some research (Kohn, 1971) actually sees formalization, in the form of bureaucracy, as one mechanism by which individuals can experience personal growth and development. So the question really is, How do people react to formalization?

Some insights can be found in the literature on professionals in organizations. There has been a strong interest in this topic, since increasing numbers of professionals of all sorts are working in organizations, and many occupations are attempting to professionalize. Analyses of the relationships between professionals and their employing organizations formerly proceeded from the premise that there are built-in strains between professional and organizational principles and values (see, for example, Kornhauser, 1963; Blau and Scott, 1962). More recent research has challenged that assumption. It is now viewed as quite possible that there can be situations in which professionals are able to carry out their work with a minimum amount of interference from the organization, and the organization is able to integrate the work of the professionals for its own benefit.

This approach is followed in a study of the degree of alienation experienced by scientists and engineers employed in a large corporation in the aerospace industry (Miller, 1967). These professionals reported that they felt more alienation when their supervisor used directive, rather than participative or laissez-faire, supervisory practices and less alienation in situations in which they themselves had some control over the decisions affecting their work. The same general pattern was found in regard to other incentives that the organization provided professionals. There was less alienation when the scientists and the engineers had some part in deciding the nature of their own research efforts, when the company provided opportunities and a climate for the pursuit of their own professional careers, and when the company encouraged purely professional activities, such as the publication of papers or pursuit of additional training.

Miller also found that the length of professional training was associated with the extent of alienation felt. The more training people have, the more they are likely to feel alienation under those conditions that produce it for the group of professionals as a whole. That is, for a Ph.D. scientist, the absence of encouragement of professional activities is more likely to produce alienation than it is for an M.A. scientist.

Utilizing the idea of intraorganizational variations in structure, Miller also examined the extent of alienation felt by the professionals when the specific work location was considered. Some of the professionals worked in a basic research-and-development laboratory in the company, but most were employed in research and development in one of the major production units. The personnel in the basic research laboratory experienced much less alienation than those in the production-oriented unit.

This study is most relevant for the analysis here. Professionals were examined because they bring to the organization a set of externally (professionally) derived standards by which they can guide their own behavior. The presence of organizational guidelines (formalization) is thus a duplication of norms that are probably perceived as less valid than are the norms of the profession involved. For professionals, therefore, the greater the degree of formalization in the organization, the greater the likelihood of alienation from work.

This point is supported further when two additional research reports are considered. Part of the research of Aiken and Hage (1966) was concerned with the degree of alienation felt by the professionals in the sixteen social welfare agencies they examined. They, too, were concerned with alienation from work, but they also looked at alienation from expressive relations. This was measured by responses to questions asking the degree of satisfaction felt about superiors and co-workers. The less satisfaction felt, the more the individual is alienated from expressive relations.

As would be expected from the direction of this discussion, the greater the degree of formalization of the organization, the more alienated were the workers in both areas of alienation. Alienation was much more strongly felt in regard to the job itself. "This means that there is great dissatisfaction with work in those organizations in which jobs are rigidly structured; rigidity may lead to strong feelings of work dissatisfaction but does not appear to have such a deleterious impact on social relations in the organization" (p. 504). Strict enforcement of rules was strongly related to both forms of alienation; social relations are also disturbed when rules are strictly enforced. It was also found that both forms of alienation were high when authority in the organizations was centralized and the members had little opportunity to participate in decision making.

A different approach was taken in my analysis of the relationships between professionalization and bureaucratization (Hall, 1968). Bureaucratization is a broader concept than formalization, but it contains many of the same implications, as indicated in earlier discussions of the topic. I attempted to demonstrate that professionalization, like formalization, is a continuous variable, with some occupations being more professionalized than others. The study included physicians, nurses, accountants, teachers, lawyers, social workers, stockbrokers, librarians, engineers, personnel managers, and advertising account executives. After the occupations were ranked according to their attitudes toward several professional values, the average scores for each occupation were matched with the scores on bureaucratization measures for the organizational units in which these people worked. The results indicated that, in general, bureaucratization is inversely related to professionalization. This is consistent with the argument in this section. Examined more closely, these findings reveal some interesting patterns.

A weak relationship was found on the bureaucratic dimension involving the presence of rules. The kinds of rules the organizations developed in these cases apparently did not interfere with the work of the professionals. There was a stronger negative relationship on the procedural-specifications dimension. As more procedures were specified by the organization, the burden on the professionals apparently was stronger. In this case, the professionals were likely to want to utilize procedures that they themselves developed on the job or through their professional training.

Most of the studies that have been discussed have concluded that professionalization and formalization are incompatible. The more professionalized the workforce, the more likely that formalization will lead to conflict and alienation. A major implication of these findings is that formalization and professionalization are actually designed to do the same thing—organize and regularize the behavior of the members of the organization. Formalization is a process in which the organization sets the rules and procedures and the means of ensuring that they are followed. Professionalization, on the other hand, is a nonorganizationally based means of doing the same thing. From the organization's point of view, either technique would be appropriate, as long as the work gets done.

It is exactly at this point that the organization faces a major internal dilemma. If it allows too little freedom for its members, they are likely to feel oppressed, alienated, and "bureaucratic," and to engage in rule following for its own sake. If, on the other hand, it allows more freedom, behavior could become erratic and organizationally irrelevant. The basic factor here appears to be the kinds of guidelines for behavior that the individuals themselves bring to the organization. The more work standards they bring with them, the less the need for organizationally based standards.

It is difficult, of course, for the organization to know what kind of standards people bring with them. Even the use of a relatively common criterion, such as membership in a recognized profession, is not a perfect predictor, since not all members of a profession act in accordance with its standards and not all professional standards are good for all organizations. And when the organization moves into other personnel areas, away from the professions or established crafts, the availability of such external criteria is problematic. Because even well-developed external criteria, such as professionalization, may at times be organizationally irrelevant, the organization has to develop its own system of rules and procedures to accomplish what it is attempting to do.

Before moving to additional implications of formalization for the individual and the organization, we must draw another conclusion from the analysis of professionals in organizations. The emphasis in much of the research in this area is on conflict between the professional and the employing organization. Evidence from the Hall research suggests that such conflict is not inevitable and should not be assumed without demonstration. This research found, for example, that the legal departments of large organizations are not necessarily more bureaucratized than law firms of comparable size. Lawyers working in the trust department of a bank may actually be working in an organizational environment similar, and perhaps even identical, to the one they would find in a law firm. This suggests that it is very possible to find organizational structures that are compatible with the degree of professionalization of their members.

The finding that legal or other professional departments in organizations may not be more bureaucratized or formalized than autonomous law firms raises another issue. The legal department of a bank is clearly less formalized than the division in charge of handling, sorting, and verifying checks. As is true of complexity, there are degrees of formalization within the organization. This can be most easily seen between departments, but it also occurs between levels in the organization. In general, the higher the level, the less the formalization (Hall, 1962; Child, 1973).

Zeitz's (1983, 1984) research provides an appropriate way to conclude this section. He found that formal structuring of activities had positive effects on organizational members' levels of satisfaction and perceived organizational climate. At the same time, role constraints and rule enforcement had negative effects. Well-delineated rules apparently provide a meaningful framework in which to work. Organ and Greene (1981) also found that formalization reduced ambiguity for a sample of scientists and engineers. In these studies, the interactions between levels of formalization and organizational members' expectations were the key to the ways in which individuals reacted to their organizations.

CENTRALIZATION

Centralization refers to the distribution of power within organizations. Centralization is thus one of the best ways to summarize the whole notion of structure. As was noted earlier, structure can be viewed as constituted and constitutive (Ranson, Hinings, and Greenwood, 1980). In the case of centralization, a given distribution of power is constitutive in that it generates other actions—people comply with organizational rules and decisions. Centralization is also constituted in that power distributions are subject to change as groups and individuals gain or lose power over time. Power itself will be considered in detail in Chapter 5. Here we will consider the nature and correlates of the structural aspect of power in organizations.

Centralization has been defined in several ways, the emphasis always being on the distribution of power. Hage (1980) defines centralization as "the level and variety of participation in strategic decisions by groups relative to the number of groups in the organization" (p. 65). The greater the level of participation by a greater number of groups in an organization, the less the centralization. Hage's approach emphasizes that power is exercised in a variety of ways and in a variety of locations in an organization. For example, at my university—and at most good universities (see Blau, 1973)—the decision of whom to hire for a faculty position lies with the hiring department. The decision here is decentralized. Whether a particular department will be able to hire someone, however, is decided by the central administration, which reviews faculty vacancies and determines whether or not there needs to be a redistribution of vacancies; departments with declining enrollments and weaker programs are likely to lose positions to departments with high enrollment demands and strong programs. This is a centralized decision.

Van de Ven and Ferry (1980) define centralization as "the locus of decision making authority within an organization. When most decisions are made hierarchically, an organizational unit is considered to be centralized; a decentralized unit generally implies that the major source of decision making has been delegated by line managers to subordinate personnel" (p. 399). Van de Ven and Ferry go on to note that the substance of the decisions is an important consideration. In a highly professionalized organization, for example, decisions in regard to areas of professional competence are left to the professionals involved. Areas that are considered to be outside the limits of professional competence are likely to be more centralized.

What Is Centralized or Decentralized?

Of the several elements of centralization, the most obvious is the right to make decisions. Who or what has the right to make which kinds of decisions and when can they be very specifically spelled out. If most decision making occurs at the top, the organization is centralized. The matter is not that simple, however.

Centralization is not only a matter of who makes decisions. If personnel at lower levels in the organization are making many decisions but the decisions are "programmed" by organizational policies, a high degree of centralization remains. A low degree of centralization is found in situations of democratic, collective decision making (Rothschild and Whitt, 1986).

Another element of centralization is the evaluation of activities (Dornbusch and Scott, 1975: p. 82). The evaluation process involves the determination of whether work was done properly, well, or promptly. If evaluation is carried out by people at the top of the organization, there is centralization, regardless of the level at which decisions are made. A situation in which there is centralized evaluation would probably—but not necessarily always—also be one in which policies are centralized.

For the sake of clarity, it is important to distinguish centralization from centrality. Centrality refers to a person's or a social role's position in workflow, communications, or friendship networks. It is related to people's being perceived as influential by both supervisors and nonsupervisors (Brass, 1984).

Centralization and Other Organizational Properties

In this section we will examine the relationships between size, technology, and environmental factors as they relate to centralization. These factors will be considered in detail in the next chapter in the discussion of explanations of structure. Here, the purpose is to develop an understanding of centralization.

Size. Research evidence in regard to the relationships between organizational size and centralization is paradoxical. From their study of state employment security offices, Blau and Schoenherr (1971) conclude that "the large size of an agency produces conflicting pressures on top management, as it heightens the importance of managerial decisions, which discourages delegating them, and simultaneously expands the volume of managerial responsibilities, which exerts pressure to delegate some of them" (p. 130). The net result of increasing size is increased delegation or decentralization. The risk of delegation is lessened if personnel have expert qualifications. A centralized policy in regard to employee qualifications thus appears to contribute to delegated or decentralized power.

One problem with this line of reasoning (a variation of the chicken-egg debate) should be noted: It is impossible to determine if increased size leads to pressures to delegate and thus to utilize experts, or if the hiring of experts leads to pressures to delegate, with size not really being a factor. The question cannot be answered with the kinds of data now available, but probably a combination of the two types of answers is most appropriate.

Blau's (1973) further research on colleges and universities revealed basically the same findings. Large universities were more decentralized than smaller ones. Academic institutions and government agencies show a major difference in the qualifications of their personnel. In the government agencies, qualified personnel were utilized to carry out the organization's policies; in the academic organizations, the highly qualified personnel were able to gain power for themselves and to exercise a great deal of power over educational policies.

In a study using the Aston data and their measures on a second set of data, Mansfield (1973) reached conclusions essentially the same as those of the Blau research. Mansfield found that increasing size is related to the increasing use of rules. This leads to the decentralization of decision making but not to loss of control for the organization. In smaller organizations, specialists report directly to the top of the organization, whereas in larger ones, problems are handled at a decentralized level, but under the guidance of organizationally based rules. A study of large corporate medical practices found that important decisions shifted from clinicians to administrators. In such medical practices, decisions have ramifications for the total organization (Kralewski, Pitt, and Shatin, 1985).

The relationship between size and centralization is thus complex, with increasing size leading to delegation in some circumstances. But delegation usually takes place within a framework of rules, so larger size generally is related to greater centralization.

Technology.   The technological factor has already been implied in this discussion. Some work is delegated, with the control remaining at the top of the organization by the use of rules governing the work. Other work is delegated to specialists who make their own decisions at lower levels in the organization. Work that is delegated with controls is *routine* in its technology (Child, 1973). In a bank, for example, each teller can handle thousands of dollars if the transactions are routine, small cash deposits and withdrawals, but if a customer presents a check for $2,000 and asks for cash, that is a different matter. The handling of thousands of dollars is not delegated; rather, the decision moves back up the organization to the teller's supervisor. The routine nature of the technology, of course, is reflected in the rapid spread of ATMs, which have taken over much of the routine work of tellers.

Organizations deal with tasks that vary in the certainty with which they can be accomplished (Dornbusch and Scott, 1975). The variety of tasks performed in an organization means in essence that it has multiple technologies and thus must structure itself according to the task being performed. In a hospital, administering clinical treatment is more uncertain than processing insurance forms. Decision making in regard to which clinical treatment to provide is decentralized to the nurse, the physician's assistant, or the physician involved with a particular case. The processing of insurance forms is centralized (and formalized) by organizational procedures. These conclusions coincide with our earlier comments on intraorganizational structural variations. Variations in centralization are linked to different tasks with varied technologies.

Technology also permits organizations to monitor members' behavior. The amount of data entered, the number of telemarketing calls made, or the number of units produced are work output measures that can be monitored (Ouchi, 1977). Ouchi notes that organizations can monitor people's behavior or their work outputs. A combination of large size and homogeneous tasks contributes to the utilization of such output controls.

Another aspect of technology adds some slight confusion to the discussion. Participative management, in the form of consultation with subordinates in regard to decisions that affect them, is more likely to be successful in situations involving advanced technology (Taylor, 1971). Advanced technology here refers specifically to that concentrated at the workflow level; thus, participative management is most effective in the more automated kinds of situations.

Hage and Aiken's (1967a) work has shown that participation in decision making—a different aspect of centralization—is related to the absence of rules, thus suggesting that centralization by rules and centralization by nonparticipative decision making tend to operate together. In routine situations, rules govern the actions of the organizational members and there is likely to be little delegation of power through participation. In less routine situations, where there is task uncertainty, activities such as group meetings are likely to be held to try to resolve problems (Van de Ven, Delbecq, and Koenig, 1976).

The issue of routinization and uncertainty and their relationship to centralization is closely linked to the level of professionalization of the personnel in the organization. Lincoln and Zeitz (1980) report that individual professionals desire and achieve participation in decision making. They also find that the overall level of professionalization of an organization results in all employees experiencing an increase in influence.

There are two cautions that should be noted in regard to participation in decision making. First, the fact that there is participation by organizational members may not mean that power is actually delegated. If the final decision still rests in the hands of the superiors in the organization, little power is actually delegated and participation is advisory at best. Although participation may help in the implementation of a decision, there is no decentralization or delegation of power unless it contributes to the actual decision.

The other caution regards something that is too seldom considered by sociologists and other organizational researchers—budgetary controls, such as internal audits. Although Hofstede (1972) and Ouchi and Maguire (1975) have dealt with this issue, it has tended not to be considered, which is a loss for organizational theory. Budgetary controls have the potential for retaining a great deal of control at the top of the organization. Most of the studies that have been cited here have not included budgetary control mechanisms. It would certainly appear that budgetary matters could be centralized in ways other than the allocation of tasks or decision making on other issues.

Environmental Relations. The relationships among size, technology, and centralization have not been straightforward. The same pattern is found when studies of the relationships between organizations and their environments are considered. As we know from the Lawrence and Lorsch (1967) study, environments are critical for organizations.

A basic consideration is how much competition an organization faces in its environment. From their study of thirty business firms in India, Negandhi and Reimann (1972) suggest that competitive market conditions make decentralization more important for organizational success than do less competitive situations. This study was a successful replication of the Lawrence and Lorsch (1967) contingency theory previously discussed. Further analysis of these data indicated that the degree of dependence on other organizations was actually more strongly associated with decentralization than were the factors of size, technology, and market competitiveness. The perceptions of the organizational decision makers are a critical mediating variable between the organization and the environment. It is those decision makers who make the strategic choices about the environment and about how the organization will respond to it. In this set of findings, the competitiveness of the environment affects the degree of decentralization (Negandhi and Reimann, 1973a, b).

A very different conclusion was reached in a study of thirty-eight small manufacturing firms in the United States (Pfeffer and Leblebici, 1973). This study found that a more competitive environment led to a greater demand for control and coordination. There was a greater frequency of reporting, more emphasis on written communications, and a greater specification of decision-making procedures—in short, a much greater degree of centralization. The study also found that in less competitive environments, there were more changes in product design, production processes, and number of products.

The contradictory findings seem to offer few conclusions about the effects of competition on centralization. A good part of the difficulty may lie in the fact that the more general characteristics of the organizational environments were not specified. For example, in an expanding economy in which the competing organizations are all gaining, decentralization may occur. In a contracting economy, where one organization's gain is the other's loss, the tightening up and centralization that Pfeffer and Leblebici found would occur (Khandwalla, 1972).

Another aspect of organizational environments is their degree of stability. Research on this topic reaches contradictory findings, as did that on competition (Whetten, 1980). Authors such as Burns and Stalker (1961) and Aldrich (1979) have argued that decentralization is more appropriate for conditions of turbulence or nonstability in the environment, whereas others (Hawley and Rogers, 1974; Yarmolinsky, 1975; Rubin, 1979) have argued in favor of centralization in such situations. Again, a resolution of the differences in these findings might be possible if it were possible to determine if the environment was expanding or contracting, as was suggested in the case of competition. In a situation of growth, decentralization might be the more appropriate response to turbulence, whereas centralization might be necessary in periods of contraction.

Competition and stability are important general environmental characteristics. Another important component of the environment is the degree of uncertainty experienced. When the environment is quite uncertain, organizations are likely to decentralize (Alexander, 1991). This same study also found that spatial dispersion and previous practices (historical precedent) were related to decentralization.

Closely related to centralization is the notion of "loose coupling" (Weick, 1976; Aldrich, 1979; Orton and Weick, 1990). This idea was developed to describe situations in which organizational units have low levels of interdependence. There is agreement that loosely coupled organizations tend to be more flexible and responsive to environmental pressures (Whetten, 1980). The degree of coupling can be misleading. For example, school organizations are commonly considered to be loosely coupled. In actuality, administrators can retain control through the allocation of resources such as curricular materials (Gamoran and Dreeben, 1986).

Loose coupling is not the same as decentralization, since the degree of coupling refers to the level of interdependence among units rather than to the distribution of power. In general, a loosely coupled organization would also be decentralized. An example of a loosely coupled organization is the business conglomerate. If the consumer products division is having a difficult time because of high interest rates, that will not affect the heavy-machinery division whose market is growing. Such an organization is loosely coupled. Each division may be more or less centralized in such a situation.

Centralization and Macropolitical Considerations

The overriding importance of organizations for the social order is underscored by considering some examples of their use for political purposes. Organizations can be shaped to be part of the process of political change and development. We have already seen how the Bolsheviks used their "organizational weapon" (Selznick, 1960). During the Cultural Revolution, the People's Republic of China used its organizations as a means of continuing political indoctrination and involvement. This was high centralization of both government and enterprise. The former Yugoslavia developed a program of "self-management" in which the workers in an enterprise elected a workers' council that in turn elected the management of the enterprise. This is not participative management of the sort discussed earlier but, rather, management by participation. Enterprises in the Israeli kibbutz system (composed of small organizations) have a socialist ideology that is promoted by a system of rotation of all people through all positions. These ideological purposes are not always met. In Yugoslavia, participation was lower and alienation was higher than the ideology indicated or political leaders desired (see Rus, 1972).

A major study of differing patterns of centralization in ten nations has been conducted by Tannenbaum and his colleagues (1974, 1986). The original research was carried out in manufacturing plants in Austria, Italy, Israel, Yugoslavia, and the United States. Austria and Italy are basically capitalist, like the United States; the Israeli kibbutzim is socialist, and the Yugoslav economy was socialist. Israel and the United States contained the plants that were most successful, as defined not only by the standards used in the country in question but also by such universal factors as efficiency and morale. The kibbutz plants are highly decentralized, and the effects of hierarchy are virtually eliminated. In the United States, hierarchy is present, but its effects are mitigated by several factors. There is a limited potential for upward worker mobility in the American plants, but it is greater than in the Italian plants. There is also greater participativeness in the American plants. Workers are consulted and treated more as equals, even though they are not equal in power, and the rewards are higher.

Some of the Tannenbaum researchers believed that American workers had a form of "false consciousness," since they did not have opportunities for advancement, and that they were being duped by human relations efforts of the American managers.

This Marxist approach gets at the very heart of the macropolitical issues involved in centralization. Management by participation, as in the case of Israel and Yugoslavia, is a direct attempt to alter traditional power arrangements within a society.

China offers a different picture of macropolitical conditions and organizational centralization. Chinese policies were not at all participative but, rather, were designed to strengthen the power of the regime and emphasized political indoctrination and loyalty. The country was highly centralized. In China today, there is a move to decentralize the social system. Here also, there has been rapid growth in small, local enterprises (Nee, 1992; Hall et al., 1993). In the Hall et al. study, the small Chinese enterprises were found to be much more centralized than a sample of small firms in the United States. This could be a carryover from the earlier, highly centralized era or even perhaps a reflection of Confucian family values.

The American approach, which increasingly features some degree of participation in decision making, does not attempt to redistribute power. It does, however, minimize the perceptible effects of power differences. Those of the Tannenbaum et al. researchers who judge this as immoral and misleading miss an important consideration. Even if it is agreed that workers are exploited to even a small degree, the end result remains in question. What is better—a situation such as that in Italy, where the exploitation is definitely experienced and verbalized, or a situation such as that in the United States, where it is experienced more blandly and scarcely verbalized? This would be up to each reader to decide.

It is possible, for example, that at some time in the future, American workers, having experienced at least symbolic participation, would press very hard for actual participation. Those who had never experienced participation might not necessarily want to move in this direction.

The final consideration, developed by the Dutch sociologist Cornelius Lammers (1975), is that participative management involves taking part in decision making, whereas both management by participation and self-management involve workers taking over organizational management. Participative management is a functional form of decentralization that may lead to greater efficiency and effectiveness, and the other two forms are structural forms of decentralization that lead to power equalization.

True power equalization in organizations is extremely unlikely. The very nature of organizations requires some form of hierarchy, once organizations move beyond very small size, simple technologies, and low levels of complexity. As in the wider society, power differences are ubiquitous. The effects of such power differences can perhaps be minimized by making them less abrasive through participative schemes.

Centralization and Micropolitical Considerations

Organizations are part of the political system. They also contain their own internal political system, which is an important consideration for centralization. There are contradictions between traditional control structures and new forms of organizing, such as along the lines of professional organizations (Heydebrand, 1977). As noted earlier, the presence of professionals increases the level of participation in the organization. The increased participation is not accomplished benignly. Instead, it is fought for and over, since those who had decision-making power are not likely to give it up easily to the professionals coming into the organization.

Some authors view the internal politics of an organization as a reflection of the external political system. One view is that the technology employed in many factories is there not so much for technical efficiency as to be a means by which maximal control over labor can be achieved (Marglin, 1974). Ongoing labor–management negotiations and battles over the prerogatives of management and workers can reflect wider political schisms. This is true particularly in Europe. Power can be delegated to lower participants, and power can be taken by these same lower participants (Bacharach and Lawler, 1980). Universities in the late 1960s and early 1970s exemplified the give-and-take of power as students gained in power and thus had the right to make decisions that previously had been made by faculty or administrators. This internal organizational power struggle was a reflection of the larger political context.

The exercise of power within organizations will be considered in a later chapter. In regard to centralization, it is critical to note that the micropolitics of organizations involves the continuing power struggles that occur within organizations, whether among departments, hierarchical levels, or individuals (Pfeffer, 1978). Although the micropolitical approach emphasizes power struggles, the fact that power is distributed at one point in time (the pattern of centralization) will have a crucial impact on the distribution of power at succeeding points in time.

The Outcomes of Centralization

The degree of centralization in organizations says a great deal about the society in which they are found. A society in which the majority of organizations are highly centralized is one in which the workers have little say about their work. The same would probably be true of their participation in the society. The degree of centralization of organizations is also an indication of what the organization assumes about its members: High centralization implies an assumption that the members need tight control, of whatever form; low centralization suggests that the members can govern themselves. In both cases, it should be remembered, the control is in behalf of the organization. Professionals and other expert personnel in organizations do not work in behalf of their professions. Their expertise is intended to be in behalf of their organization.

A major outcome of varying degrees of centralization is for the organization itself. High levels of centralization mean greater coordination, but less flexibility; consistent organization-wide policies, but possibly inappropriate policies for local conditions; and the potential for rapid decision making during emergencies, but overloaded communications channels during normal operations as communications flow up and down the hierarchy.

SUMMARY AND CONCLUSIONS

This chapter has considered the basic organizational characteristics of complexity, formalization, and centralization. These characteristics have outcomes for the individuals who are in the organizations and who have contacts with it. They also have outcomes for the organizations themselves and for the wider society of which they are a part.

We have already begun an examination of the topic of the next chapter—the explanations of structure. Issues such as size, technology, and relationships with the environment have loomed large in analyses of structure. We will examine these issues and also pay attention to some broader explanations that have been recently introduced.

chapter 4

Organizational Structure: Explanations

In this chapter we will attempt to explain the forms of organizations that were described in the last chapter. Obviously, degrees of complexity, formalization, and centralization are neither random nor accidental. We have already developed the points that size, technology, and environment play roles in determining organizational forms. We will return to those factors here and then add some important considerations. Our conclusion will be that organizational structures are a consequence of the simultaneous impact of multiple factors.

The idea of structure is basically simple, and we will return to our building analogy to illustrate this. Buildings have structures, in the form of beams, interior walls, passageways, roofs, and so on. The structure of a building is a major determinant of the movements and activities of the people within it. Buildings are supposed to have structures that fit the activities that go on within them. An office building is different from a factory. Factories where automobiles are made are different from those where computers are made. Buildings are designed to fit the needs of the activities that are to be carried out within them. They are designed to accommodate populations of various sizes—no sane architect would design a huge cathedral for a small congregation—and to withstand the environment in which they are located. Buildings in upstate New York are different from those in Arizona (although there is a rumor that my campus in Albany was actually designed for Arizona). Just as the size, the major activity or technology to be used, and the environment are important in building design, so is the element of choice—of style, color, and so on. Buildings also reflect the values and ideologies of the persons in control; corporate headquarters and state capitols do not take the form they do by accident.

The analogy of organizational structures to those of buildings is not perfect, since organizations are not built by architects but by the people within them. Those people are not necessarily in agreement about how the organization should be arranged. Just as one building can be a copy of another; organizational structures can be copies of other organizations. Like buildings, they can also reflect the particular fads or fashions popular at the time of their construction. And, just as buildings can be renovated, organizations can be redesigned.

The present chapter is an attempt to explain the variations in organizational structures or forms. There is no single explanation for the forms of organizations. Rather, multiple explanations are needed to understand organizational structure. This is not a simple matter. Some factors operate together in a positively correlated manner, as when large size and routine technology combine to yield a highly formalized situation. In another situation size and technology might operate in a negatively correlated fashion, as when large size and nonroutine technology are present. These relationships could themselves be affected by differences in national cultures or by historical events.

Explanations of factors affecting structure fall into two major categories. The first is the *context* in which organizations operate. Contextual explanations include organizational size, technology, internal culture (or organizational climate), the environment, and national cultural factors. Context here means the situation in which an organization is currently operating. This situation is simultaneously within and beyond an organization's control. For example, an organization can decide to expand its operations and in so doing expand its size. Once the size is expanded, it is part of the context of the organization, since the sheer factor of size has an influence on structure. The same process operates in the technologies employed by an organization, the environments with which it deals, its internal culture, and the national culture in which it is embedded. These contextual conditions are a result of earlier decisions that were made in and for an organization. In keeping with the theme of our analysis, the decisions were made to move the organization toward a higher level of effectiveness. Whether this worked or not is another matter.

The second category of explanations of structure is *design*. By design we mean the choices made in an organization about how the organization is to be structured. The major approaches here are strategic choice and institutional models of structure. Any study of design must consider that not all actors within an organization will have the same judgment in regard to the design of structure. Organizational design is by definition a political issue but, again, a political issue linked to our notion of effectiveness.

CONTEXTUAL EXPLANATIONS

Size

At first glance, organizational size appears to be a simple variable—the number of people in an organization. The size issue is much more complicated than that, however. The discussion of organizational boundaries suggested that it sometimes is problematic who is in or out of an organization. In a penetrating article, Kimberly (1976) demonstrated that size actually has four components.

The first component of size is the physical capacity of the organization. Hospitals have a fixed number of beds. Production organizations have a relatively fixed capacity, such as the number of assembly lines and their speed, to transform raw materials. Universities have capacities in regard to classroom or dormitory space.

The second component of size is the personnel available to the organization. This is the most commonly used measure and conceptualization of size, having been used in 80 percent of the studies reviewed by Kimberly. The basic problem with using this component is that the meaning of the number of personnel is ambiguous. For some religious organizations and universities, size in this form is sometimes a goal. Larger size can mean an increased budget. For other organizations, the goal is to keep the size at a minimum to reduce costs.

The third component of size is organizational inputs or outputs. Inputs can be such factors as the number of clients or students served and the number of inmates housed in a prison. A college or university's graduation rate is an output and an important one when intercollegiate athletic programs are considered. Sales volume is an important output measure for many businesses. Kimberly correctly suggests that this measure is limited in its usage to comparisons between organizations of a similar type.

The final component of size is the discretionary resources available to an organization, in the form of wealth or net assets. For a college or a university, the size of its endowment is an important consideration. This is conceptually distinct from the other aspects of size.

The components of size may be highly intercorrelated in some instances, and indeed they are, but the conceptual distinctions among them are so great that each should be treated separately. These structural characteristics may be a consequence, a covariant, or a determinant of size, making the utility of the size variable even more uncertain.

Much of the work relating size to organizational structure was conducted before Kimberly's analysis. We will review some of that literature now, with the realization that these studies are based almost exclusively on the number of personnel available. These studies do indicate the directions that have been taken in research on size; some authors argue that size is the determinant of structure, and others argue the opposite.

The major proponents of the importance of size as a determinant of structure have been Peter M. Blau and his associates (see Blau, Heydebrand, and Stauffer, 1966; Blau, 1968, 1970, 1973; Blau and Schoenherr, 1971; Meyer, 1968a, 1968b, 1971; also Blau, 1972; and Klatzky, 1970a). Their data were collected primarily from studies of government agencies, such as state employment services and municipal finance divisions, with supplementary data from universities and department stores. The data reveal some fascinating anomalies in organizations and also some important considerations about the role of organizations in contemporary society.

Blau's studies are concerned primarily with organizational size and differentiation. Differentiation is measured by the number of levels, departments, and job titles within an organization. This is the same as the concepts of vertical and horizontal complexity discussed in Chapter 3. The research findings indicate that increasing size is related to increasing differentiation. The rate of differentiation decreases, however, with increasing size. Administrative overhead is lower in larger organizations, and the span of control for supervisors is greater. Since administrative overhead is inversely related to size, and the span of control is directly, or positively, related to size, larger organizations are able to achieve an economy of scale. It is here that the first anomaly is demonstrated. Size is related to differentiation, and differentiation, bringing increased need for control and coordination, is related to increased requirements for administrative overhead. Size and differentiation thus work at cross-purposes. Blau concludes that the size factor is the more critical and that economy of scale still results from large size.

The second major set of studies that find size to be the major determinant of organizational structure are those of the Aston group in England (see Pugh et al., 1963; Pugh et al., 1968; Hickson, Pugh, and Pheysey, 1969; Inkson, Pugh, and Hickson, 1970; Child and Mansfield, 1972; Donaldson and Warner, 1974; and Hickson et al., 1974). These works represent the original Aston studies. The major conclusion of these studies is that increased size is related to increased structuring of organizational activities and decreased concentrations of authority. Most of the data come from manufacturing organizations, but some are based on studies in government agencies and labor unions.

There is still other evidence in regard to the importance of size. Managerial practices are related to the size of the unit being supervised. Flexibility in personnel assignments, the extent of delegation of authority, and an emphasis on results rather than procedures are related to larger unit sizes (Mahoney et al., 1972). At the same time, subunit size has been found to be negatively related to subunit performance (Gooding and Wagner, 1985). The size factor thus does not act in a unitary manner.

The evidence presented thus far has emphasized the strong positive relationship between size and structure. Other researchers question that emphasis. My own research, for example, has not found such strong relationships. In one study, which used a subjective approach, we found only a modest relationship between size and perceived degree of bureaucratization (Hall and Tittle, 1966). In another study, utilizing an approach similar to that of Blau and the Aston group, we came up with mixed findings in regard to size and structure. Using data from a set of seventy-five organizations of highly varied types, we concluded:

> In general, the findings of this study in regard to size are similar to those of previous research which utilized size as a major variable; that is, the relationships between size and other structural components are inconsistent. . . . There is a slight tendency for larger organizations to be both more complex and more formalized, but only on a few variables does this relationship prove to be strong. On others, there is little, if any, established relationship. (Hall, Haas, and Johnson, 1967b: pp. 908–9)

These findings do not suggest that size is unimportant but, rather, that factors other than size must be taken into account to understand structure. These additional factors will be discussed in the sections that follow.

Research on size has met with additional criticisms. Argyris (1972) has analyzed Blau's research and found it wanting in several regards. He first questions the reliance on official descriptions of organizational structures. Citing several studies that have found that organization charts are nonexistent or inaccurate, and that members of top management cannot always accurately describe their own organization, Argyris wonders if the approach that Blau has taken might not invalidate the results. He also suggests that size may be correlated with, but not generate or cause, differentiation.

Another major criticism the view that size is the determinant of structure comes from a reanalysis of the Aston data (Aldrich, 1972a; Hilton, 1972; Aldrich, 1972b; and Heise, 1972). Aldrich suggests that size is actually a dependent variable: " . . . the more highly structured firms, with their greater degree of specialization, formalization, and monitoring of role performance, simply need to employ a larger work force than less structured firms" (Aldrich, 1972a: p. 38). In Aldrich's reanalysis, technology emerges as the major determinant of structure.

Before turning to technology, we should note some additional matters related to size. First, as we saw in Chapter 1, most organizations are small. Within small organizations, the effects of organizational design efforts are likely to have more direct consequences for the organization. Geeraerts (1984) found that the heads of small organizations who were professional managers were more likely to adopt bureaucratic practices than were heads of small organizations who were owner-managers. Geeraerts attributes this to the education and professional careers of the professional managers. A study of airlines found that small airlines are more active in initiating competitive challenges in the airline industry than are the big carriers (Chen and Hambrick, 1995). Small organizations can be nimble.

At the same time, small organizations are highly vulnerable. Most new organizations are small. Research has consistently shown (see Starbuck and Nystrom, 1981) that new organizations have a low survival rate. Starbuck and Nystrom note that "nearly all small organizations disappear within a few years" (p. xiv). Interestingly, they provide data that support this conclusion for both governmental agencies and corporations. Apparently, governmental organizations are not as protected as many people think. The corollary of this research, of course, is that large organizations are more likely to survive and are less vulnerable than small ones.

Large organizations are also more likely to have more resources. This would permit them to enter new markets. At the same time, large organizations do tend to be more bureaucratic, and this would operate against entering new markets (Haveman, 1993). Large organizations are also more likely to have more highly developed internal labor markets. Paradoxically, rapid growth may hinder the development of internal labor markets as growing organizations bring in personnel from outside the organization (Van Buren, 1992). Larger organizations do provide better pay and fringe benefits (Kalleberg and Van Buren, 1996)—these are not aspects of structure, but they certainly are important.

Organizational size is a crucial factor for much of what goes on in and around organizations. It is just one of the contextual factors that are important, however, as we move to a consideration of technology.

Technology

The relationship between technology and organizational structure is not easy to understand. It may seem easy if you consider something like the routine processing of checks in a bank. This is usually done in a situation of high division of labor, high formalization, and high centralization. Technology is not easy to understand, however, in more complex situations.

I will use a situation in which I am currently involved to illustrate this. At my university I serve as Chair of the Intercollegiate Athletics Advisory Board (IAAB). This is the body that oversees our intercollegiate athletics program. All colleges and universities that are NCAA members have IAABs or their equivalents. We dealt with the issue of gender equity in our athletic programs a few years ago. After some months of deliberation, we recommended a program in which the proportion of women and men participating in intercollegiate athletics is very close to the proportion of men and women in the student body.

Where is technology in this example? Well, it is in the processing of the issue of gender equity. Technology involves "acting on and/or changing an object from one state to another. . . . The object can be a living being, a symbol, or an inanimate object" (Goodman, Griffith, and Fenner, 1990: p. 48). We were dealing with complex symbols. Our technology involved discussion, consultation, looking at our own values, thinking about the coaches and players involved, and considering the ramifications for the future. This was a very imprecise technology. Organizationally, it was high on complexity and low on formalization and centralization.

Interest in technology as a major component of organizational analysis was sparked by the work of Woodward (1958, 1965) and Perrow (1967). (See also Burns and Stalker, 1961; Blauner, 1964; Emery and Trist, 1965; Lawrence and Lorsch, 1967; and Thompson, 1967). Woodward's work is particularly interesting because she stumbled onto the importance of technology during the course of a research project in the United Kingdom. She found that several critical structural variables were directly linked to the nature of the technology of the industrial firms being studied. The organizations were categorized into three types: first, the small-batch or unit-production system, as exemplified by a shipbuilding or aircraft-manufacturing firm; second, the large-batch or mass-production organization; third, the organization that utilizes continuous production, as do chemical or petroleum manufacturers.

Woodward's findings show that the nature of the technology vitally affected the management structures of the firms studied. The number of levels in the management hierarchy, the span of control of first-line supervisors, and the ratio of managers and supervisors to other personnel were all affected by the technology employed. Not only was structure affected, but also the success or effectiveness of the organizations was related to the "fit" between technology and structure. The successful firms of each type were those that had the appropriately structured technical systems.

"Raw materials" are central to Perrow's (1967) approach to technology. This raw material

> may be a living being, human or otherwise, a symbol or an inanimate object. People are raw materials in people-changing or people-processing organizations; symbols are materials in banks, advertising agencies and some research organizations; the interactions of people are raw materials to be manipulated by administrators in organizations; boards of directors, committees and councils are usually involved with the changing or processing of symbols and human interactions, and so on. (p. 195)

The nature of the raw material affects how the organization is structured and operated. According to Perrow, the critical factors in the nature of the raw material, and hence the nature of the technology employed to work on it, are the number of "exceptional cases encountered in the work" and the nature of the "search process" that is utilized when exceptional cases are found (pp. 195–96). Few exceptional cases are found when the raw material is some object or objects that do not vary in their consistency or malleability over time. Many exceptions are found in the obvious cases of human beings and their interactions, or the less obvious cases of many craft specialties or frontier areas within the sciences. Search processes range from those that are logical and analytical to those that must rely upon intuition, inspiration, chance, guesswork, or some other such unstandardized procedure. The first form of search may be found in the engineering process in many industries. The second form of search may be found in some activities in the aerospace industry. Thus, within "industry" we have a wide array of technologies and organizational forms.

Perrow's framework has been tested several times with mixed results. Most studies find that routineness is related to high formalization and centralization (Hage and Aiken, 1967a; Lawrence and Lorsch, 1967; Comstock and Scott, 1977; Mohr, 1971). An interesting twist is reported by Miller et al. (1991). They found that the routineness-centralization relationship operates in small organizations but not in large ones. It would seem that large organizations are probably dispersed, and thus decentralization would be necessary. Interestingly, the original Aston studies did not find a strong relationship between technology and organizational structure.

The mixed results in regard to technology appear to be based on several factors. In the first place, there has been uncertainty about the level at which technology is operative in the organization. The Aston group sheds some light on the subject. Hickson, Pugh, and Pheysey (1969) break down the general concept of technology into three components: operations technology—the techniques used in the workflow activities of the organization; materials technology—the materials used in the workflow (a highly sophisticated technique can conceivably be applied to relatively simple materials); and knowledge technology—the varying complexities in the knowledge system used in the workflow. In their own research, these authors have been concerned with operations technology.

In the English organizations they studied, operations technology had a secondary effect in relationship to size. They conclude:

> Structural variables will be associated with operations technology only where they are centered on the workflow. The smaller the organization, the more its structure will be pervaded by such technological effects; the larger the organization, the more these effects will be confined to variables such as job-counts of employees on activities linked with the workflow itself, and will not be detectable invariables of the more remote administrative and hierarchical structure. (pp. 394–95; italics in original)

These findings mean that operations technology will intervene before the effects of size in these work organizations. They also imply that the administrative element in large organizations will be relatively unaffected by the operations technology. It is here that the form of the knowledge technology, which was not examined, becomes important.

The importance of knowledge technology can be seen in Meyer's (1968a) examination of the introduction of automated procedures into the administrative structures of state and local departments of finance. This resulted in more levels of hierarchy, a wider span of control for first-line supervisors,

fewer employees under the direction of higher supervisors, and fewer responsibilities—but more communications responsibilities—for members who are
nominally in supervisory positions. In these particular organizations, the
knowledge technology changed from simple to relatively complex.

In the second place a basic problem with the studies on technology has
been the kinds of organizations studied. The Aston group is most confident of
its data when service and administrative units are removed from the sample.
The type of industry and its technology are related—for example, the steel industry versus the book publishing industry—so that sampling differences between studies could increase or decrease the relationship between technology
and structure (Child and Mansfield, 1972).

The technology-structure issue has been approached in a diametrically
different manner by Glisson (1978). He found that the structural attributes
of division of labor and procedural specifications determined the degree of
routinization and thus the nature of service delivery among a set of human-
service organizations. Glisson thus reverses the causal argument. The issue,
then, may be one of those chicken-versus-egg phenomena. Additional research, particularly longitudinal studies, is needed to begin to resolve this
particular issue.

A good part of the literature on size and technology has been presented
in an either-or fashion, with either technology or size being proposed as the
key structural determinant. This was, in fact, a major debate in the early 1970s.
Fortunately, researchers dropped the debate and began to examine size and
technology together.

A study of a large state employment security agency examined task uncertainty, task interdependence (technological variables), and work-unit size as
they related to coordination mechanisms (Van de Ven, Delbecq, and Koenig,
1976). As tasks increased in uncertainty, mutual work adjustments through
horizontal communications channels and group meetings were used instead of
hierarchical and impersonal forms of control. As task interdependence increased, impersonal coordination decreased and more personalized and interactive modes of coordination, in the form of meetings, increased. Increasing
size, on the other hand, was related to an increased use of impersonal modes
of coordination, such as policies and procedures and predetermined work
plans. In a related study, Ouchi (1977) found that both size and homogeneous
tasks were related to output controls on workers.

A study of architectural firms revealed that structural complexity and
task diversity were dependent upon size when there were uniform tasks, but
the cognitive ideas and a professional orientation were more important in
nonuniform tasks (Blau and McKinley, 1979). Thus, size is important under
one technological condition but under another.

The idea that size is important for certain structural variables but technology is important for other aspects of structure receives additional support
from the research of Marsh and Mannari (1981). Using data from Japanese

factories, they found that structural differentiation and formalization were more a function of size than of technology. On the other hand, labor inputs, cybernetic complexity, costs and wages, differentiation of management from ownership, span of control of the chief executive, and union recognition varied more with technology than with size.

In the last section on size, the work of Peter Blau and his associates was prominent in the discussion of the importance of size. Beyer and Trice (1979) reexamined the original Blau and Schoenherr (1971) study and suggest that the earlier findings, with their strong emphasis on size, were probably a result of the type of organizations studied—state employment agencies that had very routine technologies. Beyer and Trice's own data show that in nonroutine organizations, personnel specialization generates horizontal differentiation. They correctly suggest that a search for a single or primary cause of organizational complexity is doomed to failure. They also suggest that there should be a focus on the strategic choices that decision makers select, which may be an important step forward in the analysis of structure. We will consider this issue at a later point.

The final study to be considered in regard to the size-technology issue is that of Daft and Bradshaw (1980). In a study of universities, they found that growth in administrative departments was related to large size, whereas growth in academic departments had more of a technological base. Daft and Bradshaw go on to consider some additional explanations. They suggest that factors in an organization's environment, such as pressures from the community or the government, contribute to differentiation among the academic departments. They also suggest that the decision-making process is critical and offer the interesting notion that there are two levels of decisions—the formal decision to add a department or a program and an earlier decision by someone who senses a problem and becomes an "idea champion" who pushes for the formal decision. They are correct in this regard, of course, since the idea to make some kind of structural change has to begin somewhere. They do miss the fact that decisions in organizations are highly political and that many ideas that are developed never see the light of day in the sense that there is no formal action on them because they died in some committee. A final suggestion of Daft and Bradshaw's is that financial resources affect decisions about structural change. This is almost never considered by organizational analysts (economists aside, of course), but it would appear to be of great importance.

We have been treating technology as some sort of impersonal force. In many ways it is, even with interacting computers. At the same time, people certainly do react to technology and technological change (Weick, 1990; Barley, 1990). Some people show fear and loathing toward computers, and others literally fall in love with their computers. These individual reactions cannot be ignored, but they are not central to our concerns here.

We have also been treating technology only at the organizational level. Just as it is important to note that there are impacts on individuals, so is it important to note that technology and technological change affect entire industries, nations, and the world itself. "It is increasingly apparent that the causal influences flow in both directions. Organization at the level of the firm, the industry, and the nation affect technological advance. In turn, technical advance affects organizational structure at all three of these levels and at the level of the world economy" (Tushman and Nelson, 1990: p. 2). For our purposes here, of course, technology is just one of the factors affecting organizational structure.

Internal Culture

The importance of the internal culture factor has received varying degrees of attention by organizational scholars and practitioners. It received prominence in Barnard's (1938) important analysis of the functions of the executive. One of the major functions of the executive was to "set the tone" for the entire organization.

The emphasis returned with a vengeance in the 1980s as organizations sought a culture of "excellence" (Peters and Waterman, 1982). Culture became a buzzword in much of the management literature.

According to Smircich (1985), organizational culture "is a possession— a fairly stable set of taken-for-granted assumptions, shared meanings, and values that form a kind of backdrop for action" (p. 58). Another formulation considers culture to be "shared values and beliefs, assumptions, perceptions, norms, artifacts, and patterns of behavior (Ott, 1989; p. 1). Culture includes jargon and slang, humor and jokes, and other such forms (Trice and Beyer, 1993). It can also include strong ideologies, as Hyde's (1992) analysis of feminist health centers indicates. Strong ideologies make an organization conservative, since actions and decisions are made within a particular ideological framework.

Internal organizational cultures are relatively stable. People come and go, but the culture remains robust (Harrison and Carroll, 1991). The stability and robustness of internal cultures make it puzzling that culture became such a theoretical and managerial buzzword in the 1980s and early 1990s (Smith, 1993). After all, if culture is stable, it is hard to change and thus not a real management tool.

Internal cultures are a organizational context in which structures are formed. Along with size and technology, it is part of the configuration of internal organizational factors that have been formed in interaction to yield structure and that compose the context in which future structural arrangements are developed. Like size and technology, culture is an internal contingency variable (Pheysey, 1993). It is a factor that affects preferences, such as one for centralization or decentralization, and interacts with other contextual factors. We will turn now to a consideration of external contextual factors.

The Environment

In later chapters we will deal with organizational environments in detail; here our concern is simply to trace some of the implications of organizational environments for organizational structure. Of primary interest is the social environment of organizations; but the physical environment, such as climate or geography, can also be important, particularly for organizations that utilize or affect that physical environment.

Environmental characteristics are constraints on organizations, affecting their scale of operations and their mode of technical production (Ranson, Hinings, and Greenwood, 1980). These characteristics refer specifically to the socioeconomic infrastructure in which organizations are located. The demographic situation, including factors such as the racial and ethnic mixes present, constrains organizations, as do the institutionalized values surrounding the organization. Thus, they suggest that as clergy revise their theology, the structural forms of religious organizations will be altered. Similarly, if teachers modify their pedagogical frames of reference, schools will change. The value changes are brought into the organization from outside. Organizational decision makers are faced with making the organizational structure congruent with the demands placed on it.

A study of school districts found that the administrative complexity of the districts is related to the environmental complexity that the districts face. If schools receive federal funds, for example, the administration is most complex and fragmented, because of all the various reporting requirements (Meyer, Scott, and Strang, 1987).

Another way of looking at environments is to determine whether they are "hostile" or "friendly" (Khandwalla, 1972). A friendly environment is supportive, providing funds and value support. In a hostile environment the very underpinnings of the organization are threatened. The grave doubts raised about the nuclear energy industry in the wake of the Three Mile Island accident in Pennsylvania, plus other assorted problems with the industry, made the environment hostile for organizations in that industry in the United States. Colleges and universities had friendly environments during the 1960s and early 1970s. Money poured in for new facilities and personnel, and there was a general belief that education was the key to solving social and international problems. Obviously, that environment has moved from one of friendliness to one of neutrality, if not hostility.

Khandwalla suggested that in a friendly environment, organizations will be structurally differentiated. The environment will be monitored by differentiated personnel who are then integrated by a series of mechanisms, such as committees and ad hoc coordinating groups. If the environment turns hostile, the organization will "tighten up" by centralizing and standardizing its operations.

In a slightly different approach to the same issue, Pfeffer and Leblebici (1973) analyzed the effects of competition on structure. They found that in more competitive situations, there is a greater demand for control and coordination. Reports are more frequent, and there are more written communications and a greater specification of decision procedures. When competition is less intense, there are more frequent changes in product design, production processes, and number of products. Less competition provides some "slack," so that the organization can afford to do more than its routine competitive activities.

Competition is an interesting phenomenon. It occurs in the public and private sectors. It also has ramifications above and beyond economic factors. A study of a set of newspaper companies found that in a competitive environment—for example, where there was more than a single newspaper in a city—the structure of the newspaper reflected the complexity of the community. If there was no competition, the newspaper did not mirror the community as closely. Thus, in the competitive situation, attention would be paid to all components of the community, such as minority groups. Without competition, those groups could be ignored (DuBick, 1978).

A study of competition among hospitals shows an additional side of the noneconomic aspects of competition (Fennell, 1980). Fennell found that hospital services increased in competitive situations. She attributes the increase in services to the competition rather than to service needs. Thus, competition here is counter to economic rationality, raising the costs of medical services as each hospital in a competitive situation adds more and more expensive equipment and services that are not actually needed.

When environmental demands are conflicting, as in the case of community mental health programs that move into drug abuse treatment, organizations can develop structures that have conflicting goals and inconsistent structures and practices (D'Aunno, Sutton, and Price, 1991).

Another approach to the analysis of environment on organizational structure is represented by those who have attempted to compare organizations in different social settings. Meyer and Brown (1977) made a historical analysis of government organizations in the United States. They found that the era of origin and subsequent environmental shifts was related to the degree of formalization, which was in turn related to multiple levels of hierarchy and the delegation of personnel decisions to lower levels in the organization. Although the era of origin effects are pervasive, the environmental shifts force the organization to continually adjust to the context in which it is found.

National Culturals

Meyer and Brown studied organizations over time in one country. It is interesting to compare organizations *across* countries. A comparison of Canadian and American firms looked at the importance of foreign control on the structure of organizations, examining Canadian-owned firms in the United States and American-owned firms in Canada, as well as domestically owned firms in each country. The study found the effects of foreign control to be problematic, with somewhat less innovation in the foreign-controlled firms but with the rest of the relationships relatively weak (Brown and Schneck, 1979). Brown and Schneck (1979) did reach an important conclusion beyond the issue of foreign control. They suggested that government policy is very important for the organizations. National policies in areas such as health care or banking appear to have a direct impact on organizational structure, with clear differences between Canada and the United States.

The nature of the environment is *perceived* by organizational decision makers and boundary spanners. The perception of the environment is then enacted in the organization through decision making (Malan, 1994). Managers in South Africa and the United States perceive different amounts and kinds of environmental turbulence. Interestingly, the decisions made in these two settings were not found to be very different.

The importance of national cultures for organizations can be examined most clearly, perhaps, in cases of multinational organizations. The use of the multinational organization permits an examination of the effects of the country of origin compared with the effects of the host country. Schollhammer (1971) suggested that the multinational firm is affected by its country of origin so that a Dutch-based firm would exhibit different characteristics from those of a Japanese-based firm in their American operations.

In an analysis of Japanese companies in the United States, Ouchi and Jaeger (1978) and Ouchi and Johnson (1978) found the following general differences between Japanese and American firms:

American	Japanese
Short-term employment	Lifetime employment
Individual decision making	Consensual decision making
Individual responsibility	Collective responsibility
Rapid evaluation and promotion	Slow evaluation and promotion
Explicit, formalized control	Implicit, informal control
Specialized career path	Nonspecialized career path

The Ouchi analyses found that the Japanese firms with operations in the United States resembled the Japanese model more than the American model, again suggesting that the country of origin is of critical importance.

Interest in national cultural differences and their impacts on organizations has risen dramatically in recent years. The easiest imagery here is the multinational enterprise, with manufacturing, distribution, sales, and administrative operations spread around the globe. But there are other imageries as well. Many international religious organizations have long had multinational operations. One only need think about the well-publicized policy differences between American Roman Catholics and the Vatican to get a glimpse of national cultural factors in operation.

How does national culture interface with internal organizational culture? One answer is provided by Geert Hofstede (1993), who is a leading scholar of multinational organizations. He sees culture as "mental programming or software" (p. 1) and believes national and organizational cultures overlap. For some issues, such as dealing with authority, national culture is most important. For other issues, such as dealing with innovations, organizational cultures are more important.

Perhaps the easiest way to frame the national culture issue is to look at the juxtaposed arguments of "culture free" versus "culture bound." The culture-free view is that organizational characteristics are based on factors other than national cultures. These other factors could be size, technology, internal culture, or factors not yet considered. The culture-bound argument is that national cultures are the dominant force in operation. As we will see, neither extreme argument can be sustained.

In their study of multinational banks in Hong Kong, Birnbaum and Wong (1985) found support for a "culture-free" determination of structure. Centralization, vertical and horizontal differentiation, and formalization were not related to the cultures in which the multinational banks studied had operations. Marsh and Mannari (1980) also report that structural relationships found in the West tend to have the same form in Japan, rather than varying with culture. Conaty, Mahmoudi, and Miller (1983) found that organizations in prerevolutionary Iran were modeled on Western organizations.

These findings are in contrast to the arguments of the "culture-bound" analysts. A study of manufacturing plants in France, West Germany, and Great Britain found that the education, training, recruitment, and promotion processes lead to a situation in which the organizational processes of differentiation and integration are carried out by logics that are particular to a society and result in nationally different organizational shapes (Maurice, Sorge, and Warner, 1980). Differences have also been found in studies of Saudi Arabia and the United States (At-Twarjri and Montansani, 1987), in multinational firms in India (Rosenweig and Singh, 1991; Gupta and Govindarajan, 1991), in business organizations in East Asia (Japan, South Korea, Taiwan, and Hong Kong), small businesses in China and the United States (Hall et al., 1993), newspapers in Finland (Dalin, 1997), and breweries in Germany and the United States (Carroll, Swaninathan, and Wiedenmayer, 1993).

There are thus contrasting findings and interpretations in regard to the importance of cultural differences for organizational structure. There are several possible explanations for these differences. Quite obviously different research methodologies were used in the various studies (Tayeb, 1987). Different conceptual frameworks were also in evidence. The most intriguing explanation for these differences is that of Birnbaum and Wong (1985). They suggest that cultural differences themselves might be the source of the different findings. Where particular organizational forms are acceptable, as in the case of Western forms in prerevolutionary Iran, one would expect to find such forms. In postrevolutionary Iran, on the other hand, one would be surprised to find a preponderance of such Western forms.

Organizations are affected by the culture and environment in which they are located, just as they are affected by size and technology. These factors interact with one another, with no single factor dominating. Lincoln, Hanada, and McBride (1986) suggest that national culture effects are additive in the sense that they are added to the variations in structure introduced by operations technology, size, and market constraints. These authors go on to note that there may be situations in which cultural factors could override technology.

Whereas Lincoln et al. believe that the effects of culture are additive, Hamilton and Biggart (1988) argue, in their analysis of South Korean, Japanese, and Taiwanese organizations, that cultural effects and market factors explain organizational growth but that authority patterns and legitimation strategies best explain organizational structure. This is the first suggestion of a theme that will be developed in later pages: that explanations of organizations must be used together rather than in opposition.

A colleague and I disagree with Hamilton and Biggart in regard to Chinese and Japanese differences (Hall and Xu, 1990). We believe that differences in family and Confucian values in the two countries contribute to crucial differences in structure between the two countries. We do not disagree in regard to using explanations in combination.

The research we have been reviewing has two important characteristics. First, national culture is being moved to the forefront of explanations of organizational structure and organizations more generally. Second, the attention being paid to culture is being done with the realization that other factors affecting structure, such as size, technology, and other environmental conditions, are not diminished in importance. They are retained in the explanatory equations.

Our attention now shifts to the ways in which organizational design affects structure, but there is a final point to be made in regard to our contextual factors. Organizational design strategies are themselves affected by the cultures in which the design efforts are made (Schreyogg, 1980; Schneider, 1989). American, British, Japanese, and Chinese organizations would all have their own techniques of formulating their strategies.

ORGANIZATIONAL DESIGN

The notion of organizational design has a very rational ring to it. We simply design organizations to attain their goals and be effective. Fortunately or unfortunately, the matter is not that simple. Rationality itself is hard to accomplish, regardless of what is being planned. At the same time, events in organizations are not entirely random, since the very intent of structure is to provide some degree of certainty of action. In the sections that follow, alternative approaches to organizational design will be presented and evaluated. The complicated nature of organizational design is well captured by Starbuck and Nystrom (1981):

> Evidently, people and organizations solve problems by processes that operate quite separately from the processes by which they characterize and perceive problems. . . . This separation is probably beneficial, for people and organizations misperceive problems and they characterize problems in ways that grossly distort what they do perceive. When people and organizations generate solutions, the productive solution attempts combine multiple, simultaneous attacks on the components of problems. Solution attempts produce both predicted and unpredicted effects and both good and bad ones. Consequently, solution attempts become components of the problems they address. The initial problems, if they are solved, are ultimately solved through iterative sequences of solution attempts, and these sequences succeed because the people and organizations have observed and reacted to intermediate effects. Usually, of course, environmental changes render the initial problems and early solution attempts obsolete before the initial problems are actually solved. (pp. xix–xx)

Starbuck and Nystrom's comments suggest that organizational design is problematic and uncertain. Other observers are more sanguine and offer prescriptions such as Caplow's (1976) book *How to Run Any Organization*. The very title smacks of rational organizational design. Peters and Waterman's (1982) long-running best seller, In *Search of Excellence*, contains the kinds of prescriptions that are typical of the view that organizations can be the object of rational organizational design. They prescribe the following:

1. A bias for action—do it, try it, don't analyze the problem to death.
2. Stay close to the customer and understand the service or product needs.
3. Engage in entrepreneurship and promote autonomy within the organization.
4. Productivity is through people and not technology.
5. Have high values and demand excellence.
6. Stick to the knitting—do what you do best.
7. Keep the staff lean and simple.
8. Have simultaneous looseness and tightness—allow people to be autonomous, but at the same time be disciplined. (This summary is from Van de Ven, 1983.)

From the perspective of Starbuck and Nystrom and that taken here, these prescriptions are too simplistic. They ignore the perceptual and judgmental difficulties that Starbuck and Nystrom stress and the weight of several bodies of literature. Organizational design does affect structure, but not in the simple, overly rational manner suggested by the authors of prescriptive solutions for organizations. In the sections that follow, we will consider alternative perspectives on organizational design, beginning with the idea that organizations make strategic choices in regard to how they are structured.

Strategic Choice

The idea of strategic choice is not a new one. Chandler (1962) emphasized the importance of strategic choices for business firms such as Sears, Roebuck and General Motors as they attempted to take advantage of perceived markets in their environment. The establishment of General Motors as a multidivisional form with Chevrolet, Pontiac, and the other automotive divisions was seen as a consequence of strategic choices.

Child (1972) advanced this argument by noting that the internal politics of organizations determine the structural forms, the manipulation of environmental features, and the choice of relevant performance standards that are selected by organizations. The internal politics are themselves dependent upon the existing power arrangements in the organization. Again, structure begets structure.

Strategic choices are made on the basis of "bounded rationality" (Simon, 1957). The nature of rationality as a component of the decision-making process will be considered in detail in Chapter 7, but it is important here to note that the bounded-rationality idea means that the strategic choices are not necessarily the optimal choices. Rather, they appear to be optimal as a consequence of decisions made through the political process within organizations. The concept of "equifinality" is useful here. Equifinality refers to the presence of several means (structures) available to reach a given end (goal) (Katz and Kahn, 1966). Organizations are faced with both equifinality of means to ends and the presence of multiple ends. That is why the notion of choice is important. An organization is faced with multiple environmental pressures and must choose one path among many options toward one of many objectives.

Organizations are faced with environments that differ in their rates of change and degree of uncertainty. Specific parts of organizations are affected by specific environmental elements (Miles, Snow, and Pfeffer, 1974). The legal department of an organization has different environmental interactions from those of the public relations department and would thus choose a different form.

The political context of the decision-making process has an important relationship with structure. For example, people carrying out nonroutine tasks are likely to have power because of their expertise; those doing routine tasks do not have that power source. People with expertise can claim and receive more discretion, or decentralization on a broader basis, as something won from a position of power, rather than something delegated from above (Pfeffer, 1978; Pfeffer and Salancik, 1978).

The power holders in organizations decide what are issues and what are not issues. Thus, the decision to make a strategic choice or not is based on power arrangements (Ranson, Hinings, and Greenwood, 1980). The term that is most commonly used to describe power arrangements in organizations is the dominant coalition (Thompson, 1967). The "dominant coalition comprises a direct and indirect 'representation' or cross-section of horizontal constituencies (that is, subunits) and vertical constituencies (such as employees, management, owners, or stockholders) with different and possibly competing expectations" (Pennings and Goodman, 1977: p. 152).

This approach does not see the dominant coalition as representative democracy. Rather, the dominant coalition is the outcome of the power held by the various parties in the coalition. Thus, some units are more powerful among the horizontal constituencies, and there is obvious power differentiation among the vertical constituencies. The dominant coalition, then, comprises the power center in the organization. This power center or coalition is that which makes the strategic choices in regard to the organization and its structure. In some cases, there is no dominant coalition, with a single individual or set of individuals dominating all others. In those cases, personality characteristics of powerful chief executive officers may be a key determinant of structure (Miller and Droge, 1986).

Decision makers in the dominant coalition select those parts of the environment with which they will be concerned. This selection is done within a political framework in which membership in the dominant coalition can shift, as can the distribution of power within it. On the basis of selective perception of the environment, appropriate strategies can be selected for dealing with this environment. This decision making includes utilizing the appropriate technology for implementing the strategy. In the strategic choice perspective, technology is thus brought into the organization. The decisions also involve strategies for arranging roles and relationships to control and coordinate the technologies being employed. This is done to ensure continuity of the organization, its survival and growth (Chandler, 1962).

Strategic choices take place within contexts. For example, a study of the multidivisional form, such as that employed by General Motors, found that industrial diversity and geographical dispersion were strongly related to the presence of the multidivisional form, with organizational size having an indirect effect by contributing to diversity and dispersion (Palmer et al., 1987). Conversely, the absence of diversity would limit the extent to which the multidivisional form would be used. The industrial limits to choice are evident in the fact that the petroleum and agricultural industries were less diverse than other industries. Also, firms dominated by banks or by family members were less diverse and dispersed and had fewer multidivisional forms. The industrial context in which firms operated thus had a major impact on the form adopted.

The Marxian Twist. A sharply different perspective on organizational design has been taken by Marxist scholars. Goldman and Van Houton (1977) note:

... research has shown the promise of a Marxist approach to bureaucracy. Marglin's (1974) analysis of hierarchy during the industrial revolution and Stone's (1973) discussion of the development of job ladders in the late nineteenth century steel industry show how changes in the division of labor stem as much from the desire to effect organizational control as from the need to apply continually advancing technology to production. Braverman (1974) and Edwards (1975), analyzing contemporary work organization, suggest that machinery and bureaucratic regulations in industry derive from managerial desires to effect substantial control over both labor market characteristics and the attitudes of workers. This research indicates that managerial thinking is attuned to the larger social, political, and economic setting, as well as to internal administration.

Other Marxist or quasi-Marxist research informs the study of bureaucracy, albeit in a more indirect fashion. Studies of economic elites, focusing particularly on interinstitutional relationships and the interpenetration of economics and politics, provide an alternative view of managerial behavior to that found in most literature on organizations. (pp. 108–9)

Additional fuel for this fire was supplied by Clawson (1980), who traced the spread of Taylor's (1911) principles of "scientific management" through industry in the United States. According to Clawson, this resulted in more control by capital and less control by labor. Clawson's analysis focuses on the manner in which craft work was deskilled as factory work was more and more minutely subdivided into small, routine tasks. Clawson argues that this deskilling has continued into the present, with less and less control possible for workers in a wide variety of settings.

There are two major problems with this Marxist argument. First, the evidence in regard to the extent of the deskilling of labor is actually quite mixed (Form, 1980; Spenner, 1979, 1983, 1990; Attewell, 1987; Vallas, 1990). Indeed, there is evidence of skill enhancement for some kinds of work.

The second problem is that alluded to in the initial discussion of organizational design and strategic choice. Rationality is bounded and problematic. Just as a "perfect" solution to a design issue is unlikely, so is it unlikely that managerial attempts at control will work perfectly. In addition, labor will strongly resist efforts at control (Edwards, 1979).

Despite these problems, worker control must be considered a component of organizational design. Management does have interests that are different from those of the worker. The introduction of new machines and new forms of organization are at least in part attempts to control workers (Perrow, 1983; Sabel, 1982).

The worker-control issue appears to be one among several that are faced by the dominant coalition in organizations as design attempts are made. Again, there appear to be industry effects on the forms of worker control and internal labor market strategies that are used (Baron, Jennings, and Dobbin, 1988; see also Bills, 1987). These authors argue strongly that there are multiple sources for organizations' personnel policies and that monocausal arguments are inadequate. I am in complete agreement.

The Downsizing Twist.   In recent years a new element has been added to strategic choice. Many organizations are choosing the path of downsizing (Cappelli et al., 1997). This can involve laying off employees at all levels (except the very top, of course) and "externalizing" activities—purchasing products and services outside the organization's boundaries, employing cheaper labor in a location "offshore," or buying janitorial or payroll services from an outside vendor.

Government organizations engage in a form of downsizing when they "privatize" some of their activities. Privatization is a volatile issue, particularly for government employee unions who make an interesting linkage between privatization and privateers. In any event, the privatizing of schools or prisons is another example of the downsizing approach to organizational design.

There is an important consideration here that must be highlighted. Most of the analyses of strategic choice that have been considered make the implicit assumption that choices are made to increase organizational efficiency. The downsizing argument turns this around and sees "structures as outcomes of efficiency constraints" (Meyer, 1990a: p. 209). According to this point of view, financial control has become paramount.

Strategic Choice: A Summary.   These excursions into Marxian worker control and downsizing must not blind us to the fact that choices are made about organizational structures. Strategic choices are made on an ongoing basis. As Chapter 7 will demonstrate, whether or not such choices can be rational is truly problematic. Decision makers continue to make choices. A key factor here is that these choices are made within a system of constraints. The constraints are exactly the factors we have been considering in this chapter.

I will use an example to illustrate this. A few years ago, it was announced to the local news media that our intercollegiate athletic program was making major structural changes to achieve gender equity. This choice involved dropping some men's teams and adding some women's teams. (I chaired the committee that made these recommendations to the president. He accepted the recommendations, and the director of athletics announced the decision.) At that point another part of the environment came into the picture. Students, coaches, alumni, and parents of players on the affected teams protested the decision and successfully blocked it in court. After a year of additional deliberations, the original recommendation was upheld. Decision making is not a simple process.

Our operating constraints were size, in the form of the amount of resources (money) available for intercollegiate athletics; the internal organizational culture, in the form of tradition and strong emotional support for maintaining some of the men's teams; and the environment, in the form of federal and NCAA mandates for gender equity. Technology was not a factor.

Decisions made under constraints are at the core of what has come to be known as *structural contingency theory* (Donaldson, 1995, 1996). This theory is built on the work of Lawrence and Lorsch, which was considered in the last chapter. Organizational structures are based on decisions made in the contexts in which the organizations are operating. This means, simply, that there is no one best form of structure.

The Institutional Explanation

The final explanation of organizational structure to be considered is the institutional model. This model has become a major contributor to our understanding of organizational phenomena. It is another attempt to answer the question, Why do organizations take the forms that they do? Much of the research here has been carried out in not-for-profit organizations with somewhat indeterminate technologies. DiMaggio and Powell (1983) argue that "institutional isomorphism" is now the dominant reason that such organizations assume the forms that they do. According to DiMaggio and Powell, Weber's (1952, 1968) original analysis of the driving force behind the move toward rationalization and bureaucratization was based on a capitalist market economy, with bureaucratization an "iron cage" in which humanity was bound since the process of bureaucratization was irreversible.

DiMaggio and Powell believe that major social changes have altered that situation to such a large extent that an alternative explanation is needed. Their analysis is based on the assumption that organizations exist in "fields" of other, similar organizations. They define an organizational field as follows:

> By organizational field, we mean those organizations that, in the aggregate, constitute a recognized area of institutional life: key suppliers, resource and product consumers, regulatory agencies and other organizations that produce similar services and products. The virtue of this unit of analysis is that it directs our attention not simply to competing firms, as does the population approach of Hannan and Freeman (1977b), or to networks of organizations that actually interact, as does the interorganizational network approach of Laumann et al. (1978), but to the totality of relevant actors. (p. 148)

According to this perspective, organizations are increasingly homogeneous within fields. Thus, public universities acquire a sameness, as do department stores, airlines, professional football teams, motor vehicle bureaus, and so on. DiMaggio and Powell cite three reasons for this isomorphism among organizations in a field. First, there are coercive forces from the environment, such as government regulations and cultural expectations, which can impose standardization on organizations. Government regulations, for example, force restaurants (it is hoped) to maintain minimum health standards. There is strong evidence in support of the coercive force of government mandates. Both the adoption of disciplinary and grievance processes and the formation of internal labor markets have been traced to the development of government mandates for equal employment opportunities (Dobbin et al., 1993; Sutton et al., 1994).

Second, DiMaggio and Powell note that organizations mimic or model each other. This occurs as organizations face uncertainty and look for answers to their uncertainty in the ways in which other organizations in their field have faced similar uncertainties. Rowan (1982) argues, for example, that public schools add and subtract administrative positions in order to come into isomorphism with prevailing norms, values, and technical lore in their institutional environment. DiMaggio and Powell argue that large organizations tend to use a relatively small number of consulting firms, which "like Johnny Appleseeds, spread a few organizational models throughout the land" (p. 152). A concrete example, noted by DiMaggio and Powell, is Japan's conscious modeling of its courts, postal system, military, banking, and art education programs on Western models in the late nineteenth century. As DiMaggio and Powell note:

> American corporations are now returning the compliment by implementing (their perceptions of) Japanese models to cope with thorny productivity and personnel problems in their own firms. The rapid proliferation of quality circles and quality-of-work-life issues in American firms is, at least in part, an attempt to model Japanese and European successes. (1983: p. 151)

A *New York Times* article reports that business firms are establishing formal intelligence departments to keep tabs on competitors from home and abroad. One source is quoted as saying that "understanding your competitors' positions and how they might evolve is the essence of the strategic game" (Prokesh, 1985). In DiMaggio and Powell's conceptualization, the field is more than simply competitors. The establishment of intelligence departments reflects the strong mimetic tendencies within organizations.

A third source of institutional isomorphism is normative pressure as the workforce, and especially management, becomes more professionalized. Both professional training and the growth and elaboration of professional networks within organizational fields leads to a situation in which the managerial personnel in organizations in the same field are barely distinguishable from one another. As people participate in trade and professional associations, their ideas tend to homogenize. This normative factor was found to be important in the Dobbin et al. (1993) and Sutton et al. (1994) studies cited earlier. Here, along with the importance of government mandates, professional personnel managers were instrumental in bringing about employment reforms. Additional support is found in research on the financial reporting practices in Fortune 200 business firms. This research found that financial reporting practices were based on the professionalization in the environment of the firms studied (Mezias, 1990).

The institutional perspective thus views organizational design not as a rational process based on organizational goals but as one of both external and internal pressures that lead organizations in a field to resemble each other over time. This perspective sees strategic choices as coming from the institutional order in which an organization is embedded.

The institutional perspective itself has become institutionalized (Tolbert and Zucker (1996) and perhaps even "authoritarian" within the field of organizational theory (Hirsch, 1997. p. 1703). Indeed, it is being applied, some would say misapplied, in fields far beyond the indeterminate technologies that were the focus of DiMaggio and Powell's original formulation. Sometimes it appears that structural characteristics that cannot be explained by any other reason are attributed to institutional forces.

At the same time, institutional theory is providing insights into important things that have happened in and around organizations. For example, the growing proportion of women in management and an increased awareness of work-family issues have been attributed to both normative and coercive institutional processes (Blum, Fields, and Goodman, 1994; Goodstein, 1994).

EXPLAINING ORGANIZATIONAL STRUCTURE

We have been considering a series of explanations of organizational structure. These have ranged from contextual factors such as size and technology to the design factors of strategic choice and institutional isomorphism. Which is the correct explanation? It should be obvious by now that neither "all of the above" nor "none of the above" is the appropriate answer. The explanations of structure must be considered in combination.

This has become well recognized among sociologists. For example, Tolbert (1985) combined the environmental pressure and institutional perspectives in explaining aspects of the administrative structures of universities. Fligstein (1985) studied the spread of the multidivisional form among large corporations and found support for the strategic choice, member control, and institutional perspectives. Fligstein also suggests that in a different set of organizations, other explanations might be valid. Fligstein concludes (and I concur):

> ... each school of thought has tended to view its theory as a total causal explanation of organizational phenomena. This suggests that one of the central tasks in organizational theory is to reorient the field in such a way as to view competing theories as contributing to an understanding of organizational phenomena. (p. 377)

The healthy and informed eclecticism that Fligstein calls for has essentially become the norm in organizational analyses. Hamilton and Biggart's (1988) study of the importance of national culture for organizations in the Far East is another example of this multiple-theory approach, as is Drazin and Van de Ven's (1985) analysis of the structures of a set of employment security units.

Further examples of this move toward multiple theoretical explanations are found in Kraatz and Zajac's (1996) study of private colleges and universities, where local economic and demographic conditions (environmental conditions) were more important than institutional factors in explaining structural changes. Similarly, a study of the development of the thrift industry in California found that environmental pressures operated in tandem with institutional forces (Haveman and Rao, 1997). There is a growing recognition that market and task contingencies operate along with institutional pressures (Bugra and Usdiken, 1997; Gupta et al., 1994; Sutton and Dobbin, 1996).

Organizations are structured in a context. Van Houton (1987) analyzed the various approaches to organizational design that were attempted in Sweden in the 1970s and 1980s. He concludes that these cannot be understood out of their historical context. Organizations are thus "complex structures-in-motion that are best conceptualized as historically constituted entities" (Clegg, 1981: p. 545). There are, then, multiple explanations of structure. When these explanations are taken singly, in opposition to one another, and outside their historical and cultural context, they have little to offer. When combined and in context, they enable us to understand why organizations take the forms that they do.

Organizations do not take form automatically. They do so because of decisions that are made, and that brings us back to the factor of strategic choice. But our move back is informed by the theoretical inclusiveness that we have just considered. Thus, organizations may diversify or reorganize to better fit their environments (Donaldson, 1987). They adapt their forms to fit the national culture in which they are operating (Sorge, 1991). They may also seek to differentiate themselves from other organizations and thus not conform to institutional pressures (Han, 1994). When they face multiple and conflicting environmental contingencies, they may respond with "misfits" (Gresov, 1989). Strategic choices are also made in light of the technologies available and appropriate for the organization involved.

As we turn now to a consideration of organizational processes, it should be made clear that organizational structures affect these processes and vice versa (Miller, 1987). Structure affects the flow of information and the power arrangements in organizations. Decisions made in regard to attempted strategies affect structure. Unlike the buildings in our analogy at the outset of this chapter, structures are in motion.

SUMMARY AND CONCLUSIONS

We have considered the various explanations that have been developed to explain the forms that organizational structures take. Organizational structure is dynamic. Organizations change in size, adopt new technologies, face changing environments and internal and national cultures, adopt new strategies or find old ones, and adjust to other organizations in their field.

Before turning to organizational processes, we must repeat that organizational structures are there for a purpose and that the purpose is to be as effective as possible. There are many sources of deflection from the structure-effectiveness linkage—some intentional and some accidental, some humorous and some tragic—but the linkage remains.

It has been implicit in the discussion that the structure of an organization has important outcomes—for its members and for the social system of which it is a part. It is within structure that the processes of power, conflict, leadership, decision making, communication, and change operate. We now turn to a consideration of those processes.

Power and Power
Outcomes

Organizations and power are synonymous in many ways. After all, organizations are powerful tools of the powerful when we think of organizational outcomes. They are also power systems in regard to the ways in which people conform to organizational rules. They are political systems in regard to the allocation of resources. Power is distributed between the privileged and the underprivileged. In Mintzberg's (1983) terms, we can think of power "in and around" organizations. If we think of power arrangements as being a consequence of organizational design, then power arrangements are another means by which organizations attempt to be effective.

In this chapter we will analyze the nature of power within organizations. A major focus will be the way power relationships develop over time. In many ways, power is a most puzzling phenomenon. On the one hand, power is stable and self-perpetuating. Those in power have the resources to maintain themselves in power. On the other hand, as the events in Eastern Europe and the USSR in 1989 and 1990 demonstrated, entrenched power can be overthrown with startling quickness.

There are many ways in which power can be distributed in organizations. In Chapter 3, the discussion of centralization revealed that power can be concentrated in the hands of the few or be decentralized throughout the organization. Morgan's (1986: p. 145) sixfold classification of power relationships in organizations is a good introduction to the ways power can be distributed.

First, organizations can be *autocracies*, wherein power is held by an individual or a small group with absolute control. Second, organizations can be *bureaucracies,* in which rules are written and power relationships clearly specified. Third, organizations can be *technocracies,* in which knowledge and expertise rule the system. Fourth, organizations can be governed by *codetermination,* wherein opposing parties in the organization share in the ruling system. Fifth, organizations can be *representative democracies,* in which officers are elected and serve specific terms or for as long as they have member support. This was the system in former Yugoslavia that came tragically apart. Finally, organizations can be *direct democracies,* in which everyone participates and has the right to rule. This system has characterized many cooperatives, as well as the kibbutzim in Israel. Many organizations are mixed types, with elements of more than one form of rule. Bureaucracy is the dominant form and will be the primary focus here.

THE NATURE OF POWER IN ORGANIZATIONS

Power can usually be rather simply defined. There is general agreement that it has to do with relationships between two or more actors in which the behavior of one is affected by the behavior of the other. The political scientist Dahl (1957) defines power thus: "A has power over B to the extent that he can get B to do something B would not otherwise do" (pp. 202–3). (For other general discussions of power, see Bierstedt, 1950; Blau, 1964; Kaplan, 1964; and Weber, 1947: pp. 152–93.) If we remember that the "he" in the definition can be a "she" and that the "A's" and "B's" are not necessarily individuals, this simple definition captures the essence of the power concept. It implies an important point that is often neglected: The power variable is a relational one; power is meaningless unless it is exercised. A person or a group cannot have power in isolation; power has to be in relationship to some other person or collectivity, as when a person or a group has to overcome the resistance of another person or group (Pfeffer, 1992).

Power relationships involve much more than interpersonal power. In the case of organizations, it is vital to consider interunit power relationships. The units here can be hierarchical levels, such as labor and management. The units can also be departments or divisions, such as sales and manufacturing. We will also examine interorganizational relationships from the power standpoint at a later phase of the analysis. We have already considered the power of organizations in society. Power is thus a crucial process at every level of analysis.

Power Relationships

The relational aspect of power can be clearly seen when we introduce the idea of dependency. Power relationships entail mutual dependency. This means that the two parties need each other (Emerson, 1962). Management needs workers to produce services or products. Workers need management so they can get paid.

Dependency is particularly easy to see in organizations, which by their very nature require interdependence of personnel and subunits (Bacharach and Lawler, 1980). The existence of power relationships is also generally easy to see. In highly bureaucratized organizations, "power or authority would tend to be hierarchic: each level would have just that amount of power necessary to carry out its responsibilities; ascendant levels in the hierarchy would have increasing power based on broader knowledge about the organization and/or greater task expertise" (Wamsley, 1970: p. 53). The design of these types of organizations rests largely on the power variable, with the intent of ensuring that each level in the organization has sufficient power. When an issue arises that is out of the purview of an office at a particular level, it is passed up the organization until it reaches the level where the decision can appropriately be made. Of course, few organizations approximate this ideal type, because the power arrangements are affected by informal patterns worked out over time and by personal differences in the exercise of the power available in an office. Nevertheless, in many organizations, power relationships are tightly prescribed and followed, and they are highly visible to all who enter the organization.

In such settings power is very easily seen and experienced, in others it is more obscure. In some situations it is extremely hard to isolate. When a new or unanticipated situation arises, it may be difficult to determine exactly how and where power is to be exercised. In an analysis of a confrontation between students and university administration during the 1960s, Bucher (1970) relates the following anecdote:

> According to the students' statements, the dean asserted that "nobody in the university has the authority to negotiate with the students. . . ." "Obviously somebody in the university makes policy decisions," the students said, "and until an official body comes forward, we consider the present situation a refusal to negotiate our demands." (p. 3)

In the situation described, neither the students nor the university administration in question could locate an office or an individual who had the power to negotiate with students. The students' perception that this constituted a refusal to negotiate is only partially accurate. Such a situation simply had not arisen before, and there was undoubtedly no established way to handle it because the power relationship was yet to be determined.

Power is as much a fact of university life as it is of corporate life, even if it takes a different form and is expressed in different ways. In campus situations such as these student-administration confrontations, issues and relationships are explored that have not really been part of the preexisting power system. Because more power is introduced into the system as arrangements are made to handle such incidents in the future, we see that there is not a fixed amount of power in the system for all time; the amount of power can contract or expand.

As noted earlier, the subunits or departments in an organization also have varying amounts of power. A study of industrial firms found that the sales departments were overwhelmingly regarded as the most powerful units in the organizations involved. The members of the other departments regarded them that way and apparently behaved accordingly (Perrow, 1970a).

Several important studies have examined the departmental origins of chief executives. This has been done in the belief that those departmental origins are a good clue in locating departmental power. One study found that lawyers (coming from legal departments) were disproportionately represented among corporate chief executives. The argument is that organizations face complex legal problems, and lawyers move to the top of the organization as they appear to solve the problems (Priest and Rothman, 1985). A historical analysis of the 1919–79 period reports that entrepreneurs or people who came up through manufacturing dominated corporate presidencies in the early decades of the century. The middle decades were dominated by sales and marketing. The last decades have been dominated by personnel from finance (Fligstein, 1987). The difference in the findings reported here (lawyers versus finance) is undoubtedly due to differences in samples of organizations studied. The important point is that ignoring interdepartmental power relationships by looking only at interpersonal power obscures an important facet of organizational power and organizational life.

Two additional aspects of power are important. First, power is an act; it is something that is used or exercised. Too frequently the act of power is ignored in analyses of power, which tend to focus on the results of a power act. These results can take several forms, including compliance and conflict, but the exertion of power is what is of interest to us here. To sustain power, power holders must self-consciously exercise power to signify to others their awareness of their role obligations (Biggart and Hamilton, 1984). Second, the recipients of power are crucial in determining if a power act has occurred. If recipients interpret an act as a power act, they will respond on that basis, whether or not the power wielder intended to utilize power. Interestingly, if the power recipient does not respond to the power act, power is not exercised.

Types of Power

The discussion thus far has treated power as a unitary concept, but there is a long history of distinguishing among types of power. Probably the best-known and most widely used classification system is that of Weber (1947). Weber makes a basic distinction between *power* and *authority*. Power involves force or coercion and is an important factor as an internal process in organizations only in cases such as slave-labor camps, some prisons, and some schools. Authority, on the other hand, does not imply force. Rather, it involves a "suspension of judgment" on the part of its recipients. Directives or orders are followed because it is believed that they ought to be followed. Compliance is voluntary. This requires a common value system among organizational members, and this condition is usually met (Scott, 1964).

Weber (1947) developed the widely known and widely used typology of rational-legal, charismatic, and traditional authority. *Rational-legal* authority characterizes most power relationships in contemporary organizations; it is based on the belief in the right of those in higher offices to have power over subordinates. Another, and more accurate, way of understanding rational-legal authority is to think of it as an aspect of the office or position that has authority over another office or position. For example, at the start of every semester, I hand out a course syllabus to each of my students. When the students read the assignments, write the papers, and take the exams, rational-legal authority has operated. They have accepted the legitimate power I have in my position as professor over their positions as students. This emphasis on positions takes the person out of the equation—we will put the person back in now. *Charismatic* authority stems from devotion to a particular power holder and is based on his or her personal characteristics. This type is certainly found in modern organizations, to which it can be either a threat or a benefit. If a person in an authority position can extend rational-legal powers through the exercise of charismatic authority, there is more power over subordinates than that prescribed by the organization. If the performance of the subordinates is enhanced (assuming for the moment that their performance enhancement is also beneficial to the actors themselves), such an addition is beneficial. If, on the other hand, charismatic authority is present in persons outside the formal authority system, the system itself can be threatened.

The third form, *traditional* authority, is based on belief in the established traditional order and is best exemplified by operating monarchies. Vestiges of this form can be found in organizations in which the founder or a dominant figure is still present, when terms such as "the old man wants it that way" are verbalized and the wishes of the "old man" are followed. The Roman Catholic Church serves as a good example, since traditional authority is clearly represented by the system of pope, cardinals, archbishops, and so on.

Control in organizations is at least partially based on the process of evaluation (Dornbusch and Scott, 1975). The individual who evaluates one's work has authority. Control through evaluation is most effective when the individuals being evaluated believe the evaluations are important, central to their work, and capable of being influenced by their own efforts. If people believe that the evaluations are soundly based, they will be more controlled by the evaluation process. Dornbusch and Scott also note that authority is granted from above as well as from below. In a multilevel hierarchy, people in a position to evaluate others are legitimated from subordinates and also from their own superiors. When there is opposition to authority, as there frequently is, power holders can resort to trying to manufacture consent. This manufactured-consent situation is known as *domination* (Hardy and Clegg, 1996).

There is a final type of power—*influence*. Authority involves an acceptance of the power system as one enters the organization, whereas influence is a power situation in which the decision is made, consciously or unconsciously, at the particular moment the power appeal is sent from the power holder (Bacharach and Lawler, 1980). When a persuader becomes institutionalized, in the sense of being always accepted and thus legitimated by the recipient, this influence becomes authority. Influence can be used by a person or an office to extend the amount of authority in a situation. Influence attempts can be resisted, of course.

Power Bases and Sources

Organizational units and people in organizations get their power through their control of both power bases and power sources. Power bases refer to what power holders control that permits them to manipulate the behavior of others. Power bases include the ability to reward or coerce, legitimacy, expertise, and serving as a referent for the power recipient (Etzioni, 1961; French and Raven, 1968). In addition, access to knowledge (Bacharach and Lawler, 1980) and "family ties" (Allen and Panian, 1982) have also been identified as power bases. Family ties here refers to extended friendship patterns as well as actual family linkages. To have power in a situation, the power must have a power base that is of value to the power recipient. One of the power bases of a professor is the ability to reward (and sometimes punish) students with course grades. A professor may also have bases of legitimacy, expertise, and access to knowledge.

Bacharach and Lawler (1980) go on to make an additional distinction. They note that there are four sources of power in organizations. They use the term "sources" to refer to the manner in which parties come to control the power bases. The sources are (1) office or structural position; (2) personal characteristics, such as charisma; (3) expertise, which is treated as a source and a basis of power, since individuals bring expertise with them to the organization through such mechanisms as professional training, which is then converted into a power basis at a specific point in time; and (4) opportunity or a combination of factors that gives parties the chance to utilize their power bases.

These sources of power are used in the power situations of authority and influence, which in turn utilize the bases of power that have been distinguished. Thus, an individual or a unit in an organization has a power source, such as an official position in which power in the form of authority or influence is exercised. The earlier discussion of structure emphasized that positions are set in advance of the particular persons occupying those positions. This is a key source of power (Finkelstein, 1992; Fligstein and Brantley, 1992; Brass and Burkhardt, 1993). As the power is exercised, the power holder utilizes the power bases that are available. In this formulation, the bases cannot be used unless the power holder first of all has the appropriate power source.

This is made all the more complicated by the fact that some exercises of power are issue specific, whereas others are more general (Enz, 1989). For example, the president of my university has general power but defers to the expertise of the building-and-grounds superintendent in regard to the timing of snow removal. In this situation the building-and-grounds superintendent has a combination of office and expertise as sources of power and expertise and legitimacy as bases of power.

Another example may help in understanding the somewhat abstract presentation of types, bases, and sources of power. I recently got a phone call from the university president's office asking me to attend a dinner later in the same week and to wear "business attire." I did so and it was enjoyable. Why did I do it? The answer is that the president's office has rational-legal authority. In addition, I like the president very much and she wields influence over me above and beyond the limits of the office. In this case, the president did not call me herself. Rather, one of her assistants did. The power base was family ties, since the president and I know each other well and are good friends. The power source was the charisma of her assistant, who was able to persuade me to go to the dinner. This simple incident was a power situation; it was certainly not one of lasting importance, but the types, bases, and sources of power were all operative.

HORIZONTAL POWER RELATIONSHIPS

It is easiest to conceptualize or visualize power along the vertical axis of organizations. The vertical dimension is only one part of power relationships in organizations, however. As we have already seen in the discussion of the differential power of departments, power is also exercised along the horizontal dimension. Interdepartmental, staff-line, and professional-organizational relationships are all familiar loci of the horizontal dimension.

The term "horizontal power relationships" seems to represent an inconceivable situation. If the parties in the relationship have exactly equal amounts of power, then as soon as one gains power at the expense of the other, a vertical element is introduced. But the concern here is with relationships between units and persons who have positions relative to each other that are basically lateral or equal. In these lateral relationships, the power variable can become a major part of the total relationship. "Power overtly exists when other's resistance must be overcome to get one's way" (Pfeffer, 1992: p. 176). It is conceivable that power will not enter the relationship if the parties have no reason to attempt to affect each other's behavior. However, the power variable will almost inevitably enter such relationships when issues such as budgetary allocations, output quotas, and priorities for personnel come into the picture. There are major interdepartmental power struggles on the horizontal axis in most organizations.

Staff-Line Relationships

Horizontal or lateral power relationships have been carefully analyzed by Dalton (1959). Perhaps his best-known contribution is his analysis of staff-line conflict in manufacturing organizations. Dalton found that these personnel were in almost constant conflict in several areas. The staff personnel tended to be younger, have more formal education, be more concerned with proper dress and manners, and be more theoretically oriented than the line managers in the organizations studied. That was the basis for conflict, but it was also part of the power relationship. The power aspect, aside from its importance in actual conflict situations, came in when the staff attempted to get some of its ideas implemented (expert power).

Power was also exerted in regard to the personal ambitions of the people involved. Dalton assumed that both sets of managers sought income, promotions, power in the organization, and so on. In the organizations studied, the line personnel held the power in controlling the promotion process; at the same time, they feared that the staff might come up with ideas that would make the line's modes of operations look seriously outmoded or unimaginative. This is an example of two different forms of power as a part of one power relationship. The outcome was a series of conflicts between line and staff that, viewed from outside the organization, were costly to it. There was a fairly high turnover among staff personnel, who apparently felt that they were not getting anywhere in the organization. The staff resented the line, and vice versa.

To accomplish anything in such a situation, the staff must secure some cooperation from the line. This requires giving in to the line by moderating proposals, overlooking practices that do not correspond to rigid technical standards, and being generally subservient to the line. If this is not done, the staff's suggestions will probably go unheeded. This in turn will make their output zero for the time period, and their general relevance for the organization will then be questioned. This, of course, is not a unique situation.

The staff-line power interactions were studied in manufacturing organizations. The same forms of interaction would appear to characterize schools, where the teachers are the line and personnel such as curriculum specialists are the staff. Unfortunately, there has been little additional research on staff-line relationships since Dalton's major study, although Jackall (1988) does touch on the topic briefly in his analysis of the moral development of managers in corporations.

Staff-line relationships are more difficult to analyze when an organization has multiple lines. For example, an airline has flight attendants, ground personnel, counter personnel, and pilots, all of whom would be considered line operations. Staff would consist of planners, lawyers, financial officers, and so on. Staff-line conflicts would be found in these situations, although they have not been analyzed as such. The issue is not dead. In the case of airlines, it would be fascinating to examine the power of the line pilots relative to that of the staff lawyers. My guess is that the staff would have more power than the line.

Professional-Organizational Relationships

The analysis of staff-line relationships was essentially replaced by a focus on the relationships between professionals and their employing organizations. The power situation is one in which administrators must evaluate professionals under their administrative responsibility. Professionals here could be architects, lawyers, nurses, faculty members, or scientists. The evaluation of professionals' work is difficult for someone not in that profession. This is true in many cases even if the evaluator, in an administrative position, is a member of the same profession. For example, a research scientist in an organization is likely to be under the supervision of another scientist who has been promoted to research administration. The very fact that the latter is now working in administration prevents him or her from keeping up with developments in the scientific discipline; since they occur rapidly, it is difficult even for the practicing scientist to keep abreast of what is occurring.

Since the organization must in some way control all its members, the issue becomes very difficult with respect to the professional. If the organization tries to exert legitimate control through the hierarchy, the professional is apt to resist it. If it turns over the control of the professional to other professionals, the organization not only loses control but also is uncertain whether the professionals involved are contributing to the organization exactly what the organization thinks they should. This dilemma is frequently resolved by allowing the professionals to control themselves, with a fellow professional (for example, the research administrator) held accountable for the work of that unit as a collectivity. This allows the professional to work in a situation where there is less direct scrutiny but provides the organization with a system of accountability.

The reward system in these situations is also frequently altered. Instead of promoting professionals by moving them into higher positions in the administrative system, organizations develop "dual ladders" for their promotion system, whereby professionals can advance either by being promoted in the traditional way or by staying in their professional unit with their work but at increasingly higher salaries. (At the present time, at the University at Albany, there is a faculty member who has a higher salary than the president.) Additional rewards for professionals can come through publication and participation in the affairs of their profession. As the professionals becomes better known in their field, their own power increases. At the same time, the organization continues to have power, by providing the reward system as a whole.

This discussion has involved ways in which the power issue may be resolved. But obviously, in many cases the issues are not resolved, and professionals are in conflict with the rest of the organization. They may feel that the organization is intruding into their work through unnecessary rules and regulations or that their contributions are receiving insufficient attention and reward. The members of the organization in contact with the professionals, on the other hand, may view them as hopelessly impractical and out of touch with what is really important for the organization.

One of the most visible examples of the power relationships between professionals and their employing organizations can be seen in analyses of health maintenance organizations (HMOs). HMOs attempt to control costs, sometimes by limiting referrals to other physicians and sometimes by limiting the length of hospital stays. When physicians believe that a patient needs more care than the HMO permits, the conflict situation is evident. As these situations are evolving, the new role of physician-manager has developed (Hoff and McCaffrey, 1996; Hoff, 1998).

Another form of lateral power relationship that would often involve professionals is the power of expertise. Since there is no one universal organizational or societal truth system, experts can take differing views on what is good, rational, legal, or effective for the organization. When the perspectives of accountants, lawyers, research scientists, management consultants, and executives are combined, it is extremely unlikely that a common viewpoint will emerge even after serious discussions. As the level of training and expertise increases in organizations, differences in perspective will be magnified, and the power of expertise may well become a greater source of conflict for organizations. Professionals in organizations will continue to seek more power for themselves and their point of view (Hage, 1980).

Cliques and Coalitions

In his perceptive study of industrial organizations, Dalton (1959) found that cliques were an important component of the power system. Dalton showed that personal self-interest took the form of clique formation by individual members across organizational lines. Cliques were formed to defend the members in the face of real or imagined threats to their security by automation or reorganization. Aggressive cliques were formed to accomplish some purpose, such as to halt the expansion of a department perceived as usurping some of the power of clique members. Dalton's analysis shows that organizations are constantly filled with interpersonal power situations as events and conditions shift over time. These cliques need not, and in fact usually do not, follow the established organizational hierarchical or horizontal system.

Cliques can also be based on differentiation within organizations. People in different parts of organizations deal with qualitatively different information. The sales representative, the sales manager, and the marketing vice president are in the same functional area but deal with information with different time frames and referents. Sales representatives would be differentiated from other managerial personnel at the same level in the organization and would undoubtedly form cliques on that basis (Mintzberg, 1979). Cliques can also form on the bases of age, gender, and race and ethnicity. When power is exercised (or attempted) on these bases, it can be very divisive for an organization.

Some analyses of power in organizations have focused on coalitions of individuals and groups (Bacharach and Lawler, 1980; Pfeffer, 1981). Coalitions are formed as parties seek to advance their own interests. Coalitions seek to exert power over other coalitions and advance their own interests. Analyses of coalitions suggest that organizations are highly political, with shifting alliances and power arrangements. Factors such as gender, age, departmental position in the organization, educational background, length of time in the organization, and personal values all may influence coalition formation (Pfeffer, 1981: p. 37). These factors also may lead the individual and groups into different coalitions, depending on the issue.

The analysis of cliques and coalitions can lead us to view organizations as a "bewildering mosaic of swiftly changing and conflicting cliques, which cut across departmental and traditional loyalties" (Mouzelis, 1967: p. 159). Although this view is warranted as a check on an overstructured view of organizations, it is an overreaction. Cliques and coalitions would not form if there were not a common basis for interaction or if there were not already interaction among members. Rather than being random, the formation of cliques and coalitions obviously arises from the established organizational order and then varies from that order. The fact that cliques and coalitions can form vertically and horizontally and represent personal and subunit interests reflects the constant interplay of the power variables within the organization.

Uncertainty, Dependency, and Interdepartmental Power

Crozier's (1964) analysis of French organizations gives us another view of power along the horizontal dimension. Departments in tobacco firms studied were in a constant power struggle, with maintenance personnel holding the most power because of their knowledge in repairing the equipment necessary to the production process. Production workers and their supervisors were essentially helpless unless the maintenance personnel performed their work. That, of course, gave the maintenance personnel a great deal of power in the organization. Crozier states:

> With machine stoppages, a general uncertainty about what will happen next develops in a world totally dominated by the value of security. It is not surprising, therefore, that the behavior of the maintenance man—the man who alone can handle the situation, and who by preventing these unpleasant consequences gives workers the necessary security—has a tremendous importance for production workers, and that they try to please him and he to influence them. (p. 109)

This is a vivid example of the dependence relationship inherent in a power situation. If it were not for the essential expertise of the maintenance personnel in this situation, the production workers would not be so dependent. Although the Crozier study is perhaps an extreme case, it does illustrate how lateral relationships can come to be built around the power of the parties involved.

Additional insights into this kind of power relationship are provided by Perrow's (1970a) study, which was directly concerned with the power of different departments in organizations. Using data from twelve industrial firms based on answers to the question "Which group has the most power?" Perrow found that the firms studied were overwhelmingly dominated by their sales departments. This domination is shown in Figure 5–1. Although he does not have direct evidence, Perrow believes that this would be the case in most industrial firms in the United States. As noted earlier in this chapter, finance departments have replaced sales departments as the dominating force in contemporary business organizations (Fligstein, 1987). Figure 5–1 would thus show a drastic reconfiguration were it to be drawn today.

FIGURE 5–1 Overall Power of Departments in Industrial Firms (Means of Departmental Means)
Source: Charles Perrow, "Departmental Power and Perspective in Industrial Firms," in Mayer N. Zald, ed., *Power in Organizations* (Nashville, TN: Vanderbilt University Press, 1970), p. 64.

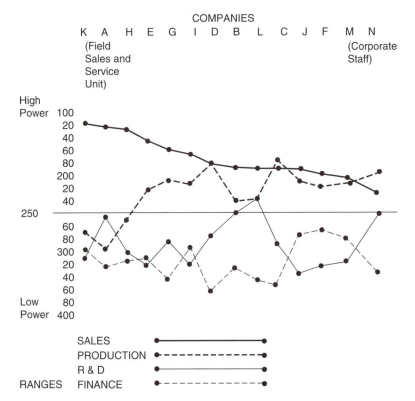

Perrow concludes that the most critical function in an organization tends to have the most power, linking his analysis to Crozier's. He notes that in the one firm that was production dominated, the production department was able to get control of the computer, inventory, and purchasing. It was in a position to tell the sales department what could or could not be done under existing conditions. Those same functions could be handled in the finance department, as was the case in another firm, with finance passing the information along to sales, thus giving sales power over production. The combination of critical function and dependence gives sales its power position in these organizations.

A PERSPECTIVE ON POWER IN ORGANIZATIONS

The discussion thus far has been largely descriptive, dealing with various studies of the forms of vertical and horizontal power relationships. In this section we will try to bring some of these considerations together in an overview of power in organizations.

The Amount of Power

The first point to be made here is a quantitative one, concerning the amount of power in an organization. Consider the following conclusion: "To sum up, managers and managed in organizations at the same time come to influence each other more effectively and thereby generate joint power as the outcome of a better command by the organization over its technological, economic, and human resources in the service of certain objectives" (Lammers, 1967: p. 204). This joint influence is actually a condition of *more* power in the organization than was the case before mutual influence entered the picture.

If the idea of power bases is utilized, it is obvious that the amount of power in an organization, as well as in a single interpersonal situation, can vary as additional elements are brought into power relationships. The power of office or of expertise can be expanded to include the referent base. The amount of power in an organization changes over time.

This view that the amount of power varies in organizations has to be considered with some caution. First, the amount does not vary dramatically from situation to situation. Factors leading to an increase or a decrease are typically not rapid or sudden in their impact—with the exception of something like a disaster, in which case the amount of power in the organization could change very dramatically. Generally, however, changes in the amount of power will be gradual. A second caution is that at any one point in time, the amount of power in an organization is fixed—a zero-sum game. If one person or group gains in power, another loses. Power acts are carried out within a fixed-amount framework. It is the framework that is altered over time.

Factors Affecting the Distribution of Power

When the focus is shifted from the amount of power to the reasons power is distributed as it is, several points stand out. The ability to cope with uncertainty has been found to make an important contribution to power differentials (Hickson, Pugh, and Pheysey, 1969). An organizational unit that can cope with uncertainty is able to deal with some issue of concern to the organization. If the concern is financial, for example, the unit able to attract resources will gain in power (Salancik and Pfeffer, 1974). In the perspective of the Aston group, coping with uncertainty is coupled with both the centrality of the organizational unit to the total organization and the unit's nonsubstitutability. Units that cope well with uncertainty and are irreplaceable and central to the workflow of the organization will have increased power.

An empirical examination of this theoretical approach revealed that this process did in fact operate but with this minor modification (Hickson et al., 1974): Some organizational units are delegated important tasks in the first place. They can increase their power by effective coping. In other instances, power can be developed when organizational units enter new and important areas of uncertainty, cope well, and develop more power. An analysis of the amount of power held by executives found essentially the same pattern. If executives coped with the dominant requirements imposed by the environment of their industry, they had high power (Hambrick, 1981). Centrality to the actual flow of work in the organization is more important than centrality in the broader, more abstract mission of the organization (Asher and Shapiro, 1988; Astley and Zajac, 1990). A study of Protestant denominations in the United States revealed, for example, that religious authority has been weakened by issues such as the maintenance and strengthening of the central office of a denomination (Chaves, 1993). The central office is in the midst of the workflow, whereas religious issues apparently are not. Congruity in values among work-unit members and top managers also contributes to unit power (Enz, 1988).

This approach implies that power is constantly shifting within organizations as units or people gain or lose power according to how well they cope with uncertainty. Although it is true that power is a component of any situation, the imagery of constantly shifting power is misleading for two reasons. First, it ignores the importance of the established hierarchy and degree of centralization. Although the coping-with-uncertainty approach is concerned with horizontal power relationships, the more vertical ones cannot be ignored. Second, once an organizational unit or person gains power by its success in coping, it tries very hard to maintain its power. Earlier success gives a unit or a person an immediate advantage over other units or people because it already has more power. Indeed, the environment present at the time an organization is formed and the background of the founding entrepreneur influence the departmental areas that come to be regarded as most important (Boeker, 1989). These historical influences carry over throughout the organization's history as "vestiges of early events" (p. 408). An organizational unit's previous power position is the main predictor of its subsequent power (Lachman, 1989). The same is true for individual managers and executives; powerful CEOs are less likely than their weaker subordinates to be dismissed when their organizations are doing poorly (Boeker, 1992).

Studies of university budget allocation decisions have found that the more powerful units receive more resources—the rich get richer and the poor get poorer. This pattern is particularly evident in times of financial adversity (Pfeffer and Salancik, 1974; Hills and Mahoney, 1978).

Power is self-perpetuating. Thus, those in power in an organization tend to remain in power. They have resources, and the power recipients do not. The very fact that legitimacy is such an important consideration in organizational power arrangements sets the stage for the perpetuation of existing power distributions (Michels, 1949).

The distribution of power in organizations has ramifications beyond those already discussed. The distribution of resources within an organization, including rewards, budget items, and personnel, is affected by the power system (Zald, 1970; Pondy, 1970). Since the allocation system is affected by the existing power system, it tends to perpetuate the existing system. Frequently overlooked is the fact that the accounting and information systems within organizations are important agents of power; they determine the emphasis given to particular kinds of activities and the information that is available to various members of the organization. The nature of the incentive system within the organization is an important power consideration, since it provides the basis, both in nature and in extent, on which rewards are distributed.

As will be discussed in Chapter 7, decision making is a critical organizational process. Power is obviously important in decision making. Power holders shape and decide what are issues and what are nonissues (Ranson, Hinings, and Greenwood, 1980; Clegg and Dunkerley, 1980). If an organizational member believes that something is a burning issue, it will become one in the organization only if power holders also define it as such.

External Factors

The primary focus of this discussion has been factors internal to the organization. Zald (1970) points out that external considerations also play an important role in the power system of the organization. Here factors such as associations of similar organizations (trade associations or baseball leagues), relationships with suppliers and users of the organization's output, regulatory agencies, and other indirectly involved parties affect the amount and distribution of power within the organization. For example, the National Labor Relations Board, after its establishment in the 1930s, facilitated the growth in power of labor unions (Peterson, 1970). At the same time, the increasing complexity of labor laws and regulations led to the development of specialists in labor relations, and these personnel also gained in power in the organization, largely as a consequence of these external factors. External economic conditions also affect the power system in organizations as markets for labor and outputs shift, the source of "raw materials" is altered, and the nature of the organization's clientele varies.

An analysis of United Fund agencies found that community organizations that were successful in raising funds themselves received greater allocations from the United Fund. These community organizations were less dependent upon the United Fund, and the United Fund feared that the successful community organizations might attempt their own fund-raising efforts (Pfeffer and Long, 1977). The external world thus invades the power structure of these organizations. These analyses emphasize the importance of external relationships for the distribution and exercise of power within organizations. External relationships also are important to the extent that they provide access to wealth and power for the organization (Aldrich, 1979). Power, like other organizational phenomena, does not exist in isolation within the organization itself.

POWER IN VOLUNTARY ORGANIZATIONS

Voluntary organizations have all the characteristics of other organizations in regard to the nature and importance of power as an internal process. They are somewhat different, however, because of the apparent need for membership participation to keep the organization viable. Most analyses point to the cruciality of the democratic process for voluntary organizations, since this form of power determination tends to assure continued participation. Craig and Gross (1970) suggest that, in addition, voluntary organizations must remain permeable to new ideas and interests if democracy is to be maintained. This permeability assures continued participation by maintaining membership interest in issues that are new and around which power can cluster, thus preventing the tendency toward oligarchy. Maintaining membership involvement is crucial for such organizations.

LOWER PARTICIPANTS

We have focused on vertical and horizontal components of power relationships in organizations. Before concluding this analysis, we will examine a final form of power relationship. This type is rare in organizations, but anyone who has had any contact with an organization has confronted it from time to time. The power of "lower participants" in organizations can be a source of both frustration and wonder. Lower participants are organizational members who have low official power but who wield much more power than their position would predict.

Mechanic (1962) has identified some of the sources of power of lower participants. As we shall see, these are not too different from the general sources of power that have been discussed in the earlier sections. What is different is that these lower members of organizations are able to amass resources far beyond the wildest imagination if only their position is considered. The first source of power is expertise coupled with the difficulty of replacing the person in question. The maintenance personnel in Crozier's study had this form of power over the managers in the tobacco industry. Another example is a person in a clerical position who gains power by being the only one in an organization who knows how to perform a particular operation. This person thereby becomes indispensable, and all work has to go through his or her hands. In some cases, patterns of personal likes and dislikes can "make or break" another person in the organization who ostensibly has a higher position; for example, requests for information can be conveniently "lost."

A second source of power is the amount of effort and interest expressed on the job. Mechanic notes the example of university departmental administrative assistants who can have "power to make decisions about the purchase and allocation of supplies, the allocation of their services, the scheduling of classes, and, at times, the disposition of student complaints. Such control may in some instances lead to sanctions against a professor by polite reluctance to furnish supplies, ignoring his or her preferences for the scheduling of classes, and giving others preference in the allocation of services" (p. 359). Removal of this power from administrative assistants involves the expenditure of time and effort. A departmental chair is unlikely to come down hard on a trusted administrative assistant, whereas he or she might on younger or disfavored faculty.

Several other factors are associated with lower participants' power. One is the attractiveness of the individual involved; personal or physical attractiveness can lead to relationships that are outside the organization's (or the individual's) intent. Physical location and position within an organization can make one person more critical than another; major information processors can have strong control over those who are dependent on them for accurate information. Coalitions among lower participants can also increase their power. Rules themselves can provide a source of power, in that strict adherence to a highly formalized rules system can impede operations in the organization. A supervisor cannot really criticize subordinates who are following the letter of the law.

THE OUTCOMES OF POWER RELATIONSHIPS

Compliance and Involvement

The most frequent consequence of a power act is *compliance*. This is frequently overlooked in analyses of power, since the resistance to power—conflict—is more dramatic and exciting. The fact of the matter is that the less dramatic phenomenon of compliance is much more frequent. And, despite the importance of conflict for organizations, compliance is really the heart of organizations, since, after all, rational-legal authority is seen as rational and legal by power recipients.

Etzioni (1961, 1975) made compliance the basis of his typology and conceptualization of organizations. It may be remembered from the discussion of typologies that Etzioni identified alienative, calculative, and moral involvement on the part of lower participants as they comply with the various forms of power used. Etzioni recognized that in many cases there are mixed reasons for compliance. Thus, schoolchildren generally believe that their teachers are to be obeyed (authority), but there is always the potential for punishment (coercive power).

The findings associated with the Etzioni scheme suggest that when organizations are able to develop moral involvement on the part of their members, their commitment to the organization is higher. This is particularly the case for voluntary organizations. Compliance and involvement are interrelated phenomena. Voluntary organizations rely on moral involvement. Moral involvement is apparently increased when members are encouraged to participate and do participate. Participation thus contributes to compliance through the process of involvement (Wood, 1975; Hougland, Shepard, and Wood, 1979; Hougland and Wood, 1980).

Compliance, and even willing compliance, is common in organizations. It is so common that it is almost boring. People come to work on time, do what their bosses desire, and produce their goods or deliver their services. Organizational units generally also comply or obey. This is not the only response to power, however. The power recipient can withdraw from the situation or attempt to circumvent the power holder (Blau, 1964). Withdrawal involves backing off from the power relationships. Circumvention is exemplified by "going over the boss's head," which is a risky move but certainly not infrequent. Another example of circumvention would be going to a department chair or college dean to appeal the acts of a professor. The power outcome of greatest interest, however, is conflict.

CONFLICT IN ORGANIZATIONS

Conflict arises whenever interests collide. The natural reaction to conflict in organizational contests is usually to view it as a dysfunctional force that can be attributed to some regrettable set of circumstances or causes. "It's a personality problem." "They're rivals who always meet head on." "Production people and marketing people never get along." "Everyone hates auditors and accountants." Conflict is regarded as an unfortunate state that in more favorable circumstances would disappear.

If our analysis ... is correct, however, then conflict is *always present* in organizations. Conflict may be personal, interpersonal, or between rival groups and coalitions. It may be built into organizational structures, roles, attitudes, and stereotypes, or arise over a scarcity of resources. It may be explicit or covert. Whatever the reason, or whatever the form it takes, its source rests in some perceived or real divergence of interests. (Morgan, 1986: p. 155; emphasis added)

Many of the major forms of conflict within organizations are already well known to anyone concerned with organizations or with society in general. Labor-management conflict is a prominent part of our social heritage as well as of organizational life. It is possible to view conflict between workers and management as inherent in organizations (Sabel, 1982). Divisions that exist along skill and ethnic lines can also be viewed as inherent sources of conflict.

Conflict in organizations involves more than simple interpersonal conflict. (Not that interpersonal conflict is necessarily simple, given the complexities of the human personality, but for our purposes it is only part of the picture.) The psychologist R. Nevitt Sanford (1964) puts this point in a historical perspective when he states: "Twenty years ago, it seemed easy to account for organizational conflict by blaming the problem behavior of individuals. But the simple formula, 'trouble is due to trouble-makers,' is unfortunately inadequate in the light of our present knowledge of the social process" (p. 95). The individualized approach to conflict is inadequate because organizational considerations and the very nature of organizations themselves contribute to conflict situations.

Bases of Conflict

Katz (1964) has identified three organizational bases of conflict. The first is "functional conflict induced by various subsystems within the organizations" (p. 105). In this form of conflict differentiation, such as that discussed in Chapter 3, leads people and units to have different and often opposing interests.

The second basis of conflict is the fact that units may have similar functions. Conflict here can take the form of "hostile rivalry or good-natured competition" (p. 106). Such competition can be beneficial, but it can also be destructive. Conflicts may also develop when there is mutual task dependence or when there is asymmetric, or unbalanced, dependence among units in regard to a task (Aldrich, 1979). These first two sources of conflict stem from horizontal power relationships between people or organizational units.

Katz's final form of organizationally based conflict is "hierarchical conflict stemming from interest-group struggles over the organizational rewards of status, prestige, and monetary reward" (p. 106). Since less than total satisfaction with the reward structure is common, and since subgroups develop their own communication systems and norms, it is normal that lower-level personnel "try to improve their lot by joining forces as an interest group against the more privileged members of the organization" (p. 106). Although one typically thinks of blue-collar workers and unions in this regard, the process would operate with white-collar workers and subgroups in the management hierarchy. Conflict can involve equity issues, such as the distribution of rewards, and equality issues regarding basic status differences (Kabanoff, 1991).

Conflict can also result from imperfect communication (Robbins, 1974). Communication can be distorted, semantic difficulties can exist, knowledge itself contains intrinsic ambiguities, and communications channels can be imperfectly used. Structural conditions also lead to conflict; large size, the heterogeneity of the staff, styles of supervision, extent of participation, the reward system, and the form of power used are among such conditions. Robbins also notes that personal-behavior variables are important in the areas of personality dimensions and interactions, role satisfactions, and individual goals. In addition, conflict can emerge from differences between occupational groups, such as different professions, or between groups with different power in the organizations, such as in labor-management conflict (see Dahrendorf, 1959; Hage and Aiken, 1970; Silverman, 1971; Hage, 1980). Furthermore, just as we cannot assume that the organization will always act rationally, so we cannot assume that individuals will not "depart from rational, reality-based behavior in their individual struggles against one another or in their participation in group struggles" (Katz, 1964: pp. 105–6).

These bases of conflict are an inherent element of organizations; thus, conflict itself must be viewed as inherent. At the same time, the fact that these antecedents or bases of conflict are present does not mean that conflict will take place. Before conflict can arise, the parties involved must perceive that they are in a position to interfere with the other party (Kochan, Huber, and Cummings, 1975; Schmidt and Kochan, 1972). A decision must be made to engage in conflict. Whether the decision is based on rational calculation or fervid emotion, or is individual or collective, it does not occur automatically.

The Conflict Situation

We have been looking at the bases of conflict situations and the parties engaged in them. We will now examine the conflict situation itself and then turn to the outcomes of conflict. There are four components in the conflict process (Boulding, 1964). The first is the parties involved. Conflict must involve at least two parties—individuals, groups, or organizations. Hypothetically, therefore, there can be nine types of conflict–person-person, person-group, and so on. Boulding suggests that there is a tendency toward symmetry in these relationships, in that person-organizational or group-organizational conflict tends to move toward organizational-organizational conflict. This is based on the power differentials that are likely to exist between these different levels in the organization.

The next component in this framework is the field of conflict, defined as "the whole set of relevant possible states of the social system. (Any state of the social system which either of the parties to a conflict considers relevant is, of course, a relevant state)" (p. 138). What Boulding is referring to are the alternative conditions toward which a conflict could move. If two parties in a conflict have a particular power relationship with each other, with one having more power than the other, the field of conflict involves a continuation of the present state, plus all the alternative conditions. These alternatives include both parties' gaining or losing power or one's gaining at the expense of the other. This concept is indicative of the process nature of conflict, in that the parties in the situation will seldom retain the same position in relation to each other after the conflict is resolved or continued. The field of conflict includes the directions of the movement as the process occurs.

The third component is the dynamics of the conflict situation. That is, each party in a conflict will adjust its own position to one that it feels is congruent with that of its opponent. If one of the parties becomes more militant, the other will probably do the same. This assumes, of course, that the power available to the two parties is at least moderately comparable. An interesting aspect of the dynamics of conflict is that conflict can "move around" in an organization (Smith, 1989). Parties in a conflict can "take it out on others" as they engage in their conflict.

The field of conflict can thus expand or contract as the dynamics of the conflict situation take place. The conflict can move around, allies can be sought or bought, and coalitions can be formed. A nonorganizational example of these dynamics can be found in international relations, where nations will intensify their own conflict efforts in anticipation of or reaction to their opponents' moves. This can escalate into all-out war and eventual destruction, or it can stabilize at some point along the way, but the conflict will seldom be limited in its scope to the parties involved. The same phenomenon occurs in organizations, with the equivalent of all-out war in the case of labor-management conflicts that end in the dissolution of the company involved. The dynamic nature of conflict can also be seen in the fact that there is an increase and decrease in the intensity of a conflict during its course. Although the field of conflict may remain the same, the energies devoted to it vary over time.

The final element in the Boulding model is the management, control, or resolution of conflict (p. 142). The terms used suggest that conflict situations are generally not discrete situations with a clear beginning and a clear end. They obviously emerge from preexisting situations and do not end forever with a strike settlement or a lowering of the intensity of the conflict. Boulding notes that organizations attempt to prevent conflict from becoming "pathological" and thus destructive of the parties involved and the larger system. One form of conflict resolution is a unilateral move; according to Boulding, a good deal of conflict is resolved through the relatively simple mechanism of the "peaceableness" of one of the participants. Although it relates primarily to interpersonal conflict, this idea can be utilized in the organizational setting. Peaceableness simply involves one of the parties backing off or withdrawing from the conflict. In most cases, the other party reacts by also backing off, even if it would prefer to continue, and the conflict is at least temporarily resolved. This kind of resolution is seen in labor-management disputes when one of the parties finally decides to concede on some points that were formerly "nonnegotiable."

Reliance upon peaceableness is potentially dangerous, however, because the parties may not exhibit this kind of behavior. For the peaceable party itself, the strategy is hazardous if the opponent is operating pathologically or irrationally to any degree. For that reason, organizations develop mechanisms to resolve or control conflict. One technique is to placate the parties involved by offering them some form of "side payment" as an inducement to stop the conflict; for example, in professional-organizational conflict, the professionals may be given concessions in the form of the relaxing of some organizational rules they feel to be excessively burdensome.

Conflicts in organizations can also be resolved through the offices of a third party. The third party may be a larger organization that simply orders the conflict behavior to cease under the threat of penalties (as when the government prohibits strikes and lockouts in a labor dispute that threatens the national interest), or it may be a mediator. Since intraorganizational conflict takes place within a larger context, the organization can simply prohibit the conflicting behavior. This does not resolve the issues, but it reduces the intensity of the conflict behavior. Mediation can do the same and can even lead to a complete resolution of the conflict by presenting new methods of solution that may not have occurred to the parties involved or by presenting a solution that would not be acceptable unless it were presented by a third party.

The Outcomes of Conflict

The resolution of a conflict leads to a stage that is known as the *aftermath* (Pondy, 1967, 1969). This is a useful concept because conflict resolution does not lead to a condition of total settlement. If the basic issues are not resolved, the potential for future, and perhaps more serious, conflicts is part of the aftermath. If the conflict resolution leads to more open communications and cooperation among the participants, that, too, is part of the aftermath (see Coser, 1956, 1967). Since an organization does not operate in a vacuum, any successful conflict resolution in which the former combatants are now close allies is not guaranteed to last forever. Changes in the environment and altered conditions in the organization can lead to new conflict situations among the same parties or with others.

Conflict is not inherently good or bad for the participants, the organization, or the wider society. Power and conflict are major shapers of the state of an organization. A given organizational state sets the stage for the continuing power and conflict processes, thus continually reshaping the organization. In this way, conflict plays an important role in the development of variations between organizations. This may contribute to or detract from their survival (Aldrich, 1979).

Any analysis of conflict would be incomplete without noting that conflict an be viewed as a means by which organizational management can manipulate situations to its advantage (Rahim, 1986, 1989). As with any management tool, the morality of using conflict in this manner is in the eye of the beholder and the activities of the managers and the managed. There are also broader potential outcomes, as we shall see shortly.

THE SOCIAL OUTCOMES OF POWER

Any consideration of the outcomes of power and organizations would be incomplete without a deliberate focus on the power of organizations in society. There are two important points here.

First, organizations are the means by which people are distributed in the social order (Baron, 1984; Hall, 1994). Since work is carried out in organizations, organizations determine the intrinsic and extrinsic rewards that people receive. Rewards are attached to organizational positions and not to individuals. For people not in the labor force, there is still organizational influence. Organizations, through parents' employment experiences, are a major determinant of the place of education for younger people. Organizations are the basis for retirement plans for older people. *Inequality in society thus has an organizational base.*

Second, organizational power in society is increasingly being understood as interorganizational power. Interorganizational relationships will be dealt with in detail in Chapter 10. The important point here is that interorganizational linkages in the form of systematic interlocks, particularly among corporations, yield enormous power (Useem, 1984; Mizruchi, 1992). Whether this is for social-class interests, as many analysts strongly argue, or for rationality and expediency, interorganizational linkages play a powerful role in society.

Organizational Conflict and Society

Organizational conflict is inevitable. Its consequences for organizations and their members are problematic. On the one hand, interdepartmental conflict can enhance organizational performance in some situations (Lawrence and Lorsch, 1967). It can also enhance individual performance as attention is focused and more energy is used. As noted earlier, some writers, such as Rahim (1986, 1989) see conflict management as a sound management tool.

Unfortunately, there is a darker side to all of this. As Clark (1988) notes:

> With unabashed commitment to the goals of negotiation, out-of-court settlements of enormous variety, and the powers of information, flexibility, and limited liability . . . risk and conflict management have become enablers of the transformation of many organizational actions from rule-guided competition to a more adventuresome conflict posture. The spirit of deregulation, the calls for improved organizational productivity, and the corporate drive to become "lean and mean," the frantic search for excellence and improved ratings all may be feeding the fires of organizational conflict at the expense of the rules of competition. (p. 154)

Like conflict, conflict management can get out of hand. Conflict becomes a tool by which the powerful can manipulate situations to the detriment of the less powerful, even without their awareness of being manipulated.

To make matters even worse, the civility with which conflict management was done until recently has disappeared. Now, with restructuring and hostile takeovers, honor and dignity have been replaced by a bottom-line mentality that can take the form of vengeance (Morrill, 1991).

SUMMARY AND CONCLUSIONS

This chapter has attempted to identify and trace the sources and the outcomes of power in organizations. Common sense suggests that these are important to the operations of any organization and that the lives and behavior of organizational members are vitally affected by their relative power positions. The analysis concluded that power is a reciprocal relational phenomenon between the parties involved and that each party is dependent on the other. The power relationships can be rigidly specified in advance or can develop as the relationship itself develops. This point reemphasizes the close connection between organizational structure and processes, since it is the structure that sets the original limits on the relationships.

Although power relationships are frequently thought of as interpersonal, power differentials between organizational units are also important. Interunit power relationships usually take place along the lateral or horizontal axis in organizations. Vertical or hierarchical arrangements by definition involve a power component. Also on the vertical dimension, but not in an organizationally planned way, are the power bases developed by lower participants that allow them to exert power over those farther up the organizational hierarchy.

In addition to this directional aspect of power, we discussed the forms of power inside and outside organizations. There is agreement that power in organizations does not take only one form—legitimate authority—and that extraorganizational considerations are important in power relationships. The empirical research reviewed provided additional insights into these relationships. From the outset it became apparent that most power relationships involve the use of more than one form of power. Because individuals and organizational units develop relationships over time, additional elements will almost surely be added to prestructured power arrangements.

The nature of the power system used in organizations has important consequences for the manner in which individuals attach themselves to organizations and for the more general issue of organizational effectiveness. If inappropriate power forms are used, the organization is likely to be less effective than it might otherwise be. Studies of power in organizations reiterate the dominant theme of this book—that organizational structure and processes are in constant and reciprocal interaction. Power relationships develop out of and then alter existing structural arrangements.

The broader look at power emphasized that power is not a fixed sum in organizations. The amount of power in the system can increase or decrease. Although a power system is often established by the organization, multiple forms of power and the reciprocity involved in the power relationship make a general growth in power almost inevitable.

It was also pointed out in this section that the power variable is vital in determining internal resource allocations. This fact leads to the conclusion that power relationships in organizations tend to be stable, since the original allocation of resources will be an important determinant of future power relationships. The fact that external considerations affect the power distribution and relationships within an organization is a reaffirmation of the general approach in our analysis. Organizational structure and processes interact with the environment, and organizational outputs affect the environment, which then in turn becomes a potentially altered form of input.

The analysis of power concluded with a consideration of the outcomes of power. Compliance is the most frequent outcome. Withdrawal and circumvention are also very possible outcomes. The outcome that typically receives the greatest amount of attention, however, is conflict. Conflict is part of the normal state of an organization. The consequences of conflict are also normal in that they are both positive and negative for individuals and for organizations.

Power and its outcomes are central organizational processes. They can contribute to and detract from organizational effectiveness. In the next chapter, we turn to another organizational process—leadership—that also has a relationship to effectiveness, but as we will see, the relationship is much more problematic than is commonly believed.

chapter 6

Leadership

Is leadership important? Of course it is. Is it the only determinant of organizational success or failure? Of course it isn't. This seeming contradiction will be addressed but not answered in this chapter.

Probably more has been written and spoken about leadership than about any other topic considered in this book. Whether the organization be the local school district, a church, an athletic team, or the nation, there seems to be a persistent assumption that new leadership will turn it, the organization, around. In every election at every level of government, the call for leadership goes out. Anyone who follows sports is aware of the air of expectation surrounding the appointment of a new coach or manager. A new school superintendent or university president is selected by a blue-ribbon committee with extensive inputs from all the parties likely to be involved. When I served as a member of the search committee for a new president of my university, I felt an air of excitement and uneasy expectation in the process. All the committee members were aware of the importance of the outcome.

The phenomenal changes in Eastern Europe and South Africa in 1989 and 1990 were frequently viewed from the perspective of leadership. Interestingly, from the point of view of this analysis, the changes were not attributed only to leadership but also to sweeping historical events. Those sweeping historical events are labeled environmental changes in this analysis.

At election time in labor unions and other voluntary organizations, the assumption is always made that the reelection of the old or the election of the new leaders will make an important difference in the continuing operation of the organization. In short, leadership would seem to be the crucial thing to understand about organizations.

The perspective presented in this chapter is quite different. The research and theory to be examined finds that leadership is heavily constrained by many of the factors discussed in previous chapters—organizational structure, power coalitions, and environmental conditions. This is not an "anti-leadership" position. Rather, it is an examination of leadership in the contexts in which leadership takes place.

WHAT IS LEADERSHIP?

Why is leadership the subject of such belief and sentiment? Why is it romanticized (Meindl, Ehrlich, and Dukerich, 1985)? Leadership seems to be an extremely easy solution to whatever problems are ailing an organization. Looking to new leadership can mask inappropriate structural arrangements, power distributions that block effective actions, lack of resources, archaic procedures, and other, more basic organizational problems.

In view of that, one might wonder why we should study leadership and why there have there been so many studies in the past. The fact is that in certain situations leadership is important, even critical. Those situations, however, are much more limited and much more constrained than most treatises on leadership consider.

Despite this conclusion, leadership continues to fascinate. As my colleague Gary Yukl (1989) notes:

> Leadership is a subject that has long excited interest among scholars and laypersons alike. The term connotes images of powerful, dynamic persons who command victorious armies, direct corporate empires from atop gleaming skyscrapers, or shape the course of nations. Much of our description of history is the story of military, political, religious, and social leaders. The exploits of brave and clever leaders are the essence of many legends and myths. The widespread fascination with leadership may be because it is such a mysterious process, as well as one that touches everyone's life. Why do certain leaders (Gandhi, Mohammed, Mao Tse-tung) inspire such intense fervor and dedication? How did certain leaders (Julius Caesar, Charlemagne, Alexander the Great) build great empires? Why were certain leaders (Winston Churchill, Indira Gandhi, the Shah of Iran) suddenly deposed, despite their apparent power and record of successful accomplishments? How did certain rather undistinguished persons (Adolph Hitler, Claudius Caesar) rise to positions of great power? Why do some leaders have loyal followers who are willing to sacrifice their lives for their leader, and why are some other leaders so despised that their followers conspire to murder them (e.g., as occurred with the "fragging" of some military officers by enlisted men in Vietnam)? (p. 1)

What is leadership? Leadership is a special form of power, closely related to the "referent" form discussed in the preceding chapter, since it involves "the ability, based on the personal qualities of the leader, to elicit the followers' voluntary compliance in a broad range of matters. Leadership is distinguished from the concept of power in that it entails influence, i.e., change of preferences, while power implies only that subjects' preferences are held in abeyance" (Etzioni, 1965: pp. 690–91).

For our purposes, Etzioni's general definition, if not the specific distinction made, is extremely useful. That followers do in fact alter their preferences to coincide with those of the leader is an important consideration. The followers want to go along with the wishes of the leader. Katz and Kahn (1978) follow this same line of reasoning when they note: "We consider the essence of organizational leadership to be the influential increment over and above mechanical compliance with the routine directions of the organization" (p. 528). Thus, leadership is closely related to power but involves more than simply the power allocated to a position in the organization or claimed by a member or members of organizations. Leadership is something that is attributed to people by their followers (Meindl, Ehrlich, and Dukerich, 1985).

Functions of Leadership

The differences between leadership and power are still insufficiently developed, since leadership can occur in any group at any level within the organization. In his seminal analysis of leadership, Selznick (1957) provides the needed distinction when he notes that leadership involves critical decisions (p. 29). It is more than group maintenance. According to Selznick, the critical tasks of leadership fall into four categories. The first is to define the institutional (organizational) mission and role. This is obviously vital in a rapidly changing world and must be viewed as a dynamic process. The second task is the "institutional embodiment of purpose," which involves building the policy into the structure or deciding upon the means to achieve the ends desired. The third task is to defend the organization's integrity. Here values and public relations intermix: Leaders represent their organizations to the public and to their own members as they try to persuade them to follow their decisions. The final leadership task is the ordering of internal conflict (pp. 62–63).

Selznick's focus is on top leadership. At the same time, most analyses of leadership recognize that leadership can be found at all levels in organizations. This has inadvertently created a major problem for leadership studies. The problem is that many studies of leadership have been concerned with lower-level leadership, such as that exerted by the first-line supervisor. It is crucial to remember that what might contribute to leadership at one level might be totally inappropriate at another level. Leadership at the top level in the organization has the greatest impact on the organization but involves behaviors and actions very different from those taken by leaders at the first-line supervisor position (Hunt, 1991).

One further set of distinctions should be made before we proceed with our analysis of leadership. Studies carried out in laboratories have consistently found that leadership is actually a differentiated process, with task or instrumental activities clearly separated from socioemotional or expressive activities. (See, for example, Bales, 1953; Bales and Slater, 1955.) Drawing on the work of Bales and his associates, Etzioni (1965) developed a "dual leadership" approach to organizations, suggesting that in most cases leadership rests in the hands of more than one person and that the demands of the two forms may conflict. Organizational demands determine which form will be successful, with socioemotional more effective in normative organizations and task in instrumental organizations. Etzioni concludes that, at least for first-line supervisors, attempts to improve socioemotional leadership qualities are doomed to failure, since these efforts will run headlong into the existing socioemotional leader, who has risen to the position in the interactions of the work group. This type of interpretation, of course, runs counter to the ideas and ideals of the "human relations" school of management, which stresses the utility of socioemotional interactions in the leadership process. There appears to be growing agreement that the use of human relations in leadership positions is no guarantee that any form of behavioral change by members of the organization will take place (Perrow, 1979: pp. 132–38).

It is critical to repeat that leadership at the top of an organization is vastly different from leadership at the first-line supervisory level. The distinctions between task and socioemotional leadership are applicable at the first-line supervisory level. They are largely meaningless for top leadership, since the people at the top do not really engage in direct supervisory behavior.

Components of Leadership

Every organization has an individual or a set of individuals at the top decision-making level who can exercise power simply by giving orders and making decisions. This is simple power of position and does not involve leadership as we will approach it here. Our view of leadership involves what a person does above and beyond the basic requirements of his position. It is the persuasion of individuals and innovativeness in ideas and decision making that differentiate leadership from the sheer possession of power (Bass, 1985; Bass and Avolio, 1990, 1993). A mechanical reliance on organizational position would bring about a situation in which the characteristics of the individuals filling top positions would make no difference whatsoever. The organization would be totally constrained by precedent and its own structure.

The ideas expressed thus far have implied strongly that individual characteristics are crucial for the leadership role. Although this appears to be the case, extreme care must be taken to put it in the proper perspective. There is a very real danger in assuming that because individual characteristics are crucial for the leadership function, there is a set of traits that leaders possess. The literature regarding leadership took this approach at one time, a major goal of the research being identification of the key leadership traits.

The trait approach didn't get very far because common leadership traits could not be identified. No set of characteristics is possessed by leaders and not by followers. Once researchers realized that, they increasingly turned their attention to the *situation* in which leadership is exhibited (Gouldner, 1950).

The situational approach takes the position that the set of conditions of the moment—the situation—defines by whom and in what manner leadership will be exercised. In one situation, one individual will emerge as the leader; in another situation, another individual. This approach has largely dominated the sociological approach to leadership, especially in small-group studies. The situational approach has come under fire for its inattention to the characteristics of those who rise to leadership positions. The emergent position is that although different situations demand different forms of leadership and thus generally different individuals, particular skills and behaviors will be called for in each different situation. This is a blending of the trait and situational approaches to avoid the serious pitfalls of each. (See Yukl, 1981, 1989 for an extended discussion of these points.)

The trait and situational approaches both tell us something about leadership but not the whole story. There is also the important element of interaction between leader and followers. The leader influences followers in the interaction process, and their reactions, of course, have an impact on the leader's own behavior (Hollander and Julian, 1969).

Organizational leadership is thus a combination of factors. The most obvious is the position in the organization. This gives the leader the power base and leads followers to the expectations that there is a legitimate right to that position and that the leader will in fact engage in the leadership process by shaping their own thoughts and actions and performing the leadership functions for the organization as a whole. These expectations can be seen even in periods of dissidence within the organization, when there is leadership succession and the followers express the hope that the new person will provide what the old one did not.

In addition to the position held, the leadership role demands that the individual behave in such a way that the expectations of the followers are fulfilled. Here the interrelationships between the characteristics of the individual and the position filled become crucial. Rather than suggesting that there is one set of leadership "traits," the evidence indicates that the particular characteristics giving rise to leadership behavior vary with the situation.

A very useful synthesis of the factors involved in leadership is provided by Yukl (1981). Figure 6–1 indicates how leader traits and skills affect behaviors and power. These in turn interact with external, or exogenous, situational variables and intervening variables and contribute to end-result variables, such as group performance and organizational goal attainment (effectiveness in this conceptualization).

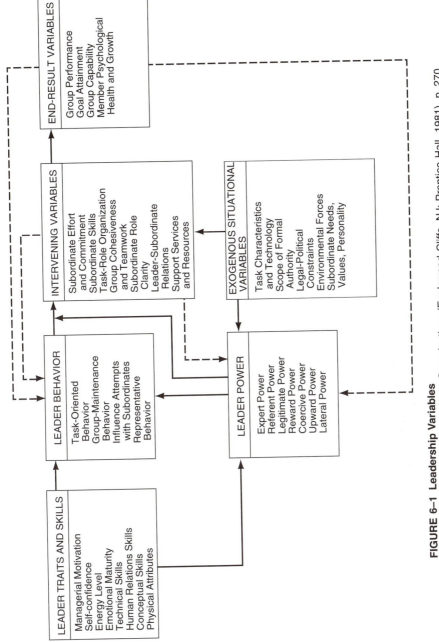

FIGURE 6–1 Leadership Variables
Source: Gary A. Yukl, *Leadership in Organizations* (Englewood Cliffs, NJ: Prentice Hall, 1981), p. 270.

LEADER TRAITS AND SKILLS
Managerial Motivation
Self-confidence
Energy Level
Emotional Maturity
Technical Skills
Human Relations Skills
Conceptual Skills
Physical Attributes

LEADER BEHAVIOR
Task-Oriented Behavior
Group-Maintenance Behavior
Influence Attempts with Subordinates
Representative Behavior

INTERVENING VARIABLES
Subordinate Effort and Commitment
Subordinate Skills
Task-Role Organization
Group Cohesiveness and Teamwork
Subordinate Role Clarity
Leader-Subordinate Relations
Support Services and Resources

END-RESULT VARIABLES
Group Performance
Goal Attainment
Group Capability
Member Psychological Health and Growth

LEADER POWER
Expert Power
Referent Power
Legitimate Power
Reward Power
Coercive Power
Upward Power
Lateral Power

EXOGENOUS SITUATIONAL VARIABLES
Task Characteristics and Technology
Scope of Formal Authority
Legal-Political Constraints
Environmental Forces
Subordinate Needs, Values, Personality

The advantage of the Yukl framework is that it identifies the factors that contribute to leadership and those that could block leadership efforts. For example, it is quite possible that subordinate individuals will not have the necessary skills (intervening variable) or that the technology available (exogenous situational variable) will be insufficient for the tasks at hand, so that leadership efforts are thwarted. Another advantage of Yukl's framework is that it can deal with leadership at various levels within the organization. There is an understated element in the Yukl approach that must be noted here. Significant environmental considerations, such as shifting market stages, can have an overwhelming impact on leadership efforts (Eisenhardt and Schoonhoven, 1990). The Yukl framework does focus attention on end-result, or outcome, variables, and it is these to which we now turn.

THE OUTCOMES OF LEADERSHIP FOR ORGANIZATIONS

In this section the focus will be on leadership at the top of the organization. There is little direct evidence regarding the effect that top leaders have on organizations, simply because there has been very little research on top organizational leadership. Organizational researchers have not had access to top business and government leaders. Some organizational scholars, such as Warren Bennis and Richard Cyert, have become university presidents, but their subsequent writings have not reflected those experiences. There have been books by and about business leaders, such as Lee Iacocca and Donald Trump, but they are not informative for our purposes. To study top leadership, therefore, we will have to extrapolate from the large number of studies of supervision and the smaller number of studies of top leadership succession.

Studies of supervisory leadership in organizations are confusing, if not downright chaotic, even to those who are well versed in the literature (Cartwright, 1965: p. 3). A major factor in the confusion, aside from the ideological biases evident in some investigations, is the large number of dependent variables used in leadership analyses. If variations in the amount or the style of leadership are taken as the independent variable, then a whole series of variables has been treated as the dependent ones. These run the gamut from hard measures of productivity to the more elusive factors of morale and satisfaction.

Leadership Styles

Research regarding supervisory leadership has come to focus on two contrasting styles or approaches to the leadership role. These are the authoritarian (task) and the supportive (socioemotional) approaches. The biases alluded to earlier are evident and understandable when these two terms are brought into the discussion. (Who would want to support authoritarianism?) The supportive leader is "characterized by . . . employee oriented, democratic behavior, uses general supervision, and is considerate of his subordinates" (Filley and House, 1969: p. 399). The authoritarian leader, on the other hand, is much more likely to rely on the power of his or her position and be more punishment centered. A very evident problem for the discussion here is that the authoritarian form actually may not be leadership in the way we have defined it. A series of studies at The Ohio State University used the terms "initiating" and "consideration" to make essentially the same distinctions, and another series of studies at the University of Michigan used the terms "production orientation" and "employee orientation" with little difference in meaning.

The supportive leader utilizes socioemotional appeals to subordinates. This involves

Consideration for Subordinates. The leader considers the needs and preferences of his subordinates, whom he treats with dignity and kindness, and is not punitive in his dealings with them. Such a leader is frequently referred to as "employee centered" as opposed to "work centered" or "task centered."

Consultative Decision Making. The leader asks his subordinates for their opinions before he makes decisions. Such a leader is consultative, participative, or democratic (as opposed to unilateral, autocratic, or arbitrary) in his decision making.

General Supervision. The leader supervises in a general rather than a close manner, delegates authority to his subordinates, and permits them freedom to exercise discretion in their work rather than imposing tight controls and close (frequently overbearing) supervision. (Filley and House, 1969: pp. 399–400, gender-based terms in the original version)

In their review of the research in this leadership area, Filley and House find that supportive leadership, as opposed to autocratic leadership, is quite consistently related to several indicators of subordinate satisfaction and productivity:

1. There is less intragroup stress and more cooperation.
2. Turnover and grievance rates are lower.
3. The leader himself is viewed as more desirable.
4. There is frequently greater productivity.

The evidence here is confounded, unfortunately, by the possibility that the workers themselves may contribute to their greater satisfaction and productivity by their own attitudes and behavior, independent of those of the leader. They may be high-producing, positively oriented employees who "do not require close, autocratic supervision, and therefore it is possible for the supervisor of such employees to be more human-relations oriented" (p. 462). Despite this possibility, the weight of the evidence is that supportive leadership does lead to more positive attitudinal responses, particularly on the part of subordinates. This pattern seems to hold even in organizations that are thought to favor more authoritarian leadership styles. For example, a study of police units found that satisfaction and commitment to the organization were related to more supportive leadership (Jermier and Berkes, 1979).

The productivity issue is not as clear as the attitudinal one. Although some evidence does suggest that greater productivity is associated with supportive supervision, other studies report no difference, or that there is actually more output when autocratic styles are used (Dubin, 1965). Even more confusion arises when Lawler and Porter's (1967) conclusions are considered. They suggest that the causal ordering between satisfaction and productivity might be reversed. It is typically thought that satisfaction leads to productivity, but Lawler and Porter suggest that productivity might lead to satisfaction. For the analysis of leadership, trying to increase satisfaction in order to increase productivity may be futile.

An obvious question here is, What does the organization want? Another obvious question is, What do the workers want? If satisfied employees are desired, then the supportive approach has clearly been shown to be more effective. But what if the workers and the organization both want high productivity and high pay? Short-run output gains may well be more easily achieved under an autocratic system. There is also evidence to suggest that when workers expect to be supervised in an autocratic style, supportive supervision can be counterproductive and threatening to satisfaction.

In summarizing these leadership studies, Filley and House conclude that supportive leadership behavior is most effective when

1. Decisions are not routine in nature.
2. The information required for effective decision making cannot be standardized or centralized.
3. Decisions need not be made rapidly, allowing time to involve subordinates in a participative decision-making process.

and when subordinates

4. Feel a strong need for independence.
5. Regard their participation in decision making as legitimate.
6. See themselves as able to contribute to the decision-making process.
7. Are confident of their ability to work without the reassurance of close supervision. (pp. 404–5)

This particular kind of organization is similar to some that have already been described in the section on organizational structure—the less formalized organizations that must rely on the inputs of their own members if they are to be effective. Their technology is such that there is a constant search for new ideas and solutions to problems. The obvious corollary of the findings as to the kind of organization in which supportive leadership styles are likely to be effective is that in the opposite kind of organization such forms of leadership are least likely to be effective. That is, in organizations in which decisions are routine, information is standardized, and so on, effective leadership is more likely to take the task-oriented form, because inputs from the individual members of the organization are not so important and there is not the same need to spend time in the decision-making process. In addition, there may be organizational members who either are threatened by the decision-making process or have no wish to participate in it and for whom the provision of ready-made answers in the form of formal procedures or decisions made for them is a satisfying, or at least a nonthreatening, situation.

These interpretations are strongly buttressed by the findings emerging from Fiedler's (1967, 1972, 1982, 1987) continuing studies of the leadership process. Fiedler finds that in stable, structured situations, a stricter, more autocratic form of leadership is more likely to be successful, whereas in a situation of change, external threat, and ambiguity, the more lenient, participative form of supervision would work better. Of course, in many organizations conditions will change in one direction or another, suggesting that an effective leader in one situation may not be such in another. Thus, another contingency approach is evident.

Factors Affecting Leadership Outcomes

Most of the studies just cited have been performed with personnel from relatively low echelons in the organization. Regardless of the level within the organization, it is clear that the situation being faced and the personnel being led are important determinants of the form of leadership likely to be most effective. It can be argued that it would be good, from an individual or a societal perspective, if all personnel were self-motivating and desirous of participating in decision making, and that the organization as a whole would be healthier if it were constantly innovating and engaging in continual interactions with its environment; but the facts suggest that neither condition necessarily exists in practice. This then leads to the conclusion that a revamping of leadership styles in organizations is no cure-all to be applied to all organizations and all members therein.

The important aspect of the research for our purposes is the demonstrated fact that leadership at this level does make a difference in objective performance indicators and the attitudes of the personnel involved. The question is not one of style but one of impact. If production can be increased or the acceptance of a new mode of organization quickened, leadership is an important process. The extrapolation from this conclusion to top leadership is relatively easy, if unsupported by existing research. The range of behavior affected by first- or second-line supervisors is actually quite small. If the jump is made to the range of behavior that can be affected by those at the top of the organization, the potential for a real impact of leadership can be readily seen. Even in performance and attitudes, the high-level subordinates of top administrators can be affected, and their performance in turn has an impact right down through the organization.

All these conclusions must be tempered by the realization that organizations face limits on what leaders can do. The limits can be technological—there are only so many ways to run a hospital or a computer manufacturer—or environmental—rising oil costs or labor costs cannot be eliminated by leadership alone. The nature of the limits on leadership and the leadership process itself can be further understood by evidence from studies of changes in personnel at the top of the organization.

Leadership Succession

Leadership or managerial succession takes place when a person in a leadership position is replaced. Replacement can occur for many reasons—transfer, resignation, firing, death, and so on. Succession provides a "test case" for the impact of leadership, since there are seemingly clear before-and-after conditions.

Probably the best-known case study of managerial succession is Gouldner's *Patterns of Industrial Bureaucracy* (1954), an analysis of a gypsum plant and mine that underwent a major and dramatic change in top personnel. The former manager had been loose, almost indulgent, in enforcing rules and observing other standards. The parent organization, concerned about the production record of the plant, replaced the old manager with a new manager, who had the specific mandate of increasing production. The new manager knew he would be judged by his record of production, so he could either continue the established pattern—a procedure that probably would not have worked in any event, since he did not have the personal ties of his predecessor—or enforce the already-existing rules of conduct and performance. He chose the latter course, and as a result the total system became "punishment centered." That led to a severe increase in internal tension and stress.

This example is in direct contrast to classic case described by Guest (1962). Guest's study was made from observations in a large automobile factory. He states:

> Both studies [his and Gouldner's] examine the process by which organizational tensions are exacerbated or reduced following the succession of a new leader at the top of the hierarchy. Succession in Gouldner's case resulted in a sharp increase in tension and stress and, by inference, a lowering of overall performance. The succession of a new manager had the opposite results in the present case. Plant Y, as we chose to call it, was one of six identical plants of a large corporation. At one period in time the plant was poorest in virtually all indexes of performance—direct and indirect labor costs, quality of output, absenteeism and turnover, ability to meet schedule changes, labor grievances and in several other measures. Interpersonal relationships were marked by sharp antagonisms within and between all levels.

Three years later, following the succession of a new manager, and with no changes in the formal organizational structure, in the product, in the personnel, or in its basic technology, not only was there a substantial reduction of interpersonal conflict, but Plant Y became the outstanding performer among all of the plants. (p. 48)

The dramatic differences between these two cases might lead one to some sort of "great person" theory of leadership, with Gouldner's successor a nongreat person and Guest's a great one. Guest correctly rejects that approach and instead attributes the differences to the actions each manager took when confronted with an existing social structure. A major aspect of this social structure was the expectations of higher management in the organizations involved. Although both new managers were expected to improve the situation, the new manager at the gypsum plant felt that he was expected to get rid of the personnel who were not performing properly by enforcing rules to the letter—dismissing men, for example, for offenses that had previously been largely ignored. He felt that he was—and he probably actually was—under severe pressure to turn the organization around in a short period of time.

There were some other important differences in the organizations. The tradition in the gypsum plant was that new top managers came from "inside," but this was not the case here. In addition, the former manager had been active in the community surrounding the plant. The successor thus came into a situation in which there were negative feelings from the outset. The former manager also had a cadre of subordinates tied to him through personal loyalty. The successor had little recourse but to use the more formal bureaucratic mechanisms of control. At the automobile factory, on the other hand, the total social setting was different. The factory was in a large metropolitan area in which the previous managers had not become involved. The history of top management succession was one of relatively rapid turnover (three to five years), with the new manager coming from outside the plant itself. Thus, unlike the gypsum plant personnel, the auto plant personnel were used to the kind of succession they experienced.

Another, more subtle difference that Gouldner describes is that in the gypsum plant the indulgency pattern and the developed social structure among the personnel were such that there was no orientation toward cutting costs and improving productivity. The previous system was a comfortable one in which rewards, both intrinsic and extrinsic, came without an orientation toward efficiency and productivity.

The predecessor at the auto plant had attempted to use his formal powers to increase productivity. Like his successor, he was under great pressure to improve the operation, but he chose to attempt this by close and punitive supervision. The successor decided to take a different path by using more informal contacts with his subordinates and bringing them into the decision-making process and by relegating "rule enforcement to a second level of importance." This manager also worked through the existing organizational hierarchy, whereas the new manager at the gypsum plant, after some failures with the established subordinates, brought in some of his own supporting staff, thus setting up a formal hierarchy that was in a sense superimposed on the existing social structure.

Guest moves beyond his data and draws a conclusion from the comparison between his and Gouldner's cases. He suggests that the success of the auto plant manager was due in large part to gaining the consent of the governed, or democratization of the leadership process. Gouldner, in a comment regarding Guest's research, notes that the total situations in which the successions occurred were different. The gypsum plant event occurred during a period of recession, with labor relatively plentiful, but with the pressures for improvement probably more intense. The implication here is that when the total situation is viewed, it is incorrect to conclude that one or another approach to the leadership process is always the correct one, even though in both of these cases the autocratic approach was less successful.

From the evidence presented in these two studies, it should be clear that top management has the potential for drastic impacts on the organization, although it cannot yet be stated what proportion of the variance of organizational performance can be accounted for by this leadership role. Indeed, it would appear that this would vary according to the situation, since the range of alternatives even formally allowed would vary widely. Nevertheless, leadership can be seen as having a major impact on what happens to and within the organization.

An indication of the extent of the difference that leadership can make in the organization can be found in some rather offbeat research regarding baseball, football, and other sports. Baseball managers stand in an unusual organizational position. In relation to the total baseball organization, their role is similar to that of the first-line supervisor; but in relation to the playing team only, their role is similar to that of the top executive. Baseball teams are convenient units for analysis, since they "ideally, were identical in official goals, size, and authority structure" (Grusky, 1963: p. 21). Grusky was concerned with the relationship between managerial succession and organizational effectiveness. Here again, baseball teams are ideal because effectiveness is reflected directly in the won-lost statistics; how you play the game is not a crucial variable in professional sports.

The findings from the analysis were that the teams with the poorest records had the highest rates of succession. In interpreting these findings, Grusky rejects the commonsense notion built around succession as the dependent variable—that low effectiveness leads to a vote of confidence from the owner, then a firing. Instead, he develops a more complicated analysis:

> If a team is ineffective, clientele support and profitability decline. Accordingly, strong external pressures for managerial change are set in motion and, concomitantly, the magnitude of managerial role strain increases. A managerial change may be viewed in some quarters as attractive in that it can function to demonstrate publicly that the owners are taking concrete action to remedy an

undesirable situation. The public nature of team performance and the close identification of community pride with team behavior combine to establish a strong basis for clientele control over the functioning of the team. These external influences tend to increase the felt discrepancy between managerial responsibility and actual authority. Since the rewards of popularity are controlled externally, individual rather than team performance may be encouraged. Similarly, the availability of objective performance standards decreases managerial control and thereby contributes to role strain. The greater the managerial role strain, the higher the rates of succession. Moreover, the higher the rates of succession, the stronger the expectations of replacement when team performance declines. Frequent managerial change can produce important dysfunctional consequences within the team by affecting style of supervision and disturbing the informal network of interpersonal relationships. The resulting low primary-group stability produces low morale and may thereby contribute to team ineffectiveness. Declining clientele support may encourage a greater decline in team morale and performance. The consequent continued drop in profitability induces pressures for further managerial changes. Such changes, in turn, produce additional disruptive effects on the organization, and the vicious circle continues. (p. 30)

This rather complicated explanation is challenged by Gamson and Scotch (1964). Based on a different approach to baseball teams' won-lost records, Gamson and Scotch advance a "ritual scapegoating no-way casualty theory" (p. 70). This theory essentially suggests that the manager doesn't make any difference:

In the long run, the policies of the general manager and other front-office personnel are far more important. While judicious trades are helpful (here the field manager may be consulted but does not have the main responsibility), the production of talent through a well-organized scouting and farm system is the most important long-run determinant. The field manager, who is concerned with day-to-day tactical decisions, has minimal responsibility for such management functions. (p. 70)

Gamson and Scotch note that the players are a critical factor, suggesting that at one point in baseball history, regardless of who was manager, the Yankees would have done as well and the Mets would have (or more accurately, could have) done no worse. When the team is doing poorly, the firing of the field manager is ritual scapegoating. "It is a convenient, anxiety-reducing act which the participants of the ceremony regard as a way of improving performance, even though (as some participants may themselves admit in less stressful moments) real improvements can come only through long-range organizational decisions" (pp. 70–71). Gamson and Scotch add that there does seem to be at least a short-run improvement in team performance in cases where the manager is changed in midseason. They suggest that this might be attributable to the ritual itself.

Grusky (1964), in a reply to the Gamson-Scotch criticism, further analyzes the data regarding midseason changes. Adding the variable of whether the new manager came from inside or outside the organization, he finds that the inside manager is more successful. He takes this as partial evidence that his more complicated theory is more reasonable, since the inside manager is likely to be aware of the interpersonal arrangements and the performance of his predecessor and thus more likely not to make the same mistakes again. These analyses were carried out over thirty years ago, when major league baseball was a kinder and gentler business, without expansion and franchise shifts and huge player salaries.

The analyses of managerial succession, however, remain interesting and timely, since sports teams provide a unique opportunity for analyzing leadership effects. Further studies of college basketball teams and major league baseball teams conclude that succession doesn't really change things—poor performance in the past leads to poor performance after succession (Eitzen and Yetman, 1972; Allen, Panian, and Lotz, 1979). A study of coach succession in the National Football League concluded that succession is cosmetic, which is consistent with the ritual scapegoating approach. The head coach is fired and replaced by a successor with little opportunity to change policies, procedures, or personnel in the short run (Brown, 1982).

This may seem at first glance to be a lot of words spilled over a relatively minor matter in the larger scheme of things, but the points that these authors are addressing are very relevant for the present analysis. Although Gamson and Scotch follow the line of reasoning taken here, that those at the very top of the organization have a greater impact than those further down the hierarchy, the argument that external and internal pressures for success affect performance is directly in line with the evidence presented by Gouldner and Guest. The kinds of personnel available are modified by the social system of which they are a part. It is within this framework that leadership behavior takes place. Although the important question of just how much leadership behavior actually contributes to the organization is left unanswered, the sports studies do suggest that both positive and negative results ensue with managerial succession. Few cases of neutral effects are found in the analyses.

Research findings on rates of executive succession provide additional insights into the processes that are being considered. An analysis of a military installation came to the conclusion that rapid rates of succession are associated with limitations on executive control. In the military, which is characterized by a high degree of formalization, thereby limiting the discretion of any one individual, there is intentionally high turnover among all ranks (Grusky, 1970). Another study examined the length of tenure of academic department heads or chairs and found that an important consideration was the "paradigm development" of the various disciplines. This refers to the extent to which there is agreement on and use of a common theoretical basis. With higher paradigm development, the tenure of the head was longer. Larger size operated against long tenure. The effects of both size and paradigm development were found to be more pronounced in periods of environmental scarcity (Pfeffer and Moore, 1980). This is in line with the conclusion that the situation in which leadership is embedded needs study. In periods of uncertainty, in regard to both the environment and the nature of the organization itself (low-paradigm-development departments), there is likely to be a greater rate of succession. In this sense, executive succession is the easy answer to organizational problems. Like most easy answers, it appears not to make as much difference as people might hope.

The argument thus far has been that organizational structural conditions affect how much impact leadership can have. There are several other important considerations. As noted earlier, Grusky believes that whether the successor is an insider or an outsider (to the organization) makes a difference, suggesting that, for baseball teams at least, the insider is more successful. In regard to overall change in the organization, however, it appears that the person brought in from the outside will be more able to institute greater changes. The outsider is able to replace subordinates with selected lieutenants of his or her own choice. The constellation of immediate personnel around the outsider can be changed more easily than the insider's could be (Helmich and Brown, 1972). A choice between an insider and an outsider is not always available, of course. Political considerations within an organization, its financial situation, and a dearth of outsiders may force an organization to go with insiders, thus limiting the amount of change possible. (In many cases, of course, change is not necessary or seen as desirable, so that the question of insider versus outsider is not a critical one.)

The overall context is the critical factor in successions. A study of the relationship between executive succession and stock-price changes related to the succession found significant positive effects of succession, in the form of stock-price increases, but only for external appointments in small firms—again, the size factor is operative. These stock-price increases were found when the departure of the former officeholder was announced along with the appointment of the successor (Reinganum, 1985). The size factor was also found important in a study of the rates of failure among newspaper organizations, following the succession of the newspapers' founders (Carroll, 1984). These newspaper organizations would be small organizations, which are vulnerable to high failure rates to begin with, and the succession of the publisher would make the situation even more risky.

Several studies highlight the political nature of the succession process. Allen and Panian (1982) studied the effects of the locus of control in organizations and succession. Direct family control of firms exists when the chief executive is a member of the family controlling the organization. Indirect family control exists when the chief executive is not a family member. Managerial control of firms exists when management dominates the board of directors. On the basis of data regarding 242 large industrial firms in the United States, Allen and Panian conclude:

> To begin with, there was a direct relationship between managerial power and corporate performance, on the one hand, and managerial tenure and longevity,

on the other. Chief executives of more profitable firms and those who were members of controlling families usually had longer tenures and were usually older at the time of their succession than the chief executive officers of less profitable firms and those who were not members of controlling families. Similarly, there was an inverse relationship between managerial power and the probability of managerial succession during periods of poor corporate performance. Chief executive officers who were members of controlling families were somewhat less likely to experience succession during unprofitable or only marginally profitable years than chief executives who were not members of controlling families. (pp. 545–46)

These results were contingent on the extent of stock ownership of the controlling family. It obviously helps to have ties to the controlling family, even more so when that control is extensive. What is interesting about this piece of research is that family ties made top leadership succession less sensitive to performance variation than was the case when a chief executive officer did not have these family ties.

Chief executive officers tend to be succeeded by individuals with the same career specialization, such as finance, sales, or legal (Smith and White, 1987). This succession process is based on previous strategies and power coalitions within the organization. This process can involve poor strategy following poor strategy, so that the process is not necessarily beneficial. It is based on the notion of strategic contingencies developed in the chapter on power.

The political process can be seen in yet another light. Managers of unstable firms strategically manipulate causal attributions to manage the impression of the degree to which they are in control of the situation, even though they may not have any real control over organizational outcomes. They go so far as to claim responsibility for positive and negative outcomes, indicating their awareness and attempts at controlling the situation. These strategies are designed to maintain their positions (Salancik and Mindl, 1984).

Any person coming into a top leadership position is, in a very real sense, caught by the organization. For many substantive decisions involving pricing, investment, merchandising, and new products, the chief executive of an organization is actually the "victim" or "captive" of the organization (Galbraith, 1974). The chief executive does, of course, have powers of appointment to critical positions and can initiate studies that bring about major changes over time.

Another set of constraints on what the top leadership of an organization can do consists of the external environment of the organization. This is dramatically seen in an analysis of 167 major U.S. corporations by Lieberson and O'Connor (1972), who were concerned with the sales, earnings, and profit margins of the corporations over a twenty-year period. Their ingenious research considered the issue of executive succession and its impact on these performance criteria. The authors analyzed the effects of succession over one-, two-, and three-year periods to permit the maximum impact of leadership change to demonstrate itself. They also considered the economic behavior of the industry (for example, steel versus air transportation), the position of the corporation within the industry, and the state of the economy as a whole. Their findings are startling to those who really believe in leadership: *"All three performance variables are affected by forces beyond a leader's immediate control"* (p. 124; italics added).

For sales and net earnings, the general economic conditions, the industry, and the corporation's position within it were more important than leadership. Leadership was important for profit margins but still heavily constrained by the environmental conditions. These findings were replicated (with slight modification) by Weiner (1977) and Salancik and Pfeffer (1977).

Lieberson and O'Connor's findings have created a great deal of controversy, since they fly in the face of much conventional wisdom and in the face of scholars who believe in leadership. Thomas (1988) reexamined the evidence of the sort that Lieberson and O'Connor used and came up with an interesting interpretation. He notes that changes in the order in which variables are entered into the regression equation regarding performance can essentially reverse the findings. Rather than reversing Lieberson and O'Connor's findings, which Thomas believes would be implausible, Thomas suggests that leadership has little impact at the aggregate level but a substantial impact at the *level of the individual firm*. Cases of effective leadership would cancel out cases of ineffective leadership.

Another criticism of Lieberson and O'Connor is presented by Day and Lord (1988), who conclude that the impact of organizational size and some contextual effects were not considered sufficiently by Lieberson and O'Connor. They also argue that leadership ability was not considered, which, unfortunately, brings us back to a "great person" perspective.

Lieberson and O'Connor do not claim that leadership is unimportant, nor is that claim made here. Leadership is clearly important in changing organizational directions, developing new activities, considering mergers or acquisitions, and setting long-run policies and objectives. At the same time, from all of the evidence that has been presented, it must be realized that organizational and environmental constraints drastically limit the likelihood of significant change on the basis of leadership alone. The implications of such findings are crucial for organizational analysis. In established organizations, the impact of leadership is heavily constrained, and leadership change may not make much of a difference. For the new organization, leadership is obviously more important. Leadership is also crucially important in times of organizational crisis.

The impact of leadership is variable. On the one hand, it can be "transformational" (Bass, 1985; Bass and Avolio, 1990, 1993), in which both behaviors and emotions of followers are altered and the entire organization is changed. This contemporary view sees leadership as a process in which charismatic leaders develop trust, pride, and respect in followers, along with inspiration (high expectations and modeling appropriate behavior in the followers), individualized attention (respect and responsibility in the followers), and intellectual stimulation in the form of challenging new ideas and directions by the followers. On the other hand, leadership can be "transactional," in which contingent rewards are linked to performance targets, "management by exception," in which leadership takes charge when things are not going according to plan. These views of leadership conceive of it as the "heroic chief executive" (Bryman, 1996, p. 292).

This heroic view of leadership can be contrasted with one that sees leadership as helpless to do anything about the events happening to the organization.

Neither view of leadership, heroic or helpless, is really helpful. What is helpful is to realize that, statistically, half of all leaders are below average. Leadership is neither the solution nor the problem. Leadership is an important, even crucial, activity in some situations; in others there is little that a "leader" can do. Most situations, of course, fall between these extremes.

This discussion of leadership has ignored an important consideration—the *motivations* of the leaders. More than two generations ago, Berle and Means (1932) argued that corporate executives have become technical managers, separated from the concerns of capitalist owners. More recently, others have argued that corporate leadership is the modern capitalist class with phenomenal power and wealth in their organizations and in society as a whole (Allen, 1976; Zeitlin, 1974, 1976). From this perspective, organizational decisions are made on the basis of continued acquisition of power and wealth for owners.

An analysis of corporate presidents found that they are fired on the basis of poor profit performance, regardless of whether they are owners or managers, thus disconfirming the Berle and Means hypothesis about the separation of ownership and management (James and Soref, 1981). We have already noted that such changes in top leadership may be little more than cosmetic. It may not matter if the top leaders are interested in their own power or wealth, if they are really controlled by owners, or if they are simply technocratic managers, since their organizational roles and impacts would not differ. The question of the organization's outcomes for society remains an important one, however, since what is good for the organization may not be good for society. This is true whether the organizations are corporations, school systems, or churches.

LEADERSHIP IN THE VOLUNTARY ORGANIZATION

The discussion thus far has concerned work organizations, in which the leader is appointed on the basis of criteria set up in advance. The situation is somewhat different in the voluntary organization, in which the leader is elected to office. It has long been noted that in voluntary organizations there is a tendency toward oligarchy, in that the group in power wants to stay there and will endeavor to ensure its continuation in office (Michels, 1949). In looking at union leadership, Tannenbaum (1968) notes that leaders have higher incomes than the rank and file they represent. In fact, they are more likely to live like their adversaries in management than like their own union members. They have a strong personal desire to stay in office.

This personal desire to stay in the leadership position is linked with several other factors that can lead to oligarchy. The leaders may be able to develop a monopoly on the kinds of skills required for leadership—verbal ability, persuasive techniques, and so on. They obtain political power within the organization through patronage and other favors. Given their position, it is relatively easy to groom their successors. Since the nature of unions involves a time cycle in regard to contract negotiations, the leaders can provide the membership with continual reminders of what they have achieved and what they are going to try to achieve the next time. The skills developed in this phase of the union's operation are unlikely to be part of the rank and file's repertoire.

The tendency toward oligarchy is apparently found in most voluntary organizations where there is a wide gap between members and leaders in the rewards (intrinsic and extrinsic) received. Where the gap is not so great, there is a great tendency toward democracy. Lipset, Trow, and Coleman's (1956) classic analysis of the International Typographical Union demonstrates this point. The members of this union enjoy relatively high pay and a strong sense of community with their fellow members and leaders alike, and it is quite democratic.

Voluntary organizations can also be differentiated from work organizations on the basis of the strong likelihood of a form of "dual leadership." Analyses of political parties have indicated the existence of both public and associational leadership. The public leaders are those who run for and hold public office, whereas the associational leaders operate behind the scenes. An exception is the British parliamentary system, where the two forms of leadership tend to coincide. Although unofficial power arrangements certainly exist in work organizations, they appear to be more fully developed in the voluntary organization, since the latter is characterized by much looser structural arrangements. And this looser structuring would appear to be related to another important consideration: In voluntary organizations the leader is more likely to have a strong impact than in more structured organizations, because there are more possibilities for variation in the voluntary setting.

SUMMARY AND CONCLUSIONS

In this chapter the attempt was made to place a human factor, leadership behavior, within the larger framework of analysis. It was first noted that the current conceptualization of leadership involves a combination of factors. The position in the organization itself, the specific situations confronted, the characteristics of the individuals involved, and the nature of the relationships with subordinates all affect leadership behavior and the impact of that behavior. Since all of these except the position itself are variable, it is exceedingly difficult to develop single standards or prescriptions for leadership. From the many studies of leadership effectiveness at lower levels in the organization, the conclusion was reached that there is no one style of leadership that is successful at all times. The total situation must be viewed if leadership is to be understood.

The important question of whether or not leadership makes any difference in the organization was of necessity also approached indirectly. Since it has been found that leadership behavior affects both behavior and attitudes at lower levels in the organizations, the extrapolation was made that it is important at the top. The studies of top management succession led to the same conclusion, tempered by the many other factors that also determine what happens to the organization. It is unfortunate that we do not know exactly in what ways and under what conditions such impacts occur. From the perspective of the total analysis, it is clear that top leadership is important for the organization as a whole as it seeks to be effective. But we cannot specify how much more or less important it is, or under what conditions it is important, when compared with some of the other factors considered, such as the existing organizational structure, informally derived power relationships, pressures from the environment, and relations with other organizations. We can state, however, that it is important and hope that future research will begin to assess the relative strengths of these factors under various conditions. We do know that leadership involves decision making, and it is to that topic that we now turn.

chapter 7

Decision Making

The theme of this chapter can perhaps be illustrated best with an example—that of the tragic *Challenger* space shuttle, which exploded so dramatically, killing all on board. The decision to launch *Challenger* was an organizational one and was based on three factors: the competitive environment and the struggle for scarce resources; organizational conditions in NASA that contributed to the censoring of information; and a regulatory environment that was insufficient for the task (Vaughan, 1992, 1996). Economic, organizational, and environmental factors all shaped the decision to launch. There are additional factors in the decision-making process, which will be considered in this chapter.

The *Challenger* launch ended in tragedy. It was not intended to. The launch decision was not made by stupid and cruel people. It was made by people like you and me, who were trying to do the best they could. That is the way it is with decisions. We may intend that our decisions result in the best for our organizations (to be effective), but we may not have enough information, we may not understand the information we have, or we may be influenced by ideological or even moral ideas that push us into decisions that are not the best for us or our organizations. The purpose of this chapter is to analyze the decision-making *process*. It is a complicated but interesting process.

Decisions come in all sizes and shapes. Some are trivial. Others momentous. We will see that it is a mistake to think of decision making as a rational and clearly calculated process. It is also a mistake to think of decision making as simply a random process.

155

This chapter itself is a result of decision making. In earlier editions of this book, the topic of decision making was incorporated into the chapter on leadership. The decision to have a separate chapter on decision making was the consequence of discussions with students and colleagues. I would not claim that the decision was rational; I had no idea what the outcome of the decision would be or even if there would be any outcome at all. At the same time, the decision was not a shot in the dark.

Just as leadership takes place throughout organizations, so does decision making. And, in the interest of symmetry, just as the primary focus of the last chapter was leadership at the top of the organization, so the primary focus here will be decision making at the top of the organization.

STRATEGIC DECISIONS

Decisions at the top of organizations are usually labeled strategic decisions (Hickson, 1987; Heller et al., 1988). They are the big, high-risk decisions that are made. They can involve entering new markets, developing new services or products, starting new programs, closing existing programs or facilities, or more generally breaking new ground in the areas of personnel, priorities, programs, and initiatives.

From the outset it must be made clear that no assumptions of rationality are being made. Just consider the fact that people and organizations can become committed to losing courses of action and continue to make decisions that make matters even worse. These are called escalation situations. Escalation situations occur when organizational projects have little salvage value, when decision makers want to justify their own past behavior, when people in a project are bound to each other, and when organizational inertia and internal politics combine to prevent a project from being shut down (Staw and Ross, 1989). A classic example is the process by which a power company on Long Island, New York, persisted in their decision to construct a nuclear power plant in the face of fierce opposition. The power company "stuck to its guns," or escalated, for twenty-three years. The cost of the project went from $75 million in 1966 to $5 billion, when the project was abandoned in 1989 (Ross and Staw, 1993).

Several writers have developed some vivid imagery to try to portray the complexity and intricacy of strategic decision making. Weick (1976), for example, claims that it is an "unconventional soccer match," with players coming and going as they like, the field sloping and round, and goals scattered about apparently at random. Hickson (1987) likens it to an American football game:

> It is seen as a game of powerful groups in which some teams are much bigger and have thicker protective padding and harder helmets. Boundaries are elastic, the field is bumpy, and the number of teams in play fluctuates. They disagree as to where the ends of the field are, but eventually one team or coalition of teams pushes through holding the ball to where it says the end is (Hickson et al., 1986).

This is a game in which the heavier or better protected players have a greater chance of shaping what is going on and where it is going to. The shape of the ball itself can be changed. (p. 166)

The players are the participants in the decision making. Scores are made by the powerful, who define the rules (rationality) of the game. The key point here is that there is not a single, invariant rationality.

The components of the decision-making process can be seen graphically in Figure 7-1, which differentiates between high-risk or strategic decisions and decisions involving less risk. This figure contains most of the elements that we will be considering. For example, in the high-risk decision section, note that the terms "coalitions" and "intensity" and "extensity" of conflict are used. This is consistent with the idea that the exercise of power is an important component of decision making. Notice, also, that information search and discussion are important components. This involves the communication process, which is itself problematic. The fact that there is information search and discussion is also a component of the issue of rationality. The search process and discussions do not yield clear answers on many issues. In fact, the more important the strategic decisions, the higher the levels of uncertainty.

FIGURE 7–1 Decision Characteristics and Decision Trajectory
Source: Jerald Hage, *Theories of Organizations* (New York: John Wiley, 1980), p. 121.

In some ways, Figure 7-1 can be misleading. It can appear that once a decision is made, some action will take place. Actually, it is more complicated than that. External (exogenous) events can trigger decisions. Actions can take place that are not the result of decisions. Decisions can be made when there is not consensus. Even the linkage between decisions and action is not completely clear (Butler, 1990; Mintzberg and Waters, 1990). Nonetheless, Figure 7-1 does illustrate a basic model for decision making.

VARIABLES AND CONSTRAINTS

A useful approach to the kinds of decisions that have strategic importance for the organization was provided by James Thompson some years ago (1967). Thompson noted that "decision issues always involve two major dimensions: (1) beliefs about cause/effect relationships and (2) preferences regarding possible outcomes" (p. 134). "Beliefs about cause and effect" refers to whether or not there is certainty about the outcome of a decision. If we decide A, we are sure that B and only B will be the result—this is high certainty about cause and effect. "Preferences regarding outcomes" refers the degree to which there is consensus about what the organization wants.

These basic variables in the decision-making process can operate at the conscious or the unconscious level. As an aid in understanding the process, Thompson suggests that each variable can be (artificially) dichotomized as indicated in Figure 7-2. In the cell with certainty on both variables, a "computational" strategy can be used. In that case the decision is obvious. For example, in simple inventorying, when the supply of a particular item dwindles to a particular level, it is automatically reordered by a computer. Obviously, this is in no way a strategic situation and will not be of concern to us here. The other cells present more problems and are thus more crucial for the organization.

When outcome preferences are clear, but cause/effect relationships are uncertain, we will refer to the judgmental strategy for decision making. Where the situation is reversed and there is certainty regarding cause/effect but uncertainty regarding outcome preferences, the issues can be regarded as calling for a compromise strategy for decision making. Finally, where there is uncertainty on both

FIGURE 7–2 Decision Processes
Source: James D. Thompson, *Organizations in Action* (New York: McGraw-Hill, 1967), p. 134.

dimensions, we will speak of the inspirational strategy for decision making, if indeed any decision is forthcoming. (Thompson, 1967: pp. 134–35)

One obvious critical factor in this framework is information. The amount and kind of information determine the certainty in the decision-making process. The implication is that the more certain that knowledge, the easier and better the decision making. Unfortunately, information does not flow automatically into or through an organization. Whatever is happening inside or outside an organization is subject to the perceptions and interpretations of the decision makers (Duncan, 1972). Miles, Snow, and Pfeffer (1974) suggest that decision makers can take four stances in their perceptions. They can be "domain defenders," who attempt to allow little change to occur; "reluctant reactors," who simply react to pressures; "anxious analyzers," who perceive change but wait for competing organizations to develop responses and then adapt to them; or "enthusiastic prospectors," who perceive opportunities for change and want to create change and to experiment. These different perceptual bases are developed through the individual decision maker's experiences in the organization. Thus, the same external or internal conditions can be viewed differently, depending upon who is doing the perceiving. Decision makers are more likely to discern threats than opportunities (Jackson and Dutton, 1988). Decision makers are thus not automatons or computers who respond to all messages in equal ways, except in the computational situation.

Information is part of the communication process within organizations. As will be seen in the next chapter, the communication process itself is almost guaranteed to withhold, expand, or distort information. In addition, organizations scan different environments in different fashions. For example, although they usually use as much information as they can from outside the organization, they apparently cease to do so when they develop bases in other countries as multinational corporations have (Keegan, 1974). In these cases, the information-scanning process turns inside the organization, with the potential that much will be missed on the outside.

Although information is a critical component of decision making, equally important are beliefs about cause and effect. In some areas of knowledge, certainty about cause and effect is quite well developed, whereas in others, the knowledge is probabilistic at best. Since all organizations are social units interacting with society, any involvement of humans in either the cause or the effect part of the equation introduces an element of uncertainty. Complete knowledge is undoubtedly rare in the kinds of decisions with which we are concerned. In discussing the effects of the incompleteness of knowledge and information, Thompson noted that in organizations working at the frontiers of new knowledge—such as those in the aerospace industry and in medical research—the presence of imperfections and gaps in knowledge leads to the use of the judgmental strategy, even though all the variables that are known to be relevant are controlled as far as possible. Knowledge about cause and effect is further weakened when some elements of the process are beyond the organization's control. Welfare programs, for example, are affected by the people being served and the wider community that supports or rejects the total program. Still another situation in which the cause-and-effect relationship becomes unclear is when the organization is in competition with another organization over which it cannot exercise control. In that case the judgmental strategy is also used, since the organization cannot decide for sure exactly what will happen as a result of its own efforts.

In addition to changes in the nature of the cause-effect knowledge system that occur as new knowledge becomes available—as in the case of new medical discoveries that alter the approach of HMOs and hospitals to their patients—another important component of the system must be specified. The nature of cause and effect is actually really certain in only a few cases. Cause-and-effect "knowledge" is vitally affected by the belief or truth system that is prevalent in the organization. The importance of this can be seen clearly in the case of welfare systems that have two major alternative truth systems, which can lead to different interpretations of the same knowledge inputs. The organizations can believe, on the one hand, that those on some form of welfare assistance are in that condition through their own fault or, on the other hand, that the condition exists because of societal imperfections. Although there would seldom be a complete acceptance of either extreme position, the dominant truth system would serve as the mechanism by which information coming into the system is interpreted on a cause-and-effect basis, leading to the making of different kinds of decisions. Similar examples can be noted concerning the strategies adopted in regard to outsourcing or downsizing, international expansion, and most other organizational decisions. From the cause-effect standpoint, then, information is a key factor, but interpretation of it remains a variable that, although usually constant in most organizations, still affects the outcomes of the decisions that are made. The adoption of a different truth system could lead to entirely different decisions, based on the same information.

The outcome-preference side of the Thompson paradigm contains even more ambiguities for the organization than the cause-effect side. The choice among outcome preferences, or goals, is a major issue in which *power* is exercised and over which *conflicts* occur. There can be structured decision making when there is agreement on goals and anarchic decision making when there is not agreement. In cases of structured decision making, problems can arise because the participants and the environments can change. At the same time, a focus on anarchy overlooks the regularities inherent in organizations because of the ongoing structure (Pinfield, 1986). The imagery here is intended to lead to the conclusion that decision making is a process in which both rationality *and* power are problematic.

We must not lose track of the point that organizational decision making takes place *within* organizations. For example, higher levels of strategic change decisions were found in organizations that were in situations of poor performance, long tenure of both chief executives and the management team, and diversity of background of the management team (Boeker, 1997a). Fewer strategic-change decisions would be found in situations of higher performance, shorter tenure, and less diverse management teams.

RATIONALITY

Any analysis of decision making and rationality must begin with, and then discard, the notion of "economic man." "*Homo economicus* is characterized by the following: acting only in his self-interest, possessing full information about the decision problem, knowing all the possible solutions from which he has to choose as well as the consequences of each solution, seeking to maximize utility, having the ability to rank alternatives in order of likelihood of maximizing outcomes" (Zey, 1992: p. 11).

There is actually a very limited amount of rationality available in the decision-making process. As Simon (1957) has so ably pointed out, decisions are made on the basis of "bounded rationality." Limits on rationality are linked to the inability of the system as a whole to provide maximum or even adequate information for decision making and to the inability of the decision maker to intellectually handle even the inadequate information that is available. Leaving the issue of information aside for the moment, it is clear that the more important a decision is for the organization, the greater the number of factors contributing to the condition of the organization at the moment that the decision has to be made and the more far-reaching the consequences of the decision. The intellectual ability to handle these multitudinous factors is just not available among current and past organizational leaders to the degree that they and those affected by the decisions would desire. This approach, by the way, contributed to Simon's Nobel Prize in Economics in 1998.

Despite Simon's celebrated critique of the "economic man" model, such a model has been the model of choice for much of the literature in economics and psychology. There is a growing wave of criticism, however, that threatens to topple the simplistic assumptions of the economic model. One base of criticism is the recognition that values (even morals) other than simply economic interest come into play in decision making and that feelings, or affect, also play an important role (Etzioni, 1988). In addition to their values and feelings, people have habits (Camic, 1985) that guide their behavior and that may have little or nothing to do with economics, moral values, or feelings.

There are also criticisms of the economic model that are based on social considerations that extend beyond the behavior of individuals. It is quite clear that individuals act on the basis of their social relations with others, such as their family, and that many actions are social in nature (Granovetter, 1985). In addition, different industries create their own institutionalized rationality (Fligstein, 1992), which leads organizations in different industries to create their own rationalities. The environments in which organizations operate can turn from being civil to being "hostile" (Morrill, 1991), which in turn can alter the decision-making process within organizations. Even more broadly, different national cultures affect the scanning and interpretation process as organizations bring information in for decision making (Schneider, 1989). These points are made not to destroy the economic model but to augment it.

Empirical evidence of the inadequacy of the economic rationality model is appearing with increasing frequency. One of the best examples comes from an analysis of General Motors (GM) in the United States. GM was hailed as a classic case of the "M-Form" (Multi-Divisional) organization (Chandler, 1962). This form was supposedly selected because of its efficiency. Instead, for most of its history, GM sought not efficiency but consent among its managers (Freedland, 1997). A study of hospitals and their use of cesarean sections found that the rates of the use of this childbirth procedure were related not to institutional standards of best medical practice but to organizational standards of procedure (Goodrich and Salancik, 1996). These two studies are impressive. They do not disprove the rational economic model. They *do* mean that other considerations must be brought into the decision-making equation.

Some analysts have essentially abandoned the economic rationality model. This is best exemplified by the "garbage can" model of decision making, in which it essentially is argued that organizations have a repertoire of responses to problems, which are located in their garbage cans (Cohen, March, and Olsen, 1972). If a proposed solution to a problem appears to be satisfactory or appropriate, it is applied to the problem. Interestingly, this model suggests that the garbage can also contains the problem. That means that organizational decision makers do not perceive that something is occurring about which a decision has to be made until the problem matches one with which they have already had some experience. Human decision making is a symbol-driven search activity (Masuch and LaPotin, 1989). The garbage can approach stresses that we look for the familiar symbols that we have used in the past.

The garbage can imagery has elements of both truth and cuteness. Too-quick acceptance of the imagery can miss an important consideration in decision making. Garbage cans of organizations, as well as those of individuals, do not contain random responses, problems, or other debris. Instead, garbage cans reveal a great deal about the lifestyles and interests of organizations and individuals. Thus, organizations turn to previous decisions that have been discarded or put aside, and thus little in the way of new decisions enters the decision-making situation. Managers make decisions in small increments that make sense to them and generate actions that will make them look good (Starbuck, 1983). Indeed, an analysis of decision making during the Cuban missile crisis led to the conclusion that decisions were made to avoid failure rather than to achieve success (Anderson, 1983).

Another examination of rationality in decision making concluded that the choices which determine outcomes in organizational contexts are made informally and intuitively, before the consequences of the decisions are evaluated (Alexander, 1979). The suggestion here is that top decision makers make their decisions and then develop the rational-sounding reasons for those decisions after the fact.

There clearly are limits to rationality. At the same time, decisions are not entirely random. There is a "lid on the garbage can" (Levitt and Nuss, 1989). Decision making and access to decision making are constrained by forces in organizations' institutional environments. I would add organizational structural constraints to the environmental constraints.

A new form of rational model is emerging. It is based loosely on Granovetter's (1985) concept of *social embeddedness*. The basic point of this model is that people *and* organizations are embedded in social networks that lead them to try to maximize or at least utilize social embeddedness, along with economic rationality in decision making. An example of this is the finding that repeated alliances between firms lead to trust, which in turn becomes the basis for additional alliances (Gulati (1995). A study of the semiconductor industry examined the formation of SEMATECH, a research-and-development consortium among highly competitive firms, and found that individuals and firms developed a "moral community" in which individuals and firms made contributions to the industry without regard for immediate and specific paybacks (Browning, Beyer, and Shetler, 1995, p. 113). A study in a completely different setting, the garment industry in New York City, found that embeddedness, in the form of trust between and networks among garment firms, was related to higher survival rates than those among firms that relied solely on "arms-length" economic transactions (Uzzi, 1996, 1977).

These studies do not prove that embeddedness rationality is more important than economic rationality. Nor do they claim that there is not bounded rationality in embeddedness-based decisions. Instead, they give us a new and exciting way to add to our understanding of the substance of organizational decisions. To make matters all the more complex, just as variance among types of rationality is present, so there is variance in the *power* to participate in decision making.

POWER AND DECISION MAKING

Since our primary focus is strategic decision making, it should be obvious that these decisions are made at or near the top of organizations. The top of the organization may or may not include boards of directors, since their involvement is variable (Judge and Zeithaml, 1992; Finkelstein, 1992). Ideologies and values commonly enter the decision-making process (Beyer, 1981). Decisions are made by coalitions of individuals and groups (Hage, 1980; Bacharach and Lawler, 1980; Gargiulo, 1993). Interest-group interests may or may not coincide with the best interests of the organization. They certainly will not coincide with the interests of those groups not in power. Those in power have an economic incentive to manipulate information to influence decisions in their favor (Milgrom and Roberts, 1988). There are social incentives here, as well.

A study of a university found that in times of adversity, decisions were shaped by power considerations rather than by more bureaucratic considerations, such as workload (Hills and Mahoney, 1978). In periods of affluence, the more bureaucratic approach was used. This is similar to findings that social influence and social familiarity were used more in decision making during periods of adversity than in more benevolent periods (Pfeffer, Salancik, and Leblibici, 1978).

Most strategic decisions are centered at the top of organizations, since that is where the power lies. At the same time, there are instances in which subordinates are brought into the process. As we have seen previously, participation by subordinates has mixed consequences for the organization and the participants. The same is true of decision making. Greater participation can actually be dysfunctional if the participants already feel satisfied or even saturated with their role in decision making (Alutto and Belasco, 1972). If they feel deprived, bringing them into the decision-making process will increase their acceptance of the decision that is made. A useful insight on participation in decision making is that if a decision is important for the organization, a nonparticipative style is likely to be used; if the decisions are important for the subordinates in regard to their own work, a more participative approach will be taken (Heller, 1973). If the organizational decision makers believe that the subordinates have something to contribute to the decision or its implementation, then participation is more likely. Again, this is done on the basis of limited or bounded rationality.

THE DECISION-MAKING PROCESS

Hickson (1987) has suggested that decision making ought to be approached from a *dual* rationality standpoint in that both problems and politics are involved. Participants in decision making must be concerned with the problems faced and the political process of developing support for the decisions that are made. Participants intend to be as economically and "embeddednessly" rational as possible, even when considering moral and personal issues. Decision making is most effective when both substantive problems (substantive or procedural rationality) and appropriate political actions are taken within the organization; if decision makers only attempt political manipulations without concern with substantive issues, decisions are less effective (Dean and Sharfman, 1996).

Organizational decisions are made in contexts. This is the point of the whole embeddedness idea, but there is another, broader aspect of embeddedness that is important. A study of the migration of manufacturing plants from New York State between 1969 and 1985 (and there was a lot of migration) found that firms with a great deal of autonomy were most free to leave. Those that had links to local communities in the form of material, social and political embeddedness were less able to make such moves, even when production costs could be considerably reduced. Not surprisingly, the less mobile firms were in more peripheral industries. Firms in core industries were more able to move (Romo and Schwartz, 1995). Again, economic factors and social embeddedness were operative at this more macro level.

There is an additional and not so incidental component of the decision-making process—the "nondecision" (Bacharach and Baratz, 1962). This refers to situations in which (1) a decision has already been made, but the decision-making process is followed as though it had not; (2) issues are not allowed to surface as matters for decision ("I wouldn't bring that up if I were you") (Hickson, 1987: p. 175); or (3) there are issues that are believed to be unthinkable in the values of the powerful groups in the organization. Added to this is the fact that there can be decisions made to take no actions at all in regard to some contingency. Thus, although decision making can usually be thought of in an active mode, there are instances in which there are no actions.

Good and Bad Decisions

"Well, it seemed like a good idea at the time." That phrase, which we have all used in our personal lives, also characterizes organizational decisions. The quality of decisions can only be judged over time. Even the time frame is problematic. The forty-plus years of Russian rule in Eastern Europe appeared to be successful decision making on the part of the Soviets. The Ford Motor Company produced both the Mustang and the Edsel. Junk bonds appeared to be good investment strategy in the 1980s for many pension funds. The list of what now appear to be good and bad decisions could be expanded for pages. For our purposes here, it is sufficient to conclude that what appear to be successful dually rational decisions at time 1 will be problematic in one or both aspects at time 2. Problems and politics both change.

SUMMARY AND CONCLUSIONS

Decision making involves both substance and politics and both economic and socially embedded rationality. It also involves limited rationality in all issues. Nonetheless, we plunge ahead. When, and if, we are participants in decision making, we do try to do the best we can. To return to our theme, decisions are made in the interest of effectiveness. They are never perfect solutions and they never last over time, but we continue to make them.

Since information is central to decision making, and since communications allow information to flow, we will now examine this process in organizations.

chapter 8

Communication

Organizations are information-processing systems. One of the most vivid metaphors sees the organization as a brain (Morgan, 1986). This imagery captures the idea that organizations receive and filter information, process it in light of what it has already learned, interpret it, change it, and finally act on it. Organizations also have memory lapses. To take the imagery even further, there are mind-altering stimulants and depressants—organizational highs and lows.

The communication process in organizations contains elements that are strongly organizational and strongly individual. At the individual level, consider the simple example of classroom examinations. If there were not individual differences in cognition and interpretation, everyone would give the same answer to an essay question. That obviously does not happen, as every student and faculty member knows. The organizational input into the communication process comes from the structured communication channels and the positions that people occupy. For example, I interpreted information very differently when I was a dean from the way I do now as a faculty member. Organizational positions strongly influence the interpretation of communications by individuals. In this chapter the factors that affect the sending, receiving, perception, and interpretation of communications will be examined.

THE IMPORTANCE OF COMMUNICATION

Organizational structures, with their varying sizes, technological sophistication, and degrees of complexity and formalization, are designed to be or evolve into information-handling systems. The very establishment of an organizational structure is a sign that communications are supposed to follow a particular path. Power, leadership, and decision making rely upon the communication process, either explicitly or implicitly, since they would be meaningless in the absence of information.

Organizational analysts have ascribed varying degrees of importance to the communication process. Barnard (1938), for example, states: "In an exhaustive theory of organization, communication would occupy a central place, because the structure, extensiveness, and scope of the organization are almost entirely determined by communication techniques" (p. 91). This approach essentially places communication at the heart of the organization. More recently, Stinchcombe (1990) also made communication the essence of his analysis. Other theorists, however, pay scant attention to the topic (for example, see Aldrich, 1979; Clegg and Dunkerley, 1980). Instead of declaring that communication is either at the heart or at the periphery of organizational analysis, a more reasonable view is that communication varies in importance according to where one is looking in an organization and what kind of organization is being studied.

Communication is crucial for organizational managers and their work. Kanter (1977) found that the managers she studied spent an overwhelming proportion of their time in communications. These communications usually involved face-to-face interactions with subordinates, superiors, peers, and customers. There were also meetings of one kind or another. Mail and phone messages had to be answered. In short, the business of the managers was communication. It is estimated that 80 percent of managers' time is spent on interpersonal communications (Klauss and Bass, 1982). As one moves away from the top of organizations, the proportion of time devoted to communications decreases. It should be noted, of course, that the work of clerical personnel is overwhelmingly concerned with information processing. Changing information technology is having a major and unfinished impact on managerial and clerical work, and thus on organizations, as we will see later in this chapter.

These intraorganizational differences are important. Equally important are interorganizational differences. Communication is most important in organizations and organizational segments that must deal with uncertainty, that are complex, and that have a technology that does not permit easy routinization. Both external and internal characteristics affect the centrality of communication. The more an organization is people and idea oriented, the more important communication becomes. Even in a highly mechanized system, of course, communications underlie the development and use of machines. Workers are instructed on usage, orders are delivered, and so on. At the same time, the routineness of such operations leads to a lack of variability in the communication process. Once procedures are set, few additional communications are required. Although communications occur almost continuously in such settings, their organizational importance is more limited unless they lead to severe distortions in the operations.

The communication process is by definition a relational one; one party is the sender and the other the receiver at a particular time. The relational aspect of communication obviously affects the process. The social relations occurring in the communication process involve the sender and the receiver and their reciprocal effects on each other as they are communicating. If a sender is intimidated by a receiver during the process of sending a message, the message itself and the interpretation of it will be affected. Intimidation is just one of a myriad of factors that have the potential to disrupt the simple sender-receiver relationship. Status differences, different perceptual models, sexual attraction, and so on can enter the picture and lead to distortions of what is being sent and received.

These sources of distortion and their consequences will occupy a good deal of attention in the subsequent discussion. Ignorance of the potentiality for distortion has been responsible for the failure of many organizational attempts to improve operations simply by utilizing more communications. Once the importance of communications was recognized, many organizations jumped on a communications bandwagon, believing that if sufficient communications were available to all members of the organization, everyone would know and understand what was going on and most organizational problems would disappear (Katz and Kahn, 1978: p. 430). This communications bandwagon was at the heart of the flurry of interest in organizational "culture" as the cure-all for organizational problems that appeared in the 1980s (Mohan, 1993). Unfortunately, organizational life is not that simple, and mere reliance on more and better communications cannot bring about major, positive changes for an organization.

Before we turn to a more comprehensive examination of communication problems and their consequences in organizations, a simple view of optimal communications should be presented. The view is simple because it is complementary to the earlier discussion of rationality and decision making.

Communications in organizations should provide accurate information with the appropriate emotional overtones to all members who need the communication content. This assumes that neither too much nor too little information is in the system and that it is clear from the outset who can utilize what is available. It should be evident that this is an impossible condition to achieve in a complex organization. Indeed, organizations gather more information than they use but also continue to ask for more (Feldman and March, 1981). This is attributed to decision makers' needs for legitimacy. In addition, the communication process is inherently paradoxical and contradictory (Brunsson, 1989; Manning, 1992). Paradoxes and contradictions permeate organizational life.

In the sections that follow, the factors contributing to the impossibility of perfect communication systems will be examined. These factors range from those that are apparently inherent (through learning) in any social grouping to those that are peculiarly organizational. The focus will be primarily on communication within organizations. Communication with the environment of organizations will be considered later.

INDIVIDUAL FACTORS

Since communication involves something being sent to a receiver, what the receiver does with or to the communicated message is perhaps the most vital part of the whole system. Therefore, the perceptual process becomes a key element in our understanding of communications in organizations.

The perceptual process is subject to many factors that can lead to important differences in the way any two people perceive the same person or message. Even physical objects can be perceived differently. Perceivers may respond to cues they are not aware of, be influenced by emotional factors, use irrelevant cues, weigh evidence in an unbalanced way, or fail to identify all the factors on which their judgments are based. People's personal needs, values, and interests enter the perceptual process. Most communications take place in interaction with others, and how one person perceives the "other" in the interaction process vitally affects how a person will perceive the communication, since other people are more emotion-inducing than physical objects are. For example, research has shown that a person's interactions, and thus perceptions, are affected even by the expectations of what the other person will look like (Zalkind and Costello, 1962).

These factors are common to all perceptual situations. For the analysis of perceptions in organizations, they must be taken as basic conditions in the communication process. So it is obvious that perfect perception—that is, perception uniform across all information recipients—is impossible in any social situation. The addition of organizational factors makes the whole situation that much more complex.

Communications in organizations are basically transactions between individuals. Even when written or broadcast forms are used, the communicator is identified as an individual. The impression that the communication receiver has of the communicator is thus crucial in the interpretation of the communication. Impressions in these instances are not created *de novo;* the receiver utilizes his or her own learned response set to the individual and the situation. The individual's motives and values enter the situation. In addition, the setting or surroundings of the act of communication affect the impression. A neat, orderly, and luxuriously furnished office contributes to a reaction different from the one given by an office that looks and smells like a locker room. Since the perceptual process itself requires putting ideas and people into categories, the interaction between communicators is also subject to "instant categorization"; that is, you cannot understand other people unless they are placed in some relevant part of your learned perceptual repertoire. This is often done on the basis of a very limited amount of evidence—or even wrong evidence, as when the receiver notes cues that are wrong or irrelevant to the situation in question (Zalkind and Costello, 1962: p. 221).

Organizational position affects how communications are perceived or sent (Wager, 1972; Roberts, Hulin, and Rousseau, 1978). In almost all organizations, people can be superordinates in one situation and subordinates in another. The assistant superintendent of a school system is superordinate to a set of principals but subordinate to the superintendent and the school board. Communications behavior differs according to one's position in a role set. If the individual is in a role in which he or she is or has been or feels discriminated against, communications are affected. Athanassaides (1974) found that women who had suffered discrimination in their roles had a lower feeling of autonomy than others in the same role. This in turn was related to distortions in the information that they communicated upward in the organization.

All these factors are further complicated by the well-known phenomenon of stereotyping. This predisposition to judge can occur before any interaction at all has taken place. It can involve the labels "labor," "management," "minority group," and any other group membership. The individuals involved are assumed to have the characteristics of the group of which they are members; in probably the vast majority of cases, however, the characteristics attributed to the group as a whole are distortions of reality. In the sense being used here, stereotyping is the imposition of negative characteristics on the members of the communication system. The reverse situation—attributing socially approved characteristics—can also occur, of course, with an equally strong potential for damage to the communication process.

Other factors that enter the communication process in somewhat the same manner are the use of the "halo effect," or the use of only one or a few indicators to generalize about a total situation; "projection," or a person's assuming that the other members of a communication system have the same characteristics as the person's own; and "perceptual defense," or altering inconsistent information to put it in line with the conceptual framework already developed. All the factors that have been mentioned here are part of the general literature on perception and must be assumed to be present in any communication system. They are not peculiar to organizations.

The characteristics of the perceived person affect what is perceived. Here are four conclusions from research regarding the perceiver:

1. Knowing oneself makes it easier to see others accurately.
2. One's own characteristics affect the characteristics that one is likely to see in others.
3. The person who is self-accepting is more likely to be able to see favorable aspects of other people.
4. Accuracy in perceiving others is not a single skill. (Zalkind and Costello, 1962, pp. 227–29)

These findings are linked to the more general considerations—tendencies to stereotype, project, and so on. It is when the characteristics of the perceived are brought into the discussion that organizational conditions become important. Factors such as age affect how a person is perceived (Zenger and Lawrence, 1989). The person may be labeled a sales manager (accurately or not) by a production worker, and the entire communication system is affected until additional information is permitted into the system. The situation in which the communication takes place also has a profound impact on what is perceived. This is particularly vital in organizations, since in most cases the situation is easily labeled and identified by the physical location.

Organizations are full of all kinds of information, including gossip (Noon and Delbridge, 1993). There is a great deal of variance in the degree to which people are in social networks and receive information, whether it is gossip or not. Thus, information itself and individuals are part of the paradoxical communication process.

ORGANIZATIONAL FACTORS

It has already been noted that organizations develop their own cultures, with language, rituals, and styles of communications (Frost et al., 1985; Morgan, 1986; Ott, 1989). It is clear that organizations attempt to socialize their personnel so that communication problems are minimized (Pascale, 1985). Despite the presence of a common culture and socialization efforts, however, organizations contain the seeds of communication problems when their vertical and horizontal components are considered.

VERTICAL COMMUNICATION

Patterns of vertical communication have received a good deal of attention, primarily because they are so vital in organizational operations. From our discussions of organizational structure, power, and leadership, it should be evident that the vertical element is a crucial organizational fact of life. Since communication is also crucial, the vertical element intersects in a most important way. Vertical communications in organizations involve both downward and upward flows.

Downward Communication. There are five elements of downward communication (Katz and Kahn, 1978: pp. 440–43). The first is the simple and common job instruction, in which a subordinate is told what to do through direct orders, training sessions, job descriptions, or other such mechanisms. The intent of job instructions is to ensure reliable and consistent job performance. The more complex and uncertain the task, the more generalized the instructions. As a rule, the more highly trained the subordinates, the less specific the instructions are, because it is assumed that those individuals will bring with them an internalized knowledge of how to do the job, along with other job-related knowledge and attitudes.

The second element is more subtle and less often stressed. It involves the rationale for a task and its relationships to the rest of the organization. It is here that different philosophies of life affect how much this sort of information is communicated. If the philosophy is to keep the organizational members dumb and happy, little such information will be communicated. The organization may feel either that the subordinates are unable to comprehend the information or that they would misuse it by introducing variations into their performance based on their own best judgment of how the task should be accomplished. Even apart from the philosophy-of-life issue, this is a delicate matter. All organizations, even those most interested in the human qualities of their members, have hidden agendas of some sort at some time. If the total rationale for all actions were known to all members, the potential for chaos would be high, since communication overload would quickly occur. The danger of too much communication is matched by the opposite danger—too little communication—which also has strong potential for organizational malfunctioning. If the members are given too little information, and do not and cannot know how their work is related to any larger whole, there is a strong possibility that they will feel alienated from the work and the organization. Obviously, the selection of the best path between these extremes is important in the establishment of communications.

The third element of downward communication is information regarding procedures and practices within the organization. Like the first element (job instruction), it is relatively straightforward and noncontroversial. Here again, whether or not this is linked to the second element is problematic.

Feedback to individuals regarding their performance is the fourth element of the downward communication system. This is almost by definition a sticky issue, particularly when the feedback is negative. If the superior has attempted at all to utilize socioemotional ties to his or her subordinates, the issue becomes even more difficult. It becomes almost impossible when the work roles are so thoroughly set in advance by the organization that the worker has no discretion on the job at all. In these cases, only a totally conscious deviation would result in feedback. In the absence of deviation, there will probably be no feedback other than the paycheck and other routine rewards. Where discretion is part of the picture, the problem of assessment deepens, because feedback is more difficult to accomplish if there are no clear criteria on which to base it. Despite these evident problems, feedback is a consistent part of downward communications.

The final element of downward communication involves attempts to indoctrinate subordinates into accepting and believing in the organization's (or the subunit's) goals. The intent here, of course, is to get the personnel emotionally involved in their work and add this to the motivational system.

Downward communication takes place at all levels, from the top down. At each level it is interpreted by individuals, so that individual factors reenter our picture as information flows and is interpreted downward.

Upward Communication.   Contrary to the law of gravity, communication in organizations must also go up, even when nothing is going down. According to Katz and Kahn (1978):

> Communication up the line takes many forms. It can be reduced, however, to what people say (1) about themselves, their performance, and their problems, (2) about others and their problems, (3) about organizational practices and policies, and (4) about what needs to be done and how it can be done. (p. 446)

The content of these messages can obviously range from the most personal gripe to the most high-minded suggestion for the improvement of the organization or the world; and the messages can have positive or negative consequences for the subordinate, from a promotion or a bonus to dismissal. Whistleblowers are constantly in fear of dismissal. The most obvious problem in upward communication is again the hierarchy.

People are unlikely to pass information up if it will be harmful to themselves or their peers. Thus, the amount and kind of information that is likely to be passed upward is affected by hierarchy. Anyone who has been in any kind of organization knows that discussions with the boss, department head, president, supervisor, or other superior are, at least initially, filled with something approaching terror, regardless of the source of the superior's power in the organization.

Another facet of upward communication is important: Whereas communications downward become more detailed and specific, those going up the hierarchy must become condensed and summarized. Indeed, a major function of those in the middle of a hierarchy is the filtering and editing of information. Only crucial pieces of information are supposed to reach the top. This can be seen in clear relief at the national level, where the president of the United States receives highly condensed accounts of the huge number of issues of national and international concern. Regardless of the party in power, the filtering and editing process is vital in the hierarchy, since the basis on which things are "edited out" can have enormous repercussions by the time the information reaches the top. Here, as well as in downward communication, the perceptual limitations we noted earlier are in operation, so there is a very real potential for distorted communications and, more important, for decisions different from those that would have been made if some other editing process were in force (Wilensky, 1967; Halberstam, 1972).

There is an interesting technological twist here. Computer-based information technology is increasingly important in the organizational communication process. The twist is that top executives may not have computers in their own offices. They leave the handling of computer-based information to their staff and subordinates (March and Sproul, 1990). Only time will tell if this situation will change.

Dysfunctions of Hierarchy and Some Positive Outcomes

There are several specific dysfunctions of hierarchy for the communication process. In the first place, hierarchical divisions inhibit communications. There is a common tendency for people at the same status level to interact more with one another than with those at different levels. At the same time, there is a tendency for those in lower-status positions to look up to and direct friendship overtures toward those in higher-status positions. This increases the flow of socioemotional communications upward, but at the same time it leaves those at the bottom of the hierarchy in the position of receiving little of this type of input. This situation is further complicated by the fact that those in higher-status positions also direct such communications upward rather than reciprocating to their subordinates, thus reducing the amount of satisfaction derived for all parties.

A second dysfunction is that approval is sought from superiors rather than from peers in such situations. Nonperformance criteria enter the communication system, in that respect from peers, which can be earned on the basis of performance, can become secondary to approval-gaining devices that may not be central to the tasks at hand. The plethora of terms ranging from apple-polishing to more profane expressions is indicative of this.

A third dysfunction has to do with the error-correcting function of normal social interaction. Interaction among peers tends to sort out errors and at least provides a common denominator through the interaction process. This is much less likely to happen in upward communication. Subordinates are unlikely to tell a superior that they think an order or an explanation is wrong, fearing for their own positions. Criticism of one's superior is not the most popular form of communication in organizations (Blau and Scott, 1962: pp. 121–24).

These problems associated with upward communication in organizations are compounded by the factors affecting individual perception, which we discussed earlier. Since rank in an organization is a structural fact, it carries with it a strong tendency toward stereotyping. The very terms management, worker, student, general, and so on are indicative of the value loadings associated with rank. Status differences are necessary and do have their positive side; but the negative connotations attached to many of the stereotypes, and the likelihood that communications will be distorted because of real or assumed differences between statuses, build in difficulties for organizational communications.

In keeping with the earlier discussion in which it was noted that complex organizations contain paradoxes and contradictions, there are also beneficial aspects to hierarchical patterns for the communication process. The studies by Blau and his associates (1966, 1968), cited earlier, are a case in point. It will be recalled that in organizations with highly trained or professionalized personnel, a tall or deep hierarchy was associated with effectiveness. The explanation was that the hierarchy provided a continuous source of error detection and correction. The presence of experts in an organization also increases the extent of horizontal communications (Hage, Aiken, and Marrett, 1971). These can take the form of scheduled or unscheduled committee meetings or more spontaneous interactions. Communications are a vital source of coordination when organizations are staffed with a diverse set of personnel offering different forms of expertise (Brewer, 1971). If a tall hierarchy is found in an organization with a low level of differentiation in expertise, it is apparently due to the need for extensive downward communications. There is an additional aspect of hierarchy that should be noted. Unless one assumes that people always rise to a level just above that of their competence (Peter and Hull, 1969), the superiors may in fact be superior. That is, they may actually have more ability than their subordinates. If this is recognized and legitimated by the subordinates, some of the hierarchical problems are again minimized.

The most obvious contribution of a hierarchy is coordination (Hage, 1980). If one accepts the common model of communications spreading out in more detail as they move down the hierarchy, then the role of the hierarchy becomes clear. It is up to the superior to decide who gets what kind of communication and when. The superior becomes the distribution and filtering center. Given the vast amount of information that is potentially available for the total organization, this role is crucial.

HORIZONTAL COMMUNICATION

Communications in organizations go in more directions than up and down. Horizontal or lateral communication is a regular and important facet of organizational life. The focus of most analyses of communication has been the vertical axis, primarily because it was the focus of the classic writers in the field (Simpson, 1969). The horizontal component has received less attention, even though a greater proportion of the communication in an organization appears to be of this type. Simpson's study of a textile factory indicates that the lower the level in the hierarchy, the greater the proportion of horizontal communication. This is not surprising, if for no other reason than that in most organizations there are simply more people at each descending level. This fact and the already noted tendency for communication to be affected by hierarchical differences make it natural for people to communicate with those at about the same level in the organization. And those at the same level are more apt to share common characteristics, making horizontal communication even more likely.

Communication within an organizational subunit is quite different from communication between subunits. Within-unit communication is "critical for effective system functioning" (Katz and Kahn, 1978: p. 444). In most cases, it is impossible for an organization to work out in advance every conceivable facet of every task assigned throughout the organization. At some point, there will have to be coordination and discussion among a set of peers as the work proceeds. The interplay between individuals is vital in the coordination process, since the organization cannot anticipate every possible contingency. Communication within subunits contains much richer content than organizational task coordination materials. Katz and Kahn state:

> The mutual understanding of colleagues is one reason for the power of the peer group. Experimental findings are clear and convincing about the importance of socio-emotional support for people in both organized and unorganized groups. Psychological forces always push people toward communication with peers: people in the same boat share the same problems. *Hence, if there are no problems of task coordination left to a group of peers, the content of their communication can take forms which are irrelevant to or destructive of organizational functioning.* (p. 445; italics in original)

The implication here is clear. It is beneficial to leave some task-oriented communications to work groups at every level of the organization so that the potentially counterproductive communications do not arise to fill the void. This implication must be modified, however, by a reference back to the general model that is being followed here. Organizational, interpersonal, and individual factors are all part of the way people behave in organizations. If the organizational arrangements are such that horizontal communications are next to impossible, then there is little likelihood of any communication. Work in extremely noisy circumstances or in isolated work locales would preclude much interaction. (These situations, of course, contain their own problems for the individual and the organization.) On the other side of the coin, too much coordination and communications responsibility left to those who, through lack of training or ability, are unable to come to a reasonable joint decision about some matter would also be individually and organizationally disruptive.

Although it is relatively easy, in abstract terms, to describe the optimal mix of vertical and horizontal communications, another element of communications among peers should be noted. Since the communications among peers tend to be based on common understandings, and since continued communications build up the solidarity of the group, work groups develop a collective response to the world around them. This collective response is likely to be accompanied by a collective perception of communications passed to or through the work group. This collective perception can be a collective *distortion*. It is clear that work groups (as well as other interest groups) can perceive communications in a totally different light from what was intended. A relatively simple communiqué, such as a memo about possible reorganization, can be interpreted to mean that an entire workforce will be eliminated. Work groups can develop complete sets of meanings that are entirely apart from what was intended.

Interaction among peers is only one form of horizontal communication. Another form, obviously vital, occurs between members of different organizational subunits. There is little research on this subject. The principal reason seems to be that such communications are not supposed to occur. In almost every conceivable form of organization, communications are supposed to go through the hierarchy until they reach the "appropriate" office, at the point where the hierarchies of the two units involved come together. That is, the communications are designed to flow through the office that is above the two departments or units involved, so that the hierarchy is familiar with the intent and content of the communications. In a simple example, problems between production and sales are supposed to be resolved through either the office or the individual in charge of both activities.

In reality, such a procedure occurs in only a minority of such lateral communications. There is a great deal more face-to-face and memo-to-memo communication throughout the ranks of the subunits involved, primarily because the communication system would be totally clogged if all information regarding subunit interaction had to flow all the way up one of the subunits and then all the way back down another. The clogging of the system would result in either painfully slow communications or none at all.

Therefore, the parties involved generally communicate directly with each other. This saves time and can often mean a very reasonable solution worked out at a lower level with good cooperation. However, it may also mean that those further up the hierarchy are unaware of what has happened, and that can be harmful in the long run. A solution to this problem is to record and pass along the information about what has been done, but that may be neglected; even if it is not neglected, it may not be noticed.

Although the emphasis in this discussion has been on coordination between subunits, it should be clear that much of the communication of this sort is actually based on conflict. Professional departments are a good example. When professionals or experts make up divisions of an organization, their areas of expertise are likely to lead them to different conclusions about the same matter (Hage, 1974: pp. 101–24). For example, in a petroleum company it is quite conceivable that the geological, engineering, legal, and public relations divisions could all come to different conclusions about the desirability of starting new oil-well drilling in various locations. Each would be correct in its own area of expertise, and the coordination of top officials would obviously be required when a final decision had to be made. During the period of planning or development, however, communications between these divisions would probably be characterized as nonproductive, since the specialists involved would be talking their own language, one that is unfamiliar to those not in the same profession. From the evidence at hand, each division would also be correct in its assessments of the situation and would view the other divisions as not understanding the "true" meanings of the situation.

This type of communication problem is not limited to professionalized divisions. Communications between subunits inevitably contain elements of conflict. The conflict will be greater if the units involved invest values in their understanding and conceptualizations. Horizontal communications across organizational lines thus contain both the seeds and the flowers of conflict. Such conflict, by definition, will contribute to distortion of communications in one form or another. At the same time, passing each message up the line to eliminate such distortion through coordination at the top has the dangers of diluting the message in attempts to avoid conflict and of taking so much time that the message becomes meaningless. Here again, the endemic complexities of an organization preclude a totally rational operation.

Both horizontal and vertical aspects of organizations create complications for communication. At the same time, there are situations in which these obstacles are overcome. An excellent example is an analysis of aircraft carrier flight decks (Weick and Roberts, 1993). When aircraft are landing, the work pace is furious, the noise is overwhelming, and the possibility for tragic error is great. Despite these conditions, flight decks operate very effectively. Communication works across ranks and organizational divisions. Weick and Roberts believe that this is based on "heedful interrelating" and a "collective mind" (p. 357). Everyone is extremely focused. Everyone is well trained. Similar situations certainly exist with successful sports teams and in other spheres of life. At the same time, the flight-deck example is striking because it is so different. In the more mundane spheres of most real life, our vertical and horizontal factors intrude on communication.

Communication Networks

Before we turn to a more systematic examination of the consequences of all these communication problems in organizations, we should note a final bit of evidence regarding the manner in which communications evolve. The communication process can be studied in laboratory situations; among organizational characteristics, it is perhaps the most amenable to such experimentation. There has been a long history (Bavelas, 1950; Leavitt, 1951) of attempting to isolate the communication system that is most efficient under a variety of circumstances. These laboratory studies are applicable to both the vertical and the horizontal aspects of communications, since the manner in which the communication tasks are coordinated is the major focus. Three primary communication networks between members of work groups have been studied. The "wheel" pattern requires all persons at the periphery of the wheel to send their communications to the hub. This is an imposed hierarchy, since those at the periphery cannot send messages to each other; it is the task of the hub to do the coordinating. The "circle" pattern permits each member of the group to talk to those on either side, with no priorities. The "all-channel" system allows everyone to communicate with everyone else.

Using success in arriving at a correct solution as the criterion of efficiency, repeated investigations have found the wheel pattern to be superior. The other patterns can become equally efficient if they develop a hierarchy, but that takes time, and meanwhile efficiency is reduced. The more complex the task, the more time is required for the communication network to become structured. The importance of these findings for our purposes is that whether the communications are vertical or horizontal, hierarchical patterns emerge. In the vertical situation, the hierarchy is already there, although the formal hierarchy can be modified through the power considerations of expertise or personal attraction. In the horizontal situation, a hierarchy will emerge. Communication takes place on the basis of organizational structure; it also contributes to the development of structuring.

COMMUNICATION PROBLEMS

It should be clear that communications in organizations are not perfect. The basic consequence of existing communication systems is that messages are transformed or altered as they pass through the system. The fact that they are transformed means that the ultimate recipient of the message receives something different from what was originally sent, thus destroying the intent of the communication process.

Omission

There are two major forms of transformation—omission and distortion (Guetzkow, 1965). Omission involves the "deletion of aspects of messages" (p. 551), and it occurs because the recipients may not be able to grasp the entire content of the message and receive or pass on only what they are able to grasp. Communication overload, to be discussed in more detail later, can also lead to the omission of materials, since some messages may not be handled because of the overload. Omission may be intentional, as when certain classes of information are deleted from the information passed through particular segments of the organization. Omission is most evident in upward communications, since more messages are generated by the large number of people and units lower in the hierarchy. As the communications are filtered on the way up, the omissions occur. As was indicated earlier, when omissions are intentional, it is vital to know the criteria for omitting some kinds of information. Omission can occur simply as a removal of details, with the heart of the message still transmitted upward. This is the ideal, of course, but is not usually achieved, since part of the content of the message is usually omitted also.

Distortion

Distortion refers to altered meanings of messages as they pass through the organization. From the earlier discussion of perceptions, it is clear that people are selective, intentionally or unintentionally, about what they receive as messages. Guetzkow (1965) states:

... because different persons man different points of initiation and reception of messages, there is much assimilation of meanings to the context within which transmission occurs. Frames of reference at a multitude of nodes differ because of variety in personal and occupational background, as well as because of difference in viewpoint induced by the communicator's position in the organization. (p. 555)

Distortion is as likely to occur in horizontal communications as in vertical, given the differences between organizational units in objectives and values. Selective omission and distortion, or "coding," are not unique properties of organizations. They occur in all communication systems, from the family to the total society. They are crucial for organizations, however, since organizations depend upon accurate communications as a basis for decision making.

Overload

The communication problem that is perhaps more characteristic of organizations than of other social entities is communication overload. Overload leads to omission and contributes to distortion. It also leads to other coping and adjustment mechanisms on the part of the organization. There are adaptive and maladaptive adjustments to the overload situation. Omission and distortion are maladaptive. They are also normal.

Another device used when overload occurs is queuing. This technique lines up the messages by time of receipt or by some other such criterion. Queuing can have positive or negative consequences. If the wrong priority system is used, less important messages may be acted upon before those that are really crucial reach the recipient. At the same time, queuing does allow recipients to act on messages as they come in without putting them in a state of inaction because of total overload. An example of this is an anecdote from a disaster following a major earthquake. Organizations dealing with the earthquake were besieged with messages. Some organizations allowed victims to plead for help face-to-face, letting them crowd into an office and all talk at once; this quickly brought the organizations involved to a halt. The overload was so great that the communications could not be filtered in any way. Another organization received its messages by telephone, a device providing an arbitrary queuing mechanism based on an operating phone and the luck of finding an open line. This organization was able to keep functioning, because the messages came in one at a time. In such a queuing situation, of course, there are no real criteria to determine which messages get through and which do not, other than time phasing and luck in getting a phone line.

A useful modification of queuing is the previously mentioned filtering process, which involves setting priorities for messages. The critical factor here is the nature of the priorities. Many organizations utilize a modified triage system in which the most important messages are permitted to come into the system if it is perceived that the organization can take relevant actions.

Less important messages are then taken in as time permits. This sort of filtering system must be set up in advance. The question always is, what is the principle on which filtering takes place?

All the communication problems discussed derive from the fact that communications in organizations require interpretation. If there is a case of extreme overload, the interpretive process becomes inundated with so much material that it becomes inoperative. Queuing and filtering are techniques designed to sort messages into priorities. Any priority system established in advance means that an interpretation of messages has already been made, with some deemed more important than others. Thus, interpretation occurs regardless of whether priorities are set in advance or simply as messages are received.

Organizations generate and receive a vast amount of material. If we think of an organization as a pyramid, the huge mass at the base is the information entering an organization's communication system. As information moves up and through the organization, it is filtered and condensed. It arrives at the top in the form of an "executive summary." The amount of information, like the pyramid, keeps getting smaller as it rises in the organization. Here the pyramid analogy must be abandoned, since the determination of which information moves up is subject to the types of human and organizationally based interpretations we have been considering.

COMMUNICATION FROM OUTSIDE THE ORGANIZATION

The focus thus far has been internal organizational communication. The complications and problems that have been identified appear even more severe when we realize that so much of what is really important for an organization comes into it from its environment—competitors, creditors, customers, regulators, taxers, constituents, and so on. In addition, there are the more general environmental messages that are sent into an organization, such as changes in prime interest rates, demographic shifts, or petroleum price increases. We will deal with the environment in detail in Chapter 10. The point here is that communication with the environment greatly compounds the communication problems that have already been identified.

POSSIBLE SOLUTIONS

With all the problems, potential and real, in the communication process, it is obvious that a "perfect" communication system is unlikely. But although perfection, like rationality, will not be achieved, organizations do have mechanisms by which they attempt to keep the communication system as clear as they can. There are several devices that are available to reduce the distortions and other complications in the communication process (Downs, 1967). Redundancy, or the duplication of reports for verification, though adding to the flow of messages and paper in an organization, allows more people to see or hear a particular piece of information and respond to it. This is a correction device. There are several ways to create redundancy, including the use of information sources external to the situation—such as reports that are generated outside the organization itself—thus ensuring that reporting units and individuals coordinate their communications.

A common solution to at least some communication problems is the ubiquitous meeting. Meetings have the potential for yielding common meanings among participants, particularly when the intent of the meetings is to achieve consensus. Although meetings are quite valuable, it is obvious that time spent in meetings is time not spent on other activities. When I have a day filled with meetings, I have a day when I will not get any research, writing, or preparation for classes accomplished.

Another way in which communication problems can be reduced is through matrix-like systems. A study of a psychiatric hospital found committees or teams that were composed of personnel from the various occupational specialties in the hospital and from the established departments in the hospital (Blau and Alba, 1982). The teams were designed to deal with various issues and programs of the hospital, and hospital personnel served on multiple teams. In addition, traditional ranks were eliminated. For example, a team could have a nurse as the team leader and psychiatrists as team members. Blau and Alba report that these overlapping circles of weak ties inhibited segmentation and sustained participation because participants were rewarded for participating. Their data indicate that there was extensive interunit communication. There are limitations to this approach, of course. Its applicability in other forms of organizations is uncertain, and the approach requires the commitment of all the participants up through the head of the organization.

Some organizations have turned to "project groups" as a means of solving communication problems. These groups, or task forces as they are sometimes called, are typically composed of personnel from a variety of organizational units. Their usual purpose is to develop a new product or service for the organization. They may be isolated from the rest of the organization in the hope that this will enable them to think and work together. One analysis of research and development project groups composed of scientists and engineers found that such groups became increasingly isolated from key information sources within and outside their own organizations (Katz, 1982). Over time, their productivity decreased, with the communication process increasingly focused inward. Such project groups or task forces are probably better off with a short span of existence and a sunset clause specifying a termination date.

A major mechanism for achieving consensus about the meaning of communication is putting things in writing, such as contracts. Even though communication in writing is subject to interpretation, lawyers and accountants make much of their living by negotiating consensus in meanings between parties. This is not the answer for all problems, of course, but it is one way to avoid communication chaos.

The nature of, problems in, and suggested solutions for communications all point to the centrality of this process in much of what happens in an organization. But it is evident that the communication system is vitally affected by other structural and process factors. Communications do not exist outside the total organizational framework. They cannot be over- or underemphasized. More and more accurate communications do not lead inevitably to greater effectiveness for the organization. The key to the communication process in organizations is to ensure that the correct people get the correct information (in amount and quality) at the correct time. All these factors can be anticipated to some degree. If organizations, their members, and their environments were all in a steady state, communication tasks would be easier. Since obviously they are not, the communication process must be viewed as a dynamic one, with new actors, new media, and new definitions constantly entering the scene. As noted at the beginning of this chapter, ambiguities and paradoxes are to be anticipated.

The *media* of communication in organizations have received little attention in our analysis here. Breakthroughs in the forms of information and word processing, faxing, electronic message sending and receiving, and the Internet continue to be developed. Advanced communication technology itself is not the cure for organizational communication problems. The problems are rooted in the nature of organizations, their participants, and their interactions with their environments. Changing information technology will be considered further in the next chapter.

SUMMARY AND CONCLUSIONS

The communication process in organizations is a complicated one—complicated by individual idiosyncrasies, biases, and abilities and complicated by organizational characteristics such as hierarchy or specialization. Nonetheless, communications within organizations are central for the other processes of power, leadership, and decision making. Communications are shaped by organizational structure and continue to reshape structure.

The "perfect" communication system is yet to be devised and probably never will be. Technological changes in various forms have contributed to the processing of information, but the issues and problems considered in this chapter are not erased by advanced technology; in fact, in some instances they are exacerbated.

Less-than-perfect communication systems and the search for improvements contribute to both changes and innovations in organizations. Change and innovation are related to more than communications, however, and it is to this topic that we now turn.

chapter 9

Change

The analyses of power, leadership, decision making, and communication have shown that organizations are dynamic. In this chapter we will analyze the ways in which organizations change and the reasons that change does and does not take place. At times change is virtually forced on an unwilling organization, and at other times change is openly embraced and sought. Change can be beneficial or detrimental to organizations. Change can bring growth or decline or an alteration in form. The analysis of change has become a dominant focus in organizational research and theorizing. Change can lead to greater effectiveness, or just the opposite. Several alternative and competing views of change will be considered in the analyses that follow.

THE NATURE OF ORGANIZATIONAL CHANGE

Organizational change can be approached from a number of directions. It can be seen from an internal political perspective, with constantly shifting coalitions and factions (Kanter, Stein, and Jick, 1992). It can also be viewed from a historical or developmental perspective, with markets entered and controlled and with ownership shifting over time (Kochan and Useem, 1992).

Another approach is to examine the "life cycle" of organizations (Kimberly and Miles, 1980). The use of this biological metaphor, though imperfect, sensitizes us to the fact that organizations do not go along in the same state for eternity. "Organizations are born, grow, and decline. Sometimes they reawaken, and sometimes they disappear" (Kimberly and Miles, p. ix).

This fact, of course, is well recognized in the stock market, as investors try to determine which organizations are in a growth phase and which are in a decline phase. Although organizational analysts are now turning to an analysis of phenomena such as the organizational life cycle, we have not yet developed the tools by which we can ascertain exactly where an organization is in the cycle at a particular time. If we could, of course, we should probably stop being academic organizational analysts and become full-time stock market investors. That consideration aside, growth and decline are important components of organizational change. A modified life-cycle approach will be used in this chapter.

Organizational change can be defined as "the alteration and transformation of the form so as to survive better in the environment" (Hage, 1980: p. 262). This is a good definition of organizational change, with a major exception. The exception is that Hage does not consider organizational goals in this formulation of change. As will be argued in detail at a later point, analyses of organizations that do not include goals are shortsighted, since organizations engage in many activities and make many decisions that are *not* related to survival in the environment but *are* related to goals.

Organizational survival, or the avoidance of death, is, of course, the ultimate test of an organization, but at any time, unless death is imminent, what goes on in an organization is based on both environmental pressures and goals. Changes are made to make more profit or to secure more members. These have both an environmental and a goal relationship.

The distinction between environmentally and goal-based change is at the heart of the major theoretical arguments currently being waged in organizational theory. We will address and comment on these debates but will not resolve them. We will begin with a consideration of the potential for change within organizations.

The Potential for Change

Some analysts view organizations as being in constant flux. Child and Kieser (1981) state:

> Organizations are constantly changing. Movements in external conditions such as competition, innovation, public demand, and governmental policy require that new strategies, methods of working, and outputs be devised for an organization merely to continue at its present level of operations. Internal factors also promote change in that managers and other members of an organization may seek not just its maintenance but also its growth, in order to secure improved benefits and satisfactions for themselves. (p. 28)

Although we may agree or disagree in regard to the attribution of managerial motivation, Child and Kieser's conclusion is that organizations are constantly in motion. An alternative and highly individualized approach to the potential for change sees individuals as constantly learning and unlearning from their actions. It views the organization as the stage on which that learning takes place; consequently, it views the organization as learning and unlearning (Hedberg, 1981).

The individual can also be taken as the point of departure for the diametrically opposed position that organizations have *limited* potential for change. For example, individuals can get locked into courses of action. Their commitment to courses of action can escalate when they have already invested previous efforts. They defend their turf and their previous behaviors by continuing to act in the same manner (Staw, 1982). At the organizational level, Staw notes that standard operating procedures are difficult to change and that powerful coalitions exist that will block change if it is not in their interests. Programs can be in motion that have the backing of key figures in the organization ("It's the president's baby"). In Staw's view there are thus individual and collective or organizational counterforces to change.

Organizational personnel are a potential source of inertia in another way. When personnel are selected on the basis of reliability and accountability, organizational structures become "reproducible." This means that the same organizational forms will remain in place because there is no differentiation among the personnel. This tendency toward inertia because of commonalties in personnel is more likely in larger, older, and more complex organizations (Hannan and Freeman, 1984).

The matter is not that simple, however. We have stressed that paradoxes and contradiction are inherent in organizations. That is borne out in the case of change. Consider large organizations. On the one hand, they are likely to have the resources necessary for changes such as entering new markets. On the other hand, they are likely to be more bureaucratic and thus resistant to change (Haveman, 1993).

Another important consideration for the potential for change is the personnel composition or organizational demography within an organization (Pfeffer, 1983). Organizational demography is affected both by organizational policies on compensation, promotion, and the like and by environmental factors such as the rate of growth of the industry in which an organization operates. Organizational demographic characteristics in turn affect the patterns of change, since they will have an impact on succession and power differences among age cohorts.

One of the premier analysts of organizational change has been Herbert Kaufman (1971), who states:

> In short, I am not saying that organizational change is invariably good or bad, progressive or conservative, beneficial or injurious. It may run either way in any given instance. But it is always confronted by strong forces holding it in check and sharply circumscribing the capacity of organizations to react to new conditions—sometimes with grave results. (p. 8)

Kaufman goes on to describe the factors within organizations that resist change. These include the "collective benefits of stability" or familiarity with existing patterns, "calculated opposition to change" by groups within the organization who may have altruistic or selfish motivations, and a simple "inability to change" (pp. 8–23). The last point refers to the fact that organizations develop "mental blinders" that preclude change capability. This happens as personnel are selected and trained to do what was done in the past in the manner in which it was done in the past. Some people attribute the earlier difficulties of American automobile manufacturers to just this factor. People were hired and trained into executive positions from only one mold. Change is resisted because it is uncomfortable and threatening.

The basic point is that organizations by their very nature are conservative. Even organizations that try to have a radical impact on society demonstrate this conservatism. The history of the Christian religion or Communist regimes is one of conservatism, with deviants subject to inquisitions, purges, or exile in Siberia.

There are additional factors that contribute to resistance to change. Kaufman (1971: pp. 23–39) calls them "systemic obstacles" to change. These are obstacles within the overall system in which organizations operate. They include such factors as "sunk costs," or investments in the status quo; the accumulation of official constraints on behavior, such as laws and regulations; unofficial and unplanned constraints on behavior in the form of informal customs; and interorganizational agreements, such as labor-management contracts.

Another systemic obstacle to change is that organizations may not have the financial or personnel resources to engage in change efforts even if the need is identified. Despite all these obstacles, of course, organizations do change. They sustain pressures that lead to both inertia and adaptability (Gersick, 1994). These dialectical pressures for and against change are not counterbalanced.

THE CHANGE PROCESS

There are multiple explanations for change in organizations. Kaufman (1971) concludes that change takes place through personnel turnover. Despite careful selection and training, successive generations of organizational personnel are not clones of one another.

At other times change is literally forced on an organization by the environment. The requirements of affirmative action have drastically altered many organizations, as have pollution control regulations. Organizations are sometimes driven to incorporate policies and practices that are a part of the prevailing ethos in the society in which they are embedded (Meyer and Rowan, 1977). The environment has institutionalized concepts of how organizations should operate, and this leads organizations to incorporate the institutionalized practices. An empirical extension of this line of reasoning analyzed the adoption of civil service reforms in city governments for the time period 1880–1935. This research found that the speed of the adoption of a policy or programs is to a great extent determined by the extent to which the change is institutionalized by law, which leads to quicker change, or by legitimation, which is a more gradual process (Tolbert and Zucker, 1983).

Although there may be a legal mandate to make a change, it does not simply happen. This was documented in an analysis of the enormous power struggles that took place within the U.S. Postal Service in 1970 and 1971 (Biggart, 1977). Biggart concludes: "The reorganization of the U.S. Postal Service unleashed incredible forces both in and out of the organization; the forces were aimed at protecting or consolidating the power of interest groups" (p. 423). This conclusion is in line with analyses that emphasize the importance of interest groups within organizations.

The idea of "punctuated equilibrium" is a useful way to conceptualize the dialectical play of forces operating for and against change in organizations (Romanelli and Tushman, 1994). Organizations go through relatively long periods of stability. These are punctuated by short periods or bursts of fundamental change, which are in turn followed by another period of stability.

Organizational Change Cycles

This section will closely follow the idea of organizational life cycles that was noted earlier. The life-cycle approach of birth, transformations, and death has informed a great deal of organizational theory, but the biological analogy is potentially confusing. The human species, for example, has a largely predictable life span, whereas organizations do not. The life expectancy of humans can be threatened or extended by their own actions or inactions. This is also true for organizations, but they have the potential to last much longer than individuals—indeed, this is one of the predominant characteristics of organizations. Hypothetically, organizations could last indefinitely. There is only one method of human conception, but organizations can be created by entrepreneurs and by legislatures. Organizations can also be created by other organizations, as when subsidiaries are founded by a parent organization. Subsidiaries are often used to try out a new product or service. We will thus utilize the life-cycle terminology, without completely accepting the analogy.

Births and Foundings.   An organizational birth is the "creation of an operating entity that acquires inputs from suppliers and provides outputs to a given public (customers, clients, patients, etc.)" (Delacroix and Carroll, 1983: p. 276). Births also take place through legislative actions as government organizations are born. Research has documented the fact that environmental conditions, such as the characteristics of metropolitan areas for industrial firms (Pennings, 1982), state policies for railroads (Dobbin and Dowd, 1997), the existing density of organizations for women's medical societies (Marrett, 1980) and for life insurance companies (Budros, 1993), and political turbulence for newspapers (Delacroix and Carroll, 1983), have been closely related to the birth frequencies for the organizations studied.

The term "founding" has now replaced "birth" in the literature, apparently as a reaction to the biological analogy. A later study of the data on newspapers suggests that political turbulence serves as part of the institutional environment or value system in which the newspapers are embedded (Carroll and Huo, 1986). This institutional environment affects both organizational foundings and organizational failures. Preexisting organizations in an environment provide important resources for similar new organizations—the preexisting organizations serve as sources of legitimation and domain definition (Wiewel and Hunter, 1985). This line of reasoning is taken a few steps further by Hannan and Freeman (1987). In a study of American labor unions, they found that the founding rate varies with the number of other recent union foundings in a curvilinear manner. A surge of recent foundings leads to imitation and more foundings and then a competition for scarce resources. The irony is that a big surge in foundings exhausts resources and thus limits future foundings.

The social environments of organizations thus affect their rates of founding. Environments also have long-lasting effects into the futures of organizations. It must be reiterated that this is also true for organizations created by an arm of government. For example, the Morrill Act of 1862, which established land-grant colleges, has had a continuing effect on those particular colleges and on higher education in general.

There is agreement among organizational analysts that a combination of available resources, supportive government policies, and legitimation in the form of cultural values is necessary for organizational foundings (Dobbin and Dowd, 1997; Fligstein and Mara-Drita, 1996; Delacroix and Rao, 1994; Hannan et al, 1995; Baum and Powell, 1995; Hannan and Carroll, 1995). This combination of explanations brings together organizational theories (population ecology, resource dependence, and institutional) in a more powerful explanation than if a single theory could be.

There is one more important step in understanding organizational foundings. The environment at the time of founding and the characteristics of the *founder* had important implications for the structure of a medical school (Kimberly, 1979). Bringing the founder back into the equation is necessary for a complete understanding of the process. Founders must adopt strategies that are appropriate for the environment that is faced (Romanelli, 1989; Boeker, 1989).

Transformations.   Once born, organizations change. The most likely change is death, since new organizations have exceptionally high death rates (Carroll and Delacroix, 1982; Freeman, Carroll, and Hannan, 1983; Starbuck and Nystrom, 1981). New organizations are usually small and suffer a liability of newness—just think of all the new restaurants that come and go (Freeman, Carroll, and Hannan, 1983). A high mortality rate is also found among new government organizations, contrary to popular opinion (Starbuck and

Nystrom, 1981). Population ecology theorists ascribe the high death rate among new organizations to their inability to find or carve a niche in their environment (McKelvey, 1982; McKelvey and Aldrich, 1983).

Ecological theory also has a great deal to say about subsequent transformations that take place among the organizations that do survive. A basic premise of ecological theory is that organizations adapt to their environment (Hannan and Freeman, 1977a, 1997b; Aldrich, 1979; McKelvey, 1982; McKelvey and Aldrich, 1983; Kasarda and Bidwell, 1984; Bidwell and Kasarda, 1985; Baum, 1996; Baum and Singh, 1996).

The ecological perspective has a second basic premise: that organizations and organizational forms are selected by the environment for survival. Again, the analogy is that of biological systems, with a heavy emphasis on evolution and "natural selection." In the discussion that follows, I will utilize McKelvey and Aldrich's (1983) summary of the ecological framework.

McKelvey and Aldrich present four principles that operate in the ecological process. These principles determine which organizations will survive and which will not. The first principle is that of variation. Any sort of change is a variation. Variations can be purposeful or blind.

> Purposeful variations occur as an intentional response, when environmental pressures cause selection of adaptations. Blind variations are those that occur independent of environmental or selection pressures; they are not the result of an intentional response to adaptation pressures but rather occur by accident or chance. (p. 114)

Organizational analysts are essentially split on the extent to which variations are blind or purposeful. Any consideration of purposefulness would have to consider the problems of decision making that were specified in Chapter 7. Despite the problems surrounding decision making, I believe that the evidence favors at least a moderate degree of purposefulness, as will be documented in a later section.

The second principle is that of natural selection. Variations differ in the degree to which they enable organizations to acquire resources from the environment. Useless or harmful variations are likely to bring in fewer resources and thus reduce the chances of survival. With the passage of time, organizations that survive are likely to have beneficial variations. Resource acquisition involves much more than financial resources, although they are of crucial importance. Other resources include personnel, power, political support, and legitimation.

The third principle is that of retention and diffusion. This involves the passing of competencies (knowledge and skills) on to succeeding members of organizations over generations. Competencies are those that have enabled organizations to survive in the first place. Competencies are diffused to other organizations as skilled and knowledgeable people change jobs and work for new and different organizations. Competencies are retained by the information flows within organizations and involve formal and informal training. In a study of the microcomputer, cement, and airline industries, Tushman and Anderson (1986) found that technological breakthroughs can enhance or destroy organizational competencies. Knowledge and skills can become highly valuable or obsolete on the basis of technological change.

The final principle is that of the struggle for existence. This involves competing with other organizations for scarce resources. As McKelvey and Aldrich note, there are periods in which resources are unusually rich for some organizations. They cite the example of solar energy companies before the Reagan administration. These organizations had tax credit and government subsidies to the extent that almost any organization could enter the field and survive. With the Reagan administration cutbacks, there was a greatly increased mortality rate among these firms.

Another concept from the ecological perspective is the niche in which organizations survive. (Bidwell and Kasarda, 1985: pp. 52–65, have a useful discussion of this concept.) Organizations enter niches in the environment. The niche contains the resources for the organization and is likely to contain other organizations fighting for the same resources. The organization that survives is the one that can make the adaptations that enable it to overcome or at least coexist with its competitors. These adaptations are organizational change.

The ecological perspective on change is a powerful explanation of the change process. Few would argue that resource acquisition within a competitive environment is not crucial for all organizations. The key aspect of this approach, for our purposes, involves variation. I have already argued that variation is more purposeful than some ecological theorists believe. An organization can take steps to safeguard or enhance its position in its environment (Baum and Singh, 1996). These steps include the following:

(a) securing the benefits of growth, (b) enhancing competitive power or public approval through efficiency and rationalization or through the incorporation of technological progress, (c) establishing a secure domain in the environment through the negotiation of agreement as to the legitimate field of activity for the organization to occupy or through the finding of ecological niches—areas of activity that are relatively protected and which suit an organization's specific competences, and (d) the creation of the capacity to respond flexibly to external change through the improvement of management techniques. (Child and Kieser, 1981: p. 32)

These suggestions contain an element that weakens the ecological argument. This is the point that an organization can develop agreements with other organizations that lessen competition. Although antitrust legislation diminishes the ability to establish monopolies, organizations do reach agreements to minimize survival-threatening competition. The presence of trade associations, which are designed to cope with forces and demands that firms within an industry face, is an example of that (Staber and Aldrich, 1983). Another example is intercollegiate athletic conferences, such as the Big 10 or the Ivy

League. Long-term contracts are another device for reducing environmental effects. Singh, Tucker, and House (1986) found that voluntary social service organizations could enhance their likelihood of surviving by obtaining legitimation from the environment. They interpreted this finding as support for both the population ecology and the institutional perspectives. There is additional research that points to bringing potential threatening forces into boards of directors and other such interorganizational linkages as techniques that can buffer an organization against its environment (Goodstein and Boeker, 1991; Miner, Amburgey, and Steams, 1990).

In addition to agreements with other organizations, organizations have constituents who work for organizational survival. In their interestingly titled book, *Permanently Failing Organizations*, Meyer and Zucker (1989) document how workers, customers, and communities can fight to keep an organization going in the face of evidence that it is about to die. Examples here would include employees buying out a failing firm, church members fighting an archdiocese and keeping a parish church open, and communities fighting to prevent plant closings.

There is yet another component of organizational transformation that a totally ecological perspective misses. This is the movement into new areas of activity. Kimberly and Quinn (1984) capture this idea well in their comments on transitions:

> A transition is a major change in organizational strategy, structure, or process. Transitions can be precipitated by a variety of factors, such as declines in performance, perceptions of new opportunities, changes in legislation, or the development of new technologies. They may take a variety of forms, such as increasing formalization of structure, redefining principal operating units, broadening or narrowing market definitions, or engineering a shift in culture. (p. 1)

According to Kimberly and Quinn, transitions can take the form of restructuring the organization, repositioning the organization in its marketplace or environment, and revitalizing an organization that is slipping. Although our interest is not in management, as is Kimberly and Quinn's, their point that organizations can take actions that are not necessarily related to environmental pressures is vital for our considerations. This involves a form of entrepreneurism within the organization. Entrepreneurism involves the process of unprogrammed recombinations of preexisting elements of reality (Peterson, 1981: p. 65). It is also possible to conceive of programmed recombinations. Peterson correctly notes that such entrepreneurship can take place outside business firms. Government agencies and universities can be quite entrepreneurial, for example, in their contracting arrangements. These new forms can again develop without environmental pressures.

There is another element that has been missing in this discussion of change: the role of decision makers (managers) as they monitor and interpret the environment (Rao and Neilsen, 1992; Isabella, 1990). Organizations that are doing poorly often change management teams. New management teams bring strategies with them and thus contribute to organizational change (Boeker, 1997a, 1997b).

These last few paragraphs have been arguing against a totally environmentally based perspective on change. This is not meant to downplay the importance of the environment but, rather, to emphasize that the environment is only one source of change. Two leading population ecologists (Carroll and Hannan, 1989) have recognized this point by noting that environments differ in their degree of density. In highly dense and competitive situations, environmental pressures are greatest. Later research on breweries sheds some additional light on the density issue (Carroll and Wade, 1991). At one time breweries were more likely to be founded in more dense urban areas than in less dense rural areas. The development of refrigeration changed that and led to more founding of breweries in rural areas and more mortality (deaths) in urban areas.

In less dense situations, there is less competition and more emphasis on achieving legitimation from sources in the environment. This argument is a key component of the institutional model. Organizational change takes place as sources of legitimation shift.

Organizational transformation thus takes place for a variety reasons. Contemporary research is now overwhelmingly supporting the view that ecological processes (particularly competition), governmental policies, and the institutional processes of legitimization of new organizational forms work together in producing organizational change (Grant, 1995; Haunschild, 1993; Sutton et al., 1994, Barnett and Carroll, 1995; Fligstein and Freedland, 1995; Kraatz and Zajac; Stearns and Allan, 1996; Haveman and Rao, 1997). These external sources of change are brought into the organization and change takes place, primarily by decisions made at the management level (Kelly and Amburgey, 1991; Mentzer and Near, 1992; Miller and Chen, 1994; Hage et al., 1993). As was noted in the chapter on decision making, decisions are not necessarily "rational." As is the case in decision making in general, the embeddedness of managers in social networks contributes to both the content of change decisions and the orientations of managers toward change itself (Palmer et al., 1995; Palmer, Barber, and Zhou, 1995; Fligstein, 1995; Davis and Greve, 1997; Bacharach, Bamberger and Sonnenstuhl, 1996).

There is a final element of the transformation process. Organizational change can happen by *accident* (March, 1981). Things just happen. In summary, then, transformations occur because of environmental forces, by accident, and by attempts at rational choice.

Once organizations do transform or change, an interesting question arises: Does the new organizational form "set back the clock" and make the organization vulnerable because of a new liability of newness (Delacroix and Swaminathan, 1991; Amburgey, Kelly, and Barnett, 1993; Haveman, 1992). Although the evidence is inconclusive, it appears that factors such as organizational size and resources overcome this threat of "new newness."

Deaths.   The idea of organizational death or mortality is important in the organizational literature (Baum and Singh, 1994).

What is an organizational death? The question may seem trivial because all agree on the unproblematic case: an organizational death occurs when an organization fails, closes down its operations, and disbands its constituent elements. But what about mergers? When two organizations combine, at least one ceases to exist and this must be considered a death. If the merger involves a dominant partner that has absorbed the resources of the other partner, then the subordinate organization dies and the dominant organization experiences a change in structure. If, however, neither merger partner assumes a dominant position, it is difficult to assign a death to one organization and a structural alteration to the other. Instead, it is useful to consider the resulting organization as new and the two merger partners as dead. (Carroll and Delacroix, 1982, p. 170)

Organizational death is the ultimate outcome of organizational decline, a process which itself has received a great deal of attention. Cameron, Kim, and Whetten (1987) define organizational decline as "a condition in which a substantial, absolute decrease in an organization's resource base occurs over a specified period of time" (p. 224). Weitzel and Jonsson (1989) suggest that there are five stages in the decline process. These are illustrated in Figure 9–1.

In this portrayal of the decline process, the first stage of decline occurs when the organization is blind to the signs of decline. The second stage occurs when the organization recognizes the need for change but takes no action. In the third stage, actions are taken, but they are inappropriate. The fourth stage is the crisis, and the final stage is dissolution.

Another highly graphic depiction of the decline process has been presented by Hambrick and D'Aveni (1988). They picture decline into failure as a downward spiral, as seen in Figure 9–2.

Here the decline process is seen as weaknesses in organizational slack and performance, followed by extreme and vacillating strategies that lead to further problems. Lest these last two studies be taken as proof that all organizations are in a decline phase, it should be noted that Hambrick and D'Aveni's study matched fifty-seven firms that went bankrupt with another fifty-seven firms that survived.

Organizational deaths are usually seen as the outcome of the decline process. This is only partially accurate (Carroll and Delacroix, 1982). Many merger partners are actually highly successful—who would want to merge with a failing organization? The many hostile corporate takeovers of recent years indicate the attractiveness of some organizations to others for the sake of merger (Morrill, 1991). Death is thus not necessarily the outcome of failure, but it is the end of the organizational change cycle.

The process of death itself is not simple. An examination of dying organizations in both the private and the public sectors found that there were repeated social occasions, such as parties and picnics, that accompanied the deaths (Harris and Sutton, 1986). The organizations included academic units,

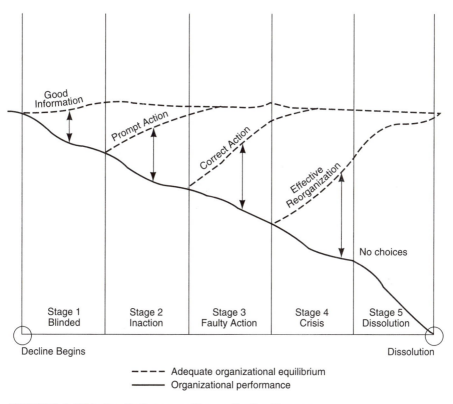

FIGURE 9–1 Widening Performance Gap as Decline Deepens
Source: Reprinted from "Decline in Organizations: A Literature Integration and Extension" by William Weitzel and Ellen Jonsson, published in *Adminstrative Science Quarterly*, 34, no. 1 (March, 1989), 102. By permission of *Administrative Science Quarterly*, © 1989.

stores, manufacturing firms, and a hospital. Some were free-standing, independent organizations, and others were part of larger organizations. In all cases, organizational deaths were traumatic for the people involved.

A further analysis of the same cases revealed that death has widespread repercussions (Sutton, 1987). For some organizations, debts were not paid, thus affecting other organizations. In other instances, the personnel from the dead organizations reconnected in new organizations. Organizational death is painful and complicated.

In this discussion of organizational change cycles, and now with a consideration of organizational deaths, we should not lose sight of the fact that many large and powerful organizations persist. The Roman Catholic Church is the best example of that. Organizational longevity has not received as much attention as decline and death, but it would be well worthy of study.

There have been studies of organizational survival in the face of strong threats. These studies suggest that the presence of institutional linkages with

Figure 9–2 Organizational Decline as a Downward Spiral
Source: Reprinted from "Large Corporate Failures and Downward Spirals" by Donald C. Hambrick and Richard A. D'Aveni, published in *Administrative Science Quarterly*, 33, no. 1 (March 1988), 14. By permission of *Administrative Science Quarterly*, © 1988.

powerful organizations for day care centers (Baum and Oliver, 1991, 1992), a focus on outputs and customer needs in business firms (D'Aveni and MacMillan, 1990), and prior records of success in Irish and Argentinean newspapers (Leventhal, 1991) contribute to survival. To make matters more confusing, Wholey, Christianson, and Sanchez (1992) report that midsized health maintenance organizations are more at risk than small or large HMOs because the midsized organizations cannot compete. This maze of rather confusing findings is reported to suggest that our research evidence does not really have an answer for *why* organizations survive. Survival is not random, but what works for one type of organization might not work for another, which brings us back to the idea that a useful typology of organizations is sorely needed.

The same array of considerations that were discussed in the section on transformations is operative in organizational deaths. Just as institutional legitimation is important for transformations, deinstitutionalization contributed to the decline and fall of the conglomerate form of business firm (Davis, Diekmann, and Tinsley, 1994). Population ecology theory would emphasize that the loss of niche leads to death. Organizational death has multiple explanations, which operate simultaneously, just as our analysis of other organizational processes demonstrates.

INNOVATION IN ORGANIZATIONS

We will now narrow our focus and consider innovations in organizations. The focus is narrower here because an innovation may have an impact on only a small part of an organization. An innovation is a departure from existing practices or technologies and represents a significant departure from the state of the art at the time it appears (Kimberly, 1981). Innovations range from minor variations in current practices to radical departures that call for major reorientations (Pennings, 1987: p. 6). The practice of organizational downsizing is a drastic form of innovation that has had repercussions that reach far beyond the downsized organization (Budros, forthcoming).

Most analyses of innovation have focused on the technological side of the coin, such as the patterns by which hospitals adopt new medical techniques or the patterns of utilization of computers. Other forms of innovation involve organizational or administrative practices. In a study of administrative practices and technological innovations in libraries, Damanpour and Evan (1984) found that technological innovations were adopted at a faster rate than innovations involving administrative practices. At the same time, adoption of an administrative innovation tended to trigger the adoption of technological innovations more readily than the reverse.

The interplay between technological and administrative innovations is illustrated by analyses that study management information systems. As organizations bring information technology into increasing use (technological innovation), they are able to decrease the number of organizational levels and personnel needed to process information (administrative innovation) (Thach and Woodman, 1994).

This interplay is graphically illustrated in Figure 9–3. The information technology (IT) industry develops new hardware and software, which organizations adopt to remain competitive and also because they copy one another. As these changes take place, organizations put pressure on the IT industry, which develops even newer hardware and software, and the cycle starts again.

Innovations within an organization are not random; innovation occurs in relation to the past and present conditions of the organization. Three forms of innovation can take place in organizations. The first is the *programmed* innovation that is planned through product or service research and development. *Nonprogrammed* innovations occur when there is "slack" in the organization; that is, more resources are available than are presently needed. Those resources are then used for innovative purposes. The innovations are nonprogrammed because the organization cannot really anticipate when extra resources will be available. Innovation is *distressed* when it is forced on the organization, such as when a crisis is perceived and new actions are taken. Innovations can develop within the organization or be imposed upon it by forces in the environment (Zaltman, Duncan, and Holbek, 1973).

The characteristics of the innovation itself are of critical importance in determining whether or not it will be adopted. Zaltman, Duncan, and Holbek note that the following characteristics of an innovation make it more or less attractive and thus more or less likely to be utilized by an organization:

1. Cost. Cost factors involve two elements, the economic and the social. Economic costs include the initial cost of adopting an innovation or a new program and the continuing costs of keeping it in operation. Social costs involve changed status arrangements within the organization as individuals and groups gain or lose power because of the new developments. Either type of cost is likely to be viewed as exorbitant by opponents and minimized by proponents of a proposed change.

FIGURE 9–3 IT Is Implemented Both as a Response to External Competition and to Institutional Influence.

IT INDUSTRY

(Competitive, Changes Need)

(Coercive, Creates Need)

ORGANIZATIONS

(Competitive, Mimetic, Normative)

2. Return on Investment. It is obvious that innovations will be selected that will yield high returns on investments. The situation is much more difficult when an innovation or a technological policy is in the nonbusiness sector.

3. Efficiency. The more efficient innovation will be selected over the less efficient status quo situation or alternative innovation.

4. Risk and Uncertainty. The less the risk and uncertainty, the greater the likelihood of adopting an innovation.

5. Communicability. The clarity of the results is associated with likelihood of innovation.

6. Compatibility. The more compatible the innovation is with the existing system, the more likely it is to be adopted. This, of course, implies that organizations are likely to be conservative in their innovations or technological policies, since what is compatible is unlikely to be radical.

7. Complexity. More complex innovations are less likely to be adapted. Again, this is a strain toward conservatism.

8. Scientific Status. If an innovation is perceived to have sound scientific status, it is more likely to be adopted.

9. Perceived Relative Advantage. The greater the advantage, the more likely that the innovation will be adopted.

10. Point of Origin. Innovations are more likely to be adopted if they originate within the organization. This is based at least partially on the perceived credibility of the source of the innovation.

11. Terminality. This involves the timing of the innovation. In some cases, an innovation is worthwhile only if it is adopted at a particular time or in a particular sequence in the organization's operations.

12. Status Quo Ante. This refers to whether or not the decision to innovate is reversible. Can there be a return to the previous state of the organization, or is the decision irreversible? A related question is whether or not the innovation or technological policy is divisible. Can a little bit at a time be tried, or does a total package have to be adopted?

13. Commitment. This involves behaviors and attitudes toward the innovation. Participation in the decision to innovate tends to raise the commitment of organizational members toward the innovation. A higher level of commitment is associated with more successful innovation.

14. Interpersonal Relations. If an innovation or a technological policy is likely to be disruptive to interpersonal relationships, it is less likely to be adopted.

15. Publicness versus Privateness. If an innovation is likely to affect a large part of the public, it will typically involve a larger decision-making body than an innovation that is limited to a private party. The larger decision-making body will tend to impede adoption.

16. Gatekeepers. This refers to the number of steps of approval an innovation must pass through. Must it pass through several or only one or two? The greater the number of gatekeepers, the more likely that an innovation will be turned down.

17. Susceptibility to Successive Modification. If an innovation itself can be modified as conditions or the technology changes, it stands more chance of adoption. This is related to the idea of reversibility, since the organization is not "locked" into a path that might begin to move away from the original objective.

18. Gateway Capacity. The adoption of one innovation or the development of a technological policy is likely to lead to the capacity to involve the organization in additional such actions.

19. Gateway Innovations. This refers to the fact that some innovations, even small changes in an organization's structure, can pave the way for additional innovations. (pp. 33–45)

What these characteristics suggest, of course, is that the less radical innovations are the ones most likely to be adopted. Innovations do not arrive at an organization's doorstep with adoption automatic. Instead, innovation characteristics interact with organizational characteristics, and both innovation characteristics and organizational conditions are embedded in an environmental situation (Damanpour, 1991).

Organizational Characteristics.   The characteristics of the innovation interact with the characteristics of the innovating organization. Hage and Aiken (1970) have found that the following organizational characteristics are related to high levels of innovation:

1. High complexity in the professional training of organizational members.
2. High decentralization of power.
3. Low formalization.
4. Low stratification in the differential distribution of rewards (if high stratification is present, those with high rewards are likely to resist change).
5. A low emphasis on volume (as opposed to quality) of production.
6. A low emphasis on efficiency in the cost of production or service.
7. A high level of job satisfaction on the part of organizational members. (pp. 30–61)

In a continuation of this line of reasoning, it is argued that more radical innovations will occur when there is a high concentration of cosmopolitan professionals or specialists. The values of the dominant coalition also are critical. If these values are prochange, then innovation is more likely (Hage, 1980: pp. 205–6).

Further research supplements the directions taken here. The adoption of innovations is related to organizational size, specialization, differentiation, and decentralization. The values of lower-level decision makers must also be considered, since their perspectives and interests must also be compatible with the innovation (Moch, 1976; Moch and Morse, 1977).

There is some controversy regarding the relative importance of organizational characteristics and the attitudes of organizational members. Baldridge and Burnham (1975), for example, have argued that organizational characteristics are more important to the innovation process than the attitudes of the members of the organization. Hage and Dewar (1973) argue the opposite, that the values of the elites in organizations are more important than structural characteristics. This is another example of the chicken-egg situation, since the interaction of elite values and organizational characteristics is undoubtedly what leads to high or low rates of change. For example, a highly specialized organization headed by a dominant coalition that favors change is much more likely to change than a nonspecialized organization headed by a coalition that values stability. Other combinations of organizational characteristics and elite values would yield different rates of change.

The role of elite values can perhaps be seen more clearly if the process of change and innovation is viewed as a political process within the organization. In a study of the Teacher Corps, a federal program of the 1960s, Corwin (1973) found that the training programs were affected by the political economy of the colleges and universities involved. The economic conditions and the internal politics of the organizations involved affected how the innovation was adopted. Organizations are characterized by power struggles. The outcome of these struggles, together with organizational characteristics, determines whether or not a particular change will be made.

Not surprisingly, the environment in which the innovation and the organization are found is an important consideration. A study done during a period of growth found that innovation increased as incentives for innovation increased, the efficiency of organizational mechanisms for developing innovative alternatives increased, and the presence of organizational characteristics enabling innovation increased (Daft and Becker, 1978). This was a study of schools during a period of relative affluence, when schools were being encouraged by federal policies and funds to try new programs.

An analysis of the rates of adoption of innovations among hospitals found that the better the hospitals' linkages with other hospitals, the higher the rates of innovation (Goes and Park, 1977).

Another study examined innovation in periods of adversity. Manns and March (1978) looked at university departments and found that under adversity, departments tended to increase the variety of course offerings, provide more attractive packaging, make courses more accessible, and increase course benefits, through such mechanisms as more credits and higher grades. A key finding of this study was that strong departments responded to adversity with fewer innovations than weaker ones. The point here is that in adversity the less successful programs had to innovate more, whereas the stronger programs were insulated from adversity. The stronger programs had access to alternative resources, such as federal grants.

The innovation process itself is not simple. Zaltman, Duncan, and Holbeck (1973) identified two stages in the innovation process—initiation and implementation. Hage (1980: pp. 209–10) expands the process to four stages—evaluation, initiation, implementation, and routinization. Regardless of the number of stages, there is agreement that successful innovation requires different organizational arrangements for each stage. Thus, decentralization might be more desirable in the initiation stage, whereas a more centralized approach might be more appropriate for the implementation stage.

As noted earlier, innovation can essentially be forced on an organization by other organizations. A study of hospitals and medical-device manufacturers documents this. The proliferation of performance standards for hospitals, based largely on federal regulations, has made the use of medical devices, such as body scanners, mandatory in hospitals. Because the quality and reliability of the devices is controlled by the manufacturers, not the hospitals, the hospitals are growing increasingly dependent on the medical-device manufacturers. Instead of deciding on their own to adopt medical devices, hospitals are being forced to do so (McNeil and Minihan, 1977).

There is an additional environmental influence on innovation. Governmental policies can encourage or discourage innovation (Hall, 1981). Japanese governmental policies—including tax, trade, tariff, and regulatory policies— were, at one time, much better coordinated and more conducive to innovation than those of the United States (Holden, 1980). The result was rapid and intense innovation by Japanese business firms.

We have now identified organizational characteristics, elite or dominant coalition values, and environmental conditions as critical factors in the adoption of innovations and in change itself. This has been largely a structural approach to change and innovation.

An alternative approach to these issues is provided by Weick (1979). He views organizations as constantly changing or "enacting" entities. He recognizes the importance of factors such as size and technology but places much greater emphasis on individual perception and interpretation than has been the case in this analysis. In Weick's approach, constantly shifting constructions of reality within the organization mean that the organization is fluid as the environment is interpreted and enacted. I view organizations as much less fluid, with both structural factors and power arrangements playing key roles in the inhibition of change and innovation. Organizations do tend toward conservatism.

SUMMARY AND CONCLUSIONS

This chapter has examined the sources and processes of change within organizations. We found that although it is useful to focus on environmental pressures as a source of change, it is impossible to ignore internal sources of organizational change. Organizations have varying potential for change. Both individual and organizational characteristics inhibit and encourage change. We have considered organizational change cycles. In this we borrowed heavily from the ecological approach to organizations, since, despite its limitations, it offers strong insights into the change process.

The chapter has also analyzed the innovation process from the perspective that there are innovation and organizational characteristics that resist and facilitate the process. From the research findings in regard to innovation, we concluded that organizational characteristics, the values of elites, and environmental pressures all contribute to change and innovation. Thus far in the book, the chapters have focused on organizational characteristics, including the interplay between power, leadership, and decision making with elite or dominant coalition values. Ever since the analysis of organizational structure, in Chapter 4 and particularly in this chapter, the environments of organizations have been seen as crucial for organizational structures and processes. The next chapter will be specifically focused on organizational environments.

In regard to innovation and change, we can conclude that these are critical processes for organizations. They are at the heart of our overall interest in effectiveness. They contribute to growth, survival, and death. The purpose here was not to do a life-cycle analysis but, rather, to demonstrate that these are not trivial processes for organizations. Again, if we could identify exactly what leads to growth or which changes or innovations are going to be successful, we would have the key to understanding and control of organizations. Although we do not have the key, we do have at least partial answers, which have been identified in the analysis thus far. Bringing in the environment will add another element to our understanding.

Organizational Environments and Interorganizational Relationships

The critical importance of organizational environments has been emphasized throughout our analysis. Terms such as "global economy" and "core and peripheral markets" emphasize the fact that all organizations are affected by their surroundings. In this chapter we will deal specifically with the nature and impact of organizational environments. By environment we mean "all phenomena that are external to and potentially or actually influence the population under study" (Hawley, 1968: p. 330; italics added). The population under study here, of course, is organizations.

This chapter has three purposes. The first purpose is to demonstrate how configurations of environmental conditions were necessary for the very formation of organizations in the first place. The second purpose is to develop categories by which organizational environments can be easily conceptualized. The third purpose is to examine how the environment "enters" organizations by means of interorganizational linkages through the use of networks and other mechanisms.

THE ENVIRONMENT AND THE FORMATION
OF ORGANIZATIONS

Organizational formation (or birth or founding) was considered in the last chapter from the perspective of the population ecology model. Here we move back in history to consider the environmental conditions necessary for the emergence of organizations as basically new forms of social interaction. Stinchcombe (1965) presented a seminal work on the interface between environments and the formation of organizations. He notes (p. 143) that special-purpose organizations took over various social functions, such as economic production, policing, education, political action, and military action, at different rates in different societies. These organizations have replaced or supplemented multipurpose groups such as the family or the community for these purposes.

If organizations take over such tasks, there must be an awareness of alternative ways of accomplishing these tasks. The alternative forms must be seen as having an attractive cost-benefit calculation; and the people involved must have sufficient wealth, legitimacy, and strength of numbers to get the new organization off the ground (Kimberly, 1975). These resources must be translated into power in order to overcome resistance from those interested in maintaining the older system.

These conditions have not been distributed randomly throughout history, but they have been present in sufficient degrees to allow new organizations and new organizational forms to emerge. Both new organizations and new organizational forms suffer the liability of newness that has been discussed. Stinchcombe notes that new organizations are more likely to survive than are new organizational forms.

Basic Environmental Conditions. The conditions just discussed are actually intermediate variables between some more-basic environmental characteristics and the rate of organizational formation. One of the basic characteristics necessary for organizational development is the general literacy and specialized advanced schooling of the population. The presence of literacy raises the likelihood that each of the intermediate variables will be sufficiently present for organizational development to occur. Stinchcombe states that

> . . . literacy and schooling raise practically every variable which encourages the formation of organizations and increases the staying power of new organizations. It enables more alternatives to be posed to more people. It facilitates learning new roles with no nearby role model. It encourages impersonal contact with customers. It allows money and resources to be distributed more easily to strangers and over distances. It provides records of transactions so that they can be enforced later, making the future more predictable. It increases the predictability of the future environment of an organization by increasing the available information and by making possible a uniform body of law over a large area. (pp. 150–51)

In addition to the key variable of education and literacy, several other factors are crucial for the conditions permitting organizational formation. Urbanization is a second factor identified by Stinchcombe in this regard. He notes that the rate of urbanization should be slow enough to allow the rural migrants to learn and develop routines of urban living. At the same time, the development of urban life is associated with greater heterogeneity of lifestyle, thus providing more alternative working and living arrangements. The urban scene requires dealing with strangers, and this too assists organizational development, since ascriptive role relationships are likely to be minimized. Impersonal laws are necessary in urban areas just as they are in organizations. Urbanization, like education, increases the organizational capacity of populations, although not to the same degree, according to Stinchcombe.

A third important factor, and one that has long been identified, is the presence of a money economy. This sort of economy

> ... liberates resources so that they can be more easily recruited by new organizations, facilitates the formation of free markets so that customers can transfer loyalties, depersonalizes economic social relations, simplifies the calculation of the advantages of alternative ways of doing things, and allows more precise anticipation of the consequences of future conditions on the organization. (Stinchcombe: p. 152)

A fourth condition is the political base of a society. For the creation of new organizations, political revolutions are held to be important because of their rearranging of vested interest groups and power systems. Resources are allocated on bases different from those in the past.

The final societal condition identified by Stinchcombe is the existing level of organizational density. The greater the density and the greater the range of organizational alternatives already available, the greater the likelihood that people will have had experience in organizations. This suggests that there is likely to be an exponential growth curve for organizations in a society—assuming, of course, that the other conditions are also present.

This analysis has been concerned with the conditions of the society that are important for the formation of new organizations and new organizational forms. Although the picture has been drawn in broad relief with historical data, the factors identified remain important for analyses at any time.

Technology and Organizational Form. Stinchcombe's analysis contains an additional set of ideas that is relevant for our purposes. He maintains that the technological conditions available at the time of the formation of an organization set the limits for the form the organization can take.

> Organizations which have purposes that can be efficiently reached with the socially possible organizational forms tend to be founded during the period in which they become possible. Then, both because they can function effectively with those organizational forms and because the forms tend to become institutionalized, the basic structure of the organization tends to remain relatively stable. (p. 153)

The emphasis on technology is consistent with the argument here, with the addition that if the newly introduced organizational form is compatible with the technology of the times, it tends to persist over time regardless of gradual changes in technology.

The emphasis in this section has been on the formation of new organizations and new organizational forms. The implication is that the environment at the time of organizational formation is critical for the form that the organization takes and that this form persists over time. That may be an oversimplification. The conditions surrounding the origins of an organization do persist in their impact on the organization, but these conditions are constantly being confronted with ongoing environmental conditions (Meyer and Brown, 1977). The organizational-environmental relationship is dynamic.

ENVIRONMENTAL DIMENSIONS

Thus far, we have treated the environment in a rather undifferentiated manner. In the next two sections we will consider two ways in which aspects of the environment can be categorized into useful dimensions.

In this section we will examine the *content* of the environment, including technological and economic considerations. In the following section we will consider the environment from a more analytical perspective that includes factors such as the stability or the turbulence of the environment. We will then combine these sets of dimensions.

Technological Conditions

Technological conditions are a convenient starting point, since this topic and the research surrounding it have already been the subject of much attention and can set the stage for the less systematically researched topics that follow.

It will be remembered, following the works of Perrow, Lawrence and Lorsch, and others, that organizations operating in an uncertain and dynamic technological environment exhibit structures and internal processes different from those operating in a more certain and unchanging technological environment. At this point we need not review the direction of the relationships and the supporting evidence, but it is important to recognize that the organization responds to this aspect of its environment. In fact, in the business firms Lawrence and Lorsch studied, special organizational divisions were established (research and development) to keep the organization current. In other organizations, departments such as industrial engineering and management information systems are so designated.

Beyond their empirical evidence that technology is salient in the operation of organizations, these findings have implications vital to our understanding of organizational-environmental interactions. In the first place, technology and other environmental characteristics are something "out there." The organization does not exist in a vacuum. Technological developments in any sphere of activity have the potential to get to the organizations related to them. New ideas come into circulation and become part of the environment as soon as they cease being the private property of any one individual or organization. Since the sciences have a norm of distributing knowledge, scientific developments become part of the public domain as a matter of course. A development that can be patented is a different matter, but if it is thought to be significant, other organizations will seek to buy it, copy it, or further extend the previous development. In any case, an organization must keep up with such developments in the technological spheres crucial to its continued success.

More subtle forms of the technological environment are found outside the hard sciences and engineering. In management and administration, new ideas are introduced through research, serendipity, or practice. In service-oriented organizations, such as schools, social-work agencies, and hospitals, the same types of technological shifts can be seen.

Organizations do not respond to technological change through simple absorption. Instead, the organization's political process operates through the advocacy of change or stability. Organizations of every kind contain their own internal "radical" and "reactionary" responses to technological and all other environmental conditions. Since the rate of technological and other environmental changes is not constant for all organizations, the degree to which organizations must develop response mechanisms varies. For all, however, technology remains an important consideration.

Legal Conditions

Another environmental dimension that is critical for organizations is the legal conditions that are part of the organization's surroundings. At one extreme are organizations that operate outside the law and respond to the legal system by attempting to evade the law at all costs and remain underground. At another extreme are local voluntary organizations that have no involvement whatsoever with safety, health, or other kinds of local, state, and national laws and regulations.

The overwhelming majority of organizations must live with federal, state, and local laws and regulations as a major part of their environments. At the very least, legal mandates set many of the operating conditions of many organizations, ranging from specific prohibitions of certain kinds of behavior to regulations requiring the periodic reporting of income and staffing. The importance of laws is exemplified by the staffs of legal and other experts who are integral to many organizations and who are specifically charged with interpreting and protecting their organizations' positions. The trend toward lawyers serving as chief executive officers is indicative of the critical nature of legal conditions for organizations (Priest and Rothman, 1985).

When a major new law is passed or an interpretation modified, organizations must make some important changes if the law has relevance to them, as analyses of civil rights laws have demonstrated (Edelman, 1990). Relatively mundane matters such as tax and employment regulations are important for nearly all organizations. More striking are the cases of major shifts that affect organizations in the public and private sectors. For example, U.S. Supreme Court decisions regarding school desegregation have had tremendous impacts on the school organizations involved. Concern for the environment has resulted in laws and regulations regarding pollution that have affected many organizations as they utilize their resources in fighting or complying with the new statutes. It should be evident that legal conditions result from actions of legislative bodies, the judicial system, and the executive branches of government at all levels.

Organizations are not benign recipients of laws and regulations. Organizations in all sectors attempt to select the appropriate legal strategy aimed at the appropriate arm of government. Organizations are important actors in the development of laws and regulations through their lobbying efforts (Champagne, Neef, and Nagel, 1981).

Political Conditions

Laws are not passed without pressure for their enactment. The political conditions that bring about new laws also have their effects on organizations. Strong political pressures to reduce or increase military and aerospace spending have led to crises or opportunities for organizations in those areas. Police departments have been buffeted back and forth between support for "law and order" and condemnation of "police brutality." School systems have drastically altered parts or all of their curricula in the face of threats from groups concerned with such topics as sex education and "left-wing" textbooks. Some organizations are directly affected by the political process because their hierarchy can be drastically changed by election results. All government units face this possibility after every election as top officials are changed at the discretion of a new administration.

Organizations in the private sector are less directly affected than public ones, but they must still be attuned to the political climate. Since lobbying for legislation that will provide of tax advantages or favorable international trade agreements is an accepted part of the legislative and administrative system of the United States, organizations must devote resources to the lobbying process. Lobbying can be very successful. Corporate tax rates are lower in states in which large corporations control a large proportion of the assets. This does not happen by accident (Jacobs, 1987, 1988).

Once legislation is passed in the legal dimension, political pressures are still brought to bear in the implementation of regulations. An analysis of the early history of the Occupational Safety and Health Administration (OSHA) in the United States documents the strong political pressures that were placed on this organization (McCaffrey, 1982). Anecdotal evidence suggests that this agency remains under intense political pressures.

Well-documented illegal corporate contributions to domestic and foreign political parties and individuals is further evidence of the importance of the political factor for organizations. In a different arena, "institutional advertising" is designed to generate public support through its presentation of the advertising organization as a good corporate citizen.

Research on the foundings (births) and mortality (deaths) of newspapers in Argentina and Ireland found that political turbulence was related to the founding of the newspapers (Carroll and Delacroix, 1982; Delacroix and Carroll, 1983). At the same time, newspapers founded during periods of turbulence are outlived by newspapers born under stable conditions. Additional research on political conditions and organizations would undoubtedly reveal more such patterns.

Politics plays a role at the local level as well as at the national or global level. A county in Texas decided to deny a tax break to Apple Computers because that company provided health benefits for unmarried partners of employees (Verhovek, 1993). Local politics in that county affected Apple and county government organizations.

We have portrayed the political environment in a rather gentle way thus far. It is hardly gentle when something like a political revolution takes place. A political revolution is a form of "environmental jolt" (Meyer, 1982). The collapse of the former East Germany is a case in point. The changed political system had ramifications for almost all organizations. Even cultural organizations, such as symphony orchestras, were affected by this jolt (Allmendinger and Hackman, 1996). Interestingly, the onset of socialism in East Germany had less impact on orchestras than its collapse.

Economic Conditions

An environmental condition that is more obvious, but again strangely neglected by most sociologists, is the state of the economy in which the organization is operating. To most business leaders, this is the crucial variable. In universities and in government work, experience also shows the importance of economic conditions when budgets are being prepared, defended, and appropriated. The sheer availability of financial resources is one of the crucial environmental conditions for the birth of organizations (Pennings, 1982). Changing economic conditions serve as important constraints on any organization. The market structure in the United States has been very stable over time, even though there are major swings through large and small recessions, depressions, inflationary periods, and so on (Burt, 1988).

Economic changes do not affect all parts of an organization equally. In periods of economic distress, an organization is likely to cut back or eliminate those programs it feels are least important to its overall goals, except, of course, for those instances in which external political pressures preclude such "rational" decisions (Freeman, 1979). Economic affluence permits government agencies to engage in a wider range of programs. For example, a study of state employment agencies found that agencies in wealthier states provided unemployment insurance to a greater proportion of the unemployed than did the agencies in the poorer states (Klatzky, 1970b). Since these agencies were paying out more, they also received a disproportionately larger share of federal funds than their less affluent peers in other states. The rich agencies get richer as the poor agencies get poorer. Of course, political changes can bring about changed economic conditions for these governmental organizations. It is impossible to disentangle political and economic factors in many cases.

Changing economic conditions are, in fact, excellent indicators of the priorities of organizations. That organizational programs vary according to the economic conditions that are confronted contributes to a paradox for most organizations. Since total rationality is not an assumption of this analysis, it can be safely assumed that an organization cannot be sure of exactly what contribution each of its parts makes to the whole. For example, research and development can be viewed as one of the luxuries that should go when an organization faces some hard times. But by concentrating on the production and distribution of what R & D has done in the past, the organization may miss the development of a new product that would be of great long-run benefit. Periods of economic difficulty do force organizations to evaluate their priorities and trim areas that are viewed as being least vital. As in the case of the communication process, the criteria by which the evaluations are accomplished are the key variables, and there is no assumption being made here that the decision process is rational.

Economic conditions surrounding organizations improve and decline with the organizations responding to the situation. Competition is an important factor in their responses in any situation. Economic competition can be most easily seen among business organizations, where success is measured in the competitive marketplace. Although the competition is not "pure," it is still an evident part of the value system in a private-enterprise economy. Economic competition among organizations takes many forms. An analysis of the patterns of corporate philanthropy among a set of business firms concluded that corporate philanthropy was a co-optive relationship, akin to advertising (Burt, 1983). The reasoning behind this conclusion was that the proportion of net income that an organization gave to charity varied with the extent to which the firms were dependent upon consumption by people who were able to do something about uncertainty in the demand for their product. A supermarket chain might thus engage in widely publicized charitable efforts in an effort to try to ensure continued patronage in a local market by appearing to be a good citizen.

Less evident than competition between business firms, but equally real, is economic competition among and within organizations outside the business sphere. From repeated experiences in government agencies at several levels, it is clear that competition is fierce during budget season (Wildavsky, 1964).

Government agencies are all competing for part of the tax revenues, which constitute a finite "pot." Organizations that rely on contributions from members, such as churches, are also affected by the general economic conditions, since the contributors have more or less income available. An interesting research question is the extent to which the severity of economic competition varies among organizations in all sectors of society. It appears almost equal, regardless of the organizations' major emphases.

Demographic Conditions

Demography is also a frequently overlooked factor. The number of people served, and their age and sex distributions, make a great deal of difference to all organizations. As a general rule, an organization can predict its probable "market" for the future from information in census data, but population shifts, such as those resulting from migration, are less predictable and can make an organization vulnerable. In a society where race, religion, and ethnicity are important considerations, shifts in these aspects of the demographic condition must also be considered.

The most striking examples of the importance of demographic change have come from organizations located in the central cities of growing and declining metropolitan areas. Businesses, schools, and police departments have different clienteles from what they once had, even though the organizations themselves might not reflect this. At least in the short run, it is the urban poor and minority group members who suffer the consequences. The organizations themselves, however, eventually undergo transitions (often painful) as they begin to realize that their clienteles have become different and that they themselves must change.

Demographic distributions within an organization have important ramifications for a wide variety of organizationally important issues, such as performance, innovation and adaptability, turnover, and interorganizational linkages (Pfeffer, 1983). For organizations that use an external labor market, demographic conditions in the environment would thus be reflected within the organization. For example, fast-food restaurants experienced a shortage of younger workers in the late 1980s and turned to older workers for their counter staff.

Ecological Conditions

Related to demography scene is the general ecological situation surrounding an organization. The number of organizations with which it has contacts and relationships and the environment in which it is located are components of the organization's social ecological system. An organization in an urban area is much more likely to have contacts with a myriad of other organizations than is one in a rural area. Since the density of other organizations around any particular organization varies widely, the potential for relationships also varies.

If we shift from social ecology to the physical environment, we find that the relationships between organizations and ecological conditions become even more evident because of the recent concerns about the total ecological system. That organizations have effects on the environment is abundantly demonstrated by the various organizations that pollute and the others that fight pollution.

A more subtle point is that the environment affects organizations. Factors such as climate and geography set limits on how organizations allocate resources. Transportation and communication costs rise if an organization is distant from its markets or clients. Even such mundane items as heating and cooling expenses must be considered limits on an organization.

Some organizations are located to take advantage of physical environmental conditions. This is most easily seen in the case of organizations using physical raw materials, such as ore or petroleum, or those using particular characteristics of the environment, such as ski areas. More subtle is the fact that organizations such as national professional associations and trade associations tend to be located in just one place in the United States—Washington, D.C. That is where their action is. It is their social ecological environment. Although ecological factors are generally constants, since only in unusual circumstances are there significant changes, these conditions cannot be ignored in a total organizational analysis involving comparisons between organizations.

Cultural Conditions

The environmental conditions discussed thus far are fairly straightforward. The culture surrounding an organization is much harder to conceptualize. In Chapter 4 the importance of national cultures for organizational structure was discussed in detail, but there is more to culture than national culture.

Although the influence of national culture is now an accepted fact, it is not clear whether culture overrides other factors in determining how an organization is shaped and operates. There is evidence suggesting that organizations at an equivalent technological level—for example, at the same degree of automation of production—are quite similar in most respects, as was indicated in the chapters on structure. The basic problem is to sort out the influences of these various environmental factors as they impinge on the organization. Unfortunately, not enough is yet known for such fine distinctions to be made. The various factors discussed so far definitely interrelate in their organizational effects in a very complex interaction pattern. For example, it appears that the more routine and standardized the technology, the less the impact of cultural factors. The production of children's toy automobiles is probably carried out in similar organizational forms in Hong Kong, London, Japan, Switzerland, and Tonka, Minnesota. When one moves to less routinized technological operations, such as local government, the administration of justice, or highway construction, the impact of culture is likely to be higher. Culture is important for organizational structuring. It also has an important impact on the ways in which organizations formulate their strategies for the future (Schneider, 1989).

Culture is not a constant, even in a single local setting. Values and norms change as events affect the population involved. If they involve conditions relevant to the organization, these shifts are significant for it. Newspaper editorials, letters to the editor, and other colorations of reports in the mass media indicate how values can change in regard to particular organizations or types of organizations. These value shifts may precede or accompany political shifts, which would have a more direct impact. Changes in consumer tastes represent another way that cultural conditions can affect organizations. Examples of this are easily found; a dramatic one is that of the Ford Motor Company's contrasting experiences with the Edsel and Mustang cars. Tobacco companies are faced with major shifts in values and continue to scramble to reduce the damage caused by the antitobacco movement (Dunbar and Wasilewski, 1985).

The culture-organization relationship is not a one-way street. Organizations attempt to shape cultural values through their public relations efforts. Organizations also shape cultures as they expand into world markets. The movement of Japanese automobile firms into the U.S. manufacturing scene has shaped the behavior of their suppliers, who had to learn to supply on a "just-in-time" basis (Florida and Kenney, 1991). Powerful organizations are very capable of changing cultural values.

ANALYTICAL DIMENSIONS

Another way of categorizing aspects of the environment is by their more analytical elements (Aldrich (1979: pp. 53–70; see also Aldrich and Marsden, 1988). As we will see, it is possible to intertwine a variation of Aldrich's dimensions with those just outlined. Aldrich's list of dimensions is described below.

Environmental Capacity

The capacity of an environment is to its "richness" or "leanness," or the level of resources available to an organization. According to Aldrich:

> Organizations have access to more resources in rich environments, but such environments also attract other organizations. Stockpiling and hoarding of resources is probably not as prevalent in rich as in lean environments. Lean environments also promote cut-throat competitive practices, and apart from rewarding organizations capable of stockpiling and hoarding, lean environments reward efficiency in the use of resources. Two alternatives are open to organizations in lean environments: move to a richer environment, or develop a more efficient structure. The latter alternative can be accomplished by improving operating practices, merging with other organizations, becoming more aggressive

vis-à-vis other organizations, or moving to a protected subenvironment through specialization. (p. 53)

There are many examples of such organizational responses. American Airlines, for instance, moved its corporate headquarters from New York City to Dallas. Although the phrase "rich and lean environment" was not used, the reasons given for the move—access to qualified personnel and more modern facilities—essentially had that meaning. At times some of the responses that Aldrich suggests are not possible. Legal requirements, for example, may prevent merger because of the threat of monopoly. In such cases, as Pfeffer and Nowak (1976) point out, organizations may engage in joint ventures. Joint ventures involve the investment of resources from several organizations in a single large project, such as the Concorde airplane developed by France and England. Joint ventures such as this are a form of interorganizational relationship that will be considered shortly.

Environmental Homogeneity-Heterogeneity

This dimension refers to the degree of similarity or differentiation within the environment. According to Aldrich, a homogeneous environment is simpler for organizations, since standardized ways of responding can be developed. Many organizations attempt to make their environment more homogeneous by limiting the kinds of products made, clients served, markets entered, and so on. Social service organizations consistently attempt to make their environment homogeneous by referring clients that do not fit within their operations to other social service organizations. The result of this, of course, is that the most difficult clients are referred and referred and referred. This yet another form of interorganizational linkage.

Environmental Stability-Instability

This term refers to the extent of turnover of elements or parts of the environment. Stability, like homogeneity, permits standardization. Instability leads to unpredictability, which organizations resist. Any aspect of an organization's environment can be stable or unstable, whether it be economic, legal, or technological conditions. An environment can be stable for a long time and then undergo a major upheaval (Gersick, 1991).

Environmental Concentration-Dispersion

Concentration or dispersion in the environment involves the distribution of the elements in the environment. Are they located in one place or are they scattered across a large area? It is easier for an organization to operate with a more concentrated environment, as in the case of customers or clients.

Domain Consensus-Dissensus

Organizations claim a domain or a market. This dimension refers to the degree to which those claims are recognized or disputed by other parties, such as government agencies. If the interested and relevant parties agree that a particular organization has the right and the obligation to operate in a particular way in a particular area, there is domain consensus. This dimension is thus concerned with organizational "turf."

Organizations attempt to achieve domain consensus by securing protective legislation or regulations, such as import quotas, tariffs, or exclusive rights to a sales territory. In the public sector, there are frequent consensus-dissensus debates about federal, state, or local responsibilities for programs in transportation, education, or social welfare. Disputes over domain are another way organizations relate to one another.

Environmental Turbulence

This is the most difficult of Aldrich's dimensions to understand, since turbulence seems a great deal like instability. Turbulence here means that there is a great deal of causal interconnection (tight coupling) among the elements in the environment. In a turbulent environment, there is a high rate of environmental interconnection. An economic shift has political and technological ramifications in a turbulent environment. The movement of business firms from the Northeast to the Sun Belt in the United States is an example of such turbulence. This movement has lowered the tax base in the Northeast, forcing increases in the tax rates to maintain essential and nonessential services, which in turn has led to additional decisions to move. These moves also affect other sectors, such as education, health, and social services.

On the basis of their research, Dess and Beard (1984) believe that the foregoing six dimensions can be reduced to three dimensions. They propose that the dimensions of munificence (capacity), complexity (homogeneity-heterogeneity and concentration-dispersion), and dynamism (stability-instability and turbulence) capture the essence of Aldrich's distinctions. On that basis, we can now intertwine the content dimensions with the analytical dimensions (see Figure 10–1). Each of the content dimensions can be characterized by its munificence, complexity, and dynamism.

Before turning to an analysis of how the environment is perceived by the organization, one other characteristic of environments, which is not included in these dimensions, must be considered. This is the degree to which the environment itself is organized (Jurkovich, 1974). This is crucial in regard to consumers, for example, since organized consumers can be much more threatening to an organization than nonorganized individuals. Most environmental pressures come from other organizations in the form of government agencies, competing organizations, cultural organizations, and the like. When

ANALYTICAL CATEGORIES

	MUNIFICENCE	COMPLEXITY	DYNAMISM
CONTENT CONDITIONS			
TECHNOLOGICAL			
LEGAL			
POLITICAL			
ECONOMIC			
DEMOGRAPHIC			
ECOLOGICAL			
CULTURAL			

FIGURE 10–1 Environmental Dimensions
Source: Andrew H. Van de Ven and Diane L. Ferry, *Measuring and Assessing Organizations* (New York: John Wiley, 1980), p. 298.

we examine interorganizational relationships, the specific linkages between organizations and their counterparts will be analyzed in detail.

THE PERCEPTION OF THE ENVIRONMENT

We have been proceeding as though the environment is simply something "out there" beyond the organization, which anyone in the organization can readily spot and identify. It would be handy if that were the case, but it is not. The environment comes into the organization as information and, like all information, is subject to the communications and decision-making problems that have been identified. Environmental information is information to be processed.

People have different positions in organizations. Some people are identified as "gate keepers" (Nagi, 1974) or "boundary spanners," who are designated to admit certain information that is relevant to the organization. Their perceptions are influenced by their positions within the organization (Leifer and Huber, 1977). Of course, it is difficult to determine where the organization stops and the environment begins. Different positions are at an organization's boundaries, depending on what the activity at the moment is. At times it can be the switchboard operator; at other times it is the president or the chief executive officer (Starbuck, 1976).

An organization selects those aspects of the environment with which it is going to deal (Starbuck, 1976: pp. 1078–80). The selection process is affected by the selection processes of other organizations with which it is in contact. At the same time, of course, interorganizational linkages are affected by environmental pressures (Provan, Beyer, and Kruytbosch, 1980). In this manner, organizations go about constructing or inventing their environments. The scope of the domain or environment claimed or selected by organizations has an impact on its operations. Narrow domain claims are associated with stability, broad and inconsistent claims with loss of functions. Broad claims coupled with technological capacity and newness lead to domain expansion (Meyer, 1975). Domain claims seldom contract.

Organizational theory has stressed the importance of perceived uncertainty in the environment (Duncan, 1973; Leifer and Huber, 1977). It is equally important to stress that much of the environment that is perceived is actually quite certain, rather than uncertain. Colleges and universities, for example, face a certain demographic profile of the number and distribution of potential students. Business firms face a certain environment of governmental regulations. The environment thus contains elements of certainty and uncertainty. Even when an environment is certain, of course, there is no guarantee that it will be perceived as such (Milliken, 1990).

Just as the perceptions of individuals are shaped by their experiences, so, are the perceptions of organizations. Organizations may actually be more realistic than individuals because of their constant comparisons with and sharing personnel among comparable organizations (Starbuck, 1976: pp. 1080–81), but it has not yet been clearly demonstrated that this is the case. It must be remembered that the perceivers of the environment are themselves individuals, all with idiosyncrasies in perception.

THE IMPACT OF THE ENVIRONMENT ON THE ORGANIZATION

What do all these environmental factors, however selected and perceived, do to organizations? There are several answers. In the first place, organizations vary in their vulnerability to environmental pressures (Jacobs, 1974). The more dependent an organization is on its environment, the more vulnerable it is. An organization with strong financial resources is less vulnerable to economic fluctuations than is one with no reserves. In the 1970s and early 1980s, petroleum manufacturers were highly dependent on and vulnerable to political shifts in their sources of raw materials and their markets. They attempted to manipulate their environment by stabilizing the political conditions. Tobacco companies attempted to manage, regulate, and reduce the damage of the antismoking movement (Dunbar and Wasilewski, 1985). It is interesting to note here that the antismoking movement *is the environment* for tobacco companies and that this environment includes government agencies, citizens' groups, airline workers, and numerous other factions. Tobacco smoke is an alien part of my environment.

When an organization is vulnerable, it reacts to the environment. Several studies have shown that strong environmental pressures are related to increased formalization and a general "tightening" of the organization (see Freeman, 1973; Khandwalla, 1972; Boddewyn, 1974; and Pfeffer and Leblebici, 1973). It is odd that the environmental pressures do this, since in many ways the loosely coupled organization is more adaptive to the environment and is more likely to develop innovations that might be beneficial over the long run (Weick, 1976). Organizations that are vulnerable to the environment, of course, face a greater risk of failure if an innovation happens not to be successful.

Every organization is dependent on its environment to some degree. Each adapts internal strategies to deal with the perceived pressures (Snow and Hrebriniak, 1980). Contingency theory strongly suggests that there is no best way to cope with environmental pressures. The specific stance that an organization takes derives from choices that are made within it. This decision-making process is a political one in the sense that different options are supported by different factions within the decision-making structure. The option finally selected is a consequence of the power of individuals and groups that support it. That environmental pressures often tighten the organization may be a consequence of the fact that this is the option that powerful segments of organizations have traditionally taken. It may not be the one most useful for the organization, of course.

Among the strategies that organizations develop for dealing with their environments, a critical one is to attempt to shape the environment itself. An analysis of pharmaceutical manufacturing firms found that they had been more successful than the typical firms in the phonograph-record industry largely because the pharmaceutical firms had been able to control relevant aspects of their environments. The pharmaceutical firms could exert control over pricing and distribution, patent and copyright laws, and external opinion leaders (Hirsch, 1975). This control of the environment was a source of greater profitability. Organizations attempt to gain and maintain power over environmental conditions that are of strategic importance to them.

It might appear that when resources are scarce, organizations might resort to illegal acts such as price fixing or other activities to restrain trade. Actually the opposite appears to be true. Counterintuitively, large firms in munificent environments were found to be more likely to commit illegal acts (Baureus and Near, 1991). Organizations compete with one another for technological, political, economic, legal, and other advantages. This competition takes place in overlapping dimensions of the environment. A political advantage can contribute to economic advantage and vice versa. For example, the interests of the financial and industrial core industries in the United States became vested interests in the U.S. State Department in the 1886–1905 period, whereas other interests were not as well protected in foreign policy (Roy, 1981; see also Carstensen and Werking, 1983; and Roy, 1983a, 1983b). In the same vein, there is evidence that indicates that corporate elites in the United States and Great Britain have inclusive and diffusely structured economic and social relationships. These transcend individual firms and lead to interactions with government that promote policies favorable to these elites (Useem, 1982). Organizational environments are thus subject to actual, attempted, and perhaps even unintentional manipulation by the organizations within them.

INTERORGANIZATIONAL RELATIONSHIPS

At this point our analysis will move from a consideration of organizational environments in a broad, general sense to a consideration of the specific organizations in contact with one another through interorganizational relationships (IORs). The relationships of any single organization with its environment take place through the actions of other organizations—organizations affect organizations (Haunschild and Miner, 1997). The legal environment is experienced through the actions of government enforcement and regulative agencies; the economic environment through competing organizations, organizations that give donations, and so on. The cultural dimension of the environment has been identified as the basis of support for small family-run firms in the knitwear industry (Lazerson, 1995). Here cooperative IORs exist among knitwear firms in a community, rather than the competitive IORs that exist among other businesses.

Individuals as well as organizations are affected by IORs. For example, clients of social service organizations are vitally affected by IORs. A common practice is client referral. Theoretically, if one agency is unable to provide the needed services for a particular client, the individual is referred to an appropriate agency for service. What happens in practice is that clients who are easily treated or provided services are not referred, and the more difficult ones are referred, with the most difficult cases sometimes eventually "falling between the cracks" of the referring set of organizations.

At the societal level, there has been a long-standing concern with the actual and potential power of the "military-industrial complex." This refers to interorganizational patterns linking the military with industry into a powerful set of organizations that can dominate other spheres of life. Linkages among powerful organizations through interlocking boards of directors have become the focus of intense scrutiny by political and organizational sociologists.

Organizational theorists began paying attention to IORs when they started looking beyond organizational boundaries into organizational environments and when urban sociologists began to recognize urban communities as networks of organizations (Cook, 1977), particularly in regard to the delivery of social services (Litwak and Hylton, 1962; Warren, 1967; Warren, Rose, and Bergunder, 1974). A consistent research finding is that integrated IORs contribute to improved health and social care at the community level (Provan and Milward, 1995; Goes and Park, 1997; Alter and Hage, 1993). To understand IORs, we will first examine the variety of forms of IORs that can be identified. We will also identify various levels of analysis that can be utilized in the understanding of IORs.

IOR: Forms and Levels

There is a general agreement that IORs have three basic forms. These are illustrated in Figure 10-2. The dyad or pairwise relationship is the simplest form of IOR and has probably received the most attention in empirical research. The interorganizational set idea was derived from analysis of role sets (Merton, 1957). Evan (1966) and Caplow (1964) introduced the organizational set idea into the literature. The emphasis is on a focal agency (FA in Figure 10–2) and its dyadic relationships with other organizations. It is very possible to trace the impact of changes in one dyadic relationship as they affect other pairwise relations within the set (Evan, 1966; Caplow, 1964; Van de Ven and Ferry, 1980).

The "action set" is a variation on the organizational set. The action set is composed of "a group of organizations formed in a temporary alliance for a limited purpose" (Aldrich, 1979: p. 280; see also Aldrich and Whetten, 1981). According to Aldrich, "Action sets may have their own formalized agreements, internal division of labor, behavioral norms vis-à-vis other organizations, and clearly defined principles for the recruitment of new members" (p. 281).

Interorganizational *networks* are more inclusive. They consist "of all organizations linked by a specified type of relation, and (are) constructed

FIGURE 10–2 Forms of Interorganizational Relationships

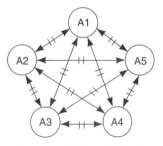

a. Pairwise or Dyadic Interorganizational Relationship

b. Interorganizational Set

c. Interorganizational Network

by finding the ties between all organizations in a population" (Aldrich, 1979: p. 281). Networks are "the total pattern of interrelationships among a cluster of organizations that are meshed together in a social system to attain collective and self-interest goals or to resolve specific problems in a target population" (Van de Ven and Ferry, 1980: p. 299). Analyses of business organizations are paying particular attention to networks. For example, when the knowledge base of an industry is both complex and expanding, the locus of innovation has been found to be in networks rather than individual firms (Powell, Koput, and Smith-Doerr, 1996). Networks have also been found to be the bases of integrative agreements that can transcend economic factors in decision making. This finding comes from an analysis of the New York garment industry (Uzzi, 1997). Embeddedness in social networks continues to be the basis of the corporate charitable contributions in the Twin Cities (Galaskiewicz, 1997) that were described in Chapter 1 and will also be considered here.

Before turning to the issue of *levels* of analysis among these patterns of IORs, we should note that an analyst can focus on a variety of dimensions within these forms. Figures 10–3, 10–4, 10–5, and 10–6 demonstrate the complexity that exists when the organizational set concept is used.

The examples are drawn from research on the social-control system for problem youth that John Clark and I conducted some years ago. Figure 10–3 indicates the organizations in interaction with a focal organization, in this case the police. The frequency of the interaction is also indicated. Figure 10–4 indicates the degree of formalization of the relationship; Figure 10–5 indicates whether the relationship is cooperative or conflictual.

These figures include only a few variables and a few members of the organization set. The complexity of the relationships is indicated by the fact that frequent interactions do not necessarily mean highly formalized or cooperative relations. In addition, it can be seen in Figure 10–5 that cooperation and conflict can exist in the same relationship. The organizations cooperate on some issues but conflict on others.

Another meaning implicit in the idea of the organization set is indicated in Figure 10–6, where the major linkages for the police are seen to be with other law enforcement agencies. Although these relationships are based on contacts in regard to law enforcement problems, they are also an important basis on which the focal police department determines how well it is doing. Organizations use other organizations of the same type both for comparison purposes and as a source of new ideas.

The analysis of IORs is complex. Not only do organizations like the police have relationships with the sets of organizations depicted in Figures 10–3 through 10–6, but they also have multiple other sets of relationships. Each organization must purchase goods and services. Many of these organizations have concerns other than problem youths. The welfare department, for example, is also involved in financial assistance programs with linkages to federal, state, and local organizations as well as to citizens' groups.

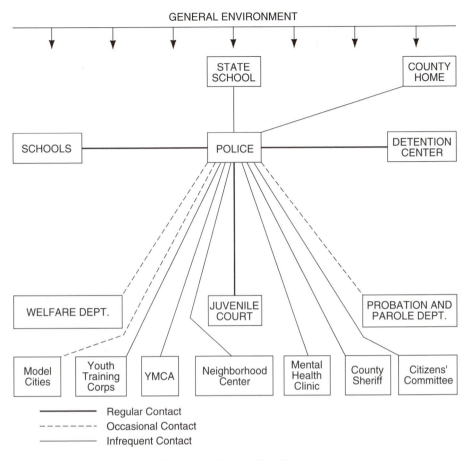

FIGURE 10–3 The Organization Set and Interaction Frequency

There is yet another form of IOR. This is the joint venture (Pfeffer and Nowak, 1976). It entails the creation of a new organizational entity by the joining of organizations in a partnership. The joint venture provides a way to avoid illegal mergers but still permits joint-capital investment on the part of the organizations involved. Pfeffer and Nowak note that joint ventures may occur in both profit and nonprofit sectors. Among profit-seeking organizations, oil and gas exploration efforts are a common form of joint venture, as the participating organizations, which have both competitive and symbiotic relationships among themselves, seek to reduce environmental uncertainty and reduce the risks for each participant. Joint ventures among nonprofit organizations are exemplified by alliances formed among private colleges. Through these alliances, they can achieve competitive advantages over independent colleges.

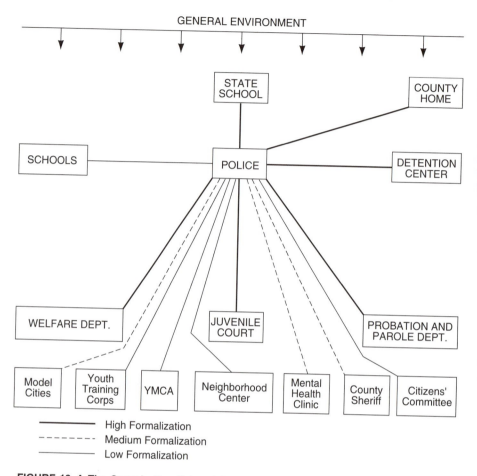

FIGURE 10–4 The Organization Set and Formalization of Relationships

The joint venture is a good place to begin to examine the issue of level of analysis. In the case of the joint venture, one could focus attention on the newly created entity—the joint venture—or on the participating organizations or on both. This is true for all forms of interorganizational interaction. In the case of the dyad, for example, the focus of interest could be on the organizations involved (Schmidt and Kochan, 1977), on the relationship itself (Hall et al., 1977), or on the environment in which the dyadic relationship is based. The focus could also be on the individuals involved, such as boundary personnel.

When the analysis is focused on sets or networks, even more complexity is introduced, since the focus can be on the set or network, a focal organization within the constellation, other organizations, the relationships themselves, or the environment in which all this is occurring, such as the community. One study examined the linkages with environmental elements that

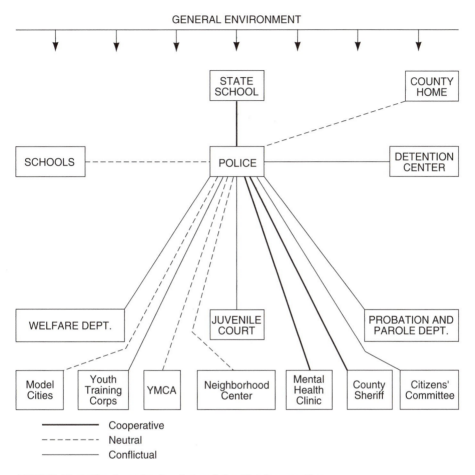

FIGURE 10–5 The Organization Set and Conflict-Cooperation

modify power relationships within an organizational set (Provan, Beyer, and Kruytbosch, 1980). Another studied the relationship between organizational characteristics and IORs at different levels of government, such as the county or state level (Klonglan et al., 1976). The focus here is on the manner in which organizational characteristics are related to interorganizational patterns. Turning the analysis in another direction, Metcalf (1976) found that IORs provide for organizations a means of adapting to, rather than merely responding to, environmental pressures, according to their own needs. Interorganizational analysis is thus a complex and potentially confusing enterprise, since various studies have had different focuses, with less clarity on the level of analysis than would be desirable.

A major difficulty in interorganizational analyses is the ordering among the units of investigation. Using a simplified set of distinctions among the

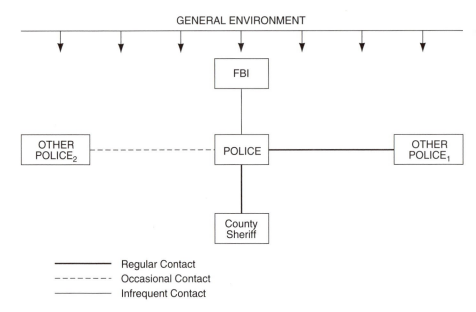

FIGURE 10–6 Another Type of Organization Set

environment, the organizations involved, and the qualities of the relationships, we can identify the following alternatives as shown in Figure 10–7.

Each alternative represents a possible assumption about causal ordering. The possibility of feedback loops for each alternative complicates the situation further. Unfortunately, we do not have the answer regarding optimal ordering. The reason for this is that each component is interactive with the others. We probably have an extended example of the chicken-versus-egg argument here, with causal priority difficult to establish and probably not worth the effort, since each component does affect and is affected by the other.

As has been noted, analyses of IORs have overwhelmingly been oriented to the delivery of human services such as health care, employment service, youth-serving organizations, welfare organizations, and the like. The reason for this has been the belief that interorganizational coordination would lead to im-

FIGURE 10–7 Alternative Causal Orders
Source: Ronald S. Burt, Kenneth Christman, and Harold C. Kilburn Jr., "Testing a Structural Theory of Corporate Co-optation: Interorganizational Directorate Ties as a Strategy for Avoiding Market Constraints on Profits," *American Sociological Review,* Vol. 45, Figure 1, p. 827.

proved service delivery and lower costs. Federal and state research support and programs reflected this emphasis, and researchers in the area responded to these emphases. The heavy emphasis on human-service IORs reflects aspects of the cultural dimension of the more general environment as the necessity of delivery of human services remains, thankfully, an ongoing cultural value. The political and economic dimensions are obviously important, also. The focus in the next section is specifically on IORs and human-service delivery.

A FRAMEWORK FOR IOR ANALYSIS: THE HUMAN-SERVICE DELIVERY AREA

This section focuses on IORs themselves, rather than on the participating organizations. The analysis is primarily inductive, based on research findings in the area. The body of accumulated knowledge here is fragmented and the scholarship is uneven, but there is enough information to serve as a guide to understanding (Galaskiewicz, 1985: p. 281). We will consider characteristics of the general environment that appear to be important, specific situational factors affecting relationships, the bases of the relationships, resource flows in relationships, actual transactions, and finally outcomes of the relationships. The framework is adapted from Morrissey, Hall, and Lindsey (1981).

General Environmental Characteristics

We earlier identified dimensions of organizational environments. These same dimensions are critical for IORs. Thus, technological, legal, political, economic, demographic, ecological, and cultural conditions have been identified. For example, legal mandates have been shown to be an important basis for interaction (Hall et al., 1977). The cultural conditions in a community could support or repress IORs. Organizations in highly complex technological environments, such as nuclear-waste management, are known to each other and can rank each other's performance (Shrum and Wuthnow, 1988).

We can also analyze the environment along a different set of dimensions. As indicated in a previous section of this chapter, environmental capacity, homogeneity-heterogeneity, stability-instability, concentration-dispersion, consensus-dissensus, and turbulence are used as analytical environmental dimensions.

Turbulence has been identified as an important factor because it refers to the increasing causal interconnection among the elements in the environment. This means that there is a greater rate of interconnection among the organizations in a system (Emery and Trist, 1965; Terreberry, 1968). As turbulence increases, we would expect a higher rate of IORs.

Environmental complexity plays a similar role, as the number of activities and situations in the environment rise with increasing complexity. Organizations deal with complexity by specializing in a limited range of activities (Aldrich, 1979). This in turn leads to a loosely coupled system in which links among organizations are necessary for organizational survival. Aldrich's emphasis on survival suggests that organizations are not tightly bound to one another but only to the extent that they need one another for survival. This is too limited a view of the importance of the environment, since other characteristics, such as legal or economic situations, may lead to tighter binding than would simply be caused by complexity.

Homogeneity-heterogeneity has an impact on the range of organizations that have interactions, with a heterogeneous environment having the capability for a wider range of interactions. A heterogeneous environment leads to a proliferation of organizational programs, which may contribute to a higher level of interorganizational interaction (Aldrich, 1979).

Environmental capacity is similar to the economic dimension but also includes other resource bases. There are contradictory interpretations of the impact of environmental capacity. Galaskiewicz and Shatin (1981), on the one hand, report that poor neighborhoods draw fewer social service organizations and thus fewer interorganizational linkages. Aiken and Hage (1968), on the other hand, report that a shortage of resources draws organizations together. Turk (1973) found that the scale of municipal government was related to the development of interorganizational relationships. A rich environment may provide the organization with resources that permit it to engage in interorganizational relationships that it otherwise might not.

The stability-instability factor also appears to have mixed consequences. Galaskiewicz and Shatin report that stable clientele provide certainty for organizations and thus less need for interaction. Stability may also permit the development of formalized or routinized relationships (Aldrich, 1979).

The concentration-dispersion dimension is more straightforward. For example, concentration of manpower agencies contributes to interagency interactions (Aldrich, 1979). Similarly, the consensus-dissensus dimension appears to have a one-directional relationship with interorganizational interactions, with domain consensus contributing to more interactions.

Obviously, more research is needed to determine the patterns of relationships between the environment, IORs, and the organizations involved. Such research is difficult to accomplish, since environmental qualities have to be measured over time, as do IORs. The problem of causal ordering referred to earlier also presents severe analytical problems. Despite these problems, a full understanding of IORs is impossible without an adequate conceptualization and eventual measurement of these general environmental properties.

Situational Factors

There is agreement that the general environment is important as a setting for IORs. The specific situations in which IORs take place are also crucial.

The situational factors that will be discussed represent preconditions for or antecedents (Halpert, 1982) of interactions. There are five factors that appear to be important here.

(1) Awareness. It has long been recognized that organizations operate in a "field" of other organizations (Warren, 1967). Less recognized is the fact that organizations vary in their awareness of the field around them. Awareness refers to both the recognition of other organizations and the recognition by organizational representatives that their organization is interdependent with other organizations in their field.

IORs do not occur automatically. A good part of interorganizational theory is predicated on the assumption that IORs will not occur unless there is awareness of potential or actual interdependence among the organizations involved (Levine and White, 1961; Litwak and Hylton, 1962; Levine, White, and Paul, 1963). There is a form of hierarchy of awareness (Klonglan et al., 1976). First is a general awareness of the existence of other organizations and their activities. The next level involves mutual acquaintance among the directors of the organizations. The focus on directors is probably too narrow, since acquaintances among staff members would be of great importance in some instances. The next levels of awareness involve specific interactions and joint board membership among directors. We will deal with these two issues separately, since they are a step beyond simple awareness.

An alternative approach suggests that there are two levels of awareness (Van de Ven and Ferry, 1980). At the more general level is the extent to which boundary spanners in organizations are knowledgeable about the goals, services, and resources present in other organizations. This awareness provides identification of alternative sources of services and resources. According to Van de Ven and Ferry, higher levels of awareness are likely to result in higher levels of interaction.

The second level of awareness involves interpersonal ties among organizational personnel (Boje and Whetten, 1981). These can involve "old school" ties, membership in common professional organizations, membership in common religious or fraternal organizations, simple friendships, or contacts that are based solely on work. Interpersonal ties are crucial for interorganizational relationships at periods of environmental turbulence (Galaskiewicz and Shatin, 1981). A higher level of interpersonal ties is seen to be linked to higher levels of interorganizational interaction.

The quality of ties is overlooked in most analyses. Obviously, friendships will yield a different form of interorganizational relationship than will animosity. Personal ties, such as those between auditors and their clients reduce the likelihood of ties breaking (Seabright, Levinthal, and Fichman, 1992). Interorganizational relationships are based on much more than the qualities of the individuals involved, but this factor should not be overlooked.

(2) Domain Consensus-Dissensus.   The domain issue has already been raised in the discussion of Aldrich's (1979) analysis of the dimensions of the general environment of organizations. The domain issue has particular salience in interorganizational relationships. Unfortunately, several meanings are embedded in the usage that the concept has received.

One meaning has a simple spatial referent. The domain is the geographical area served by an organization, such as the "service area" or "catchment area" used by neighborhood health centers or community mental health centers. In these spatial cases, the issue of domain is usually settled in advance, and domain is not really an issue except for potential clients who may reside on a border of two organizations' domains.

A more complex and important meaning of domain concerns the level of agreement about role or task differentiation among the organizations involved in IORs (Levine, White, and Paul, 1963). The roles organizations play relative to one another, in regard to their programs and services and clients to be served, are critical for the organizations involved and involve such issues as whether or not dyads of organizations serve common clients (Molnar, 1978). Domain consensus can also refer to the degree to which an organization's claim to a specific domain is disrupted or recognized by another organization (Aldrich, 1979).

Two issues are intertwined here. The first is the issue of consensus or agreement on domain; the second is that of the commonness of the domain. It is quite possible that organizations could claim the same domain with consensus or dissensus.

Another aspect of the domain issue involves ideological considerations. Ideological issues can include the compatibility of the goals of the organizations involved, conformity in treatment ideologies in social service organizations, or compatibility in understanding the nature of the issues faced (Benson et al., 1973; Boje and Whetten, 1979; Hall et al., 1977; Mulford, 1980; and Schmidt and Kochan, 1977). The ideological issue becomes important in practice. For example, police agencies typically have a different ideology toward problem youth from that of social welfare agencies. These differences, which can be severe or mild, affect the qualities of interactions among the organizations.

Some have argued that domain consensus must exist before exchange relationships among agencies are possible (Levine and White, 1961). Organizations with intersecting domains tend to be more interdependent than those that do not share domains, with intersecting domains contributing to interorganizational relationships (Molnar, 1978). Others have argued that interorganizational relationships do not depend on domain consensus (Schmidt and Kochan, 1977; Hall et al., 1977). These authors do suggest that the level of consensus does affect the qualities of relationships but not their sheer existence. Exchange relationships themselves apparently do not depend on such consensus (Cook, 1977). There is not consensus on domain consensus.

(3) Geographical Proximity. The distribution of organizations in space has received relatively little attention in the literature on organizations in general. Geographical proximity refers to the spatial distance between organizations or their subunits. It has been noted that distance can facilitate or inhibit interactions (Broskowski, 1980). It is more difficult for both organizations and individuals to establish or maintain relationships across distances. It can also be noted that the type of unit involved in an IOR interacts with the spatial issue. Modern communication techniques permit the rapid flow of information across space, but clients or staff members are more difficult to transfer.

The decision to coordinate with another organization is easier if the organizations involved are physically close to each other (Reid, 1969; Schermerhorn, 1975; Boje and Whetten, 1981; and Halpert, 1982). Proximity promotes familiarity of domains. In many communities several city or county agencies might be housed in the same building. This proximity would facilitate interactions in comparison with organizations that are spread throughout some geographical area.

(4) Localized Dependence. Related to geographical proximity is the degree to which organizations are dependent upon a local area for their resources (Galaskiewicz, 1979; Maas, 1979). Localized dependence refers to the extent to which needed resources are obtained only from a local area rather than from a more widely dispersed resource base. If organizations with localized dependence are successful in commanding localized resources, they are more powerful or central in the network of organizations in a community. If, on the other hand, there is high localized dependency with relatively weak access to resources, the organization is much more vulnerable to the power of other organizations.

(5) Size. The final situational factor is the size of the actual or potential set or network of organizations. Most analyses have focused on the actual number of organizations in a network (Van de Ven and Ferry, 1980). Size is a situational factor in that at any given time there is a finite number of organizations available for interactions. In general, the number of organizations in a relationship is related to the complexity faced by any single organization. It is also likely that large numbers of relationships weaken the quality of the relationships (John, 1977; Caragonne, 1978). An increase in the number of organizations in a relationship affects dependencies, domains, and the potential rewards or resources for participating in the relationship. Again, the analogy with individuals is appropriate here. Many ties reduce the likelihood of each tie being strong, so that there would be a greater proportion of superficial linkages in a large network than in a smaller network. Although weak ties among individuals have been shown to have great importance for their job seeking (Granovetter, 1973), there is no solid evidence regarding the impact of different forms of ties among organizations. It appears that a large set or network

would have the potential for dissipating resources and actions, but it could also provide many alternatives for an organization, in the areas of resource acquisition, client flows, and the like.

The number of relationships increases exponentially as group size increases (Caplow, 1964). The same thing would occur among organizations. The number of organizations in a relationship, or the number potentially available, thus is an important situational factor for interorganizational relationships.

Reasons for Interaction

IORs do not just happen. They occur in an environment and in a situational context. They also occur for reasons. There are three basic reasons for IORs (Galaskiewicz, 1985). The first is the *procurement and allocation of resources* such as facilities, materials, products, and revenues. These are crucial for organizational survival. The second is to form coalitions for *political advocacy and advantage*. The third is to achieve *legitimacy or public approval*. The last reason can be seen in instances of interlocking boards of directors among cultural organizations and corporations. On the basis of the study in the Minneapolis–St. Paul area, Galaskiewicz found that:

> . . . personnel from more influential companies tended to be recruited to more cultural boards and that companies tended to sit on the boards of more prestigious cultural organizations. One interpretation of these findings is that cultural organizations were striving to enhance their own reputations by aligning with the more influential companies in the area; and corporations were striving to enhance their legitimacy by aligning themselves with more prestigious cultural organizations. (pp. 296–97)

We will identify four specific reasons or bases for contact here. They range from ad hoc situations to those mandated by law or regulation. The outcome from each basis is likely to be different for the organizations involved and for the relationship itself.

(1) Ad Hoc Bases.   Relationships have an ad hoc basis when there is little or no previous patterning in the relationships among organizations. A specific need, problem, or issue may arise among two or more organizations. In the social service area, a client with an unusual problem may trigger one organization to call up another to get an opinion or to make a referral. Ad hoc bases are the least important for IORs, since they tend to be one-shot operations. If an ad hoc situation repeats itself or more elements enter the relationships among the agencies involved, other bases for a continued relationship will develop.

(2) Exchange Bases.   The exchange basis for IORs has been the dominant orientation toward such relationships since Levine and White's (1961)

seminal paper. According to Levine and White, exchange is "any voluntary activity between two organizations which has consequences, actual or anticipated, for the realization of their respective goals or objectives" (p. 120). Cook (1977) has extended this formulation beyond the two-party implication of Levine and White. She examines exchange within networks of organizations and incorporates power differentials among organizations into her formulation. The exchange idea incorporates the notion that organizations must acquire resources and that exchange is the major mechanism by which this occurs (Thompson, 1967; Jacobs, 1974; Benson, 1975).

The exchange basis can be seen as a form of bargaining in which each organization seeks to maximize its advantage in acquiring resources from another organization (Schmidt and Kochan, 1977). Although the exchange formulation seems to imply that this is bargaining among equals, modern exchange theory, as exemplified by Cook's work, does not make that assumption. Power differences among organizations are taken into account. Even when there is a great imbalance of power, the powerful organization that seeks to interact with a weaker organization can do so because of the power difference (Schmidt and Kochan, 1977). The exchange is unequal, but the participants do engage in resource exchange. The exchange basis emphasizes the importance of resource acquisition for the organizations involved. It also implies rationality, as the organizations seek to maximize their gains in interaction. All the problems associated with decision making in organizations must be considered in exchange interactions, since decisions here cannot be assumed to be any more rational than decisions made in other spheres of organizational actions. A study of business firms found that they tend to continue relationships with their auditing firms over long periods of time (Levinthal and Fichman, 1988). History has its own consequences in that relationships appear to be maintained for their own sake.

Resource exchange has far-reaching consequences (Van de Ven and Walker, 1984). Perceptions of resource dependence are an important spur for IORs. Resource dependence is a powerful direct determinant of IOR communications, resource transactions, and consensus. Monetary transactions and client referrals involve different patterns of coordination.

Exchange is an important basis for interorganizational interactions. It becomes less of a factor, however, when the interactions among organizations become formalized. Formalization is likely if resource exchanges continue (Van de Ven and Walker, 1984).

(3) Formalized Agreements.   Formalization is the degree to which the interdependency among organizations is given official sanction by the parties involved (Marrett, 1971). This official sanction or recognition is typically written down and may be legally or contractually binding (Van de Ven and Ferry, 1980). A formal agreement is based on exchange. Once the agreement is signed or otherwise authorized, the relationship changes, since interactions are

based on a specified pattern rather than ongoing through the exchange process at each interaction episode.

In our study of organizations concerned with problem youths, we (Hall et al., 1977) found that the presence of a formal agreement among organizations was related to the frequency and importance of interactions to a greater degree than to other bases of interaction. We also found that an organization did not need to evaluate other organizations when a formal agreement was in place. Apparently, the presence of a formal agreement is based on frequent and important interactions among organizations; the agreement serves to simplify interactions, since each interaction does not have to be weighed according to its contributions to the organizations involved. The organizations have agreed to interact, and the interactions take place.

Another basis for interaction has a very different source from that of agreements among the organizations involved. In many instances, interactions among organizations are mandated from outside the interacting parties.

(4) Mandatedness.　This basis for IORs has received increasing attention in recent years. Mandatedness refers to the extent to which relationships are governed by laws or regulations. These laws or regulations are imposed on the relationship by legislative or administrative rulings—the legal environmental dimension. The organizational actors are brought together because of a legal-political mandate (Raelin, 1982). For example, laws regarding unemployment compensation may require a public employment agency to interact with a welfare department to determine client eligibility. Such interaction may or may not have occurred without a mandate present. A mandated relationship may place an organization in a contradictory position (Halpert, 1982). Compliance with the mandate may disrupt established procedures. At the same time, it may be necessary for the organization if it is to receive financial support. Mandated relationships may well lead to conflict, since organizations may be forced to interact even with domain dissensus, interpersonal animosities among members, and so on.

Mandated interactions do not guarantee that interactions will take place. Unless there is some sort of enforcement mechanism, organizations may ignore a mandate. Since mandates are typically associated with some type of resource flow and with monitoring, they usually do in fact serve as an important basis for interorganizational interactions. It is quite possible that an organization can receive contradictory mandates (Gardner and Snipe, 1970). This means that an organization will have to try to serve several mandates at one time along with its own orientations from an exchange perspective. It may seek to interact with one organization but be forced to interact with one or more other organizations. Again, this moves the analysis of interorganizational interactions still further from a basis of pure rationality.

Mandated interactions continue to receive attention in research and practice. Interorganizational interactions outside the area of human services appears to be frequently based on some sort of mandate. Governmental regulatory agencies are mandated to interact with business firms. City and county government agencies are mandated to interact with state and federal agencies. Although exchange considerations enter into the passage of laws and regulations through the process of lobbying and the give-and-take of policy formulation, the presence of a strong and enforced mandate leads to IORs of a different form from those which evolve from ongoing exchanges. For example, a study found that mandated collective bargaining led to greater subunit power within organizations than was the case when mandated collective bargaining was not present (Schwochan, Fenilee, and Delaney, 1988). Another study found that the presence of mandates was related to greater frequency of interactions (Oliver, 1990). This would in turn lead to more intense interactions, and the relationship would tend to grow in many directions.

In this section we have examined ad hoc, exchange, formalized-agreement, and mandated bases of interorganizational interactions. Each basis has a different outcome. At the same time, all interorganizational interactions involve something passing between the organizations involved. We will now turn to a consideration of these resources that flow between organizations.

Resource Flows

Regardless of the environment, the situational factors, and the bases of interactions, interorganizational interactions have a content, and it is to this that we now turn. Exchange theory properly focuses on resource exchange, and we will examine resource interdependency among organizations. The flow of resources varies in intensity, so we will examine this quantitative aspect of interactions. We will then turn to the issue of joint programs, where organizations, in addition to exchanging resources, engage in activities together.

Resource Interdependence.   Situations in which two or more organizations are dependent upon one another for the resources each has access to or controls are the basis of resource interdependency. Resources take a variety of forms, such as inflows and outflows of information, money, and social support (Galaskiewicz and Marsden, 1978). There can be other resources for funds, facilities, and personnel (Molnar, 1978). Organizations that have intersecting domains tend to be more interdependent. Equipment and meeting rooms can be added to the list of resources that could be exchanged; so can clients (Mulford, 1980; Boje and Whetten, 1979).

It has long been recognized that organizations are seldom capable of controlling all the resources they require (Levine and White, 1961; Litwak and Hylton, 1962). An interorganizational division of labor can develop in which the participating organizations specialize by providing a particular service in return for a particular resource they need (Aldrich, 1979). Each organization becomes dependent upon the other in this situation. Organizations tend to resist dependence and to attempt to make other organizations dependent upon them (Benson, 1975).

It is unclear what the direction of resource flows means in regard to interdependence. On the one hand, a great outflow of some resource, such as money, could indicate great dependence, since the organization involved would appear to have to buy needed goods or services. On the other hand, money outflow may make other organizations more dependent upon the organization in question if this is their only source of funds.

There are three forms of interdependence (Pennings, 1980b). When there is horizontal interdependence, all members of an organization set compete with one another in obtaining resources and disposing of goods and services. In cases of vertical interdependence, organizations interact at different stages of the production of goods or delivery of services. For example, in the juvenile justice system, police, courts, probation services, reformatories, and halfway houses are in a sequential order. Each organization jockeys for power, but the competition is less than in horizontal interdependence. Symbiotic interdependence occurs when organizations complement one another in the rendering of service to individual clients. Here there is minimal competition, especially when agreements regarding domain have been achieved.

Intensity.   The level of resource investment required of the organizations involved in IORs determines the intensity of the relationship (Marrett, 1971; Aldrich, 1979). For service organizations, the higher the level of referrals, services provided, staff support, facilities and other resources, the greater the intensity of the relationship. Implicit in the consideration of intensity is the question of the relative proportion of an organization's resources that are invested in the relationship. The higher the proportion, the more intense the relationship and the greater the dependency (Baker, 1990).

The more intense the relationship, the more important it is for the organizations involved. The relationships that any organization has vary in their intensity from the casual to the all-consuming. The former makes little difference, whereas the latter has the potential to consume the organization if all its efforts involve interorganizational relationships and if those relationships use up all its resources.

Intensity is sometimes confused with or combined with the frequency of interactions. This is a bad mix, since frequent interactions can be casual but a very intense interactions can be infrequent. For this reason, we will consider frequency in another context. Dyadic relationships, networks, and organizational sets can all vary in intensity. Interactions become most intense in crises. For example, the tragic disappearance of a female student at my university led to intense and prolonged interaction between the campus police and the state police. Research on disasters such as earthquakes and floods reveals similarly intense interactions (Drabek et al., 1981). When there is no crisis, relationships will be less intense. The impact of intensity is both networkwide and organization specific.

Joint Programs. Joint programs are a special type of resource flow (Aiken and Hage, 1968; Mulford and Mulford, 1980). Here the emphasis is not simply on resource flows in the context of interdependency but also on substantial resource commitment and collaboration. Aiken and Hage found that joint programs were of particular importance to the welfare and health organizations that they studied. They were more salient than client, personnel, or financial support flows. Joint programs were not "minor incidents" in the lives of the organizations. Some had existed for over twenty years (p. 919). Aiken and Hage also found that joint programs tended to foster other joint programs, since the IORs grew in scope and depth.

Joint programs involve an investment of resources and an intense relationship. They also involve purposive actions in regard to some issue that is jointly confronted. Joint programs can involve a particular type of client or treatment program in the services sector or a new area of exploration for raw materials, as in the case of joint ventures (Pfeffer and Nowak, 1976). An important difference between joint programs and other forms of interactions is that the actions in a joint program are purposive and not just responsive to environmental pressures.

Transaction Forms

IORs are interaction processes between organizations and within networks and sets. We will first note how the interactions can be structured and then turn to the transaction processes themselves.

Interaction Formalization. We have already noted that organizations can have formalized agreements among themselves that can govern their interrelationships. These agreements are in place before the succeeding interactions. There is another aspect of formalization that can serve to structure the interactions. This is the presence of an intermediary organization that serves to coordinate or control interorganizational interactions.

Councils of churches, chambers of commerce, welfare boards, the NCAA, and other such mediating and coordinating organizations serve to structure the relationships among organizations (Warren, 1967; Mott, 1968). The power of these formalizing agencies can be more or less binding, so that it is important to consider the degree of interaction formalization (Van de Ven and Ferry, 1980). In some cases, the intermediary organization's decisions are binding; in other cases they are merely advisory. An example of this variation can be seen in an analysis of organizations affected by the United Fund. This study found that the power of the United Fund was inversely related to the capabilities of the member organizations obtaining funds from alternative sources (Pfeffer and Long, 1977). Those agencies that were highly dependent upon the United Fund had their interactions more formalized and controlled than those with less dependence. The presence of an intermediary organization of the sort we have been discussing leads to stability of IORs (Leblebici and Salancik, 1982).

Interaction Standardization.   There are two aspects of standardization. The first is the degree to which the resources interchanged are standardized. If organizations agree to exchange particular types of clients or personnel, high standardization is present. Low standardization occurs when the units are heterogeneous. High standardization results in more routinized interactions, with less time and energy devoted to sorting and classifying the units that are exchanged or transferred (Marrett, 1971; Aldrich, 1979).

The second form of standardization involves the procedures used in the transactions. Low standardization is represented by procedures being chosen on a case-by-case basis, and high standardization is exemplified by similar procedures being used over a period of time. When high standardization is present, there are likely to be forms and checklists that are routinely filled out as the transaction occurs. Larger and more complex organizations are more likely to standardize their transactions than are smaller and less complex organizations (Aldrich, 1979). A good example of the variance in standardization is the assignment of academic credits for students transferring from a community college to a four-year college. A large public college or university is likely to have developed procedural standardization for determining transferable credits. The small private college would treat each transfer on a case-by-case basis. The credits themselves are examples of unit standardization.

Importance.   IORs vary in their importance for the interacting organizations (Hall et al., 1977, 1978; Klonglan and Paulson, 1971; and Schmidt and Kochan, 1977). The importance of interaction is a strong predictor of the frequency of interactions. The idea of importance contains two elements. The first is the importance of another organization to the work of a focal organization. The second is the importance of the interaction itself. In either case, importance is a major contributor to the generation of IORs. Importance has been examined at the dyadic level and not at the set and network levels, but the pattern would appear to be the same. At the network level, if all mental health organizations in the network perceived that the other organizations and the interactions themselves were important, the interactions themselves would take place with greater frequency and intensity. Important interactions are likely to lead to formalized agreement among the organizations interacting (Hall et al., 1977).

Frequency.   As noted earlier, frequency of interaction and intensity are sometimes viewed synonymously. This is inappropriate, since frequency is a component of the transactions among organizations, whereas intensity is a component of the resource flow among organizations. Although importance and frequency are also closely associated, there is not a necessary relationship between the processes. A once-a-year budget meeting may be more important than weekly casual contacts. In general, however, important relationships are frequent relationships. We (Hall et al., 1978) found that frequent interactions were related to high levels of both coordination and conflict. This suggests that frequent interactions tend to include more elements of the organizations involved than do infrequent interactions. Frequent interactions contribute to heightened resource flows. Interactions can have high or low frequency on the basis of voluntary exchange, formal agreements, or mandates. Extended and frequent contacts are related to joint cooperative efforts (Heide and Miner, 1992).

Reciprocity. Reciprocity refers to the symmetry of the transactions among organizations. Resources can flow to both parties equally or in an imbalanced fashion. An examination of faculty personnel flows among graduate schools of business found that the flows were not reciprocal, with prestigious schools of business sending out more faculty members in the form of new Ph.D.'s than they received (Baty, Evan, and Rothermel, 1971). In this case, the lack of reciprocity contributed to the power of the sending schools, since the less powerful schools were dependent upon the more powerful. When there is mutual dependence, organizations will attempt to maintain reciprocal relationships.

Power. Of all the IOR transaction processes, power has received the most attention. Power in an interorganizational situation is equivalent to that in the intraorganizational situation—the ability of one party to have another party do what the other party would not otherwise do (Dahl, 1957). The power variable has been used in a variety of ways, and we will try to disentangle the various approaches that have been suggested.

One dominant theme is based on resources and views power as the possession of resources that enables an organization to use those resources to gain the compliance of others (Burt, 1977; Aldrich, 1979). Building on the perspective that sees power as residing in dependency, analysts have argued that parties in a power relationship are tied to each other by the dependence of one party on the other, or perhaps by mutual dependence. Power lies in asymmetrical dependence.

Aldrich (1979) examined the manner in which social service organization administrators deal with the power dependency issue. Four alternatives were suggested. First, an organization can build up its own resource base and thus reduce dependence. Second, the organization can seek alternative sources of needed resources, thus limiting dependency. Third, an organization can use coercion to make the other organization surrender resources without complying with its demands. This is the conflict situation as exemplified by the strike. Finally, the organization can essentially withdraw from the situation by modifying its goals or technologies. If these alternatives are not available or are not chosen, dependency will continue, and the organization will have less power than the organization with which it is interacting.

Another analysis identified expert, referent, reward, coercive, legal, and community power bases of interorganizational power (Halpert, 1974). These power bases or resources were found to be the source of organizational power in IOR transactions.

These approaches to IOR power have been applied primarily to dyadic relationships. Network analysts have frequently substituted the notion of centrality for power in their research (see Alba, 1982). Centrality refers to the relative position of an organization in a network of organizations, with those more central being viewed as having more power (Boje and Whetten, 1981; Galaskiewicz, 1979). Information and resource flows can be traced in networks. In a totally decentralized network, there is equal participation by all organizations, with perfect symmetry or reciprocity and no power differences. This is a rare situation, since networks are typically integrated by a centrally located organization (Aldrich, 1979).

There is yet another aspect to IOR power. In some IORs, the issue of exchange is not a consideration and network centrality is determined in advance. This is the situation in which power relationships are determined in advance of any interactions. In a network of organizations in which all receive their resources from a central source, such as a government agency, the power relationships are predetermined. Some bargaining will occur, but the relationship is set in advance. Organizations that are designated as information clearinghouses have a similar power role. As in the case of power within organizations, the present hierarchy of power must not be overlooked, although it has been by many interorganizational analysts.

Cooperation.   Cooperation is a process in which organizations pursue their own goals and thus retain autonomy while at the same time orienting their actions toward a common issue or outcome (Mulford, 1980; Warren, Rose, and Bergunder, 1974). We are distinguishing cooperation from coordination, since the latter process involves the pursuit of a common goal. Cooperation is typically viewed as a form of voluntary interaction (Maas, 1979) and would be found in instances of exchange-based or voluntary-agreement-based relationships. Cooperation can involve personnel interchange or products and services for clients (Klonglan and Paulson, 1971; Aiken and Hage, 1968). The cooperation process involves a relatively small investment on the part of the organizations involved, but it does mean that they have to take each other's actions into account.

Conflict.   IOR conflict is an oppositional process in which one party attempts to block or thwart the activities of another party. Conflict can occur at the individual and collective levels and within and between social systems (Galtung, 1965). For the analysis here, we are concerned with IOR conflict, whether it be interpersonal or collective in basis. Interpersonal conflict is relatively easy to understand. Collectively based conflict is more complex and refers to situations in which the organization as a whole is involved in the conflict. An example is Sebring's analysis (1977) of university-state government interactions in which unsuccessful encounters in the past led to conflicts in the present.

Conflict can take several forms in IOR transactions. Some conflict is regulated, as in competition, and other conflicts take place outside a regulatory base. As in the case of IOR processes, conflict can also be based on power differences or on domain disputes (Molnar and Rogers, 1979). It can also have ideological grounds. A study found that some police agencies are in conflict with other social service organizations, primarily because of their differing philosophies (Halpert, 1982).

The correlates of conflict are not well understood. A major reason for this is a pervasive belief that conflict is a process to be avoided. This belief appears to be misguided. Conflict and its resolution can have long-run benefits for IORs (Guetzkow, 1966; Assael, 1969). Some analysts argue that conflict is both system-integrative and system-disintegrative (Zeitz, 1980; Alter, 1990). The resolution of old conflicts sets the stage for new conflicts in a dialectic manner. Our study found that conflict was related to interaction frequency and to interactions based on both formal agreements and mandates (Hall, Clark, and Giordano, 1979). We do not see agreements or mandates as the cause of conflicts but rather interpret this relationship as being based on the fact that agreements and mandates are found in situations that are important to the parties involved. This study also found that conflict was related to power differences. Although noting that resource acquisition can be an important source of conflict, the study found that conflict also existed between organizations that had very different resource bases, such as different levels of government, as when city agencies are in conflict with county agencies.

A very different slant on interorganizational conflict is reported in a study of intergovernmental planning agencies, such as transportation, coastal zone use, energy use, and comprehensive land use (Shrum and Wuthnow, 1990). In this case, lower-level officials at the federal level interacted with higher-level officials from state and local government agencies. This status incongruence led to conflict. In this study there was no analysis of the outcome of the conflict. The apparent assumption is that the conflict got in the way of effective planning.

Conflict Resolution.   Inasmuch as there are few Hundred Years' Wars among organizations, it is safe to conclude that most conflicts are resolved. Four conflict resolution techniques that take place at the IOR level have been identified (Van de Ven and Ferry, 1980; see also Blake and Mouton, 1964; Lawrence and Lorsch, 1967; Burke, 1970; and Filley, House, and Kerr, 1976). The issues can be ignored or avoided; the issues can be smoothed over by playing down differences and emphasizing common interests; the issues can be openly confronted and differences worked through as in the case of collective bargaining; or the issues can be submitted to some hierarchical power, in the form of either some party at a higher administrative level or an outside party that is given power over the situation.

There are two other alternatives—contracting or expanding the organizational boundary (Aldrich, 1979). Contraction involves removing the organization from some aspect of its domain and thus resolving the conflict. Expansion permits an organization to encompass the other conflicting organization. Aldrich's suggestions are particularly relevant in the competitive situation. When an organization leaves a market, it is contracting; when it buys out a competitor, it is expanding its boundary.

Conflict resolution has been found to be a major contribution to coordination (Hall et al., 1978). It will be remembered that in this study conflict was based on interaction frequency and the importance of the interactions. These factors contribute to conflict, conflict resolution, and coordination. IORs are truly complex.

Coordination.   Coordination has had an interesting role in IOR analyses. Probably most studies have had coordination as an explicit or an implicit dependent variable, on the assumption that somehow coordination was good for any clients involved, could cut costs, and was good in its own right. That assumption is now being seriously questioned.

Coordination involves a process of concerted decision making or action in which two or more organizations participate with some sort of deliberate adjustment to one another (Warren, Rose, and Bergunder, 1974). A key factor here is the idea that the transactions are deliberate and involve a collective goal. This is a major point of differentiation from cooperation.

Two forms of coordination have been identified in social service organizations (Gans and Horton, 1975). Administrative coordination involves fiscal issues, personnel practices, and planning and programming. Joint budgeting and joint planning exemplify coordinated administrative practices. Coordinated direct service activities involve such things as case conferences or a case coordinator. The coordination transaction process is complex in that administrative matters can be highly coordinated while service coordination is a shambles.

In my view, coordination is an interorganizational process and not an outcome of interorganizational relationships. It may or may not be desirable. Many urban reform efforts in the 1970s believed that coordination would result from interorganizational efforts. In some cases, the coordination efforts actually got in the way of direct service delivery (Warren, Rose, and Bergunder, 1974; Perrow, 1979). Nonetheless, coordination of service delivery still is seen as a process that contributes to network effectiveness (Provan and Milward, 1995).

INTERLOCKING BOARDS OF DIRECTORS

Interlocking boards of directors are an important form of IORs. In this form a member or members of the board of directors (or board of trustees) of one organization also serve on boards of other organizations. Most research about interlocking boards has been based on studies of the private sector rather than the public service sector. Our focus thus moves away from human service organizations.

Interlocking boards of directors have been the subject of commentary and research for a long time. U.S. Supreme Court Justice Louis Brandeis warned in 1913 that such interlocks contain many evils, such as the suppression of competition (Pennings, 1980b). Pennings goes on to note that contemporary analyses of interlocks run the gamut from analyses of board interlocks as the means by which elites maintain societal control to sober scholarly analyses of the manner in which organizations attempt to control uncertainties by such interlocks.

In the basic form of director interlock, an officer or a director of one organization is a member of the board of directors of another organization. In another form of interlock, members of two organizations sit on the board of a third organization (Burt, Christman, and Kilburn, 1980). This is illustrated in Figure 10–8.

Several phenomena are represented in Figure 10–8. Firestone Tire and Rubber Company owned eight establishments in the industries indicated. According to Burt (1980), those establishments were not randomly selected.

> . . . they are, to varying extents, drawn from interdependent industries. The largest portion of supplies for the textile industry, for example, is purchased from the chemical industry, so it is to the advantage of Firestone's textile establishment to have transactions with Firestone's chemical establishment rather than being forced to deal on the open market. Similarly, the largest portion of supplies for the rubber industry is purchased from the chemical industry. Firestone's rubber establishment therefore benefits from its "inside" connection to Firestone's establishment in the chemical industry. (p. 564)

Organizations cannot purchase all organizations in their environments because of limited resources and federal merger restrictions. Interlocking boards of directors are a less direct way in which organizations can be linked. In Figure 10–8 Firestone and Western Airlines have direct interlocks, with a member from Firestone on Western's board of directors and vice versa. Indirect interlocks are present through Cleveland Trust, a banking organization. Western Airlines is a classic example of organizational death, by the way. It was acquired by Delta Airlines, which obliterated the logo and all other visible signs of Western Airlines. Only some of its routes remain.

In the world of interlocking directorates, financial institutions are the dominant actors. Commercial banks, investment banks, and insurance companies

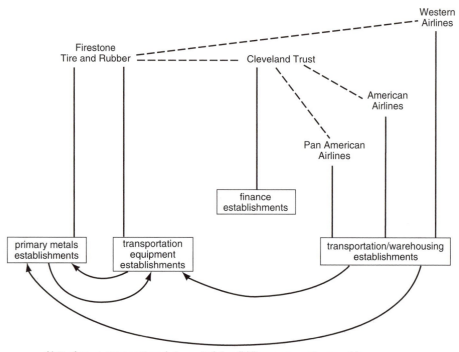

Note: Arrows represent market constraint, solid lines represent ownership, and dashed lines represent interlocking.

FIGURE 10–8 Illustrating Three Types of Directorate Ties Involving Two Firestone Tire and Rubber Establishments in 1967
Source: Ronald S. Burt, Kenneth P. Christman, and Harold C. Kilburn, Jr., "Testing a Structural Theory of Corporate Co-optation: Interorganizational Directorate Ties as a Strategy for Avoiding Market Constraints on Profits," *American Sociological Review*, 45 (October 1980), 827.

are the most likely organizations to have their members on the boards of other types of organizations (Pennings, 1980a, 1980b). These relationships are quite stable over time (Mariolis and Jones, 1982). Some analysts go so far as to conclude that the corporate system is dominated by only a handful of New York commercial banks and financial institutions (Mintz and Schwartz, 1981). This has not always been the case. Railroads, along with the telegraph and coal industries, were at the core of interlocks for the period 1886–1905 in the United States (Roy, 1983a, 1983b; see also Mizruchi and Bunting, 1981). Railroads were very powerful in that era as the nation industrialized and moved west.

Interlocks are a means by which organizations can attempt to manage uncertainty in their environments (Burt, Christman, and Kilburn, 1980; Burt, 1980, 1983; Pennings, 1980a, 1980b). Interlocks provide access to resources and can influence decisions. There are instances in which interlock occurs because an organization demands representation on another organization's board, thus lowering the autonomy of the latter organization (Aldrich, 1979).

It is imperative to note that interlocks are purposive. Purposiveness is evident for both parties. Organizations that are experiencing financial problems, such as declining solvency and declining rates of profit, seek out directors from financial institutions (Mizruchi and Stearns, 1988). At the same time, financial firms "infiltrate" the decision-making structure of firms with solvency problems. These interlocks would only take place in situations in which some hope for the future was perceived. Financial institutions would not interlock with lost causes. Interlocks tend to be reconstituted if they are broken. Breaks occur when a director dies or retires (Stearns and Mizruchi, 1986; Richardson, 1987; Palmer, Friedland, and Singh, 1986; Portugal, 1993).

Reconstitution of ties is linked to ongoing resource dependencies. These dependencies can take the form of political and community support for state colleges (Portugal, 1993) or more general financial support for organizations as diverse as hospitals (Boeker and Goodstein, 1991) and airlines (Lang and Lockhart, 1990).

So that you may understand the consequences of interlocks of boards of directors, Pennings's (1980a, 1980b) findings will be summarized. Of the 797 largest American business firms, only 62 have no interlocks with the remaining 735 firms. Financial firms are disproportionately represented in the interlocks. Interlocks are most common in concentrated industries where monopolies almost exist in the first place. Financial firms avoid interlocks with firms that appear risky, instead seeking interlocks with those that are not risky. Well-interlocked firms were found to have greater economic effectiveness. This was particularly the case with firms that rely on equity financing and that are capital intensive. The relationships between interlocks and economic effectiveness were strongest for effective organizations. Financial firms do not want to get involved with operations that they perceive as performing poorly. Pennings views these patterns of interlocks as persuasive attempts by financial firms to enhance their position with solvent firms that will be reliable customers for loans, bonds, and other forms of debt. It is a technique by which financial firms acquire good customers and by which the customers have access to financial resources. Interlocks are thus a device for managing competition to control uncertainty in corporate profits (Burt, 1983). It has also been found that interlocks have been used to try to prevent hostile takeovers—networks are used to spread the "poison pill" (Davis, 1991). The so-called poison pill is a device in which stockholders (other firms) are given the opportunity to buy a company's stock at an extremely low price on an option. This opportunity spreads through the network and prevents the hostile takeover.

These findings are hardly radical, but they are in keeping with what we understand about the ways in which organizations seek to acquire resources and enhance their position in their environment. It should be stressed that organizations in the public sector engage in the same kinds of activities through their boards of trustees, advisory boards, and the like. Research has demonstrated the importance of boards for organizations as diverse as the YMCA

(Zald, 1970) and the United Way (Provan, Beyer, and Kruytbosch, 1980). An examination of the board of any college or university would reveal similar linkages into important segments of the organization's environments.

Evidence of a slightly different slant can be found in the research carried out in the Minneapolis–St. Paul metropolitan area (Galaskiewicz et al., 1985; Galaskiewicz, 1997). Contrary to some studies, this research has not found consistent patterns of interlock among firms that constrained one another across industries. Neither local sales patterns nor labor markets affected the patterns of interlock.

This research found that social status within the community was important for interlocks. Socially elite individuals who were associated with large corporations were disproportionately represented on boards of directors. Firms tended to interlock with those of equal social standing. According to Galaskiewicz et al., both "clout and grace" (1985: p. 423) contributed to the densest interlocks. Economic clout and social grace made companies and people attractive to one another.

The Galaskiewicz studies dealt with interlocks and corporate philanthropy. There are interesting linkages at levels below the boards of directors. There are "corporate contributions officers" who hold staff positions well below the top executive level. People in these positions also have cohesion with one another, since they have similar-to-identical role relationships. This contributes to the "contagion" in philanthropy that was identified in the Minneapolis–St. Paul area (Galaskiewicz and Burt, 1991). The authors caution that there may be a regional influence on their findings.

Some analysts believe that the actual power of boards of directors is quite limited in that their power is to ratify or defeat what the chief executive officer and his or her administration propose to do. Quite frequently, the executive officer and the administration have greater knowledge than members of the board and can thus control the situation. At the same time, boards of directors can remove top administrative officers (James and Soref, 1981). The presence of external influences on a board of directors can have little affect on the behavior of managers in some cases (Fligstein and Brantley, 1992). At the same time, boards of directors are at the apex of power in organizations and there is a natural jousting for power. Powerful top managers want to maintain their power and prefer passive boards. Active boards want to maintain or increase their power (Zajac and Westphal, 1996).

Board interlocks have an additional basis, which is independent of organizational issues. Political sociologists have focused on *social class* and its relationship with interlocks. Based on Canadian evidence, Ornstein (1984) concluded that corporate imperatives and class solidarity factors operate in interlocks. Using data from a U.S. Senate committee, Kerbo and Della Fave (1983) found that there is an "intercorporate complex" of major corporations, with banks in a central coordinating position that is short of control. They also found evidence for an inner group of the "corporate class" that provides the human linkages.

The social-class argument has persuasive evidence in its behalf at the local level (Galaskiewicz et al., 1985; Palmer, Friedland, and Singh, 1986) and at the national level (Mintz and Schwartz, 1981; Useem, 1979, 1982, 1984; Domhoff and Dye, 1987). An analysis of the 1980 congressional elections found that corporate contributions to political action committees (PACs) for these elections were based on ideological conservatism (Clawson and Neustadt, 1989). They conclude that interlocks are based on classwide rational actions. Although it is hard to comprehend how classes can be more rational than organizations, the class argument is persuasive.

The class argument is especially persuasive if it is used in conjunction with an organizational perspective on interlocks. Mizruchi (1989, 1992) provides just that perspective. He examined 1,596 dyads among 57 large manufacturing firms. He found that membership in the same primary industry or several similar industries, geographical proximity of corporate headquarters (but not plant locations), market constraints, and common relations with financial institutions (through stock ownership or directorate ties) were related to similarity of political behavior. He argues that resource dependency and social class explanations were both operative.

Director interlocks are a means by which the resources that are important to organizations and their relationships flow between organizations. They can give an organization a competitive advantage through access to financing, information, and other resources.

OUTCOMES OF IOR

As might be expected, the outcomes of IOR are complex and difficult to measure. In the human-services area, much of the research has been concerned with improved service delivery, which itself is difficult to conceptualize and measure. A study of health care delivery with a focus on two hospitals found that service delivery was quite well coordinated through a complex system of formal and informal arrangements (Milner, 1980). One of the hospitals provided high-quality care to affluent patients, and the other provided lower-quality care to the poor. The interorganizational arrangements served to maintain this differentiation. IORs were thus effective on the one hand but divisive on the other.

The outcome issue is both simple and complex. Its simplicity is that it lies in the eyes and minds of the beholders. The complexity of the outcome issue is that there are multiple eyes and minds that can make this assessment. This problem is identical to the issue of organizational effectiveness, which will be considered in the next chapter. The perceived effectiveness of interorganizational interactions can be assessed from the standpoint of participants within each organization, the organization as a whole, clients served or disserved, the community in which the interactions take place, or legislative or administrative decision makers who have jurisdiction over the particular dyads, sets, or networks in question. The outcome issue is thus one of political power, resource dependence, and moral choice. Outcomes that are good for one organization may be bad for another; clients may benefit, but the organizations may suffer; relationships may be cost-effective but damaging to organizations and clients. Analyses of IORs must keep these considerations in mind.

Most of the research on which this analysis has been based was carried out in social service organizations, with the exception of the materials on director interlocks. We clearly need an expanded database from a broader range of organizations. The analysis contained relatively little reference to the organizations involved in interactions. Little is actually known of this linkage. We also suffer from a shortage of information about the individuals involved in IOR interactions. There is some limited information on boundary spanners, but this role may actually be a peripheral one, with much greater importance found in the individuals who are on interlocking boards or those who interpret and decide upon the information brought by boundary spanners. There are important political and moral issues in regard to the power of interlocking directorates.

The area of IORs is thus one of great research potential. There is a general belief that the relationships are important, even though this has not yet been demonstrated.

SUMMARY AND CONCLUSIONS

This chapter has been focused on organizational environment, a topic that has been stressed throughout our analysis of organizations. The more general content and analytical dimensions of the environment were considered. Attention was then focused on specific aspects of environments as they are played out through IORs.

There is always a danger of converting analyses of organizational environments into the primary focus of organizational analyses. That would be a huge mistake. Environments are an important component of organizational analysis, to be sure, but the real focus should be organizational effectiveness, to which we turn in the next chapter. Environments will not disappear in the consideration of effectiveness, but neither will they overwhelm the analysis.

chapter 11

Organizational Effectiveness

This whole book has been about organizational effectiveness. We study organizations primarily to understand how and why they are effective or ineffective. We may want to make them more or less effective from an economic, political, or moral perspective. It is now well recognized that the various parties concerned with any single organization can have contrasting and conflicting views on its effectiveness. We are not neutral about the organizations with which we deal as workers, clients, customers, or publics. I don't want to be abused by any organization, public or private. I also want the organizations in which I participate as a member to do well. To do well is to be effective. My perspective on effectiveness, however, varies with my position in the organization. I see effectiveness differently as a faculty member from the way I saw it as dean. I have different perspectives about the other organizations of which I am a part.

In this chapter our analysis essentially comes full circle. We began this book by considering some of the outcomes of organizations. We then examined structural characteristics, processes within organizations, and organizational environments. In essence, the outcomes of structural arrangements, processes such as decision making and leadership, and dealing with the environment are designed to contribute to organizational effectiveness. Unfortunately, like many organizations, organizational effectiveness itself is highly complex.

There are several competing models of effectiveness in the literature that have served as the bases for analyses of effectiveness. In the present chapter these models will be analyzed and their strengths and weaknesses highlighted.

Inherent in the models and in the debates about the models is the idea that organizational effectiveness as a concept contains contradictions. With that in mind, we will develop a *contradiction* model of effectiveness, which is designed to encompass the insights that previous models have identified.

For practitioners and scholars who concentrate on organizational analysis, organizational effectiveness has been a dominant explicit and implicit point of departure. This reflects the administrative-technical orientation of many people who study organizations (Benson, 1977). They wish to find ways to adjust organizations to enhance effectiveness. Benson notes that although many studies deal with effectiveness in a direct and highly visible way, even those studies that do not focus on effectiveness tend to deal with it implicitly, as an underlying or background orientation.

Not everyone is concerned with organizational effectiveness in this manner. There are many important social issues that have generated attempts to prevent organizational effectiveness. Opponents of nuclear-energy development and generation and of abortion are essentially against the effectiveness of the organizations that provide electricity and abortions. Ironically, the success of these oppositional efforts depends upon the effectiveness of the oppositional organizations.

The present analysis is an attempt to decompose the concept of organizational effectiveness and to expose and examine the contradictions inherent in the concept and its applications. The purpose is to provide a sounder basis for research, theory, and practice. It is hoped that the analysis will be more than administrative-technical and that it will be informative for individuals concerned with altering the directions that organizations take.

TOWARD A CONTRADICTION MODEL OF EFFECTIVENESS

Before we get into the specifics of the contradiction model of effectiveness that is to be introduced here, it should be made clear that the approach to be taken forces the analysis of effectiveness away from attempts to conceive of *overall* organizational effectiveness. A contradiction model requires the uncompromised acceptance of the fact that it is folly to try to conceptualize organizations as effective or ineffective (Campbell, 1977).

Although there is agreement that effectiveness as an overall concept has little or no utility, it would be a big mistake to simply ignore issues and findings that have been developed in regard to effectiveness. This seeming paradox can be resolved if a contradiction model of effectiveness is used. Put very simply, a contradiction model of effectiveness will consider organizations to be more or less effective in regard to the variety of goals that they pursue, the variety of resources that they attempt to acquire, the variety of constituents inside and outside the organization, and the variety of time frames by which effectiveness is judged. The idea of variety in goals, resources, and so on is key here, since it suggests that an organization can be very effective in some aspects of its operations and less so in others.

The contradiction idea has its roots in a research project that was discussed in the previous chapter: the study of organizations that deal with problem youths. It was found that these organizations had multiple and conflicting goals. One set of organizations in the study were juvenile detention centers. These organizations had the goals, among others, of "maintaining secure custody" and "providing healthy living arrangements." On the face of it, those are incompatible goals, since secure custody would be optimized by simply locking the youths in cells, which is hardly a healthy living arrangement.

The example of contradictory goals just noted comes from the public sector. It is frequently believed that goals here are more amorphous and contradictory than those in the private sector. Unfortunately, the private-sector picture is also one of contradictions. For example, the goal idea seems simple in the case of profit-making organizations. Indeed, much of the research on effectiveness has used this type of organization because of assumed goal clarity. The seemingly readily quantifiable profit goal is not such a simple matter, however. It is confounded by such issues as the time perspective (long-run or short-run profits); the rate of profit (in the form of returns to investors); survival and growth in a turbulent and unpredictable environment that might in the short run preclude profit making; the intrusion of other values, such as providing quality products or services or benefiting humankind; and the firm's position compared with that of others in the same industry. Even the nature of profit itself is multifaceted. It can involve return on stockholders' equity, return on total capital, sales growth, earnings-per-share growth, debt-to-equity ratio, and net-profit margin. These are not well correlated (Forbes, 1973), which alone makes the idea of goals extremely complex.

The goal approach has another complication. We have already demonstrated that organizational decisions and actions cannot be viewed simply from a rational-model framework. Decisions that at first appear to be rational turn out to be disastrous because of events beyond organizational control.

In the pages that follow, we will present and evaluate the major models of effectiveness. Each makes a positive contribution to our understanding and contributes to the contradiction model.

MODELS OF ORGANIZATIONAL EFFECTIVENESS

The system-resource model is the first effectiveness model to be examined, because an extensive analysis of the environmental-organizational interface has been presented. This model was developed by Yuchtman and Seashore (1967; Seashore and Yuchtman, 1967), who begin by noting that variables concerning organizational effectiveness could be ordered into a hierarchy. At the top of the hierarchy is some ultimate criterion that can only be assessed over time. An example of such an ultimate criterion would be the optimum use of opportunities and resources found in the environment. According to the natural-selection model, the ultimate criterion would be survival or death.

Next come penultimate criteria, which are performance measures, such as business volume and market penetration, for organizations in specific industries. Other penultimate criteria are more time specific, such as having a high proportion of new members. The utility of this approach was examined by use of a data set from insurance agencies. The data revealed that there were identifiable factors that were stable over time and that involved organizational-environmental linkages.

Seashore and Yuchtman conclude that their findings lead to a definition of effectiveness of an organization as the *"ability to exploit its environment in the acquisition of scarce and valued resources to sustain its functioning"* (p. 393; italics in original). Their reasoning is that whereas some of the penultimate criteria found, such as business volume and market penetration, could be construed as goals, others, such as a high proportion of new members, could not.

Seashore and Yuchtman also conclude that resource acquisition must be viewed as relative to the capacity of the environment. Some organizations operate in rich environments; others act in poorer ones. They also note that their definition stresses the ability to utilize the environment rather than maximum utilization of the environment, since maximum utilization could lead to the total depletion of resources.

The Seashore-Yuchtman argument is persuasive but contains some problem areas. For instance, it is actually a question of semantics whether growth in business volume is viewed as only one form of resource acquisition or as a goal. The relatively stable penultimate criteria discussed by Seashore and Yuchtman can easily be viewed as goals or as constraints on the decisions made by the insurance firms in question. The less stable criteria, such as youthfulness of members, could turn out to be predictor variables for these sorts of organizations. It is well known, for example, that young men and women who enter the life insurance sales occupation have good success at first, selling to relatives and friends. This would appear to be a means by which a goal, such as sales volume, could be achieved.

It should also be noted that resource acquisition does not just happen but is based on what the organization is attempting to achieve—namely, its goals. This is in line with our earlier discussion of decision making, in which decisions are made on the basis of perceived environmental conditions and organizational goals. It is reasonable to argue that resources are seldom acquired just for their own sake; they are also acquired according to the paths selected by the power coalitions in the organization. Seashore and Yuchtman implicitly recognize this point when they suggest that criteria for determining effectiveness must be identified.

The Seashore-Yuchtman formulation has been criticized as being too narrow in that it utilizes only the interests of the organizational directors (Scott, 1977). In the case of insurance firms, potential customers could withhold resources, but there are many forms of organizations in which potential customers do not have that option. A more basic issue is that whereas some people may benefit from the survival of an organization, others may benefit from its dissolution (Keeley, 1984).

The Goal Model

The goal model of effectiveness is both simple and complex. In the simple version, effectiveness has been defined as the "degree to which [an organization] realizes its goals" (Etzioni, 1964: p. 8). The model becomes complex as soon as it is realized that most organizations have multiple and frequently conflicting goals. Structural differentiation in organizations is related to goal diversity and goal incompatibility (Kochan, Cummings, and Huber, 1976). Since most organizations do exhibit structural diversity, such multiplicity and incompatibility can almost be taken for granted in most organizations. This makes the goal model difficult to use but does not automatically destroy its utility.

Goals involve intents and outcomes and serve as constraints on decision making. Organizational goals are by definition creations of individuals, singly or collectively. At the same time, the determination of a goal for collective action becomes a standard by which the collective action is judged. The collectively determined, commonly based goal seldom remains constant over time. New considerations imposed from without or within deflect the organization from its original goal, not only changing the activities of the organization, but also becoming part of the overall goal structure. The important point is that the goal of any organization is an abstraction distilled from the desires of members and pressures from the environment and internal system.

Thinking of goals as abstract values has the utility of indicating the reason organizational members do not just act on their feelings or whims on a particular day. At the same time, it is a mistake to take as the abstraction the official goal statements of the organization. Perrow (1961) has analyzed this situation nicely. He notes that official goals are "the general purposes of the organization as put forth in the charter, annual reports, public statements by key executives and other authoritative pronouncements." Operative goals, on the other hand, "designate the ends sought through the actual operating policies of the organization; they tell us what the organization actually is trying to do, regardless of what the official goals say are the aims" (p. 855).

In one of the early studies in the tradition of modern organizational theory, Blau (1955) found that two employment agency units, which had the same official goals, were very different in what they really were attempting to accomplish. One unit was highly competitive, with members striving to outproduce each other in the numbers of individuals placed. In the other unit, cooperation and quality of placement was stressed.

In discussing this point, Perrow (1961) notes:

> Where operative goals provide the specific content of official goals, they reflect choices among competing values. They may be justified on the basis of an official goal, even though they may subvert another official goal. In one sense they are a means to official goals, but since the latter are vague or of high abstraction, the "means" become ends in themselves when the organization is the object of analysis. For example, where profit making is the announced goal, operative goals will specify whether quality or quantity is to be emphasized, whether profits are to be short run and risky or long run and stable, and will indicate the relative priority of diverse and somewhat conflicting ends of customer service, employee morale, competitive pricing, diversification, or liquidity. Decisions on all of these factors influence the nature of the organization and distinguish it from another with an identical official goal. (pp. 855–56)

Operative goals may be linked directly to official goals. At the same time, operative goals can develop that are unrelated to official goals. Perrow goes on to note:

> Unofficial operative goals, on the other hand, are tied more directly to group interests, and while they may support, be irrelevant to, or subvert official goals, they bear no necessary connection with them. An interest in a major supplier may dictate the policies of a corporate executive. The prestige that attaches to utilizing elaborate highspeed computers may dictate the reorganization of inventory and accounting departments. Racial prejudice may influence the selection procedures of an employment agency. The personal ambition of a hospital administrator may lead to community alliances and activities which bind the organization without enhancing its goal achievement. On the other hand, while the use of interns and residents as "cheap labor" may subvert the official goals of medical education, it may substantially further the official goal of providing a high quality of patient care. (p. 856)

Operative goals are thus a derivation of and a distillation from official goals. They are developed and modified through ongoing interaction patterns within organizations. They are more than just the results of interpersonal interactions, however. They persist beyond the life of a particular interaction and become the standards by which the organization's actions are judged and around which decisions are made. Even though operative goals are developed in concrete interactions, they, like official goals, are abstractions, since they become standards by which actions and decisions are judged.

The discussion of the development of operative goals suggests that goals change over time. There are three reasons for changes in the goals of organizations. First, organizations are in direct interaction with the environment through their IORs. Organizational goal setting is affected by competitive, bargaining, co-optative, and coalitional relationships with the environment (Thompson and McEwen, 1958). Competition occurs when the rivalry between two organizations is mediated by a third party, as in the case of business firms competing for the same customers. Competition also occurs in the public sector as government agencies compete for a share of the tax dollar (Wildavsky, 1964). Competition affects the goal structure as the organization shapes its actions to try to ensure continued support. In this regard, of course, the goal model can be seen to encompass at least some aspects of the system-resource model.

Bargaining also involves resources but in a different manner. The organization is in direct interaction with suppliers, customers, and other organizations. In a bargaining situation, an organization has to "give" a little to get what it desires. Thompson and McEwen note the example of a university that bargains the right to name a building for a substantial gift to build the building. If the donor attaches strings to the gift, the university might alter its operative goals to get the money.

Co-optation is "the process of absorbing new elements into the leadership or policy-determining structure of an organization as a means of averting threats to its stability or existence" (Thompson and McEwen, 1958: p. 27). The classic study of co-optation is Selznick's (1966) analysis of the development of the Tennessee Valley Authority. The TVA shifted its emphases as segments of the community were brought into its decision-making system. Business firms engage in co-optation as they engage in board interlocks when there are market constraints (Burt, Christman, and Kilburn, 1980; Burt, 1983). Co-optation is a two-way street, of course: Both co-opters and co-optees are affected by the action.

Coalition is the actual combining of two or more organizations. This is the most extreme form "of environmental conditioning of organizational goals" (Thompson and McEwen, 1958: p. 28). In this case, the organizations in the coalition cannot set goals unilaterally.

Shifts in organizational goals as a result of direct interactions with other organizations in a focal organization's environment emphasizes the importance of dealing with operative, rather than official, goals. A reliance only on official goals would miss these sometimes subtle, sometimes dramatic shifts. This kind of analysis also indicates the importance of looking at organizational effectiveness over time, since a cross-sectional analysis might be done just before a significant shift occurs and thus be essentially meaningless.

The second reason that goals change is that internal organizational changes may occur. We have already noted the importance of power coalitions within organizations. These power coalitions can shift, sometimes as a result of external pressures, but also because of internal dynamics. Michels's (1949) classic study of the development of oligarchy in political parties and labor unions is illustrative of this. The goals of the rank and file tend to give way to those of the elites. Organizations can be seen as "battlegrounds for stakeholders, both inside and outside, who compete to influence the criteria for effectiveness so as to advance their own interests" (Kanter and Brinkerhoff, 1981: p. 322).

Organizations may begin to emphasize goals that are easily quantifiable, at the expense of those that are not so easily quantified. Universities look at the number of faculty publications rather than at the more-difficult-to-measure goal of classroom teaching; business firms look at output per worker rather than at "diligence, cooperation, punctuality, loyalty, and responsibility" (Gross, 1968: p. 295). If organizations do begin to emphasize that which is easily quantifiable, then there is a shift of goals in that direction. Goal shifts are also possible when there is slack in the organization and it is secure. A study of the National Council of Churches found that staff interactions guided by a new professional ideology and strong purposive commitments contributed to major and radical goal shifts within the organization (Jenkins, 1977). This study also suggests that threats to the organization's domain would probably lead to a more conservative stance.

The final source of goal shifts lies outside the organization and involves indirect pressures from the general environment. Economic conditions can become altered. Technological developments must be accommodated. Values shift. Organizational goals are adjusted to these environmental conditions. The classic study of this form of goal shift is Sills's (1957) analysis of the March of Dimes organization, which had been oriented toward the treatment of individuals who suffered the crippling effects of polio. The development of safe vaccines, a technological development, essentially eliminated the need for the continued existence of the organization, until it shifted its goals to include other crippling diseases.

Another example of this form of goal shift can be seen among colleges and universities as the demographic composition of the population shifts. Higher-educational organizations are now including nontraditional students as major recruitment targets, with "seminars for seniors" and a wide array of continuing-education programs. The demographic shifts are beyond the control of the organizations involved, as are the other sources of indirect pressure from the environment. Although organizations can try to influence values, manipulate the economy to their advantage, and keep up with technological developments, many situations are simply beyond organizational control. At various times, the United States has faced shortages of gasoline. Organizations, even petroleum firms, have no control over the actions of oil-producing nations. Thus, the environment can have an indirect but still crucial role in the determination of goal shifts.

Thus far, the analysis has suggested that organizations have multiple goals, which may be contradictory and which may also shift. We will now turn to a consideration of how goals can be used in analyzing effectiveness.

Goals and Effectiveness

As noted earlier, the simplest use of the goal model suggests that an organization is effective to the degree to which it achieves its goals. According to Campbell (1977):

The goal-centered view makes a reasonably explicit assumption that the organization is in the hands of a rational set of decision makers who have in mind a set of goals that they wish to pursue. Further, these goals are few enough in number to be manageable and can be defined well enough to be understood. Given that goals can be thus identified, it should be possible to plan the best management strategies for attaining them. Within this orientation, the way to assess organizational effectiveness would be to develop criterion measures to assess how well the goals are being achieved. (p. 19)

Unfortunately, for organizations and those who analyze them, the matter is not that simple. Hannan and Freeman (1977b) have examined the goal model and have pinpointed some of the problems with its use. They begin their analysis by pointing out that it would be unsatisfactory to totally drop the goal concept, since goals are part of the defining characteristics of organizations. They go on to note, however, that a first and major difficulty with the goal approach is that there is likely to be a multiplicity of organizational goals. This occurs even among the publicly legitimated or official goals, as has already been noted. Hannan and Freeman comment: "Virtually all public agencies and bureaus have very many public goals. For example, the number and diversity of goals of agencies like the Department of Health, Education, and Welfare (HEW) and the Department of Commerce boggle the imagination" (pp. 111–12).

According to Hannan and Freeman, the second broad problem with goals involves their specificity (p. 113). Universities have the very general goals of advancing the store of useful knowledge; police agencies have the goal of protecting the public. These broad goals become much more specific in actual operations, with the more specific goals taking a variety of possible forms. For the police, for example, protecting the public could be approached from the standpoint of putting more officers on foot patrol, cracking down on prostitution, putting more officers in plainclothes operations, or making public relations statements. Within the organization, units can move in divergent directions that are consistent with the broader goal but that could interfere with one another's operations.

The third problem with goals involves the temporal dimension. Hannan and Freeman (1977b) note:

Should we consider the short run or the long run or both? The many published empirical studies that employ cross-sectional data on samples of organizations (see, for example, Lawrence and Lorsch, 1967) tacitly take the short-run perspective. Whether or not this is appropriate depends on the nature of the goals function for each organization. To the extent that the goals function stresses quick return on investment (as in many business ventures, disaster relief organizations, military field units, and so on) the short-run outcomes should be given highest priority. For those organizations that orient toward continued production (for example, many other types of business ventures, universities, research and development organizations, and so on) the year-to-year fluctuations in performance should be discounted and the average performance over longer periods emphasized. (p. 113)

Hannan and Freeman note that different levels in the hierarchy can employ different time frames, making the situation even more complex. They do not deal with the fact that different units within the same organization can also have different time frames.

Hannan and Freeman also deal with the second part of the goal model, which is organizational performance or output. Outcome assessment is difficult for several reasons. The first is the time perspective used. An outcome that is successful for the short run could be disastrous for the long run. Another problem in outcome assessment involves "bounding systems" (Hannan and Freeman, 1977b: p. 116), or the problem in distinguishing the effects of events both inside and outside the organization. The issue here is that it is very difficult to determine what activity within an organization contributes to some outcome. It is equally difficult to specify if that outcome is a result of organizational actions or the result of some external force. This point is not lost on organizational management. Corporate annual reports tend to attribute unfavorable outcomes to external, unstable, and uncontrollable causes. Favorable outcomes are attributed to actions taken by management (Bettman and Weitz, 1983). Closely related findings are reported in an analysis of letters to shareholders. These letters tend to be self-serving and attribute corporate performance to the actions taken by management (Staw, McKechnie, and Puffer, 1983). Interestingly, these letters appear to be convincing, since they are related to stock price increases. They are also related to the sale of stock by corporate management.

The quality of the input of an organization affects the quality of the output. Many social service organizations, for example, select clients (inputs or external forces) who appear to have good chances of success in the treatment that the organization provides. More problematic clients are referred elsewhere or are simply passed around the social service system. This sort of situation makes the assessment of the outcome of the social service organization difficult, since it is difficult to disentangle organizational-versus-input effects.

The problem is made even more complicated by the fact that although both input quality and the contribution of units within organizations can be understood as contributors to performance, so too can the ability of the organization to control the quality of inputs. Control of environmental factors is an outcome of organizational actions. Organizations attempt to build up demands for their outputs. Success here means higher performance.

Hannan and Freeman conclude:

> Once we acknowledge that all these factors are subject to organizational strategy and action, we are faced with a serious methodological problem. All of the variables that appear in the conventional analyses are endogenous, that is, causally dependent on other variables in the model. For example, the quality of inputs may be a function of the expenditure on inputs, which is a function of output performance. If none of these factors is causally prior, or exogeneous, it is extremely difficult to obtain unique estimates of any relevant causal effects in the

system. In the technical language of econometrics, the system is underidentified. To remedy this situation one must make a considerable number of strong assumptions concerning the details of the causal structure. Unfortunately, the existing theories of organizational performance (and effectiveness) do not provide a basis for these assumptions. (p. 122)

Hannan and Freeman conclude their argument by suggesting that effectiveness be dropped as a *scientific* concept, since comparisons across organizations cannot be made to construct and test abstract theories of organizations. They then suggest that effectiveness considerations remain valid for *engineering* or *social criticism*. By this they mean that effectiveness can be used in the administrative-technical sense by individuals interested in engineering or in managing organizations toward public or private goals. Social criticism can be accomplished by demonstrating that organizations are not doing what they claim to be doing or that they are not doing it well enough. In the contradiction model that will be developed here, the intent will be to permit effectiveness considerations to remain at the scientific level.

The goal model as an engineering tool can be readily seen in analyses of performance among business organizations. Performance refers to achieving economic goals, usually with a short-term emphasis. "High-performing firms" are a sacred symbol among some business analysts, but as with many sacred symbols, many meanings can be applied to it. Indeed, there are entire industries that have been developed around measuring high performance, such as accountancy, compensation management, financial planning, and fund managing (Meyer, 1994). There is an interesting institutional twist to the engineering of performance measurement, since measures of performance can be adopted out of the fear that not to adopt particular measures would be "disadvantageous" (Meyer, 1994, p. 576). Performance measures are adopted on faith rather than on evidence.

We have now moved into the issue of who or which parties are to judge the performance of organizations in regard to goals. The views of different organizational constituents can vary widely and must be considered, as they will be in the contradiction model. In the next section, we will deal specifically with attempts to conceptualize effectiveness in terms of the satisfaction of organizational participants. One approach that has been tried, based on the goal model, has been to ask persons in superordinate positions about the effectiveness of organizational units that are subordinate to them. This approach is quite useful for performance assessments of organizational subunits. It also could be used in situations where organizations within a single political jurisdiction, such as state, county, or city organizations, are being examined. In reality, such effectiveness judgments are made at the time of budget allocations, but that process contains more than effectiveness considerations.

The approach of asking superordinates about the effectiveness of subordinates has been used with success by Mahoney and Weitzel (1969) and Duncan (1973). This approach has revealed that even superordinates stress different goals. Mahoney and Weitzel note:

General business managers tend to use productivity and efficient performance. These high-order criteria refer to measures of output, whereas lower-order criteria tend to refer to characteristics of the organization climate, supervisory style, and organizational capacity for performance. The research and development managers, on the other hand, use cooperative behavior, staff development, and reliable performance as high-order criteria; and efficiency, productivity, and output behavior as lower-order criteria. (p. 362)

Effectiveness thus lies in the eyes and minds of the beholders, with the important qualification that some beholders are more powerful than others.

Participant-Satisfaction Models

In this section we will examine models of effectiveness that, in various ways and at various levels, utilize individuals as the primary frame of reference. The emphasis in these models is not satisfaction as seen in morale or some other psychological state of the individual. This is frequently a component of the goal model, seeing morale as just one of several goals. Rather, in these models the emphasis is on individual or group judgments about the quality of the organization.

Barnard (1938) set the tone for participant-satisfaction models with his analysis of organizations as cooperative, incentive-distributing devices. "Individuals contributed their activities to organizations in return for incentives, the contribution of each in the pursuit of his particularistic ends being a contribution to the satisfaction of the ends of others. Barnard regarded the motives of the individuals participating in organizations as the critical determinants. Only if these were satisfied, could the organization continue to operate" (Georgiou, 1973: p. 300). Organizational success was not viewed as the achievement of goals but rather as survival through the ability to gain enough contributions from the members by providing sufficient rewards or incentives.

Georgiou (1973), building on the work of Barnard, has developed what he labels a "counter paradigm" to the goal model (see also, Samuel, 1979). According to Georgiou:

Thus, the essential thrust of the counter paradigm is that the emergence of organizations, their structure of roles, division of labor, and distribution of power, as well as their maintenance, change, and dissolution can best be understood as outcomes of the complex exchanges between individuals pursuing a diversity of goals. Although the primary focus of interest lies in the behavior within organizations, and the impact of the environment on this, the reciprocal influence of the organization on the environment is also accommodated. Since not all of the incentives derived from the processes of organizational exchange are consumed within the interpersonal relations of the members, organizational contributors gain resources with which they can influence the environment. (p. 308)

The implication of Georgiou's argument for effectiveness is that incentives within organizations must be adequate for maintaining the contributions of organizational members and must also contain a surplus for developing power capabilities for dealing with the environment. A basic problem with this argument is that it does not disclose how the incentives are brought into the organization in the first place. If a major incentive is money, the money must be secured. To be sure, money is brought into the organization through exchanges with the environment, but it appears that the system-resource approach or a goal model dealing with profit is necessary before considering individual inducements.

Cummings (1977) approaches effectiveness from a slightly different perspective. He states:

> One possibly fruitful way to conceive of an organization and the processes that define it is as an instrument or an arena within which participants can engage in behavior they perceive as instrumental to their goals. From this perspective, an effective organization is one in which the greatest percentage of participants perceive themselves as free to use the organization and its subsystem as instruments for their own ends. It is also argued that the greater the degree of perceived organizational instrumentality by each participant, the more effective the organization. Thus, this definition of an effective organization is entirely psychological in perspective. It attempts to incorporate both the number of persons who see the organization as a key instrument in fulfilling their needs and, for each person, the degree to which the organization is so perceived. (pp. 59–60)

According to this approach, factors such as profitability, efficiency, and productivity are necessary conditions for organizational survival and are not ends in themselves. The organization must acquire enough resources to permit it to be instrumental for its members. A loosely related approach argues that more effective organizations are those in which the members agree with the goals of the organization and thus work more consistently to achieve them (Steers, 1977).

Approaching organizational effectiveness from the perspective of individuals and their instrumental gains or their goals has three major problems. The first problem, which is particularly the case for Steers's approach, is that individuals have varying forms of linkages to the organizations of which they are a part. People's involvement in organizations can be alienative, calculative, or moral (Etzioni, 1961, 1975). These different forms of involvement preclude the possibility of individual and goal congruence in many types of organizations. Continuing for a moment with a criticism of Steers's approach, it does not appear to be unfair to note that many personnel in most organizations are probably unaware of the organizations' official or operative goals, so that agreement becomes a moot point.

A second, and more basic, problem in these psychological formulations is that their focus on instrumentality for individuals neglects the activities or operations of the organization as a whole or by subunits. Although the instrumentality approach is capable of being generalized across organizations, it misses the fact that organizational outputs do something in society. They are consumed, enjoyed, but could be environmentally harmful. They affect other organizations and people in and out of other organizations as much as people within a focal organization. The psychological approach also downplays the reality of conflicts among goals and decisions that must be made in the face of environmental pressures. The problem is basically one of overlooking a major part of organizational reality. For example, there is a positive relationship between workers' commitment to the organization and such effectiveness indicators as adaptability, turnover, and tardiness. No such relationship was found with the effectiveness indicators of operating costs and absenteeism (Angle and Perry, 1981). Reducing effectiveness considerations to the individual level misses the point that there can be conflicts between desirable outcomes, such as lowered operating costs and lowered turnover.

A third problem with this form of individualistic approach is that it misses the fact that individuals outside the organization are affected by what organizations do. A study of the juvenile justice system found that the "clients" of a juvenile justice system network had clearly different views of the effectiveness of organizations such as the police, courts, and probation departments from those of the members of those agencies (Giordano, 1976, 1977). That is hardly surprising, of course, since the clients in this case were juveniles who had been in trouble with the law. Nonetheless, a client perspective on effectiveness would seem to be a critical component of any comprehensive effectiveness analysis.

Keeley (1978, 1984) has tried to overcome the problems of focusing only on the reactions of internal organizational actors by proposing a "social justice" approach to effectiveness. Building on the work of Rawls (1971), Keeley suggests that a guiding principle for organizational evaluation might be "maximization of the least advantaged participants in a social system" (1978: p. 285). Keeley then proposes that this approach could be operationalized by minimizing the regret that participants experience in their interactions with the organization. Keeley's later work (1984) shifts to the idea of organizational harm but retains the same flavor. He recognizes the difficulties associated with the actual application of the approach but claims that the approach actually contains an optimization principle that goal models do not contain. It is possible to specify the manner in which group regret or harm can be minimized across organizations. It is not possible to specify how goal attainment can be optimized across organizations, given the diversity of goals.

Keeley (1978) concludes:

> Finally, the social-justice model—specifically the minimization of regret principle—manages to balance participant interests in an ethical, yet pragmatic, fashion. It may seem perverse to focus on regretful organizational participants rather than on those, possibly more in number, who enjoy the outcomes of cooperative activity. But the point is that generally aversive system consequences ought not, and, in the long run, probably will not, be tolerated by some participants so that positive consequences can be produced for others. Systems that minimize the aversive consequences of interaction are, therefore, claimed to be more just as well as more stable in the long run. (p. 290)

One can disagree with the practicality of Keeley's approach from the standpoint of the difficulties in determining levels of regret or harm for all system participants, but the point on ethicality is one that should remain fixed in effectiveness modeling.

Constraints, Goals, and Participants

A very different approach to the role of participants is taken by Pennings and Goodman (1977), who make a major contribution to the literature on effectiveness. They approach participants by using the concept of the dominant coalition. To show how Pennings and Goodman bring participants into effectiveness determination, it is necessary to trace their theoretical argument. Their approach is very similar to the contradiction model used in the present analysis.

Pennings and Goodman begin their argument by defining effectiveness: "Organizations are effective if relevant constraints can be satisfied and if organizational results approximate or exceed a set of referents for multiple goals" (p. 160).

The idea of constraints involves conditions or requirements that must be satisfied if an organization is to be effective. Constraints involve policies or procedures, set in advance. They guide decision making and behavior in the organizations. Examples of constraints are "maintaining market share at a certain percentage, maintaining quality at a certain level, and not doing business in foreign countries requiring political kickbacks" (p. 160).

Organizational goals, on the other hand, refer to desired end states or objectives specified by the dominant coalition. Pennings and Goodman are explicit in their inclusion of multiple goals. Both constraints and goals are used in the assessment of effectiveness, but there are important differences between the two concepts. Goals receive special attention and concern from the dominant coalition. They are closely related to the motivations of the dominant coalition. Interestingly, goals and constraints can be on the same dimension or area of activity, but the difference lies in the attention paid by the dominant coalition. Pennings and Goodman state:

> Whether achieving a particular quantity or quality level is a goal or constraint depends partially on which is more central to the organization's dominant coalition. For example, some U.S. universities emphasize the number of students enrolled as a constraint for quality of academic excellence, whereas other universities emphasize high enrollment but are constrained by the need of maintaining a minimum level of academic excellence. (p. 161)

A second difference between goals and constraints is that "goals may or may not approximate a referent, whereas constraints must be satisfied as a necessary condition of organizational effectiveness. Degrees (or the relative amount) of organizational effectiveness can be assessed by the degree to which a goal approximates or exceeds a referent" (p. 161). This is obviously a complicated set of ideas and requires some discussion. Referents are the standards by which constraints and goals are evaluated. They involve the dominant coalition's standards of evaluation. Constraints must be met if an organization is to be effective, but just meeting the constraint does not mean effectiveness. *Achieving a goal on top of the constraint is effectiveness.* Pennings and Goodman use the example of a business firm that wants to increase its profits (a goal) and at the same time maintain the quality of service (a constraint). A failure in maintaining quality of service would contribute to ineffectiveness, but exceeding the quality of service standard would not lead to effectiveness. Only by increasing its profitability and maintaining the quality of service would the organization be effective. Effectiveness is based on the degree to which the goal is achieved.

Interestingly, Pennings and Goodman do not bring in resources as constraints. It would appear that the system-resource and goal models could be nicely joined in this constraint-goal terminology. Certainly, resources are required, and the resource level required for operations is a constraint on the organization. This may be the most appropriate usage of the system-resource model—for example, viewing resources as important constraints that must be satisfied before movements toward goals can be realized.

Pennings and Goodman recognize that there are multiple goals and constraints and that the time frame for these is not constant. They also recognize that for each constraint or goal there may be multiple referents. They do not note that different referents for a single goal or constraint may have contradictory elements. They recognize that effectiveness must always be measured after the fact.

An important contribution of the Pennings-Goodman formulation is the specification that organizations have internal and external constituencies. These are the components of the dominant coalition that decide goals and determine constraints. Effectiveness criteria are defined by the dominant coalition on the basis of consensus agreements that are achieved. Consensus is achieved by negotiation among the parties involved. This is not a simple process, since the various constituencies themselves have differing and multidimensional preferences.

The process of achieving consensus has the effect of focusing attention on the goals, constraints, and referents. It also forces the dominant coalition to consider alternative arrangements among these elements, adjusting levels of constraints so that goals might be achieved, or altering goals in the face of constraints that cannot be adjusted. Pennings and Goodman view organizations as being made up of multiple constituencies that influence the setting of constraints, goals, and referents. The internal dominant coalition determines the forms and emphases that these take. According to Pennings and Goodman, "although constituencies may hold many referents and constraints with which to evaluate the organization, it is only to the extent that these constraints and referents can be imposed on the organization that they become useful tools for assessing effectiveness" (p. 171).

There is an additional element that is important. Goals, constraints, and referents are determined by the dominant coalition. As the dominant coalition experiences changes in its composition that accompany power shifts or top leadership succession, goals, constraints, and referents will change. Changes take place over time in the perceptions of effectiveness and in evolving constituent preferences (Cameron and Whetten, 1981; Zammuto, 1982). Goals, constraints, and referents are thus moving targets over time.

The approach to be taken in our contradiction model is quite similar to that of Pennings and Goodman. A major difference is the utilization of resources as constraints. Another important difference is that whereas the Pennings-Goodman formulation stresses consensus achieved in the dominant coalition, the contradiction model will not assume consensus. To be sure, decisions have to be made, but there may be times when the consensus that is achieved for a particular decision is so tenuous that it is very short lived, and the decision is soon reversed. The contradiction model stresses that the various constituencies of an organization may have irreconcilable differences and that effectiveness for one party may be the opposite for another.

The Pennings-Goodman formulation is much more comprehensive than the other participant-satisfaction models considered earlier. The importance they attribute to the consensus achieved through the dominant coalition led to its placement here. The placement here is also based on the importance given to the political process in effectiveness determination. Both system-resource and goal modeling tend to imply rational decision making, with strategies adopted on the basis of how best to acquire resources or survive to minimize goal attainment. The present approach also assumes that decisions will be made on the basis of some degree of rationality, but tempered with the political facts of organizational life.

Effectiveness for Whom?

Charles Perrow has been a consistently perceptive analyst of organizations. This perceptiveness is exemplified in his analysis of effectiveness studies (1977). He first notes that most studies of effectiveness are what he calls the "variable analysis" type (p. 96). This type of study involves trying to isolate those variables that are somehow related to measures of effectiveness. This is in the administrative-technical tradition. In place of this form of analysis, Perrow suggests that analysts engage in two other types of effectiveness studies— "gross-malfunctioning analysis" and "revelatory analysis." Both involve the question, Effectiveness for whom?

Gross-malfunctioning analysis is proposed as a method to isolate poorly operating organizations with an eye toward improving their services or products.

This is proposed as an alternative to the common practice of looking at high-performance organizations and trying to find the correlates of this high performance. Revelatory analysis deals more precisely with the effectiveness-for-whom question. Perrow views organizations as

> ... intentional human constructions but not necessarily rational systems guided by official goals; as bargaining arenas, rather than cooperative systems; as systems of power rather than crescive institutions reflecting cultural norms; and as resources for other organizations and groups rather than closed systems. If we define organizations, then, as intentional human constructions wherein people and groups compete for outputs of interest to them under conditions of unequal power, we have posed the issue of effectiveness quite differently than in the other two perspectives. We now have to ask, what does the organization produce? (p. 101)

In answer to this question, Perrow notes that human-service organizations, such as hospitals, prisons, schools, and welfare organizations, have outputs that are more critical than the services provided to clients. Employment opportunities, segregation and control of people who are thought to be deviant or of the wrong age to be part of society, business opportunities for legitimate business, and markets for organized crime are some of the major outputs of such social service organizations. Perrow believes that revelatory analysis would

> ... reveal what most managers know but social scientists cannot afford to acknowledge, namely, that complex social systems are greatly influenced by sheer chance, accident, luck; that most decisions are very ambiguous, preference orderings are incoherent and unstable, efforts at communication and understanding are often ineffective, subsystems are very loosely connected, and most attempts at social control are clumsy and unpredictable. (p. 103)

Perrow is suggesting two things here. First, organizations should not be analyzed with preconceived notions about what the function of the organization is. He is calling for an explicit recognition of the parties involved in organizational operations and their stake in the survival of the organization. The fact that different groups have different stakes suggests that an approach to organizations that looks at decisions and actions as a simple ordering around goals or environmental pressures is naive.

The effectiveness-for-whom issue is crucial in any effectiveness formulation. That different parties are affected in different ways by organizational actions should be clear. Actions that are successful in one direction may be unrelated to actions in another direction. For example, corporate social responsibility may be unrelated to the stock market performance of corporations, even though a good financial performance may yield the reputation of social responsibility (Alexander and Buchholz, 1978; McGuire, Sundgren, and Schneeweis, 1988). Efforts in one arena may have little impact in another.

THE CONTRADICTION MODEL

There is growing evidence that most organizational analysts are now realizing that effectiveness is a truly multifaceted phenomenon. Research on colleges and universities found that effectiveness is a "multidomain" phenomenon and concludes:

> Effectiveness in one domain may not necessarily relate to effectiveness in another domain. For example, maximizing the satisfaction and growth of individuals in an organization . . . may be negatively related to high levels of subunit output and coordination. . . . Specifically, publishing a large number of research reports may be a goal indicating a high level of effectiveness to faculty members (on an individual level) while indicating low effectiveness at the subunit or organizational level (e.g., poor teaching quality, little time with students, little personal attention for students, graduate student teaching instead of professors) to legislators and parents of undergraduates. (Cameron, 1978: p. 625)

This point has a great deal of substantive validity. It is also quite close to the contradiction model. It does not deal with power differences among constituents or with temporal shifts in environmental pressures as we will do here.

Based on the evidence presented throughout this book and on the effectiveness models considered, the contradiction model can now be presented in a relatively simple manner:

1. *Organizations face multiple and conflicting environmental constraints.* These constraints may be imposed on an organization; they may be bargained for; they may be discovered; or they may be self-imposed (Seashore, 1977). Imposed constraints are beyond organizational control. They involve our familiar environmental dimensions, such as legal or economic positions. To be sure, organizations lobby for legal and regulative advantage, but taxes and regulations are essentially imposed on organizations. This imposition is not just from government. A computer or software manufacturer, such as Microsoft, that develops new systems is imposing this environment on users, if those users must adopt the new system to stay "state of the art." Bargained constraints involve contractual agreements and competitive pressures in markets. Discovered constraints are environmental constraints that appear unexpectedly, as when a coal company finds that its vein of ore has run out. Self-imposed constraints involve the definitions of the environment that organizations utilize. For example, a study of newspaper coverage of an oil spill documented the fact that newspapers differed markedly in the amount of space given to the spill (Molotch and Lester, 1975). Organizational policy thus defines the importance of environmental elements.

Regardless of the source of the constraints, their conflicting nature must be stressed, since efforts to deal with one constraint may operate against the meeting of another. Indeed, organizational units facing multiple contingencies are more prone to face design misfit and lower performance than those in simpler situations (Gresov, 1989). As a general rule, the larger and more complex the organization, the greater the range and variety of constraints it will face. Organizations have to consider their environments, recognize and order the constraints that are confronted, and attempt to predict the consequences of their actions—all within the limitations on decision making and rationality we have considered.

2. *Organizations have multiple and conflicting goals.* This point has been beaten to death, but one more pass is necessary here. A case from my university—The University at Albany—is instructive. It involved a threatened budget cut, which is an annual event that sometimes results in real cuts and sometimes does not. In the case I am describing, the threatened cuts were severe. Each vice president had to make up a list of "target" positions in his or her area. We know that decisions that are made in such situations are the result of power coalitions. At the same time, goals do not just disappear. Issues such as the emphasis on research, needs for the continued recruitment and retention of high-quality students and faculty to achieve the goal of being a high-quality university, and reiterations of the importance of having a safe and attractive campus were voiced and were much more than rhetoric. When the cuts were made, they were based on goals and power coalitions. Both contained contradictions that were played out in actions.

3. *Organizations have multiple and conflicting internal and external constituencies.* The strict meaning of constituency is the people in a legislative district. Here the term refers to those people affected by an organization (Tsui, 1990; Marcus and Goodman, 1991). They may be employees, members, customers, clients, or the public at large. The degree to which constituents are themselves organized varies widely. On the one hand are organized groups, such as labor unions, opponents of nuclear power, and PTAs. There are also spontaneous coalitions that form within organizations. On the other hand are people affected by an organization who are completely unaware of one another's existence. There are also constituents who are affected by organizations who are unaware that they are being affected—some of Perrow's (1984) victims. In any event, we know that constituents are affected. They may or may not be considered in organizational decision making, and they may or may not themselves be organized. They must be part of any effectiveness consideration.

4. *Organizations have multiple and conflicting time frames.* The issue of time frames is closely intertwined with our consideration of goals. Consider the following:

> To the extent that the goals function stresses quick return on investment (as in many business ventures, disaster relief organizations, military field units, and so on) the short-run outcomes should be given the highest priority. For those organizations that orient toward continued production (for example, many other types of business ventures, universities, research and development organizations, and

so on) the year-to-year fluctuations in performance should be discounted and the average performance over longer periods emphasized.

The conceptual problem is that we do not know how organizations discount time. Two organizations with the same goals operating with the same structure in the same environment may place a very different emphasis on speed of return on investment. One organization may capitalize on some situations in a way that increases both the probability of quick favorable outcomes and the risk of long-term decline. The other may eschew the quick return in favor of the long term security. . . . the analyst must also know the premium placed on speed of return. (Hannan and Freeman, 1977a: pp. 113–14)

There are also intraorganizational variations in the time frame that is used (Lawrence and Lorsch, 1967). These differences occur between units and across levels on the vertical dimension.

The degree and mix of environmental constraints also vary over time. Constraints that were critical at one point may disappear as threats. New problems arise. Time also plays a role in the history of an organization, since new organizations are more vulnerable. Similarly, organizations in industries or sectors that are declining face different problems from those in growth industries or sectors.

The temporal dimension of effectiveness is essentially one of judgment. Decisions must be made with regard to the time frame of reference for analyzing goal attainment, the nature and phasing of environmental constraints, and the historical situation of the organization. Failing to recognize this can lead the analyst and the practitioner to real problems. For the analyst it is only a poor study; for the practitioner it is organizational decline or death.

We have considered contradictions in environmental constraints, goals, constituents, and time. These are the realities constructed in and for all organizations. They are the basis for judgment and action. They lead to the conclusion that no organization is effective. Rather, organizations can be viewed as effective (or ineffective) to some degree in specific constraints, goals, constituents, and time frames.

Some Applications

When considering the issue of applications from a contradiction model, the first conclusion we must reach is that efforts to be effective always involve less than total rationality. It is now a matter of faith in organizational theory that organizations do not optimize in their decision making, as shown in the discussion of decision making.

The analysis presented here goes beyond those considerations and has emphasized that there are compromises that must be made among pressing constraints, goals, constituents, and time frames. The ordering of the compromises is based on power relationships and coalitions within the organizations, coupled with external pressures. This is done with the knowledge that if once an action is selected, others are not possible, particularly with constant or diminishing resources. Before we consider these matters further, it is imperative that we address a relatively neglected topic—constraints over which organizations can have *no control.*

Constraints Beyond Organizational Control. Organizations attempt to control those constraints which they perceive to be central to them. Devices such as industrial vertical integration, utilization of boards of directors, political intervention, and advertising are all efforts to reduce environmental uncertainty or shape the environment to the benefit of the organization. At the same time, some events are uncontrollable.

A simple example of this is the weather. An organization may be dependent upon particular weather patterns, but it can do little about the forces of nature. Cloud seeding has yet to become truly feasible, and no device has been developed to control the external temperature. Agricultural organizations are thus subject to droughts, floods, and prolonged hot or cold spells. Winter recreational organizations, such as ski resorts, suffer when there is no snow and when warm temperatures prevent snowmaking. A bad weather year can cause death of some areas.

Organizations that are weather dependent can engage in activities that minimize the influence of nature, such as stockpiling food or making snow (even this does not work if the temperature is above freezing), but these organizations face a basically uncontrollable constraint.

More complex examples come in the forms of world political and economic shifts. The collapse of the Soviet regime essentially destroyed many existing organizations. The old organizations are simply gone.

There are other, less dramatic forces than the sweep of world events that are important for organizations but that they cannot control. These include such things as demographic patterns and local or regional economic developments. When a major employer leaves a community or goes out of business, all the other organizations in the community are affected.

Uncontrollable events and forces happen to organizations. They are part of the constraint package that is faced. What is important for the discussion here is that they cannot be manipulated. They are conditions to which organizations must adjust as they deal with other constraints, goals, constituents, and time frames.

Environmental Constraints That Are Potentially Manipulable. Organizations attempt to manipulate their environment. A major task of top management is to enhance the position of their organization in the environment. Analyses of interlocking corporate boards of directors have suggested that such interlocking can serve four major external functions. The selection of directors can be a means by which financial, legal, or other information or expertise can be brought to the organization. Directors can also be selected with the intent of facilitating the organization's search for capital or other resources. This is the primary reason that bank officials are so heavily represented on the corporate boards across the array of business firms. Community leaders on the boards of hospitals or colleges serve to bring in the resource of legitimacy. Board composition can also serve a political function. The selection of the appropriate director can assist in coping with federal and state agencies, since the presence of politically powerful groups can serve to blunt vigorous governmental actions. Finally, board composition has been viewed as a means by which the interests of powerful external organizations, such as banks, insurance companies, or controlling blocks of family interests, are served (Aldrich, 1979: p. 297). These interlocking directorates do not create certainty for the organizations involved.

That aspects of the environment are only potentially manipulable can be seen in an analysis of the pharmaceutical and popular-music industries (Hirsch, 1975). The pharmaceutical industry had great success in protecting itself from competition by securing the passage of state and federal legislation. It also was successful in getting organized medicine, through the American Medical Association, to permit the industry to advertise drugs by their brand names rather than by their generic names. Prescriptions were sold by brand rather than by compound. Hirsch found that the popular-music (recording) industry had a similar structure to begin with but was unable to obtain protective legislation and exclusive rights to the profits possible whenever a song was played on the radio. The popular-music industry lobbied and used other techniques to try to protect itself, but it failed and had severe problems as musical tastes, as well as many other cultural elements, changed in the 1960s. One industry was successful in manipulating its environment; the other was not.

This is an area of uncertainty for organizations. If someone were to come up with a sure technique for controlling the environment, as the early and later monopolists have, every organization would adopt it. Antimonopoly laws are specifically designed to prevent environmental control. Organizations attempt to control as much as they legally can or as much as they can without being caught.

The discussion thus far has focused on the private sector. Public organizations also seek to control their environment. The public budgetary process is one in which resources are sought for organizational maintenance and growth. Public organizations send messages to their constituents and others. These messages are designed to protect the organization and further its interests. This "propaganda" may be quite detrimental to the public in many instances (Altheide and Johnson, 1980).

In this section we have argued that organizations engage in a variety of activities designed to manipulate their environment in their favor. Whether through interlocking boards of directors, purchasing suppliers, seeking to have favorable legislation passed, or propaganda, the attempt is to manipulate the environment on behalf of the organization. These efforts have only the potential for success, since other organizations with other purposes are interacting with the same components of the environment. Organizations can be most sure of the consequences of their actions when the organization itself is considered.

Organizational Characteristics.   Organizations have the capability of being structured and restructured in accordance with the outcomes of decision making and political processes within their own boundaries. Much of the thinking that has emerged from the contingency model has dealt directly with this issue. The basic notion is that there are multiple organizational forms that are most likely to be successful, depending upon the situations the organization is confronting. One of the major tasks of top management is to determine what the most appropriate organizational form is for various situations. It is not uncommon to find business firms in rapidly changing technological fields with no formal tables of organization or organizational charts because the organization is in a constant change mode. There is a reciprocal relationship between strategy and structure (Miller, 1987).

Organizations are not completely flexible. Union contracts, custom, and laws militate against total self-determination. Nonetheless, it is possible to structure or restructure organizations to bring about greater adaptability or rigidity or more or less participation in the decision-making process. The organizational form is more subject to organizational control than the other factors affecting effectiveness that we have considered. Whether or not organizational form is most crucial for organizational effectiveness is unclear. It would appear that ultimate survival might well be a function of factors beyond organizational control. The more controllable a particular situation is, perhaps the less important it is. It is quite clear that controlling the relevant environment, over time and across conditions, and structuring the organization to acquire sufficient resources and to pursue and move to accomplish major goals is a key to any consideration of effectiveness.

The purpose of this chapter has been to develop a perspective on effectiveness that is applicable across all types of organizations. As a parenthetical note, organizational crime has also been approached from the perspectives presented here. Building on the seminal works of Sutherland (1940, 1949), Finney and Lesieur (1982) developed a "contingency model of organizational crime." This included the familiar concepts of performance emphasis, internal constraints, and legal and social environments. The contradiction model works.

SUMMARY AND CONCLUSIONS

This chapter has been an attempt to make some sense out of the critical area of organizational effectiveness. Conceptual and methodological contradictions in the analysis of effectiveness were presented, and a contradiction model was developed. The model contains key elements of the resource-acquisition and goals models and is an attempt to combine them in a manner that retains their key insights but adds the important factor of inherent contradictions. Organizational effectiveness will remain the major concern for organizational practitioners and analysts. Ignoring the contradictions will not advance knowledge or practice. Ignoring the fact that there are factors beyond organizational control or that are only potentially manipulable will also not contribute to theory or practice. It is only when theorists and practitioners realize the limited range of options open to organizations, as they confront constraints and mandates and attempt to move toward goal achievement and cope with the issues of multiple constituents and conflicting time frames, that both usable and theoretically interesting developments will take place.

In the next and final chapter, we will consider organizational theory. It will be a short chapter, because many of the issues have already been considered in this chapter and throughout the analysis.

Organizational
Theory

The objective of this chapter is to examine contemporary theories about organizations. The various theories to be considered permit us to see and understand the different facets of organizations. The intent is not to advocate the
superiority of any one theory but to argue that theoretical integration is necessary for full comprehension of organizational processes (see Budros, 1992).
There are interesting sets of debates surrounding some of the theories to be
considered, and I will attempt to steer through these debates among the various "paradigm warriors" (Aldrich, 1988) involved.

In the sections that follow, we will consider five alternative schools of
thought about organizations. These schools of thought can be labeled theories,
models, or perspectives, depending on the analyst. Each school yields insights; none has been empirically verified as *the* explanation of organizational
phenomena.

Before beginning the consideration of the alternative schools, I want to
make it clear that the history of organizational theory will not be included in
this analysis. Pugh (1966) and Clegg and Dunkerly (1980) are useful resources
for people interested in tracing the historical roots of contemporary organizational theory.

The approach taken here is inductive. The inductive approach permits us
to build on the empirical research that has been summarized in earlier chapters. Indeed, the theories themselves have already been identified and critically
evaluated at many earlier points.

The theories to be considered are grouped similarly to Pfeffer's (1982, 1997) and Donaldson's (1995) overviews and critiques of organizational theory Our focus is the organizational level of analysis. Pfeffer bases his analysis of organizational theories on the perspectives on action that are taken. One such perspective sees organizational actions as externally constrained and controlled, and thus we will consider the population-ecology and resource-dependence models as Pfeffer does. At almost the opposite extreme are models of organizational action that see such actions as purposive and rational, with an emphasis on goal direction. Included in this category are the rational-contingency model, which includes the Marxist or class twist to the traditional model, and the transaction-cost model, which has developed out of the field of economics. A final perspective on action sees organizations as based on ideas contained in an organization's field or emergent from the values of organizational actors. This is the institutional approach to organizations. Donaldson's approach is designed to counter the "antimanagement" bias that characterizes American organizational theory (p. 1) and to press for a single model based on the rational-contingency model.

THE POPULATION-ECOLOGY MODEL

The population-ecology model is associated with the works of Aldrich and Pfeffer (1976), Hannan and Freeman (1977b), Aldrich (1979), Kasarda and Bidwell (1984), Bidwell and Kasarda (1985), McKelvey (1982), McKelvey and Aldrich (1983), Carroll (1988), Carroll and Hannan (1989), Hannan and Freeman (1989). Baum and Singh (1994) and Baum (1996). This approach "posits that environmental factors select those organizational characteristics that best fit the environment" (Aldrich and Pfeffer, 1976: p. 79).

The population-ecology approach (sometimes known as the natural-selection model) was a major orientation in our consideration of organizational change and transformation. According to Aldrich and Pfeffer, the model differs from Campbell's (1969) analysis of systemic evolution in that no assumption of progression is made. The natural-selection model does not assume that changes are necessarily in the direction of more complex or better organizations. The direction of change in organizations is simply toward a better fit with the environment.

According to Aldrich and Pfeffer, the population-ecology model does not deal with single organizational units but is concerned with forms or populations of organizations. Organizational forms that have the appropriate fit with the environment are selected over those that do not fit or fit less appropriately.

Following Campbell, Aldrich and Pfeffer suggest that there are three stages in the natural-selection model. In the first stage variations occur in organizational forms. These variations can be planned or unplanned. Once variations have occurred, the second stage, selection, is reached. The analogy here is with organic evolution, in which some mutations work and others do not. Organizational forms that fit are selected over those that do not. The final stage is retention. The forms that are selected are "preserved, duplicated, or reproduced" (p. 81). Retention is accomplished, in the contemporary situation, through devices such as business schools that train future organizational managers and executives (Aldrich, 1979). The training contains lessons learned from organizational forms that have been successful or selected. Studies in the population-ecology mode have also focused on organizational foundings or births and on organizational mortality or death.

Organizational forms fill niches in the environment. Niches are "distinct combinations of resources and other constraints that are sufficient to support an organizational form" (Aldrich, 1979: p. 28). The notion of niches raises the fascinating possibility that there are unfilled niches "out there" just waiting for the right organizational form. Aldrich (p. 112) suggests that home video games and pocket electronic calculators were examples of unfilled niches being filled, but those are poor examples, since they are not organizational forms but simply consumer products. A better example of a once-unfilled but now-filled niche is the conglomerate corporation, in which a set of unrelated industries are brought together under a single ownership. This was a new organizational form that was selected by the environment as appropriate. This organizational form is now in decline (Davis, Diekmann, and Tinsley, 1994). Another example of a niche now filled is the fast-food restaurant form of organization.

Research on niches (Carroll, 1985; Freeman and Hannan, 1983) has shown that narrow niches tend to support organizations that are specialized, whereas wider niches support more generalist organizations. In Carroll's research, for example, he found that narrow niches in ethnic groups, neighborhoods, and religious and professional groups provided support for specialized newspapers. Freeman and Hannan's research involved restaurants with much the same result.

Aldrich and Pfeffer identify some problems with the population-ecology model. The sources of the original variations are not specified. Managerial processes within organizations are ignored. Inasmuch as only the successful organizational forms will survive in the long run, the processes by which the fit between the organization and the environment is achieved are ignored. The model also has the problem of being analogous to economic theories that assume perfect competition. Perfect competition does not exist in almost all instances.

Van de Ven (1979) provides some additional criticisms of this model. Van de Ven suggests that the notion of "fit" between the environment and organizations is unclear. According to Van de Ven, population ecologists appear to use fit as

> ... either an unquestioned axiom or inductive generalization in a causal model that asserts that organizational environment determines structure because effective or surviving organizations adopt structures that fit their environmental

niches relatively better than those that do not survive. To avoid a tautology, the proposition implicitly reduces to the hypothesis that organizational survival or effectiveness moderates the relationship between environment and structure. (p. 323)

This is interesting, because effectiveness is scarcely mentioned in the population-ecology modeling efforts. Van de Ven goes on to criticize the population-ecology model for drawing too heavily on analogies with biological systems. This biological analogy is ill-founded, since it does not deal with human decisions and motives. Ethical problems are ignored, and the whole process is viewed as inevitable.

Young (1988, 1989) has also severely criticized the population-ecology model, specifically the form presented by Hannan and Freeman, because of its reliance on biological theory. Freeman and Hannan (1989) believe that the population-ecology approach is well suited for viewing organizations as complex systems with limited flexibility, but Young argues that the approach may be suited for only a narrow range of organizational phenomena.

Van de Ven also criticizes the model because of its downplaying of strategic choices made on behalf of organizations. The variations in forms that occur have some source and, according to Van de Ven, that source is the strategic choices made within organizations. The idea of strategic choice will be incorporated in the present analysis at a later point.

There is another aspect of choice that is not considered in the population-ecology model. Some federal agencies have been created as last-resort responses to socioeconomic or technological difficulties. These agencies fill a niche, to be sure, but the niche is defined by governmental decision makers (Grafton, 1975).

There is an additional troublesome aspect of the population-ecology model. Organizations are not inert masses, even though they seem so at times. Even organizations that are seemingly inert have an impact by their very inertia, but that is not the point. The point is that organizations do things. They transform inputs into outputs. Those outputs have an impact on the society. Individuals, groups, and other organizations respond to organizational outputs. We are harmed and benefited by organizational outputs. In this sense *we* are the environment of organizations. Therefore, if we respond to organizations with support or opposition, and if we have power or can influence power holders, the environment responds to organizations. The population-ecology model tends to portray an environment not as filled with human actors but, rather, as an unfeeling, uncaring condition in which organizations must operate. The model removes power, conflict, disruption, and social-class variables from the analysis of social processes (Perrow, 1979: p. 243).

Carroll's (1988) anthology includes several papers that do in fact deal with institutional, cultural, and political forces, which suggests that population ecologists are paying heed to the criticisms. Hannan and Carroll's (1992) own research includes legitimation, which is a major consideration from institutional theory, as a major variable. The population ecologists are thus responding to some of the criticisms of their model.

These criticisms of the population-ecology model are not intended to suggest that it has no utility. The model has utility primarily in two areas. As some sort of "ultimate test" of effectiveness, survival is a positive indication and organizational death a negative indication. The natural-selection model can thus give a historical perspective that other approaches do not. It does not work well, however, with large contemporary private and public organizations that are almost guaranteed survival for a short time and even a medium length of time (Aldrich and Pfeffer, 1976: p. 88). The natural-selection model is also useful as a sensitizing concept to the importance of environmental factors. If an organizational form is in a period of growth or decline, because of an expanding or a shrinking niche, any model must take that into consideration. Medical technology in developed countries has now permitted many people to live until old age, with all the attendant infirmities. The organizational form of the hospital is inappropriate for the aging and ill individual who is not faced with a life-threatening emergency. The organizational form of the hospice appears to be filling the niche that was created. Evaluations of hospices will have to take survival and the growth potential into account.

Population-ecology theorists are very careful to note that their approach is concerned with organizational populations rather than with individual organizations. Unfortunately, many of the examples provided by theorists in support of the population-ecology approach have tended to be focused on individual organizations. Part of the difficulty has been semantic and part has been due to insufficient specification of the level of analysis being used. Carroll (1984a) has provided a useful set of distinctions among levels of analysis. He notes that the organizational level can be used when referring to life-cycle processes among organizations. At the population-ecology level, the growth and decline of entire populations of organizations can be traced. Finally, there is the community-ecology level. At this level populations of organizations that exist together within the same region can be examined. According to Astley (1985), the community-population perspective permits an examination of similarities within a population of organizations and also permits analyses of between-population differences. Astley believes that a community-ecology perspective has the room to allow factors such as opportunism and choice to be included in organizational analyses.

THE RESOURCE-DEPENDENCE MODEL

The population-ecology model downplays the role of organizational actors in determining the fate of organizations. There is an alternative model, the resource-dependence model, which brings organizational decisions and actions back into consideration (Aldrich and Pfeffer, 1976; Pfeffer and Salancik,

1978). The discussion that follows relies heavily on Aldrich and Pfeffer's analysis, with some additions and extensions.

The resource-dependence model has strong ties to what has been labeled the political-economy model of organizations (Wamsley and Zald, 1973; Benson, 1975) and the dependence-exchange approach (Hasenfeld, 1972; Jacobs, 1974). The basic premise of the resource-dependence model is that decisions are made within organizations. These decisions are made within the internal political context of the organization. The decisions deal with environmental conditions faced by the organization (Schreyogg, 1980). Another important aspect of the model is that organizations attempt to deal actively with the environment. Organizations will attempt to manipulate the environment to their own advantage. Rather than being passive recipients of environmental forces, as the population-ecology model implies, organizations will make strategic decisions about adapting to the environment. The role of management is vital in this process. The earlier analysis of IORs is based heavily on resource-dependence theory.

The resource-dependence model begins with the assumption that no organization is able to generate all the various resources that it needs. Similarly, not every possible activity can be performed within an organization to make it self-sustaining. Both of these conditions mean that organizations must be dependent on the environment for resources. Even seemingly self-sustaining organizations, such as isolated monasteries, must recruit new members or they will go out of existence. The resources that are needed can be in the form of raw materials, finances, personnel, or services or production operations that the organization cannot or does not perform for itself. Resources would also include technological innovations (Marple, 1982). The sources of resources in the environment are other organizations, the exception being farming and extractive industries that have the potential of owning the raw-material physical base. Even these organizations are dependent on other organizations for other resources. The fact that resources are obtained from other organizations means that the resource-dependence model can be thought of as an interorganizational resource-dependence model.

Since the resource-dependence model portrays the organization as an active participant in its relationship with the environment, it also contains the idea that the administrators of organizations "manage their environments as well as their organizations, and the former activity may be as important, or even more important, than the latter" (Aldrich and Pfeffer, 1976: p. 83). This is the institutional level of operations, in which the organization is linked to the social structure by its top executives (Parsons, 1960).

A key element of the resource-dependence model is strategic choice (Chandler, 1962; Child, 1972). This concept implies that a decision is made among a set of alternatives in regard to the strategy that the organization will utilize in its dealings with the environment. The assumption is that the environment does not force the organization into a situation in which no choice is possible. The organization is faced with a set of possible alternatives in dealing with the environment. Aldrich and Pfeffer note that the criteria by which choices are made and by which structures are determined are both important and problematic. There is not just one optimal structure or course of action. The resource-dependence model stresses the importance of internal power arrangements in the determination of the choices made. Both internal power arrangements and the demands of external groups are central to the decision-making process. The resource-dependence model does not include the idea of goals as part of the decision-making process.

The resource-dependence model suggests that organizations are, or attempt to be, active in affecting their environment. This contributes to the variation among organizations, since variations are the result of conscious, planned responses to environmental contingencies. Organizations attempt to absorb interdependence and uncertainty, either completely, as through merger (Pfeffer, 1972b), or partially, as through cooperation (Pfeffer, 1972a; Allen, 1974) or the movement of personnel among organizations (Pfeffer and Leblebici, 1973; Aldrich and Pfeffer, 1976: p. 87). The conglomerate corporation is a striking example of variation in organizational form brought about by strategic choice. It is also striking that the conglomerate form has recently been disappearing or selected out.

The resource-dependence model does deal with the selection process, which was central to the population-ecology model. Instead of viewing selection solely from the standpoint of the environment selecting appropriate organizational forms, the resource-dependence model considers the ways in which organizations interact with their environments to ensure that they survive and thrive. The environment is still the key factor, however. Aldrich and Pfeffer (1976: p. 89) argue that the environment contains many of the constraints, uncertainties, and contingencies faced by organizations. Organizational units that have the capability of dealing with constraints, uncertainties, and contingencies are those that obtain the most power within the organization (Hickson et al., 1971). The power distribution within the organization is critical in determining the nature of the choices made, thus linking the environment to the choices made through the power process operating within the organization. The emphasis on power within the organization is a necessary one, since decisions are made in a political context. The resource-dependence model emphasizes interunit power differentials and tends to ignore hierarchical power differences. Hierarchical power differences must be considered in any analysis of strategic choice, since such differences can override interunit power struggles. It is quite possible that interunit power developments, as between marketing and production departments, have a crucial role in determining who rises in the hierarchy, but once the hierarchy is set, the power of the positions at the top of the organization would appear to be most central to the strategic decisions that are made. Regardless of the source of the power, of course, the strategic choices remain tied to environmental pressures. Again, the idea of goals, in the area of decision making, is not included in this model.

There are three ways in which strategic choices are made about the environment (Aldrich and Pfeffer, 1976). The first is that decision makers in organizations do have autonomy. This autonomy is much greater than would be suggested by a strict adherence to environmental determinism. The autonomy of the decision makers is reflected in the fact that more than one kind of decision can be made about the environmental niche being occupied—more than one kind of structure is suitable for given environments. In addition, organizations can enter or leave niches. This is illustrated by the fact that business firms can decide to try new markets or abandon old ones. Similarly, many colleges and universities are attempting to expand their niches, obviously in the face of decreasing demand by traditional students, by offering more and more courses and programs designed for nontraditional, older students.

The second way in which strategic choices are made about the environment involves attempts to manipulate the environment itself. Business firms attempt to create a demand for their products; they may also enter into arrangements with other firms to regulate competition, legally or illegally. Operating through the political process, business firms may also secure the passage of tariffs or quotas to restrict competition from foreign firms. Organizations in the public sector do essentially the same thing when they expand or fight for the retention of their jurisdiction. Organizations seek to reduce their dependency on other organizations (Dunford, 1987). It is also to an organization's advantage to have other organizations dependent on it. Dunford notes that some organizations even suppress technological development, through manipulating patents, as a means of controlling resource dependence.

The third way in which the strategic choices are made about the environment is based on the fact that particular environmental conditions are perceived and evaluated differently by different people. This point is a crucial one and requires some elaboration. Organizational actors define reality in terms of their own background and values. A study documented the manner in which recruitment policies for executives in a large business firm resulted in the firm's having executives of very homogeneous backgrounds (Kanter, 1977). Kanter suggests that this permits the executives to have a great deal of trust in one another, since they will experience things in the same ways and, by implication, make the same kinds of decisions. The problem with such homogeneity, of course, is that the single point of view may be unable to detect errors.

The environment is perceived, interpreted, and evaluated by human actors within the organization. The perception becomes the reality, and environmental conditions are important only as they are perceived by organizational decision makers. Different actors can perceive the same phenomenon quite differently. The point is that the environment is acted upon by organizational decision makers on the basis of their perceptions, interpretations, and evaluations. Although there may be commonality because of homogeneity of background within an organization, and even this will not be perfect, there will not be commonality between organizations. Thus, different organizations will act differently toward the same environmental conditions, if the perceptions are different. In this regard, the critical question is the extent to which organizational perceptions vary from objective indicators of environmental conditions (Starbuck, 1976).

Aldrich and Pfeffer correctly note that there are limitations on the range of choices that are available to organizational decision makers. There may be legal barriers that prevent an organization from moving into a particular area. Economic barriers also exist. Some projects may be too expensive. Markets can be so dominated by a few firms that it is impossible for a new, small firm to enter.

In addition to barriers that preclude certain decisions, decisions to attempt to alter the environment may not be possible for many organizations. Small organizations, for example, have much less power than large organizations to modify their environments. A small state college has much less impact on the educational environment than does Harvard University.

The final aspect of the resource-dependence model is the manner in which the retention of organizational forms takes place. Aldrich and Pfeffer suggest several mechanisms that organizations utilize to retain previously successful adaptations. In many ways, these retention mechanisms represent tactical decisions about how the organization is to operate once strategic decisions have been made.

One such retention device is bureaucratization. Organizations develop documentation and filing systems. Examples from the organizational past serve as precedents for the organizational present. The development of organizational policy serves the same function. Records and policies can provide the framework and content for decisions to be made. This provides continuity for the organization and ensures that the past forms are retained. Role specialization and standardization, with related job descriptions, also ensure the policies are followed. Another important characteristic of bureaucracy, advancement based on performance, also aids in continuity. If people are advanced through the system, their experiences will be quite common and they will react in ways similar to the ways in which people have reacted in the past. Finally, the bureaucratic mechanism of a hierarchical structure also helps the retention process. The power of those at the top of the organization is viewed as legitimate. Authority is exercised, and each decision is not questioned. Bureaucratization is probably the most efficient form of administration, and all organizations will move toward this form if they seek efficiency (Perrow, 1979).

Another retention device is the socialization process. Persons entering an organization are continually socialized in formal and informal ways (Dornbusch, 1955), with the result that "the culture of the organization is transmitted to new members" (p. 97). Part of the culture of the organization involves folk wisdom and operating "rules of thumb" that persist over time.

Finally, the leadership structure of organizations tends to be consistent over time. As has been noted, people are screened and filtered as they move to the top of organizations. The screening and filtering is done by people already at the top of the organization, and they are very likely to select people who are like themselves.

> Furthermore, since the promotion of leaders is based on their experience and expertise in dealing with critical organizational contingencies, to the extent that the definition of organizational uncertainties remains the same, similarity in leadership characteristics is further assured. Organizations that are marketing-oriented, such as consumer goods companies, may tend to promote people with sales or marketing experience, who because of similar backgrounds and socialization, will have fairly similar ideas about organizational policy. (Aldrich and Pfeffer, 1976: p. 98)

There are thus several mechanisms that ensure that organizational forms that have been successful will be retained. The emphasis of the resource-dependence model is on the manner in which organizations deal with environmental contingencies.

Resource acquisition is a major activity of organizations and the resource-dependence model captures this, but it sidesteps the issue of goals. As will be seen shortly, I believe that this model must be augmented by a model that views organizational actions as being goal based as well.

THE RATIONAL-CONTINGENCY MODEL

The resource-dependence model ignores goals, as does the population-ecology model. Both approaches appear to run counter to the reality of actual decision making. In the sections that follow, we will again consider the issue of goals and then turn to the theories linked to a goals-based perspective.

The goal-based approach does not make assumptions about the rationality involved in decision making, nor does it take the simplistic view that organizations are merely instruments designed to carry out goals. Rather, the approach adds goals back into the reasons that organizations act as they do. Goals are part of the culture of organizations and part of the mind-sets of decision makers. Organizations, like the individuals who compose them, are purposive creatures. The purposiveness can be overcome by external pressures, to be sure, and the organization may die or have to drastically alter its operations. The models that emphasize the environment are correct in pointing out the importance of the environment for the births and deaths of organizations. They err, however, in abandoning the consideration of goals.

It is now widely accepted (Lehman, 1988) that organizations have multiple and conflicting goals. This means that priorities among goals are problematic for organizations. Priorities are established by dominant coalitions within organizations. The dominant coalition is a direct or an indirect

. . . representation or cross-section of horizontal constituencies (that is, subunits) and vertical constituencies (such as employees, management, owners, or stockholders) with different and possibly competing expectations. Consensus about the importance of the various criteria of effectiveness is hypothesized to be a function of the relative weights that the various constituencies carry in the negotiated order which we call organization. Consensus among members of the dominant coalition can be employed as a vehicle for obtaining effectiveness data. For example, how important is market share versus employee satisfaction? What should be the trade-off between research and development, between teaching and research, between patient care, medical research, and physicians' education? And so on. The consensus of the coalition allows the identification of such effectiveness criteria. These criteria may have different degrees of importance for the different constituencies in the dominant coalition; but somehow the preferences and expectations are aggregated, combined, modified, adjusted, and shared by the members of the dominant coalition. By invoking the concept of dominant coalition it is possible to preserve the notion of organizations as rational decision making entities. (Pennings and Goodman, 1977: p. 152)

Pennings and Goodman's term "effectiveness criteria" has the same meaning, for our purposes here, as goals. Their emphasis on rationality is correct but perhaps overstated. If we return for the moment to the environmental-based models, we can see that things happen around an organization that cannot be foreseen. And there may be competing external pressures or internal issues that cannot be rationally resolved because of their clearly contradictory nature. Nonetheless, the Pennings and Goodman approach is useful as a way of bringing goals back into the consideration of politics and decisions made by organizations.

The importance of goals should be approached from another standpoint. Simon (1964) argues that the idea of organizational goals is a reification, or a case of "treating [the goal] as a superindividual entity having an existence and behavior independent of the behavior of its members" (p. 2). The analysis here accepts such reification as necessary and correct. Interestingly, Simon goes on to note:

In the decision-making situations of real life, a course of action, to be acceptable, must satisfy a whole set of requirements, or constraints. Sometimes one of these requirements is singled out and referred to as the goal of the action. But the choice of one of the constraints, from many, to a large extent is arbitrary. For many purposes it is more meaningful to refer to the whole set of requirements as the (complex) goal of the action. This conclusion applies both to individual and organizational decision making. (p. 7)

Thus, to Simon and for our purposes here, goals are constraints for organizational decision making. So too are the environmental constraints discussed in the earlier sections. As a way of combining important elements from the perspectives of multiple and conflicting goals and environmental constraints, many analysts advocate the rational-contingency model (Donaldson, 1995, 1996).

The rational-contingency idea has been developed from contingency theory that emerged from Lawrence and Lorsch's (1967) seminal work. Later writers such as Galbraith (1974, 1977), Becker and Neuhauser (1975), and Negandhi and Reimann (1973a, 1973b) developed the basic ideas further. Donaldson (1985) claims that contingency theory is a part of "normal science" (p. ix). His strong advocacy of contingency theory (see also Hinings, 1988) is based on his conclusion that empirical evidence strongly supports its utility—a point with which I agree.

Contingency theory can be summarized in the following manner: *"The best way to organize depends on the nature of the environment to which the organization must relate"* (Scott, 1981: p. 114; italics added). Thus, in Lawrence and Lorsch's study, successful plastics firms were those that were differentiated to deal with an uncertain and changing environment, whereas beer bottle firms, with a less differentiated environment, were less differentiated internally. For our purposes, goals would be equally as important as the environment.

Contingency theory has been heavily criticized as being tautological. It has also been criticized as not being a theory, since it doesn't explain why or how a best way to organize develops (Schoonhoven, 1981; Tosi and Slocum, 1984). In addition, the idea of a best way to organize for a particular environment ignores political considerations, such as demands for collective bargaining, for a minimum wage, or for a union contract (Katz and Kahn, 1978: p. 249). High efficiency could be the result of paying low wages or of inducing workers to work long hours or to work harder. Consumers and regulators are also vital for organizational operations (Pfeffer and Salancik, 1978). Despite these problems, contingency theory has become an important part of the literature on organizations. This importance has been questioned by Meyer, Tsui, and Hinings (1993), who propose that a "configurational" approach be substituted for the contingency model. They claim that the configurational approach is more dynamic, but, in my opinion, it does not add much.

When the idea of contingency is added to the notion of rationality, we have the rational-contingency model. Organizations are viewed as attempting to attain goals and deal with their environments, with the realization that there is not one best way to do so. Findings as diverse as Burt's (1983) on corporate philanthropy and Langston's (1984) analysis of the British pottery industry are supportive of this approach. In the case of corporate philanthropy, it was found that the proportion of business firms' net incomes contributed to charity varied with the extent to which the firms were in sectors dependent upon consumption by individuals rather than other organizations. The organizations perceived charitable contributions as contributing to their profitability through their attempts to enhance their public relations image. In the British pottery example, bureaucratic elements were retained by the pottery firms because the bureaucratic elements increased profitability. Langston implies that this can be interpreted in either a rational-contingency manner or as a Marxist, worker-control strategy.

The Marxian Twist

Marxist scholars have taken a very different perspective on rationality and rational-contingency approaches to organizations. According to Pfeffer (1982):

> ... Marxist analysis blends environmental determinism with rational, strategic choice. After all, Marx argued that the evolution of economic systems was inevitable and, in his analysis of social forces, saw the presence of certain inexorable historical trends. . . . Marxist analyses relevant to understanding organizations have proceeded from the premise of conscious, rational, strategic action taken on the part of the capitalist class and organizations controlled by that class. In this sense, it is an analysis quite consistent with other approaches presuming conscious, foresightful behavior. As Goldman (1980: 12) has noted, "The Marxist position sees a high degree of managerial consciousness and intentionality even omnipotence not only in technical decisions but also in ostensibly benign programs such as welfare work early in the Twentieth Century or the democratization experiments of the 1970's." (p. 163)

Pfeffer suggests that Marxian perspectives are useful in considering two important organizational issues. The first is that of worker control and the employment relationship. The second is that of interorganizational relationships in the form of interlocking boards of directors, which are seen as an expression of "classwide rationality" as much as organizationally based rationality. Classwide rationality (Useem, 1979, 1982; Moore, 1979) exists wherein elites seek to enhance and protect their position through their active participation in the governance of organizations.

There is mixed evidence in regard to the extent to which the worker control and deskilling of labor arguments can be supported. There is strong evidence in regard to the presence and role of interlocking boards of directors.

The Marxist approach suffers from the same problems that afflict the rational-contingency perspective more generally in that although outcomes are intendedly rational, there is no guarantee that they will be so. Just as goals may not be achieved and the environment not be effectively confronted, so may worker-control efforts and classwide rational actions be thwarted. Managers and directors cannot be assumed to be more rational and controlling in a Marxian analysis than they are in any other decision-making and implementation context. Nonetheless, as Pfeffer (1982) notes, the Marxian perspective is more successful than other approaches in linking organizational properties to the broad sweep of history.

The rational-contingency model does *not* assume that rationality can necessarily be achieved, simply that it is attempted. Whether from a Marxist or a non-Marxist perspective, the rational-contingency model views organizational actions as the result of choices made among a set of goals in an environmental context of constraints and opportunities (Drazin and Van de Ven, 1985).

THE TRANSACTION-COST MODEL

The transaction-cost model has developed out of the field of economics and has captured a great deal of attention among sociologists. This model is based primarily on the work of Oliver Williamson (1975, 1981, 1985; Williamson and Ouchi, 1981). The purpose of this model is to explain the existence and operation of organizations, particularly in the private sector.

The starting point for the model is the transaction or exchange of goods and services. It assumes that individuals will act in their own self-interests (the economist's rational "man"). Simple transactions happen in "on-the-spot" situations and are conducted in the free marketplace. Over time, simple markets were replaced by more complex and uncertain situations. The environment in which transactions took place became increasingly uncertain, and simple trust in relationships became more problematic. One consequence was the emergence of hierarchies or organizations.

It is important to note that Williamson takes a turn away from the route favored by most economists. By focusing on the costs of transactions, rather than production, Williamson introduces a new factor into the economics and sociology of organizations.

> The typical neoclassical economic model conceived of firms as systems for managing production functions, with the primary decisions focused on the optimal mix of production factors—resources, labor, capital. In this model, variations in organizational structure are largely irrelevant. By contrast, the transaction costs perspective assumes that not the production but the exchange of goods and services is critical, and it emphasizes the importance of the structures that govern these exchanges. (Scott, 1987a: p. 148)

Organizations are seen as the response to uncertain environments. Included in these environments are potential exchange partners whose trustworthiness is unknown and who might behave in opportunistic ways. Bringing transactions under the hierarchy of the organization allows monitoring of behavior through direct supervision, auditing, and other control mechanisms. Behaviors come under the context of the employment contract. Transaction costs are thus reduced or at least controlled by the presence of the hierarchy. The logical extension here, of course, is that organizations would seek continued growth of control through the formation of trusts and monopolies. This has indeed happened, and the government has stepped in with antitrust regulations.

It is also possible for organizations to go in the opposite direction—they can go back to markets as is done with outsourcing, temporary help, and subcontracts (Lindberg, Campbell, and Hollingsworth, 1991). There is not a necessary one-way movement toward organizations from markets.

Williamson does not claim that the transaction-cost approach is the complete answer to all organizational phenomena. Indeed, in 1985 he noted:

"Given the complexity of the phenomena under review, transaction cost economics should often be used in addition to, rather than to the exclusion of, alternative approaches. Not every approach is equally instructive, however, and they are sometimes rival rather than complementary" (p. 18). Despite this caveat, Williamson continues to argue for the strong explanatory power of the transaction-cost approach.

As might be expected, the transaction-cost approach has raised the consciousness level of sociologists of organizations. Some have sought to attack the approach, whereas others have sought to incorporate it in their analyses of organizations. Typical of the latter are Eccles and White (1988) who studied multiprofit center firms. They note that there are transaction costs within firms, which may actually exceed the costs of external transactions. This is exemplified, in an entirely different setting, by the notion of indirect costs or overhead charged on grants and contracts made by government agencies to colleges and universities. The overhead charges can exceed the direct costs of the programs involved in some instances. Eccles and White do not believe that this negates Williamson but that their findings point to the fact that the traditional concerns of economists and sociologists cannot be isolated from each other, a point with which I agree completely.

In a study that does partially negate Williamson, Lazerson (1988) found that small Italian companies expanded through vertical and horizontal integration. The Italian firms created new small firms, which they controlled. The firms replaced market relations to insulate themselves from competition. At the same time, they increased their dependence on markets by their intensified subcontracting. They created internal markets within the firms, but the important point is that hierarchies did not develop.

A different but still critical twist is found in an analysis of the reforms attempted by the People's Republic of China (Boisot and Child, 1988). In the early to mid-1980s, China attempted to introduce free enterprise in the form of markets—this is seen as a form of bureaucracy failure. This was not a complete success, because, according to Boisot and Child, the traditional patrimonial fief system continued to intrude on true market operations.

The most systematic attack on the transaction-cost approach is being developed by Granovetter (1985; see also Knapp, 1989). He criticizes the markets-and-hierarchies framework on the basis of his belief that economic transactions are actually embedded in social relationships. Granovetter develops the position that in modern societies economic transactions are linked to trust, which is in turn linked to social relationships rather than to economic relationships.

The transaction-cost model, whether the costs are economic or social, is undoubtedly best used in combination with other explanations of organizational phenomena, as Williamson had noted earlier. Transaction-cost theory must be used in combination with population-ecology, resource-dependency, and contingency theory (Robins, 1987).

My conclusion is that the transaction-cost approach is a necessary addition to the theories discussed earlier. Regardless of whether transactions take place for social or economic reasons, and regardless of whether collegiality ranks with markets and hierarchies as a place where transactions can take place, the transaction-cost approach is important in that it informs us about the origins of organizations. Transaction-cost considerations then operate in conjunction with the theoretical perspectives that have already been discussed.

THE INSTITUTIONAL MODEL

The final theoretical model to be considered is the institutional model. We first introduced this model in the discussion of organizational structure. It can best be appreciated by looking at the ways in which the model seeks to explain why organizations take the forms that they do. Much of the research here has been carried out in not-for-profit organizations with relatively indeterminate technologies. DiMaggio and Powell (1983) argue that "institutional isomorphism" is now the dominant reason that such organizations assume the forms that they do. According to DiMaggio and Powell, Weber's original (1952, 1968) analysis of the driving force behind the move toward rationalization and bureaucratization was based on a capitalist market economy, with bureaucratization an "iron cage" in which humanity was bound, since the process of bureaucratization was irreversible.

DiMaggio and Powell believe that major social changes have altered this situation to such a large extent that an alternative explanation is needed. Their analysis is based on the assumption that organizations exist in "fields" of other, similar organizations. They define an organizational field as follows:

> By organizational field, we mean those organizations that, in the aggregate, constitute a recognized area of institutional life: key suppliers, resource and product consumers, regulatory agencies and other organizations that produce similar services and products. The virtue of this unit of analysis is that it directs our attention not simply to competing firms, as does the population approach of Hannan and Freeman (1977b), or to networks of organizations that actually interact, as does the interorganizational network approach of Laumann et al. (1978), but to the totality of relevant actors. (p. 148)

According to this perspective, organizations are increasingly homogeneous within fields. Thus, public universities acquire a sameness, as do department stores, airlines, professional football teams, motor vehicle bureaus, and so on. DiMaggio and Powell cite three reasons for this isomorphism among organizations in a field. First, coercive forces from the environment, such as government regulations and cultural expectations, can impose standardization on organizations. Government regulations, for example, force restaurants (we hope) to maintain minimum health standards. Organizations take forms that are institutionalized and legitimated by the state (Meyer and Rowan, 1977).

Second, DiMaggio and Powell also note that organizations mimic or model each other. This occurs as organizations face uncertainty and look for answers to their uncertainty in the ways in which other organizations in their field have faced similar uncertainties. Public schools add and subtract administrative positions to come into isomorphism with prevailing norms, values, and technical lore in their institutional environment (Rowan, 1982). DiMaggio and Powell argue that large organizations tend to use a relatively small number of consulting firms that, "like Johnny Appleseeds, spread a few organizational models throughout the land" (p. 152). A concrete example, noted by DiMaggio and Powell, is Japan's conscious modeling of its courts, postal system, military, banking, and art education programs on Western models in the late nineteenth century.

A *New York Times* article reports that business firms are establishing formal intelligence departments to keep tabs on competitors from home and abroad. One source is quoted as saying that "understanding your competitors' positions and how they might evolve is the essence of the strategic game" (Prokesh, 1985). In DiMaggio and Powell's conceptualization, the field is more than simply competitors. The establishment of intelligence departments reflects the strong mimetic tendencies within organizations.

Third, normative pressures push organizations toward isomorphism as the workforce, and especially management, becomes more professionalized. Both professional training and the growth and elaboration of professional networks within organizational fields lead to a situation in which the managerial personnel in organizations in the same field are barely indistinguishable from one another. As people participate in trade and professional associations, their ideas tend to homogenize.

The institutional perspective thus views organizational design not as a rational process but as one of both external and internal pressures that lead organizations in a field to resemble one another over time. In this perspective strategic choices or attempts at member control would be viewed as coming from the institutional order in which an organization is embedded.

Institutional theory also places a strong emphasis on symbols. We were given a strong symbol of the place of institutional theory when *Administrative Science Quarterly* placed Scott's (1987b) theoretical review of institutional theory as its lead article. These placements are hardly accidental.

The work of DiMaggio and Powell (DiMaggio and Powell, 1983; Powell, 1985; DiMaggio, 1988; Powell and DiMaggio, 1991) emphasizes the ways in which institutionalized practices are brought into organizations as noted above. Organizations in the same field develop isomorphism as they exchange professional personnel and face common exigencies such as governmental policies.

An alternative institutional approach is associated with the works of Meyer, Scott, and Zucker (Meyer and Scott, 1983; Scott, 1987b; Zucker,

1988). This approach contains a healthy dose of concern for environmental issues but basically turns our attention more inward. The focus is on ways in which practices and patterns are given values and how interaction patterns and structures are legitimated. It is a grand extension of Berger and Luckman's (1967) view that reality is socially constructed. Zucker's (1988) anthology provides an intellectually exciting view of organizations from this institutional perspective. In this set of papers individual actors are viewed as having feelings and meanings. They are not narrow, technocratic decision makers. Organizations are not shaped by the impersonal forces of technology or by the demands of a relentless environment.

Despite the attractiveness of the institutional formulations, I see four problems looming that raise serious issues for institutional theory (Hall, 1992; see also Hirsch, 1997).

The first problem is potential tautological reasoning. This form of reasoning was a major contributor to the demise of functional theory within sociology. "A tautology is circular reasoning in which variables are defined in terms of each other, thus making causes and effects obscure and difficult to assess" (Turner and Maryanski, 1979: p. 124; see also Turner, 1979). This problem appears to creep into DiMaggio's (1988) analysis when he notes:

> Put simply, the argument of this section is that institutionalization is a product of the political efforts of actors to accomplish their ends and that the success of an institutionalization project and the form that the resulting institution takes depend on the relative power of actors who support, oppose, or otherwise strive to influence it. I refer to the politics of institutionalization as *structural* because they follow an internal logic of contradiction, such that the success of an institutionalization process creates new sets of legitimated actors who, in the course of pursuing distinct interests, tend to delegitimate and deinstitutionalize aspects of the organizational form to which they owe their own autonomy and legitimacy. Central to this line of argument is an apparent paradox rooted in the two senses in which the term *institutionalization* is used. Institutionalization as an *outcome* places organizational structures and practices beyond the reach of interest and politics. By contrast, institutionalization as a *process* is profoundly political and reflects the relative power of organized interests and the actors who mobilize around them. (p. 13; italics in original)

If that is not tautological reasoning, it is uncomfortably close to it. This quotation also contains the seeds of a problem that will be noted later—the tendency to bring all organizational phenomena under the institutional label. This problem also plagued the functionalists.

The second problem is that institutional theory has paid almost no attention to what is institutionalized and what is not. This can be seen in the weirdly ironic case of Talcott Parsons. Parsons wrote fairly extensively about organizations and even specified the institutional level of analysis (Parsons, 1960). This is not even mentioned in Scott's (1987b), DiMaggio's (1988), or Zucker's (1988) works, although Parsons does reappear in Scott (1995). This is not a call to go back to Parsons but, rather, empirical evidence that not everything that says institutional is institutionalized.

This is a critical problem. There is a tendency to apply institutional theory in an ex post facto manner. This can be done almost mystically. Ideas and practices come and go for no reason other than institutionalization. It would appear that, in reality, some performance criteria are applied in assessing the success of a practice. I will later argue that the adoption of structures or practices is much more than institutionalized whim.

The third problem is essentially ontological. The prime interest rate and changes in it are very real to borrowing organizations; the number of eighteen-year-olds is very real to college administrators; and the number of twenty-one-year-olds is very real to brewers. Institutional theory can be very useful at this point. Individual and collective organizational myths develop about the meanings of these realities. This point has been very well demonstrated. The danger, however, is in making the reality that was the source of the myth into the myth itself.

The fourth problem is overextension. There is a tendency, as noted above, to apply institutional theory to a vast array of situations and organizations. DiMaggio and Powell (1983) were careful to hypothesize that institutional effects were more likely in situations of indeterminate technology and ambiguous goals.

There are additional criticisms of institutional theory. It is seen as ignoring deinstitutionalization processes. Some ideas are rejected, and others are replaced (Oliver, 1992). There is also a strong tendency to overlook or downplay issues such as efficiency (Abbott, 1992). Institutional theory essentially captured organizational theory in the 1990s. It became "institutionalized" itself (Tolbert and Zucker, 1996). In so doing, it has almost become "authoritarian" as it has swept our theoretical landscape (Hirsch, 1997). Undoubtedly, a new perspective will emerge to sweep the institutional approach aside, although that perspective is not yet in sight. Although an exciting new perspective is not in sight at the moment, there is excitement in the form of attempts to combine the perspectives that we have been considering.

COMBINING THE PERSPECTIVES

As organizational research moved through the 1990s, there was widespread acceptance of the need to apply these theories in combination, rather than as competing explanations. Fligstein's (1985) research is an exemplar here, as is that by Pfeffer and Davis-Blake (1987), Singh, Tucker, and House (1986), Mezias (1990), and Palmer, Jennings, and Zhou (1993). These researchers do not test theories against one another. Rather, they seek to explain the largest amount of variance that they can. No single set of combinations is dominant.

Fligstein and Mara-Drita (1996) examined rational and environmental factors in the emergence of a single market in the European Union. Goodstein (1994) combined institutional and rational-contingency approaches in an examination of the extent to which organizations get involved with work-family issues. A similar combination of perspectives is found in an analysis of the U.S. Government Accounting Office (Gupta, Dirsmith, and Fogarty, 1994). Resource-dependence theory and institutional theory were combined in an analysis of the proportion of women in management (Blum, Fields, and Goodman (1994). These are examples of a trend that is solidly growing.

SUMMARY AND CONCLUSIONS

It is almost common sense to realize that organizations must acquire resources as they simultaneously seek to achieve their goals and keep up with their competitors. There appears to be a strong sentiment among organizational theorists that the time has come to cease being "paradigm warriors" (Aldrich, 1988) and instead seek fuller explanations through combining perspectives. As this is done, theoretical growth will be evident. We may even be able to move toward the elusive goal of specifying which theoretical explanations work in which settings and thus have truly meaningful explanations of organizations. This book has been an effort in that direction.

References

Abbott, Andrew (1989). "The New Occupational Structure: What Are the Questions?" *Work and Occupations,* 16, 273–91.

——— (1992). "An Old Institutionalist Reads the New Institutionalism." *Contemporary Sociology,* 21, 754–56.

Acker, Joan (1992). "The Future of Women and Work: Ending the Twentieth Century." *Sociological Perspectives,* 35: 139–58.

Adler, Paul S., and Bryan Borys (1996). "Two Faces of Bureaucracy: Enabling and Coercive." *Administrative Science Quarterly,* 41: 61–89.

Aiken, Michael, Robert Dewar, Nancy Ditomaso, Jerald Hage, and Gerald Zeitz (1975). *Coordinating Human Services.* San Francisco: Jossey-Bass.

Aiken, Michael, and Jerald Hage (1966). "Organizational Alienation: A Comparative Analysis." *American Sociological Review,* 31, 497–507.

——— (1968). "Organizational Interdependence and Interorganizational Structure." *American Sociological Review,* 33, 912–30.

Alba, Richard D. (1982). "Taking Stock of Network Analysis: A Decade's Results," in *Research in the Sociology of Organizations: A Research Annual,* ed. Samuel B. Bacharach. Greenwich, CT: JAI Press.

Aldrich, Howard E. (1971). "Organizational Boundaries and Interorganizational Conflict." *Human Relations,* 24, 279–87.

——— (1972a). "Technology and Organizational Structure: A Reexamination of the Findings of the Aston Group." *Administrative Science Quarterly,* 17, 26–43.

——— (1972b). "Reply to Hilton: Seduced and Abandoned." *Administrative Science Quarterly,* 17, 55–57.

——— (1974). "The Environment as a Network of Organizations: Theoretical and Methodological Implications." Paper presented at the International Sociological Association Meetings, Toronto.

——— (1979). *Organizations and Environments.* Englewood Cliffs, NJ: Prentice Hall.

——— (1988). "Paradigm Warriors: Donaldson versus the Critics of Organization Theory." *Organization Studies,* 9, 18–25.

Aldrich, Howard E., and Peter V. Marsden (1988). "Environments and Organizations," in *Handbook of Sociology,* ed. Neil J. Smelser, 361–92. Newbury Park, CA: Sage Publications.

Aldrich, Howard E., and Jeffrey Pfeffer (1976). "Environments of Organizations." *Annual Review of Sociology,* Vol. 2. Palo Alto, CA: Annual Reviews, Inc.

Aldrich, Howard E., and David Whetten (1981). "Organization-sets, Action-sets, and Networks: Making the Most of Simplicity," in *Handbook of Organizational Design,* Vol. 1, ed. Paul C. Nystrom and William H. Starbuck. New York: Oxford University Press.

Alexander, Ernest R. (1979). "The Design of Alternatives in Organizational Contexts." *Administrative Science Quarterly,* 24, 382–404.

Alexander, Gordon J., and Roger A. Buchholz (1978). "Corporate Social Responsibility and Stock Market Performance." *Academy of Management Journal,* 21, 479–86.

Alexander, Jeffrey A. (1991). "Adaptive Change in Corporate Control Practices." *Academy of Management Journal,* 34, 162–93.

Allen, Michael Patrick (1974). "The Structure of Interorganizational Elite Cooptation: Interlocking Corporate Directorates." *American Sociological Review,* 39, 393–96.

——— (1976). "Management Control in the Large Corporation: Comment on Zeitlin." *American Journal of Sociology,* 81, 885–94.

Allen, Michael Patrick, and Sharon K. Panian (1982). "Power, Performance, and Succession in the Large Corporation." *Administrative Science Quarterly,* 27, 538–47.

Allen, Michael Patrick, Sharon K. Panian, and Roy E. Lotz (1979). "Managerial Succession and Organizational Performance: A Recalcitrant Problem Revisited." *Administrative Science Quarterly,* 24, 167–80.

Allison, Paul D., and J. Scott Long (1990). "Departmental Effects on Scientific Productivity." *American Sociological Review,* 55, 469–78.

Allmendinger, Jutta, and J. Richard Hackman (1996). "Organizations in Changing Environments: The Case of East German Symphony Orchestras." *Administrative Science Quarterly,* 41, 337–69.

Alter, Catherine (1990). "An Exploratory Study of Conflict and Coordination in Interorganizational Service Delivery Systems." *Academy of Management Journal,* 33, 478–502.

Alter, Catherine, and Jerald Hage (1993). *Organizations Working Together.* Newbury Park, CA: Sage.

Altheide, David L., and John M. Johnson (1980). *Bureaucratic Propaganda.* Boston: Allyn & Bacon.

Alutto, Joseph, and James A. Belasco (1972). "A Typology for Participation in Organizational Decision Making." *Administrative Science Quarterly,* 17, 117–25.

Amburgey, Terry, Dawn Kelly, and William P. Barnett (1993). "Resetting the Clock: The Dynamics of Organizational Change and Failure." *Administrative Science Quarterly,* 38, 51–73.

Anderson, Paul A. (1983). "Decision Making by Objection and the Cuban Missile Crisis." *Administrative Science Quarterly,* 28, 201–22.

Angle, Harold L., and James L. Perry (1981). "An Empirical Assessment of Organizational Commitment and Organizational Effectiveness." *Administrative Science Quarterly,* 26, 1–14.

Antonio, Robert J. (1979). "Domination and Production in Bureaucracy." *American Sociological Review,* 44, 895–912.

Argote, Linda (1982). "Input Uncertainty and Organizational Coordination in Hospital Emergency Units." *Administrative Science Quarterly,* 27, 420–34.

Argranoff, R., and A. Pattahas (1979). *Dimensions of Services Integration: Service Delivery, Program Linkages, Policy Management, Organizational Structure,* Human Services Monograph Series 13, Project SHARE, DHEW Publication No. 02-76-130. Washington, DC: U.S. Government Printing Office.

Argyris, Chris (1972). *The Applicability of Organizational Sociology.* London: Cambridge University Press.

——— (1973). "Personality and Organization Theory Revisited." *Administrative Science Quarterly,* 18, 141–67.

Aronowitz, Stanley (1973). *False Promises.* New York: McGraw-Hill.

Arum, Richard (1996). "Do Private Schools Force Public Schools to Compete?" *American Sociological Review,* 61, 29–46.

Asher, Hanna, and Jonathan Z. Shapiro (1988). "Managing Centrality: A Note on Hackman's Resource Allocation Theory." *Administrative Science Quarterly*, 33, 275–83.

Assael, Henry (1969). "Constructive Role of Interorganizational Conflict." *Administrative Science Quarterly*, 14, 573–82.

Astley, W. Graham (1985). "The Two Ecologies: Population and Community Perspectives on Organizational Evolution." *Administrative Science Quarterly*, 30, 224–41.

Astley, W. Graham, and Edward J. Zajac (1990). "Beyond Dyadic Exchange: Functional Interdependence and Sub-unit Power." *Organizational Studies*, 11, 481–501.

Athanassaides, John C. (1974). "On Investigation of Some Communication Patterns of Female Subordinates in Hierarchical Organizations." *Human Relations*, 27, 195–209.

Attewell, Paul (1987). "The De-skilling Controversy." Work and Occupations, 14, 323–46.

At-Twarjri, Mohammad I., and John R. Montansani (1987). "The Impact of Context and Choice on the Boundary Spanning Process: An Empirical Extension." *Human Relations*, 40, 783–98.

Azumi, Koya, and Charles J. McMillan (1974). "Subjective and Objective Measures of Organizational Structure." New York: American Sociological Association.

Bacharach, Peter, and Morton S. Baratz (1962). "The Two Faces of Power." *American Political Science Review*, 56, 947–52.

Bacharach, Samuel B., and Edward J. Lawler (1980). *Power and Politics in Organizations*. San Francisco: Jossey-Bass.

Bacharach, Samuel B., Peter Bamberger, and Walter Sonnenstuhl (1996). "The Organizational Transformation Process: The Micropolitics of Dissonance Reduction and the Alignment of Logics of Action." *Administrative Science Quarterly*, 41, 477–506.

Baker, Wayne E. (1990). "Market Networks and Corporate Behavior." *American Journal of Sociology*, 96, no. 3, 589–625.

Baldridge, J. Victor, and Robert A. Burnham (1975). "Organizational Innovation: Individual, Organizational, and Environmental Impacts." *Administrative Science Quarterly*, 20, 165–76.

Bales, Robert F. (1953). "The Equilibrium Problem in Small Groups," in *Working Paper in Theory of Action*, ed. Talcott Parsons, Robert F. Bales, and Edward Shils. New York: Free Press.

Bales, Robert F., and Philip E. Slater (1955). "Role Differentiation in Small Decision Making Groups," in *Family Socialization and Interaction Processes*, ed. Talcott Parsons and Robert Bales. New York: Free Press.

Barley, Stephen R. (1990). "The Alignment of Technology and Structure through Roles and Networks." *Administrative Science Quarterly*, 35, 61–103.

Barnard, Chester I. (1938). The Function of the Executive. Cambridge: Harvard University Press.

Barnett, William P., and Glenn R. Carroll (1995). "Modeling Internal Organizational Change," in *Annual Review of Sociology*, ed. John Hagan and Karen S. Cook. Palo Alto, CA: Annual Reviews, Inc.

Baron, James N. (1984). "Organizational Perspectives on Stratification," in *Annual Review of Sociology*, ed. Ralph Turner. Palo Alto, CA: Annual Reviews, Inc.

Baron, James N., and William T. Bielby (1980). "Bringing the Firms Back In: Stratification, Segmentation and the Organization of Work." *American Sociological Review*, 45, 737–65.

Baron, James N., P. Devereaux Jennings, and Frank R. Dobbin (1988). "Mission Control? The Development of Personnel Systems in U.S. Industry." *American Sociological Review*, 53, 497–514.

———— (1984). "The Organization of Work in a Segmented Economy." *American Sociological Review*, 49, 454–73.

Barton, Allen H. (1961). *Organizational Measurement*. Princeton, NJ: College Entrance Examination Board.

Bass, Bernard M. (1985). *Leadership and Performance Beyond Expectations*. New York: Free Press.

Bass, Bernard M., and B. J. Avolio (1990). "The Implications of Transactional and Transformational Leadership for Individual, Team, and Organizational Development." *Research in Organizational Change and Development*, 4, 231–72.

———— (1993). "Transformational Leadership: A Response to Critiques," in *Leadership Theory and Research: Perspectives and Directions*, ed. M. M. Chemers and R. Ayman. New York: Academic Press.

Baty, Gordon, William Evan, and Terry Rothermel (1971). "Personnel Flows as Interorganizational Relations." *Administrative Science Quarterly,* 16, 430–43.

Baum, Joel A. C. (1966). "Organizational Ecology," in *Handbook of Organization Studies,* ed. Stewart R. Clegg, Cynthia Hardy, and Walter R. Nord. Thousand Oaks, CA: Sage.

Baum, Joel A. C., and Christine Oliver (1991). "Institutional Linkages and Organizational Mortality." *Administrative Science Quarterly,* 36, 187–218.

——— (1992). "Institutional Embeddedness and the Dynamics of Organizational Populations." *American Sociological Review,* 57, 540–59.

Baum, Joel A. C., and Walter W. Powell (1995). "Cultivating an Institutional Ecology of Organizations: Comments on Hannan, Carroll, Dundon and Torres." *American Sociological Review,* 60, 529–38.

Baum, Joel A. C., and Jitendra V. Singh (1994). "Organizational Niches and the Dynamics of Organizational Mortality." *American Journal of Sociology,* 100, 346–30.

——— (1996). "Dynamics of Organizational Responses to Competition." *Social Forces,* 74, 1261–97.

Baureus, Melissa S., and Janet P. Near (1991). "Can Illegal Corporate Behavior Be Predicted: An Event History Analysis." *Academy of Management Journal,* 34, 9–36.

Bavelas, Alex (1950). "Communication Patterns in Task Oriented Groups." *Journal of the Acoustic Society of America,* 22, 725–30.

Becker, Selwyn W., and Duncan Neuhauser (1975). *The Efficient Organization.* New York: Elsevier.

Benson, J. Kenneth (1975). "The Interlocking Network as a Political Economy." *Administrative Science Quarterly,* 20, 229–49.

——— (1977). "Innovation and Crisis in Organizational Analysis." *Sociological Quarterly,* 18, 3–16.

Benson, J. Kenneth, Joseph T. Kunce, Charles A. Thompson, and David L. Allen (1973). *Coordinating Human Services.* Columbia: Regional Rehabilitation Institute, University of Missouri.

Berger, Peter, and Thomas Luckman (1967). *The Social Construction of Reality.* Garden City, NY: Anchor.

Berle, Adolph A., and Gardiner C. Means (1932). *The Modern Corporation and Private Property.* New York: Macmillan.

Bettman, James R., and Barton A. Weitz (1983). "Attributions in the Board Room: Causal Reasoning in Corporate Annual Reports." *Administrative Science Quarterly,* 28, 165–83.

Beyer, Janice M. (1981). "Ideologies, Values, and Decision Making in Organizations," in *Handbook of Organizational Design,* Vol. 2, ed. Paul C. Nystrom and William H. Starbuck, 166–202. New York: Oxford University Press.

Beyer, Janice M., and Harrison M. Trice (1979). "A Reexamination of the Relations between Size and Various Components of Organizational Complexity." *Administrative Science Quarterly,* no. 1 (March), 48–64.

Bidwell, Charles E., and John D. Kasarda (1985). *The Organization and Its Ecosystem: A Theory of Structuring in Organizations.* Greenwich, CT: JAI Press.

Bierstedt, Robert (1950). "An Analysis of Social Power." *American Sociological Review,* 15, 730–38.

Biggart, Nicole Woolsey (1977). "The Creative-Destructive Process of Organizational Change: The Case of the Post Office." *Administrative Science Quarterly,* 22, 410–26.

——— (1989). *Charismatic Capitalism: Direct Selling Organizations in America.* Chicago: University of Chicago Press.

Biggart, Nicole Woolsey, and Gary G. Hamilton (1984). "The Power of Obedience." *Administrative Science Quarterly,* 29, 540–49.

Bills, David (1987). "Costs, Commitment, and Rewards: Factors Influencing the Design and Implementation of Internal Labor Markets." *Administrative Science Quarterly,* 32, 202–21.

Birnbaum, Phillip H., and Gilbert Y. Y. Wong (1985). "Organizational Structure of Multinational Banks from a Culture-Free Perspective." *Administrative Science Quarterly,* 30, 262–77.

Blake, Richard R., and Jane S. Mouton (1964). *The Managerial Grid.* Houston: Gulf Publishing Co.

Blau, Judith R. (1966). "Organizations as Overlapping Jurisdictions: Restoring Reason in Organizational Accounts." *Administrative Science Quarterly,* 41, 172–79.

Blau, Judith R., and Richard D. Alba (1982). "Empowering Nets of Participation." *Administrative Science Quarterly,* 27, 363–79.

Blau, Judith R., and William McKinley (1979). "Ideas, Complexity, and Innovation." *Administrative Science Quarterly,* 24, 200–219.

Blau, Judith R., and Gordana Rabrenovic (1989). "Dominant Concerns and Interorganizational Relations." San Francisco: Annual Meetings, American Sociological Association/Department of Sociology, University of North Carolina, Chapel Hill.

Blau, Peter M. (1955). *The Dynamics of Bureaucracy.* Chicago: University of Chicago Press.

———— (1964). *Exchange and Power in Social Life.* New York: John Wiley.

———— (1968). "The Hierarchy of Authority in Organizations." *American Journal of Sociology,* 73, 453–67.

———— (1970). "Decentralization in Bureaucracies," in *Power in Organizations,* ed. Mayer N. Zald. Nashville: Vanderbilt University Press.

———— (1972). "Interdependence and Hierarchy in Organizations." *Social Science Research,* 1, 1–24.

———— (1973). *The Organization of Academic Work.* New York: John Wiley.

———— (1974). *On the Nature of Organizations.* New York: John Wiley.

Blau, Peter M., Wolf Heydebrand, and Robert E. Stauffer (1966). "The Structure of Small Bureaucracies." *American Sociological Review,* 31, 179–91.

Blau, Peter M., and Richard A. Schoenherr (1971). *The Structure of Organizations.* New York: Basic Books.

Blau, Peter M., and W. Richard Scott (1962). *Formal Organizations.* San Francisco: Chandler.

Blauner, Robert (1964). *Alienation and Freedom.* Chicago: University of Chicago Press.

Blum, Terry C., David Fields, and Jodi Goodman (1994). "Organizational-Level Determinants of Women in Management." *Academy of Management Journal,* 37, 241–68.

Boddewyn, John (1974). "External Affairs: A Corporate Function in Search of Conceptualization and Theory." *Organization and Administrative Sciences,* 5, 67–106.

Boeker, Warren (1989a). "The Development and Institutionalization of Subunit Power in Organizations." *Administrative Science Quarterly,* 34, 388–410.

———— (1989b). "Strategic Change: The Effects of Founding and History." *Academy of Management Journal,* 32, 489–515.

———— (1992). "Power and Managerial Dismissal: Scapegoating at the Top." *Administrative Science Quarterly,* 37, 400–421.

———— (1997a). "Strategic Change: The Influence of Managerial Characteristics and Organizational Growth." *Academy of Management Journal,* 40, 152–70.

———— (1997b). " Executive Migration and Strategic Change: The Effect of Top Manager Movement on Product Market Entry." *Administrative Science Quarterly,* 42, 213–36.

Boeker, Warren, and Jerry Goodstein (1991). "Organizational Performance and Adaptation: Effects of Environment and Performance on Changes in Board Composition." *Academy of Management Journal,* 34, 805–26.

Boisot, Max, and John Child (1988). "The Iron Law of Fiefs: Bureaucratic Failure and Problem of Governance in the Chinese Economic Reforms." *Administrative Science Quarterly,* 33, 507–27.

Boje, David M., and David A. Whetten (1981). "Effects of Organizational Strategies and Contextual Constraints on Centrality and Attributions of Influence in Interorganizational Networks." *Administrative Science Quarterly,* 26, 378–95.

Boulding, Kenneth E. (1964). "A Pure Theory of Conflict Applied to Organizations," in *Power and Conflict in Organizations,* ed. Robert L. Kahn and Elise Boulding. New York: Basic Books.

Bozeman, Barry (1987). *All Organizations Are Public: Bridging Public and Private Organizational Theories.* San Francisco: Jossey-Bass.

Brass, Daniel J. (1984). "Being in the Right Place: A Structural Analysis of Individual Influence in an Organization." *Administrative Science Quarterly,* 29, 518–39.

Brass, Daniel J., and Marlene E. Burkhardt (1993). "Potential Power and Power Use: An Investigation of Structure and Behavior." *Academy of Management Journal,* 36, 441–70.

Braverman, Harry (1974). *Labor and Monopoly Capital: The Degradation of Work in the Twentieth Century*. New York: Monthly Review Press.

Brewer, John (1971). "Flow of Communication, Expert Qualifications, and Organizational Authority Structure." *American Sociological Review,* 36, 475–84.

Broskowski, Anthony (1980). "Literature Review on Interorganizational Relationships and Their Relevance to Health and Mental Health Coordination." Tampa, FL: Northside Community Mental Health Center (final report), NIMH Contract #278-00300P.

Brown, John L., and Rodney Schneck (1979). "A Structural Comparison between Canadian and American Industrial Organizations." *Administrative Science Quarterly,* 24, 24–47.

Brown, M. Craig (1982). "Administrative Succession and Organizational Performance: The Succession Effect." *Administrative Science Quarterly,* 27, 1–16.

Brown, Richard Harvey (1978). "Bureaucracy as Praxis: Toward a Political Phenomenology of Formal Organizations." *Administrative Science Quarterly,* 23, 365–82.

Browning, Larry D., Janice M. Beyer, and Judy C. Shetler (1995). "Building Cooperation in a Competitive Industry: SEMATECH and the Semiconductor Industry." *Academy of Management Journal,* 38, 113–51.

Brunsson, Nils (1989). *The Organization of Hypocrisy: Talk, Decisions, and Actions in Organizations*. New York: John Wiley.

Bryman, Alan (1996). "Leadership in Organizations." in *Handbook of Organization Studies,* ed. Stewart R. Clegg, Cynthia Hardy, and Walter R. Nord. Thousand Oaks, CA: Sage.

Bucher, Rue (1970). "Social Process and Power in a Medical School," in *Power in Organizations.* ed. Mayer N. Zald. Nashville: Vanderbilt University Press.

Budros, Art (1992). "The Making of an Industry: Organizational Births in New York's Life Insurance Industry." *Social Forces,* 70, 1013–33.

———— (1993). "An Analysis of Organizational Birth Types: Organizational Start-up and Entry in the Nineteenth-Century Life Insurance Industry." *Social Forces,* 72, 199–221.

———— (forthcoming). "Organizational Types and Organizational Innovation: Downsizing among Institutionalized Market, Market, and Institutionalized Firms." *Sociological Forum.*

Buğra, Ayşe, and Behlül Üsdiken (1997). "Introduction: State, Market and Organizational Form," in *State, Market and Organizational Form,* ed. Ayşe Buğra and Behlül Üsdiken. Berlin: Walter de Gruyter.

Burke, John P. (1986). *Bureaucratic Responsibility.* Baltimore: Johns Hopkins University Press.

Burke, Ronald J. (1970). "Methods of Resolving Superior-Subordinate Conflict: The Constructive Use of Subordinate Differences and Disagreements." *Organizational Behavior and Human Performance,* 5, 393–411.

Burns, Tom (1967). "The Comparative Study of Organizations," in *Methods of Organizational Research,* ed. Victor H. Vroom. Pittsburgh: University of Pittsburgh Press.

Burns, Tom, and G. M. Stalker (1961). *The Management of Innovation.* London: Tavistock Publications.

Burrell, Gibson, and Gareth Morgan (1979). *Sociological Paradigms and Organizational Analysis.* London: Heinemann.

Burt, Ronald S. (1977). "Power in a Social Typology." *Social Science Research,* 6, 1–83.

———— (1980). "Cooptive Corporate Action Networks: A Reconsideration of Interlocking Directorates Involving American Manufacturing." *Administrative Science Quarterly,* 25, 557–82.

———— (1983). "Corporate Philanthropy as a Cooptive Process." *Social Forces,* 62, 419–49.

———— (1988). "The Stability of American Markets." *American Journal of Sociology,* 94, no. 2 (September), 356–95.

Burt, Ronald S., Kenneth P. Christman, and Harold C. Kilburn, Jr. (1980). "Testing a Structural Theory of Corporate Cooptation: Interorganizational Directorate Ties as a Strategy for Avoiding Market Constraints on Projects." *American Sociological Review,* 45, 821–41.

Butler, Richard (1990). "Decision Making Research: Its Uses and Misues." *Organizational Studies,* 11, 11–16.

Cameron, Kim (1978). "Measuring Organizational Effectiveness in Institutions of Higher Education." *Administrative Science Quarterly,* 23, 604–32.

———— (1986). "Effectiveness as Paradox." *Management Science,* 32, 539–53.

Cameron, Kim, Myung U. Kim, and David A. Whetten (1987). "Organizational Effects of Decline and Turbulence." *Administrative Science Quarterly,* 32, 222–40.

Cameron, Kim, and David A. Whetten (1981). "Perceptions of Organizational Effectiveness over Organizational Life Cycles." *Administrative Science Quarterly,* 26, 524–44.

———— (1983). *Organizational Effectiveness: A Comparison of Multiple Models.* New York: Academic Press.

Camic, Charles (1985). "The Matter of Habit." *American Journal of Sociology,* 91, 481–510.

Campbell, Donald (1969). "Variation and Selective Retention in Socio-Cultural Evolution." *General Systems: Yearbook of the Society for General Systems Research,* 16, 69–85.

Campbell, John P. (1977). "On the Nature of Organizational Effectiveness," in *New Perspectives on Organizational Effectiveness,* ed. Paul S. Goodman and Johannes M. Pennings. San Francisco: Jossey-Bass.

Campbell, John P., et al. (1974). *The Measurement of Organizational Effectiveness,* Final Report, Navy Personnel Research and Development Center Contract N 00022-73-C-0023. Minneapolis: Personnel Decisions.

Caplow, Theodore (1964). *Principles of Organization.* New York: Harcourt Brace Jovanovich.

———— (1976). *How to Run Any Organization.* New York: Holt, Rinehart & Winston.

———— (1983). *Managing Any Organization.* New York: Holt, Rinehart & Winston.

Cappelli, Peter, Laurie Bassi, Harry Katz, David Knoke, Paul Osterman, and Michael Useem (1997). *Change at Work.* New York: Oxford University Press.

Caragonne, P. (1978). "Service Integration: Where Do We Stand?" Paper prepared for the 39th National Conference on Public Administration, April, in Phoenix, Arizona.

Carper, William B., and William E. Snizek (1980). "The Nature and Types of Organizational Taxonomies: An Overview." *Academy of Management Review,* 5, 65–75.

Carroll, Glenn R., (1984a). "Organizational Ecology." *Annual Review of Sociology,* Vol. 18. Palo Alto, CA: Annual Reviews, Inc.

———— (1984b). "Dynamics of Publisher Succession in Newspaper Organizations." *Administrative Science Quarterly,* 29, 93–113

———— (1985). "Concentration and Specialization: Dynamics of Niche Width in Populations of Organizations." *American Journal of Sociology,* 90, 1262–83.

————, ed. (1988). *Ecological Models of Organizations.* Cambridge, MA: Ballinger.

Carroll, Glenn R., and Jacques Delacroix (1982). "Organizational Mortality in the Newspaper Industries of Argentina and Ireland: An Ecological Approach." *Administrative Science Quarterly,* 27, 169–98.

Carroll, Glenn R., and Michael T. Hannan (1989). "Density Dependence in the Evolution of Populations of Newspaper Organizations." *American Sociological Review,* 54, 524–41.

Carroll, Glenn R., and Yangchung Paul Huo (1986). "Organizational Task and Institutional Environments in Ecological Perspective: Findings from the Local Newspaper Industry." *American Journal of Sociology,* 91, 838–73.

Carroll, Glenn, Peter Preisendoerfer, Anand Swaninathan, and Gabriele Wiedenmayer (1993). "Brewery and Branerei: The Organizational Ecology of Brewing." *Organizational Studies,* 14, 155–88.

Carroll, Glenn R., and James Wade (1991). "Density Dependence in the Organizational Evolution of the American Brewing Industry across Different Levels of Analysis." *Social Science Research,* 20, 271–302.

Carstensen, Fred V., and Richard Hume Werking (1983). "The Process of Bureaucratization in the U.S. State Department and the Vesting of Economic Interests: Toward Clearer Thinking and Better History." *Administrative Science Quarterly,* 28, 56–60.

Cartwright, Dorwin (1965). "Influence, Leadership, and Control," in *Handbook of Organizations,* ed. James G. March, 1–47. Chicago: Rand McNally.

Cartwright, Dorwin, and A. Zander (1968). "Motivational Processes in Groups: Introduction," in *Group Dynamics,* 3rd ed., ed. D. Cartwright and A. Zander. New York: Harper and Row.

Champagne, Anthony, Marian Neef, and Stuart Nagel (1981). "Laws, Organizations, and the Judiciary," in *Handbook of Organizational Design*, Vol. 1, ed. Paul C. Nystrom and William H. Starbuck. New York: Oxford University Press.

Chandler, A. D., Jr. (1962). *Strategy and Structure*. Cambridge: MIT Press.

Chaves, Mark (1993). "Intraorganizational Power and Internal Secularization in Protestant Denominations." *American Journal of Sociology*, 99, 1–48.

Chen, Ming-Jer, and Donald Hambrick (1995). "Speed, Stealth, and Selective Attack: How Small Firms Differ from Large Firms in Competitive Behavior." *Academy of Management Journal*, 38, 453–82.

Child, John (1972). "Organizational Structure, Environment, and Performance: The Role of Strategic Choice." *Sociology*, 6, 1–22.

——— (1973). "Strategies of Control and Organizational Behavior." *Administrative Science Quarterly*, 18, 1–17.

——— (1976). "Participation, Organization, and Social Cohesion." *Human Relations*, 29, 429–51.

Child, John, and Alfred Kieser (1981). "Development of Organization over Time." *Handbook of Organizational Design*, ed. Paul C. Nystrom and William H. Starbuck, 169–98.

Child, John, and Roger Mansfield (1972). "Technology, Size and Organizational Structure." *Sociology*, 6, 369–93.

Christenson, James A., James G. Hougland, Jr., Thomas W. Ilvento, and Jon M. Shepard (1988). "The 'Organization Man' and the Community: The Impact of Organizational Norms and Personal Values on Community Participation and Transfers." *Social Forces*, 66, 808–26.

Clark, John P. (1988). "Presidential Address on the Importance of Our Understanding Organizational Conflict." *Sociological Quarterly*, 29, 149–61.

Clawson, Dan (1980). *Bureaucracy and the Labor Process: The Transformation of U.S. Industry, 1860–1920*. New York: Monthly Review Press.

Clawson, Dan, and Alan Neustadt (1989). "Interlocks, PACs and Corporate Conservatism." *American Journal of Sociology*, 94, 749–73.

Clegg, Stewart (1981). "Organization and Control." *Administrative Science Quarterly*, 26, 545–62.

Clegg, Stewart, and David Dunkerly (1980). *Organization, Class, and Control*. London: Routledge and Kegan Paul.

Clinard, Marshall B., and Peter Yeager (1980). *Corporate Crime*. New York: Free Press.

Cohen, Michael D., James G. March, and Johan P. Olsen (1972). "A Garbage Can Model of Organizational Choice." *Administrative Science Quarterly*, 17, 1–25.

Coleman, James S. (1974). *Power and the Structure of Society*. New York: W. W. Norton.

Colignon, Richard (1997). *The New Deal and Intellectuals: The Institutionalization of the TVA*. Albany: State University of New York Press.

Comstock, Donald, and W. Richard Scott (1977). "Technology and the Structure of Subunits: Distinguishing Individual and Work Group Effects." *Administrative Science Quarterly*, 22, 177–202.

Conaty, Joseph, Hoda Mahmoudi, and George A. Miller (1983). "Social Structure and Bureaucracy: A Comparison of Organizations in the United States and pre-Revolutionary Iran." *Organization Studies*, 4, 105–28.

Cook, Karen S. (1977). "Exchange and Power in Networks of Interorganizational Relations." *Sociological Quarterly*, 18, 62–82.

Corwin, Ronald (1973). *Reform and Organizational Survival: The Teacher Corps as an Instrument of Educational Change*. New York: John Wiley.

Coser, Lewis (1956). *The Functions of Social Conflict*. New York: Free Press.

——— (1967). *Continuities in the Study of Social Conflict*. New York: Free Press.

Craig, John G., and Edward Gross (1970). "The Forum Theory of Organizational Democracy: Structural Guarantee as Time Related Variables." *American Sociological Review*, 35, 19–33.

Crittenden, Ann (1978). "Philanthropy, The Business of the Not-So-Idle Rich." *New York Times*, July 23, sec. F.

Crozier, Michael (1964). *The Bureaucratic Phenomenon*. Chicago: University of Chicago Press.

—— (1973). *The Stalled Society,* trans. Rupert Sawyer. New York: Viking Press.

Cummings, Larry L. (1977). "The Emergence of the Instrumental Organization," in *New Perspectives on Organizational Effectiveness,* ed. Paul S. Goodman and Johannes M. Pennings. San Francisco: Jossey-Bass.

Daft, Richard L., and Selwin W. Becker (1978). *Innovation in Organizations: Innovation Adoption in School Organizations.* New York: Elsevier.

Daft, Richard L., and Patricia J. Bradshaw (1980). "The Process of Horizontal Differentiation: Two Models." *Administrative Science Quarterly,* 25, 441–56.

Dahl, Robert (1957). "The Concept of Power." *Behavioral Science,* 2, 201–15.

Dahrendorf, Ralf (1959). *Class and Class Conflict in Industrial Society.* London: Routledge and Kegan Paul.

Dalin, M. Tina (1997). "Isomorphism in Context: The Power and Prescription of Institutional Norms." *Academy of Management Journal,* 40, 46–81.

Dalton, Melville (1959). *Men Who Manage.* New York: John Wiley.

Damanpour, Fariborz (1991). "Organizational Innovation: A Meta-Analysis of Effects of Determinants and Moderators." *Academy of Management Journal,* 34, 555–90.

Damanpour, Fariborz, and William M. Evan (1984). "Organizational Innovation and Performance: The Problems of 'Organizational Lag.' " *Administrative Science Quarterly,* 29, 392–409.

Danet, Barbara (1981). "Client-Organization Relationships," in *Handbook of Organizational Design,* Vol. 2, ed. Paul C. Nystrom and William H. Starbuck. New York: Oxford University Press.

D'Aunno, Thomas D., Robert I. Sutton, and Richard H. Price (1991). "Isomorphism and External Support in Conflicting Institutional Environments: A Study of Drug Abuse Treatment Units." *Academy of Management Journal,* 34, 636–61.

D'Aveni, Richard D., and Ian G. MacMillan (1990). "Crisis and the Content of Managerial Communications: A Study of the Focus of Attention to Top Managers in Surviving and Failing Firms." *Administrative Science Quarterly,* 35, 634–57.

Davis, Gerald F. (1991). "Agents Without Principles? The Spread of the Poison Pill through the Intercorporate Network." *Administrative Science Quarterly,* 36, 583–613.

Davis, Gerald F., Kristina A. Diekmann, and Catherin H. Tinsley (1994). "The Decline and Fall of the Conglomerate Firm in the 1980s: The Deinstitutionalization of an Organizational Form." *American Sociological Review,* 59, 547–70.

Davis, Gerald F. and Henrich R. Greve (1997). "Corporate Elite Networks and Governance Change in the 1980s." *American Journal of Sociology,* 103, 1–37.

Davis-Blake, Allison, and Brian Uzzi (1993). "Determinants of Employment Externalization: A Study of Temporary Workers and Independent Contractors." *Administrative Science Quarterly,* 38, 195–223.

Day, D. V., and R. G. Lord (1988). "Executive Leadership and Organizational Performance: Suggestions for a New Theory and Methodology." *Journal of Management,* 14, 453–64.

Dean, James W., Jr., and Mark P. Sharfman (1996). "Does Decision Process Matter? A Study of Strategic Decision-Making Effectiveness." *Academy of Management Review,* 39, 368–96.

Delacroix, Jacques, and Glenn R. Carroll (1983). "Organizational Foundings: An Ecological Study of the Newspaper Industries of Argentina and Ireland." *Administrative Science Quarterly,* 28, 274–91.

Delacroix, Jacques, and Hayagreeva Rao (1994). "Externalities and Organizational Theory Unbundling Density Dependence.," in *Evolutionary Dynamics of Organizations,* Joel A. C. Baum and Jitendra V. Singh. New York: Oxford University Press.

Delacroix, Jacques, and Anand Swaminathan (1991). "Cosmetic, Speculative, and Adaptive Organizational Change in the Wine Industry: A Longitudinal Study." *Administrative Science Quarterly,* 36, 631–61.

Dess, Gregory G., and Donald W. Beard (1984). "Dimensions of Organizational Task Environment." *Administrative Science Quarterly,* 29, 52–73.

Dewar, Robert D., and Jerald Hage (1978). "Size, Technology, Complexity and Structural Differentiation: Toward a Theoretical Synthesis." *Administrative Science Quarterly,* 23, 111–36.

Dewar, Robert D., David A. Whetten, and David Boje (1980). "An Examination of the Reliability and Validity of the Aiken and Hage Scales of Utilization, Formalization, and Task Routineness." *Administrative Science Quarterly*, 25, 120–28.

DiMaggio, Paul J. (1988). "Interest and Agency in Institutional Theory," in *Institutional Patterns and Organizations: Culture and Environment*, ed. Lynne G. Zucker. Cambridge, MA: Ballinger.

DiMaggio, Paul J., and Helmut K. Anheiser (1990). "The Sociology of Nonprofit Organizations and Sectors," in *Annual Review of Sociology*, ed. W. Richard Scott and Judith Blake, 137–59. Palo Alto, CA: Annual Reviews, Inc.

DiMaggio, Paul J., and Walter W. Powell (1983). "The Iron Cage Revisited: Institutional Isomorphism and Collective Rationality in Organizational Fields." *American Sociological Review*, 48, 147–60.

Dobbin, Frank, and Timothy J. Dowd (1997). "How Policy Shapes Competition: Early Railroad Foundings in Massachusetts." *Administrative Science Quarterly*, 42, 501–29.

Dobbin, Frank, John R. Sutton, John M. Meyer, and W. Richard Scott (1993). "Equal Opportunity Law and the Construction of Internal Labor Markets." *American Journal of Sociology*, 99, 396–427.

Domhoff, G. William, and Thomas R. Dye, eds. (1987). *Power Elites and Organizations*. Newbury Park, CA: Sage.

Donaldson, Lex (1985). *In Defense of Organizational Theory: A Reply to the Critics*. Cambridge: Cambridge University Press.

———— (1987). "Strategy and Structural Adjustment to Regain Fit and Performance: In Defense of Contingency Theory." *Journal of Management*, 24, 1–24.

———— (1995). *American Anti-Management Theories of Organization: A Critique of Paradigm Proliferation*. Cambridge: Cambridge University Press.

———— (1996). "The Normal Science of Structural Contingence Theory," in *Handbook of Organization Studies*, ed. Stewart R. Clegg, Cynthia Hardy, and Walter R. Nord. Thousand Oaks, CA: Sage.

Donaldson, Lex, and Malcolm Warner (1974). "Bureaucratic and Electoral Control in Occupational Interest Associations." *Sociology*, 8, 47–59.

Dornbusch, Sanford M. (1955). "The Military Academy as an Assimilating Institution." *Social Forces*, 33, 316–21.

Dornbusch, Sanford M., and W. Richard Scott (1975). *Evaluation and the Exercise of Authority*. New York: Basic Books.

Downs, Anthony (1967). *Inside Bureaucracy*. Boston: Little, Brown.

Drabek, Thomas E., Harriet L. Tamminga, Thomas S. Kilijanek, and Christopher R. Adams (1981). *Managing Multiorganizational Emergency Responses: Emergent Search and Rescue Networks in Natural Disaster and Remote Area Settings*. Boulder: Institute of Behavioral Science, University of Colorado.

Drazin, Robert, and Andrew H. Van de Ven (1985). "Alternative Forms of Fit in Contingency Theory." *Administrative Science Quarterly*, 30, 514–39.

DuBick, Michael A. (1978). "The Organizational Structure of Newspapers in Relation to Their Metropolitan Environments." *Administrative Science Quarterly*, 23, 418–33.

Dubin, Robert (1965). "Supervision and Productivity: Empirical Findings and Theoretical Considerations," in *Leadership and Productivity*, ed. Robert Dubin, George Homans, Floyd Mann, and Delbert Miller. San Francisco: Chandler.

Dunbar, Roger L. M., and Nikolai Wasilewski (1985). "Regulating External Threats in the Cigarette Industry." *Administrative Science Quarterly*, 30, 540–59.

Duncan, Robert B. (1972). "Characteristics of Organizational Environments and Perceived Environmental Uncertainty." *Administrative Science Quarterly*, 17, 313–27.

———— (1973). "Multiple Decision-Making Structures in Adapting to Environmental Uncertainty: The Impact on Organizational Effectiveness." *Human Relations*, 26, 273–91.

Dunford, Richard (1987). "The Suppression of Technology as a Strategy for Controlling Resource Dependence." *Administrative Science Quarterly*, 32, 512–25.

Dun's Census of American Business (1995). Parsippany, NJ: Dun and Bradstreet.

Eccles, Robert G., and Harrison C. White (1988). "Price and Authority in Inter-Profit Center Transactions." *American Journal of Sociology*, 94, Supplement, S17–S51.

Edelman, Lauren B. (1990). "Legal Environments and Organizational Governance: The Expansion of Due Process of the American Workplace." *American Journal of Sociology,* 95, 1401–40.

Edelman, Lauren B., and Mark C. Suchman (1997). "The Legal Environment of Organizations," in *Annual Review of Sociology,* vol. 23, ed. John Hagan and Karen Cook. Palo Alto, CA: Annual Reviews, Inc.

Edwards, Richard C. (1975). "The Social Relations of Production in the Firm and Labor Market Structure." *Politics and Society,* 5, 83–108.

——— (1979). *Contested Terrain.* New York: Basic Books.

Egelhoff, William G. (1982). "Strategy and Structure in Multinational Corporations: An Information Processing Approach." *Administrative Science Quarterly,* 27, 435–58.

Eisenhardt, Kathleen M., and Claudia Bird Schoonhoven (1990). "Organizational Growth: Linking Founding Team, Strategy, Environment and Growth among U.S. Semiconductor Ventures, 1978–1988." *Administrative Science Quarterly,* 35, 504–29.

Eitzen, D. Stanley, and Norman R. Yetman (1972). "Managerial Change, Longevity and Organizational Effectiveness." *Administrative Science Quarterly,* 17, 110–18.

Emerson, Richard M. (1962). "Power-Dependence Relations." *American Sociological Review,* 27, 31–40.

Emery, F. E., and E. L. Trist (1965). "The Causal Texture of Organizational Environments." *Human Relations,* 18, 21–32.

Enz, Cathy A. (1988). "The Role of Value Congruence in Intraorganizational Power." *Administrative Science Quarterly,* 33, 284–304.

——— (1989). "The Measurement of Perceived Intraorganizational Power: A Multi-Respondent Perspective." *Organizational Studies,* 10, 241–51.

Etzioni, Amitai (1961). *A Comparative Analysis of Complex Organizations.* New York: Free Press.

——— (1964). *Modern Organizations.* Englewood Cliffs, NJ: Prentice Hall.

——— (1965). "Dual Leadership in Complex Organizations." *American Sociological Review,* 30, 688–98.

——— (1968). *The Active Society: A Theory of Societal and Political Processes.* New York: Free Press.

——— (1975). *A Comparative Analysis of Complex Organizations,* rev. ed. New York: Free Press.

——— (1988). "Normative Affective Factors: Toward a New Decision-Making Model." *Journal of Economic Psychology,* 9, 125–50.

——— (1991). *A Responsive Society: Collected Essays on Guiding Deliberate Social Change.* San Francisco: Jossey-Bass.

——— (1993). *The Spirit of Community Rights, Responsibilities and the Communitarian.* New York: Crown Publishers.

Evan, William (1966). "The Organization Set: Toward a Theory of Interorganizational Relations," in *Approaches to Organizational Design,* ed. James Thompson. Pittsburgh: University of Pittsburgh Press.

Farberman, Harvey A. (1975). "A Criminogenic Market Structure: The Automobile Industry." *Sociological Quarterly,* 16, 438–57.

Feldman, Martha S., and James G. March (1981). "Information in Organizations as Signal and Symbol." *Administrative Science Quarterly,* 26, 171–86.

Fennell, Mary C. (1980). "The Effects of Environmental Characteristics on the Structure of Hospital Clusters." *Administrative Science Quarterly,* 29, 489–510.

Fiedler, Fred E. (1967). *A Theory of Leadership Effectiveness.* New York: McGraw-Hill.

——— (1972). "The Effects of Leadership Training and Experience: A Contingency Model Explanation." *Administrative Science Quarterly,* 17, 453–70.

Fiedler, Fred E., and M. M. Chemers (1982). *Improving Leader Effectiveness: The Leader Match Concept,* 2nd ed. New York: John Wiley.

Fiedler, Fred E., and J. E. Garcia (1987). *New Approaches to Leadership: Cognitive Resources and Organizational Performance.* New York: John Wiley.

Filley, Alan C., and Robert J. House (1969). *Managerial Processes and Organizational Behavior.* Glenview, IL: Scott, Foresman.

Filley, Alan C., and Steven Kerr (1976). *Managerial Process and Organizational Behavior.* Glenview, IL: Scott, Foresman.

Finkelstein, Sydney (1992). "Power in Top Management Teams: Dimension, Measurement and Validation." *Academy of Management Journal,* 35, 505–38.

Finney, Henry C., and Henry R. Lesieur (1982). "A Contingency Theory of Organizational Crime," in *Research in the Sociology of Organizations,* Vol. 1, ed. Samuel B. Bacharach. Greenwich, CT: JAI Press.

Fligstein, Neil (1985). "The Spread of the Multidivisional Form among Large Firms." *American Sociological Review,* 50, 377–91.

———— (1987). "The Intraorganizational Power Struggle: Rise of Financial Personnel to Top Leadership in Large Corporations, 1919–1979." *American Sociological Review,* 52, 44–58.

———— (1992). "The Social Construction of Efficiency," in *Decision Making: Alternatives to Rational Choice Models,* ed. Mary Zey, 351–76. Newbury Park, CA: Sage.

———— (1995) "Networks of Power or the Financial Conception of Control? Comment on Palmer, Barber, Zhou, and Soysal (1995). *American Sociological Review,* 60, 500–503.

Fligstein, Neil, and Peter Brantley (1992). "Bank Control, Owner Control, or Organizational Dynamics: Who Controls the Large Modern Corporation." *American Journal of Sociology,* 98, 280–307.

Fligstein, Neil, and Robert Freedland (1995). "Theoretical and Comparative Perspectives on Corporate Organization," in *Annual Review of Sociology,* ed. John Hagan and Karen S. Cook. Palo Alto, CA: Annual Reviews, Inc.

Fligstein, Neil, and Iona Mara-Drita (1996). "How to Make a Market: Reflections on the Attempt to Create a Single Market in the European Union." *American Journal of Sociology,* 102, 1–33.

Florida, Richard, and Martin Kenney (1991). "Transplanted Organizations: The Transfer of Japanese Industrial Organization to the U.S." *American Sociological Review,* 56, 381–98.

Fombrun, Charles J. (1986). "Structural Dynamics within and between Organizations." *Administrative Science Quarterly,* 31, 403–21.

Forbes (1973). "The Numbers Game: The Larger the Company, the More Understanding the Accountant?" 112, 33–35.

Form, William (1980). "Resolving Ideological Issues on the Division of Labor," in *Sociological Theory and Research: A Critical Appraisal,* ed. Hubert M. Blalock, Jr., 110–55. New York: Free Press.

Freedland (1997). "The Myth of the M-Form? Governance, Consent, and Organizational Change." *American Journal of Sociology,* 102, 483–526.

Freeman, John H. (1973). "Environment, Technology, and the Administrative Intensity of Manufacturing Organizations." *American Sociological Review,* 38, 750–63.

———— (1979). "Going to the Well: School District Administrative Intensity and Environmental Constraints." *Administrative Science Quarterly,* 24, 119–33.

Freeman, John H., Glenn Carroll, and Michael Hannan (1983). "The Liability of Newness: Age-dependence in Organizational Death Rates." *American Sociological Review,* 48, 692–710.

Freeman, John H., and Michael T. Hannan (1983). "Niche Width and the Dynamics of Organizational Populations." *American Journal of Sociology,* 88, 1116–45.

———— (1989). "Setting the Record Straight: Rebuttal to Young." *American Journal of Sociology,* 95, 425–39.

Freidson, Eliot (1973). *The Professions and Their Prospects.* Beverly Hills, CA: Sage.

French, John R. P., and Bertram Raven (1968). "The Bases of Social Power," in *Group Dynamics,* 3rd ed., ed. Dorwin Cartwright and Alvin Zander. New York: Harper and Row.

Frost, Peter J., Larry F. Moore, Meryl Reis Louis, Craig C. Lundberg, and Joanne Martin, eds. (1985). *Organizational Culture.* Beverly Hills, CA: Sage.

Galaskiewicz, Joseph (1979). "The Structure of Community Organizational Networks." *Social Forces,* 57, 1346–64.

———— (1985). "Interorganizational Relations." *Annual Review of Sociology,* Vol. 11. Palo Alto, CA: Annual Reviews, Inc.

———— (1997). "An Urban Grants Economy Revisited: Corporate Charitable Contributions in the Twin Cities, 1979–81, 1987–89." *Administrative Science Quarterly,* 42, 445–71.

Galaskiewicz, Joseph, and Ronald S. Burt (1991). "Interorganizational Contagion in Corporate Philanthropy." *Administrative Science Quarterly,* 36, 88–105.

Galaskiewicz, Joseph, and Karl R. Krohn (1984). "Positions, Roles, and Dependencies in a Community Interorganizational System." *Sociological Quarterly,* 25, 527–50.

Galaskiewicz, Joseph, and Peter J. Marsden (1978). "Interorganizational Resources Networks: Formal Patterns of Overlap." *Social Science Research,* 7, 89–107.

Galaskiewicz, Joseph, and Deborah Shatin (1981). "Leadership and Networking among Neighborhood Human Service Organizations." *Administrative Science Quarterly,* 26, 434–48.

Galaskiewicz, Joseph, and Stanley Wasserman (1989). "Mimetic Processes within an Interorganizational Field." *Administrative Science Quarterly,* 34, 454–79.

Galaskiewicz, Joseph, Stanley Wasserman, Barbara Rauschenbach, Wolfgang Bielefeld, and Patti Mullaney (1985). "The Influence of Corporate Power, Social Status, and Market Position on Corporate Interlocks in a Regional Network." *Social Forces,* 64, 403–31.

Galbraith, John Kenneth (1974). "The U.S. Economy Is Not a Free Market Economy." *Forbes,* 113, 99.

Galbrieth, Jay (1973). *Designing Complex Organizations.* Reading, MA: Addison-Wesley.

——— (1977). *Organization Design.* Reading, MA: Addison-Wesley.

Galtung, Johan (1965). "Institutionalized Conflict Resolution: A Theoretical Paradigm." *Journal of Peace Research,* 2, 348–96.

Gamoran, Adam, and Robert Dreeben (1986). "Coupling and Control in Educational Organizations." *Administrative Science Quarterly,* 31, 612–32.

Gamson, William, and Norman Scotch (1964). "Scapegoating in Baseball." *American Journal of Sociology,* 70, 69–72.

Gans, Sheldon P., and Gerald T. Horton (1975). *Integration of Human Services: The State and Municipal Levels.* New York: Praeger.

Gardner, Elmer A., and James N. Snipe (1970). "Toward the Coordination and Integration of Personal Health Services." *American Journal of Public Health,* 60, 2068–78.

Gargiulo, Martin (1993). "Two-step Leverage: Managing Constraints in Organizational Politics." *Administrative Science Quarterly,* 38, 1–19.

Geeraerts, Guy (1984). "The Effects of Ownership on the Organization Structure in Small Firms." *Administrative Science Quarterly,* 29, 232–37.

Georgiou, Petro (1973). "The Goal Paradigm and Notes Toward a Counter Paradigm." *Administrative Science Quarterly,* 18, 291–310.

Gersick, Connie J. G. (1991). "Revolutionary Change Theories: A Multilevel Explanation of the Punctuated Equilibrium Paradigm." *Academy of Management Review,* 16, 10–36.

——— (1994). "Pacing Strategic Change: The Case of a New Venture." *Academy of Management Journal,* 37, 9–45.

Giordano, Peggy C. (1974). "The Juvenile Justice System: The Client Perspective." Ph.D. diss., University of Minnesota.

——— (1976). "The Sense of Injustice: An Analysis of Juveniles' Reaction to the Justice System." *Criminology,* 14, 93–112.

——— (1977). "The Client's Perspective in Agency Evaluation." *Social Work,* 22, 34–39.

Glisson, Charles A. (1978). "Dependence of Technological Routinizations on Structural Variables in Human Service Organizations." *Administrative Science Quarterly,* 23, 383–95.

Goes, James B., and Seung Ho Park (1997). "Interorganizational Linkages and Innovation: The Case of Hospital Services." *Academy of Management Journal,* 40, 673–96.

Goldman, Paul (1980). "The Marxist Analysis of Organizations: Values, Theories, and Research." Unpublished manuscript, Department of Sociology, University of Oregon.

Goldman, Paul, and Donald R. Van Houten (1977). "Managerial Strategies and the Worker: A Marxist Analysis of Bureaucracy." *Sociological Quarterly,* 18, 108–25.

Gooding, Richard C., and John A. Wagner III (1985). "A Meta-Analytic Review of the Relationship between Size and Performance: The Productivity and Efficiency of Organizations and Their Subunits." *Administrative Science Quarterly,* 30, 462–81.

Goodman, Paul S., Terri L. Griffith, and Deborah B. Fenner (1990). "Understanding Technology and the Individual in an Organizational Context," in *Technology and Organizations,* ed. Paul S. Goodman, Lee Sproul, and Edwin Amenta, 45–86. San Francisco: Jossey-Bass.

Goodman, Paul, and Johannes Pennings (1977). *New Perspectives on Organizations' Effectiveness.* San Francisco: Jossey-Bass.

Goodrich, Elizabeth, and Gerald Salancik (1996). "Organizational Discretion in Responding to Institutional Practices: Hospitals and Cesarean Births." *Administrative Science Quarterly,* 41, 1–28.

Goodstein, Jerry D. (1994). "Institutional Pressures and Strategic Responsiveness: Employer Involvement in Work-Family Issues." *Academy of Management Journal,* 37, 350–82.

Goodstein, Jerry, and Warren Boeker (1991). "Turbulence at the Top: A New Perspective on Governance Structure Changes and Strategic Change. *Academy of Management Journal,* 34, 306–30.

Gouldner, Alvin, ed. (1950). *Studies in Leadership.* New York: Harper and Row.

———— (1954). *Patterns of Industrial Bureaucracy.* New York: Free Press

Grafton, Carl (1975). "The Creation of Federal Agencies." *Administration and Society,* 7, 328–65.

Granovetter, Mark (1973). "The Strength of Weak Ties." *American Journal of Sociology,* 78, 1360–80.

———— (1984). "Small Is Bountiful: Labor Markets and Establishment Size." *American Sociological Review,* 49, 323–34.

———— (1985). "Economic Action and Social Structure: The Problem of Embeddedness." *American Journal of Sociology,* 91, 481–510.

Grant, Don Sherman II (1995). "The Political Economy of Business Failures across the American States, 1970–1985; The Impact of Reagan's New Federalism." *American Sociological Review,* 60, 851–73.

Gresov, Christopher (1989). "Exploring Fit and Misfit with Multiple Contingencies." *Administrative Science Quarterly,* 34, 431–53.

Gronbjerg, Kristen A. (1992) "Nonprofit Human Service Organizations," in *Human Services as Complex Organizations,* ed. Yeheskel Hasenfeld. Thousand Oaks, CA: Sage.

Gross, Edward (1968). "Universities as Organizations: A Research Approach." *American Sociological Review,* 33, 518–43.

Grusky, Oscar (1963). "Managerial Succession and Organizational Effectiveness." *American Journal of Sociology,* 69, 21–31.

———— (1964). "Reply." *American Journal of Sociology,* 70, 72–76.

———— (1970). "The Effects of Succession: A Comparative Study of Military and Business Organization," in *The Sociology of Organizations,* ed. Oscar Grusky and George Miller. New York: Free Press.

Guest, Robert (1962). "Managerial Succession in Complex Organizations." *American Journal of Sociology,* 68, 47–54.

Guetzkow, Harold (1965). "Communications in Organizations," in *Handbook of Organizations,* ed. James G. March. Chicago: Rand McNally.

———— (1966). "Relations Among Organizations," in *Studies in Behavior in Organizations: A Research Symposium,* ed. R. V. Bowers. Athens: University of Georgia Press.

Gulati, Ranjay (1995). "Does Familiarity Breed Trust? The Implications of Repeated Ties for Contractual Choices in Alliances." *Academy of Management Journal,* 38, 85–112.

Gupta, Anil, and Vjay Govindarajan (1991). "Knowledge Flows and the Structure of Control within Multinational Corporations." *Academy of Management Review,* 16, 768–92.

Gupta, Parveen P., Mark W. Dirsmith, and Timothy J. Fogarty (1994). "Coordination and Control in a Government Agency: Contingency and Institutional Theory Perspectives on GAO Audits." *Administrative Science Quarterly,* 39, 264–84.

Gusfield, Joseph R. (1955). "Social Structure and Moral Reform: A Study of the Women's Christian Temperance Union." *American Journal of Sociology,* 61, 221–32.

———— (1963). *Symbolic Crusade.* Urbana: University of Illinois Press.

Haas, J. Eugene, Richard H. Hall, and Norman J. Johnson (1966). "Toward an Empirically Derived Taxonomy of Organizations," in *Studies on Behavior in Organizations,* ed. Raymond V. Bowers. Athens: University of Georgia Press.

Hage, Jerald (1965). "An Axiomatic Theory of Organizations." *Administrative Science Quarterly,* 10, 289–320.

———— (1967). "A Framework for the Comparative Analysis of Organizations." *American Sociological Review,* 32, 194–208.

———— (1974). *Communications and Organizational Control.* New York: John Wiley.

———— (1980). *Theories of Organizations.* New York: John Wiley.

Hage, Jerald, and Michael Aiken (1967a). "Relationship of Centralization to Other Structural Properties." *Administrative Science Quarterly,* 12, 72–91.

———— (1967b). "Program Change and Organizational Properties." *American Journal of Sociology,* 72, 503–19.

———— (1969). "Routine Technology, Social Structure, and Organizational Goals." *Administrative Science Quarterly,* 14, 366–77.

———— (1970). *Social Change in Complex Organizations.* New York: Random House.

Hage, Jerald, Michael Aiken, and Cora Bagley Marrett (1971). "Organizational Structure and Communications." *American Sociological Review,* 36, 860–71.

Hager, Jerald, Paul D. Collins, Frank Hull, and Jay Treadman (1993). "The Impact of Knowledge on the Survival of American Manufacturing Plants." *Social Forces,* 72, 223–46.

Hager, Jerald, and Robert Dewar (1973). "Elite Values versus Organizational Structure in Predicting Innovation." *Administrative Science Quarterly,* 18, 279–90.

Halberstam, David (1972). *The Best and the Brightest.* New York: Random House.

Hall, Richard H. (1962). "Intraorganizational Structural Variation: Application of the Bureaucratic Model." *Administrative Science Quarterly,* 7, 295–308.

———— (1963). "The Concept of Bureaucracy." *American Journal of Sociology,* 69, 32–40.

———— (1968). "Professionalization and Bureaucratization." *American Sociological Review,* 33, 92–104.

———— (1975). *Occupations and the Social Structure,* 2nd ed. Englewood Cliffs, NJ: Prentice Hall.

———— (1981). "Technological Policies and Their Consequences," in *Handbook of Organizational Design,* Vol. 2, ed. Paul C. Nystrom and William H. Starbuck, 320–35. New York: Oxford University Press.

———— (1987). *Organizations: Structures, Processes, and Outcomes,* 4th ed. Englewood Cliffs, NJ: Prentice Hall.

———— (1992). "Taking Things a Bit Too Far: Some Problems with Emergent Institutional Theory," in *Issues, Theory, and Research in Industrial/Organizational Psychology.* ed. Kathryn Kelley. New York: Elsevier Science Publishers.

———— (1994). *Sociology of Work: Perspectives, Analyses, and Issues.* Thousand Oaks, CA: Pine Forge Press.

Hall, Richard H., John P. Clark, and Peggy C. Giordano (1978). "Interorganizational Coordination in the Delivery of Human Services," in *Organization and Environment: Theory, Issues, and Reality,* ed. Lucien Karpik. Beverly Hills, CA: Sage.

———— (1979). *The Extent and Correlates of Interorganizational Conflict.* Albany: State University of New York Press.

Hall, Richard H., John P. Clark, Peggy Giordano, Paul Johnson, and Martha Van Roekel (1977). "Patterns of Interorganizational Relationships." *Administrative Science Quarterly,* 22, 457–74.

Hall, Richard H., J. Eugene Haas, and Norman Johnson (1967a). "An Examination of Blau-Scott and Etzioni Typologies." *Administrative Science Quarterly,* 12, 118–39.

———— (1967b). "Organizational Size, Complexity, and Formalization." *American Sociological Review,* 32, 903–12.

Hall, Richard H., Shanhe Jiang, Karyn A. Loscocco, and John K. Allen (1993). "Ownership Patterns and Centralization: A China and U.S. Comparison." *Sociological Forum,* 8, 595–608.

Hall, Richard H., and Charles R. Tittle (1966). "Bureaucracy and Its Correlates." *American Journal of Sociology,* 72, 267–72.

Hall, Richard H., and Weiman Xu (1990). "Run Silent, Run Deep: A Note on the Ever Pervasive Influence of Cultural Differences on Organizations in the Far East." *Organization Studies,* 11, 569–76.

Halpert, Burton P. (1974). "An Empirical Study of the Relationship Between Power, Conflict, and Cooperation on the Interorganizational Level." Doctoral dissertation, Department of Sociology, University of Minnesota.

——— (1982). "Antecedents," in *Interorganizational Coordination: Theory, Research, and Implementation,* ed. David L. Rogers and David A. Whetten and Associates. Ames: Iowa State University Press.

Hambrick, Donald C. (1981). "Environment, Strategy and Power within Top Management Teams." *Administrative Science Quarterly,* 26, 253–76.

Hambrick, Donald C., and Richard A. D'Aveni (1988). "Large Corporate Failures as Downward Spirals." *Administrative Science Quarterly,* 33, 1–23.

Hamilton, Gary L., and Nicole Woolsey Biggart (1988). "Market, Culture, and Authority: A Comparative Analysis of Management and Organization in the Far East." *American Journal of Sociology,* 94, Supplement, S52–S94.

Han, Shin-Kap (1994). "Mimetic Isomorphism and its Effect on the Audit Service Market." *Social Forces,* 73, 637–63.

Hannan, Michael T., and Glenn R. Carroll (1992). *Dynamics of Organizational Population.* New York: Oxford University Press.

——— (1995). "Talk about Legitimation: Reply to Baum and Carroll." *American Sociological Review,* 60, 539–44.

Hannan, Michael T., Glenn R. Carroll, Elizabeth Dundon, and John Charles Torres (1995). "Organizational Evolution in a Multinational Context: Entries of Automobile Manufacturers in Belgium, Britain, France, Germany, and Italy." *American Sociological Review,* 60, 509–28.

Hannan, Michael T., and John H. Freeman (1977a). "Obstacles to Comparative Studies," in *New Perspective on Organizational Effectiveness,* ed. Paul S. Goodman and Johannes Pennings. San Francisco: Jossey-Bass.

——— (1997b). "The Population Ecology of Organizations." *American Journal of Sociology,* 82, 929–64.

——— (1984). "Structural Inertia and Organizational Change." *American Sociological Review,* 49, 149–64.

——— (1987). "The Ecology of Organizational Founding: American Labor Unions, 1836–1985." *American Journal of Sociology,* 92, 910–43.

——— (1988). "The Ecology of Organizational Mortality: American Labor Unions, 1836–1985." *American Journal of Sociology,* 94, 25–52.

——— (1989). *Organizational Ecology.* Cambridge: Harvard University Press.

Hardy, Cynthia, and Stewart R. Clegg (1966). "Some Dare Call It Power," in *Handbook of Organization Studies,* ed. Stewart R. Clegg, Cynthia Hardy, and Walter R. Nord. Thousand Oaks, CA: Sage.

Harris, Stanley G., and Robert I. Sutton (1986). "Functions of Parting Ceremonies in Dying Organizations." *Academy of Management Journal,* 29, 5–30.

Harrison, J. Richard, and Glenn R. Carroll (1991). "Keeping the Faith: A Model of Cultural Transmission in Formal Organizations." *Administrative Science Quarterly,* 36, 552–82.

Hasenfeld, Yeheskel (1972). "People Processing Organizations: An Exchange Approach." *American Sociological Review,* 37, 256–63.

Haunschild, Pamela R. (1993). "Interorganizational Imitation: The Impact of Corporate Acquisition Activity." *Administrative Science Quarterly,* 38, 564–92.

Haunschild, Pamela R., and Anne S. Miner (1997). "Modes of IOR Imitation: The Effect of Outcome Salience and Uncertainty." *Administrative Science Quarterly,* 42, 477–500.

Haveman, Heather (1992). "Between a Rock and a Hard Place: Organizational Change under Conditions of Fundamental Environmental Transformation." *Administrative Science Quarterly,* 37, 48–75.

——— (1993). "Organizational Size and Change: Diversification in the Savings and Loan Industry after Deregulation." *Administrative Science Quarterly,* 38, 20–50.

Haveman, Heather A., and Hayagreeva Rao (1997) "Structuring a Theory of Moral Sentiments: Institutional and Organizational Coevolution in the Early Thrift Industry." *American Journal of Sociology,* 102, 1606–51.

Hawley, Amos H. (1968). "Human Ecology," in *International Encyclopedia of the Social Sciences*, ed. D. L. Sills. New York: Macmillan.

Hawley, W. E., and L. D. Rogers (1974). *Improving the Quality of Urban Management.* Beverly Hills, CA: Sage.

Hedberg, Bo (1981). "How Organizations Learn and Unlearn," in *Handbook of Organizational Design*, Vol. 2, ed. Paul C. Nystrom and William H. Starbuck. New York: Oxford University Press.

Heide, Jan B., and Anne S. Miner (1992). "The Shadow of the Future: Effects of Anticipated Interaction and Frequency of Contact on Buyer-Seller Cooperation." *Academy of Management Journal*, 35, 265–91.

Heilbroner, Robert (1974). "Nobody Talks about Busting General Motors in 500 Companies." *Forbes*, 113, 61.

Heise, David R. (1972). "How Do I Know My Data? Let Me Count the Ways." *Administrative Science Quarterly*, 17, 58–61.

Heller, Frank A. (1973). "Leadership Decision Making and Contingency Theory." *Industrial Relations*, 12, 183–99.

Heller, Frank, Pieter Drenth, Paul Coopman, and Veljko Rus (1988). *Decisions in Organizations: A Three Country Comparison.* Newbury Park, CA: Sage.

Helmich, Donald, and Warren B. Brown (1972). "Succession Type and Organizational Change in the Corporate Enterprise." *Administrative Science Quarterly*, 17, 371–81.

Heydebrand, Wolf V. (1973). *Comparative Organizations: The Results of Empirical Research.* Englewood Cliffs, NJ: Prentice Hall.

———— (1977). "Organizational Contradictions in Public Bureaucracies: Toward a Marxian Theory of Organizations." *Sociological Quarterly*, 18, 83–107.

———— (1990). "The Technocratic Organization of Academic Work," in *Structures of Power and Constraint: Papers in Honor of Peter M. Blau*, ed. Craig Calhoun, Marshall W. Meyer, and W. Richard Scott, 271–320. New York: Cambridge University Press.

Hickson, David J. (1987). "Decision Making at the Top of Organization." *Annual Review of Sociology*, 13, 165–93. Palo Alto, CA: Annual Reviews, Inc.

Hickson, David J., J. Butler, D. Cray, G. R. Mallory, and D. C. Wilson (1986). *Top Decisions: Strategic Decision Making in Organizations.* San Francisco: Jossey-Bass.

Hickson, David J., C. R. Hinings, C. A. Lee, R. E. Schneck, and J. M. Pennings (1971). "A 'Strategic Contingencies' Theory of Interorganizational Power." *Administrative Science Quarterly*, 16, 216–29.

Hickson, David J., C. R. Hinings, C. J. McMillan, and J. P. Schwitter (1974). "The Culture Free Context of Organizational Structure: A Tri-National Comparison." *Sociology*, 8, 59–80.

Hickson, David J., Derek S. Pugh, and Diana C. Pheysey (1969). "Operational Technology and Organizational Structure: An Empirical Reappraisal." *Administrative Science Quarterly*, 14, 378–97.

Hild, John, Hans-Dieter Ganter, and Alfred Kieser (1987). "Technological Innovation and Organizational Conservatism," in *New Technology in Organizational Innovation: The Development and Diffusion of Microelectronics*, ed. Johannes M. Pennings and Arend Buitendam, 87–115. Cambridge, MA: Ballinger.

Hills, Frederick S., and Thomas A. Mahoney (1978). "University Budgets and Organizational Decision Making." *Administrative Science Quarterly*, 23, 454–65.

Hilton, Gordon (1972). "Causal Inference Analysis: A Seductive Process." *Administrative Science Quarterly*, 17, 44–54.

Hinings, C. R. (1988). "Defending Organizational Theory: A British View from North America." *Organization Studies*, 9, 2–7.

Hirsch, Paul M. (1975). "Organizational Effectiveness and the Institutional Environment." *Administrative Science Quarterly*, 20, 327–44.

———— (1997) "Sociology without Social Structure: Neo-Institutional Theory Meets Brave New World." *American Journal of Sociology*, 102, 1702–23.

Hirschhorn, Larry (1985). "On Technological Catastrophe." *Science*, 28, 846–47.

Hirschman, Albert O. (1972). *Exit, Voice, and Loyalty.* Cambridge: Harvard University Press.

Hochschild, Arlie Russell (1983). *The Managed Heart: Commercialization of Human Feeling.* Berkeley and Los Angeles: University of California Press.

Hoff, Timothy (1998). "Same Profession, Different People: Stratification, Structure, and Physicians' Employment Choices." *Sociological Forum,* 13, 133–156.

Hoff, Timothy, and David McCaffrey (1996). "Resisting, Adapting, and Negotiating: How Physicians Cope with Organizational and Economic Change." *Work and Occupations,* 23, 165–89.

Hofstede, Geert H. (1972). *Budget Control and the Autonomy of Organizational Units.* Proceedings of the First International Sociological Conference on Participation and Self-Management, Zagreb, Yugoslavia.

——— (1993). "Intercultural Conflict and Synergy in Europe," in *Management in Western Europe,* ed. David J. Hickson, 1–8. Berlin: Walter de Gruyter and Co.

Holden, Constance (1980). "Innovation—Japan Races Ahead as U.S. Falters." *Science,* 210, 751–54.

Hollander, Edwin P., and James W. Julian (1969). "Contemporary Trends in the Analysis of Leadership Processes." *Psychological Bulletin,* 71, 387–97.

Hougland, James G., Jon M. Shepard, and James R. Wood (1979). "Discrepancies in Perceived Organizational Control: Their Decrease and Importance in Local Churches." *Sociological Quarterly,* 20, 63–76.

Hougland, James G., and James R. Wood (1980). "Control in Organizations and Commitment of Members." *Social Forces,* 59, 85–105.

Hrebeniak, Lawrence G., and William F. Joyce (1985). "Organizational Adaptation: Strategic Choice and Environmental Determinism." *Administrative Science Quarterly,* 30, 336–49.

Hsu, Cheng-Kuang, Robert M. March, and Hiroshi Mannari (1983). "An Examination of the Determinants of Organizational Structure." *American Journal of Sociology,* 88, 975–96.

Hunt, James G. (1991). *Leadership: A New Synthesis.* Newbury Park, CA: Sage.

Hyde, Cheryl (1992). "The Ideational System of Social Movement Agencies: An Examination of Feminist Health Centers," in *Human Services as Complex Organizations,* ed. Yeheskel Hasenfeld. Thousand Oaks, CA: Sage.

Inkson, J., Derek S. Pugh, and David J. Hickson (1970). "Organizational Context and Structure: An Abbreviated Replication." *Administrative Science Quarterly,* 15, 318–29.

Isabella, Lynn A. (1990). "Evolving Interpretations as a Change Unfolds: How Managers Construe Key Organizational Events." *Academy of Management Review,* 33, 7–41.

Jackall, Robert (1988). *Moral Mazes: The World of Corporate Managers.* New York: Oxford University Press.

Jackson, Susan E., and Jane E. Dutton (1988). "Discerning Threats and Opportunities." *Administrative Science Quarterly,* 33, 370–87.

Jacobs, David (1974). "Dependency and Vulnerability: An Exchange Approach to the Control of Organizations." *Administrative Science Quarterly,* 19, 45–59.

——— (1987). "Business Resources and Taxation: A Cross-Sectional Examination of the Relationship between Economic Organization and Public Policy." *Sociological Quarterly,* 28, 437–54.

——— (1988). "Corporate Economic Power and the State: A Longitudinal Assessment of Two Explanations." *American Journal of Sociology,* 93, 852–81.

James, David R., and Michael Soref (1981). "Profit Constraints on Managerial Autonomy: Managerial Theory and the Unmaking of the Corporate President." *American Sociological Review,* 46, 1–18.

Jenkins, J. Craig (1977). "Radical Transformation of Organizational Goals." *Administrative Science Quarterly,* 22, 568–86.

Jermier, John M., and Leslie J. Berkes (1979). "Leader Behavior in a Police Command Bureaucracy: A Closer Look at the Quasi-Military Model." *Administrative Science Quarterly,* 24, 1–23.

John, D. (1977). *Managing the Human Service System: What Have We Learned from Services Integration?* Project SHARE Monograph Series. Rockville, MD: National Institute of Mental Health.

Johnston, George P. III, and William Snizek (1991). "Combining Head and Heart in Complex Organizations: A Test of Etzioni's Dual Compliance Structure Hypothesis." *Human Relations,* 44, 1255–72.

Judge, William Q., Jr., and Carl P. Zeithaml (1992). "Institutional and Strategic Choice Perspectives on Board Involvement in the Strategic Decision Process." *Academy of Management Journal,* 35, 766–94.

Julian, Joseph (1966). "Compliance Patterns and Communication Blocks in Complex Organizations." *American Sociological Review,* 31, 382–89.

Jurkovich, Ray (1974). "A Core Typology of Organizational Environments." *Administrative Science Quarterly,* 19, 380–89.

Kabanoff, Boris (1991). "Equity, Equality, Power, and Conflict." *Academy of Management Review,* 16, 416–41.

Kahn, Robert (1977). "Organizational Effectiveness: An Overview," in *New Perspectives on Organizational Effectiveness,* ed. Paul S. Goodman and Johannes M. Pennings. San Francisco: Jossey-Bass.

Kahn, Robert, Donald M. Wolfe, Robert P. Quinn, J. Diedrick Snoek, and Robert A. Rosenthal (1964). *Organizational Stress: Studies in Role Conflict and Ambiguity.* New York: John Wiley.

Kalleberg, Arne (1983). "Work and Stratification: Structural Perspectives." *Work and Occupations,* 10, 251–59.

Kalleberg, Arne, and Ivar Berg (1987). *Work and Industry: Structures, Markets, and Processes.* New York: Plenum.

Kalleberg, Arne L., and Mark E. Van Buren (1996). "Is Bigger Better? Explaining the Relationship Between Organizational Size and Job Rewards." *American Sociological Review,* 61, 47–76.

Kalleberg, Arne L., David Knoke, Peter V. Marsden, and Joe L. Spaeth (1996). "Organizational Properties and Practices," in *Organizations in America: Analyzing Their Structures and Human Resource Practices,* ed. Arne L. Kalleberg, David Knoke, Peter V. Marsden, and Joe L. Spaeth. Thousand Oaks, CA: Sage.

Kanter, Rosabeth Moss (1977). *Men and Women of the Corporation.* New York: Basic Books.

Kanter, Rosabeth, and Derick Brinkerhoff (1981). "Organizational Performance: Recent Developments in Measurement." *Annual Review of Sociology,* 7, 321–49.

Kanter, Rosabeth, Barry A. Stein, and Todd D. Jick (1992). *The Challenge of Organizational Change: How Companies Experience It and Leaders Guide It.* New York: Free Press.

Kaplan, Abraham (1964). "Power in Perspective," in *Power and Conflict in Organizations,* ed. Robert L. Kahn and Elise Boulding. New York: Basic Books.

Kasarda, John D., and Charles E. Bidwell (1984). "A Human Ecological Theory of Organizational Structuring," in *Sociological Human Ecology: Contemporary Issues and Applications,* ed. Michael Micklin and Harvey M. Choldin. Boulder, CO: Westview Press.

Katz, Daniel (1964). "Approaches to Managing Conflict," in *Power and Conflict in Organizations,* ed. Robert L. Kahn and Elise Boulding. New York: Basic Books.

Katz, Daniel, Barbara A. Gutek, Robert L. Kahn, and Eugenia Barton (1975). *Bureaucratic Encounters.* Ann Arbor, MI: Institute for Social Research.

Katz, Daniel, and Robert L. Kahn (1966). *The Social Psychology of Organizations,* rev. ed. New York: John Wiley.

——— (1978). *The Sociology Psychology of Organizations,* rev. ed. New York: John Wiley.

Katz, Ralph (1982). "The Effects of Group Longevity on Project Communication and Performance." *Administrative Science Quarterly,* 27, 81–104.

Kaufman, Herbert (1971). *The Limits of Organizational Change.* University, AL: University of Alabama Press.

Keegan, Warren J. (1974). "Multinational Scanning: A Study of the Information Sources Utilized by Headquarters Executives in Multinational Companies." *Administrative Science Quarterly,* 19, 411–21.

Keeley, Michael (1978). "A Social Justice Approach to Organizational Evaluation." *Administrative Science Quarterly,* 23, 272–92.

——— (1984). "Impartiality and Participant-interest Theories of Organizational Effectiveness." *Administrative Science Quarterly,* 29, 1–12.

Kelly, Dawn, and Terry L. Amburgey (1991). "Organizational Inertia and Momentum: A Dynamic Model of Strategic Choice." *Academy of Management Journal,* 34, 591–612.

Kerbo, Harold R., and L. Richard Della Fave (1983). "Corporate Linkage and Control of the Corporate Economy: New Evidence and a Reinterpretation." *Sociological Quarterly*, 24, 201–18.

Khandwalla, Pradip N. (1972). "Environment and Its Impact on the Organization." *International Studies of Management and Organization*, 2, 297–313.

Kieser, Alfred (1989). "Organizational, Institutional, and Societal Evolution: Medieval Craft Guilds and the Genesis of Formal Organizations." *Administrative Science Quarterly*, 34, 540–65.

Kimberly, John R. (1975). "Environmental Constraints and Organizational Structure: A Comparative Analysis of Rehabilitation Organizations." *Administrative Science Quarterly*, 20, 1–19.

——— (1976). "Organizational Size and the Structuralist Perspective: A Review, Critique, and Proposal." *Administrative Science Quarterly*, 21, 577–97.

——— (1979). "Issues in the Creation of Organizations: Initiation, Innovation, and Institutionalization." *Academy of Management Journal*, 22, 437–57.

——— (1980). "Initiation, Innovation, and Institutionalization in the Creation Process," in *The Organizational Life Cycle*, ed. John R. Kimberly and Robert H. Miles and Associates. San Francisco: Jossey-Bass.

——— (1981). "Managerial Innovation," in *Handbook of Organizational Design*, Vol. 1, ed. Paul C. Nystrom and William H. Starbuck. New York: Oxford University Press.

Kimberly, John R., and Robert A. Miles and Associates, eds. (1980). *The Organizational Life Cycle*. San Francisco: Jossey-Bass.

Kimberly, John R., and Robert E. Quinn (1984). "The Challenge of Transition Management," in *Managing Organizational Transitions*, ed. John R. Kimberly and Robert E. Quinn. Homewood, IL: Richard D. Irwin.

Klatzky, Sheila (1970a). "The Relationship of Organizational Size to Complexity and Coordination." *Administrative Science Quarterly*, 15, 428–38.

——— (1970b). "Organizational Inequality: The Case of Public Employment Agency." *American Journal of Sociology*, 76, no. 3 (November), 474–91.

Klauss, Rudi, and Bernard M. Bass (1982). *Interpersonal Communication in Organizations*. New York: Academic Press.

Klonglan, Gerald E., and Steven K. Paulson (1971). *Coordinating Health Organizations: The Problem of Cigarette Smoking*. Final report submitted to the National Clearinghouse for Smoking and Health, United States Public Health Service.

Klonglan, Gerald E., Richard D. Warren, Judy M. Winkelpleck, and Steven K. Paulson (1976). "Interorganizational Measurement in the Social Services Sector: Differences by Hierarchical Level." *Administrative Science Quarterly*, 21, 675–87.

Knapp, Tim (1989). "Hierarchies and Control: A New Interpretation and Reevaluation of Oliver Williamson's Markets and Hierarchies Story." *Sociological Quarterly*, 30, 425–40.

Knoke, David, and David Prensky (1984). "What Relevance Do Organizational Theories Have for Voluntary Organizations?" *Social Science Quarterly*, 65, no. 1 (March), 3–20.

Kochan, Thomas A., Larry C. Cummings, and George P. Huber (1976). "Operationalizing the Concepts of Goals and Goal Incompatibility in Organizational Behavior Research." *Human Relations*, 29, 527–44.

Kochan, Thomas A., George P. Huber, and Larry C. Cummings (1975). "Determinants of Interorganizational Conflict in Collective Bargaining in the Public Sector." *Administrative Science Quarterly*, 20, 10–23.

Kochan, Thomas A., and Michael Useem (1992). *Transforming Organization*. New York: Oxford University Press.

Kohn, Melvin (1971). "Bureaucratic Man: A Portrait and Interpretation." *American Sociological Review*, 36, 461–74.

Kohn, Melvin, and Carmi Schooler (1973). "Occupational Experience and Psychological Functioning: An Assessment of Reciprocal Effects." *American Sociological Review*, 38, 97–118.

——— (1978). "The Reciprocal Effects of Substantive Complexity of Work and Intellectual Flexibility: A Longitudinal Assessment." *American Journal of Sociology*, 84, 1–23.

——— (1982). "Job Conditions and Personality: A Longitudinal Assessment of the Reciprocal Effects." *American Journal of Sociology*, 87, 1257–86.

Kornhauser, William (1963). *Scientists in Industry.* Berkeley and Los Angeles: University of California Press.

Kraatz, Matthew S. and Edward J. Zajac (1996). "Exploring the Limits of the New Institutionalism: The Causes and Consequences of Illegitimate Organizational Change." *American Sociological Review,* 61, 812–36.

Kralewski, John E., Laura Pitt, and Deborah Shatin (1985). "Structural Characteristics of Medical Practice Groups." *Administrative Science Quarterly,* 30, 34–45.

Lachman, Ron (1989). "Power from What? A Reexamination of Its Relationship with Structural Conditions." *Administrative Science Quarterly,* 34, 231–51.

Lammers, Cornelius J. (1967). "Power and Participation in Decision Making." *American Journal of Sociology,* 73, 201–16.

——— (1975). "Self-Management and Participation: Two Concepts of Democratization in Organizations." *Organization and Administrative Sciences,* 5, 35–53.

——— (1981). "Contributions of Organizational Sociology: Part II: Contributions to Organizational Theory and Practice—A Liberal View." *Organization Studies,* 2, 361–76.

Lang, James R., and Daniel E. Lockhart (1990). "Increased Environmental Uncertainty and Changes in Board Linkage Patterns." *Academy of Management Journal,* 33, 106–28.

Langston, John (1984). "The Ecological Theory of Bureaucracy: The Case of Josiah Wedgwood and the British Pottery Industry." *Administrative Science Quarterly,* 29, 330–54.

Laumann, Edward O., Joseph Galaskiewicz, and Peter Marsden (1978). "Community Structure as Interorganizational Linkage." *Annual Review of Sociology,* 4, 455–84.

Laumann, Edward O., and David Knoke (1987). *The Organizational State: Social Choice in National Policy Domains.* Madison: University of Wisconsin Press.

Laumann, Edward O., David Knoke, and Yong-Hak Kim (1985). "An Organizational Approach to State Policy Formation: A Comparative Study of Energy and Health Domains." *American Sociological Review,* 50, 1–19.

Lawler, Edward E., and Layman W. Porter (1967). "The Effect of Performance on Job Satisfaction." *Industrial Relations,* 7, 20–28.

Lawrence, Paul R., and Jay W. Lorsch (1967). *Organization and Environment.* Cambridge: Harvard University Press.

Lazarsfeld, Paul S., and Herbert Menzel (1961). "On the Relationship between Individual and Collective Properties," in *Complex Organizations: A Sociological Reader,* ed. Amitai Etzioni. New York: Holt, Rinehart & Winston, Inc.

Lazerson, Mark H. (1988). "Organizational Growth of Small Firms: An Outcome of Markets and Hierarchies?" *American Sociological Review,* 53, 330–42.

——— (1995). "A New Phoenix? Modern Putting-Out in the Modern Knitwear Industry." *Administrative Science Quarterly,* 34, 40–59.

Leavitt, Harold J. (1951). "The Effects of Certain Communications Patterns on Group Performance." *Journal of Abnormal and Social Psychology,* 46, 38–50.

Leblebici, Huseyin, and Gerald Salancik (1982). "Stability in Interorganizational Exchanges: Rulemaking Processes of the Chicago Board of Trade." *Administrative Science Quarterly,* 27, 227–42.

Lehman, Edward W. (1988). "The Theory of the State versus the State of Theory." *American Sociological Review,* 53, 807–23.

Leicht, Kevin T., Toby L. Parcel, and Robert L. Kaufman (1992). "Measuring the Same Concept across Diverse Organizations." *Social Science Research,* 21, 149–74.

Leifer, Richard, and George P. Huber (1977). "Relations among Perceived Environmental Uncertainty, Organizational Structure, and Boundary Spanning Behavior." *Administrative Science Quarterly,* 22, 235–47.

Leventhal, Daniel A. (1991). "Random Walks and Organizational Mortality." *Administrative Science Quarterly,* 36, 397–420.

Levine, Adeline Gordon (1982). *Love Canal: Science, Politics, and People.* Lexington, MA: D. C. Heath.

Levine, Sol, and Benjamin D. Paul (1963). "Community Interorganizational Problems in Providing Medical Care and Social Services." *American Journal of Public Health,* 53, 1183–95.

Levine, Sol, and Paul E. White (1961). "Exchange as a Conceptual Framework for the Study of Interorganizational Relationships." *Administrative Science Quarterly,* 5, 583–610.

Levinthal, Daniel A., and Mark Fichman (1988). "Dynamics of Interorganizational Attachments: Auditor-Client Relationships." *Administrative Science Quarterly,* 33, 345–69.

Levitt, Barbara, and Clifford Nuss (1989). "The Lid on the Garbage Can: Institutional Constraints on Decision Making in the Technical Core of College-Text Publishers." *Administrative Science Quarterly,* 34, 190–207.

Lieberson, Stanley, and James F. O'Connor (1972). "Leadership and Organizational Performance: A Study of Large Corporations." *American Sociological Review,* 37, 117–30.

Liedholm, Carl, and Donald Mead (1993). "The Structure and Growth of Microenterprises in Southern and Eastern Africa: Evidence from Recent Surveys." Unpublished manuscript, Department of Economics, Michigan State University.

Lincoln, James R., Mitsuyo Hanada, and Kerry McBride (1986). "Organizational Structures in Japanese and U.S. Manufacturing." *Administrative Science Quarterly,* 31, 338–64.

Lincoln, James R., Jon Olson, and Mitsuyo Hanada (1978). "Cultural Effects on Organizational Structure: The Case of Japanese Firms in the United States." *American Sociological Review,* 43, 829–47.

Lincoln, James R., and Gerald Zeitz (1980). "Organizational Properties from Aggregate Data." *American Sociological Review,* 45, 391–405.

Lindberg, Leon N., John L. Campbell, and J. Rogers Hollingsworth (1991). "Economic Governance and the Analysis of Structural Change in the American Economy," in Governance of the American Economy, ed. John L. Campbell, J. Rogers Hollingsworth, and Leon N. Lindberg, 3–34. New York: Cambridge University Press.

Lipset, Seymour Martin (1960). *Agrarian Socialism.* Berkeley and Los Angeles: University of California Press.

Lipset, Seymour Martin, Martin A. Trow, and James S. Coleman (1956). *Union Democracy.* New York: Free Press.

Litwak, Eugene (1961). "Models of Organizations Which Permit Conflict." *American Journal of Sociology,* 76, 177–84.

Litwak, Eugene, and Lydia Hylton (1962). "Interorganizational Analysis: A Hypothesis on Coordinating Agencies." *Administrative Science Quarterly,* 6, 395–420.

Long, J. Scott, and Robert McGinnis (1981). "Organizational Context and Scientific Productivity." *American Sociological Review,* 46, 422–42.

Lorsch, Jay W., and John J. Morse (1974). *Organizations and Their Members: A Contingency Approach.* New York: Harper and Row.

Lozano, Beverly (1989). *The Invisible Work Force: Transforming American Business with Outside and Home-Based Workers.* New York: Free Press.

Maas, Meridean Leone (1979). "A Formal Theory of Organizational Power." Doctoral dissertation, Department of Sociology, Iowa State University.

Mahoney, Thomas A., Peter Frost, Norman F. Crandall, and William Weitzel (1972). "The Conditioning Influence of Organizational Size on Managerial Practice." *Organizational Behavior and Human Performance,* 8, 230–41.

Mahoney, Thomas A., and William Weitzel (1969). "Managerial Models of Organizational Effectiveness." *Administrative Science Quarterly,* 14, 357–65.

Malan, Leon (1994). "Organizational Responses to Turbulent Environments." Ph.D. diss. State University of New York at Albany.

Manning, Peter K. (1992). *Organizational Communication.* New York: Aldine de Gruyter.

Manns, Curtis L., and James G. March (1978). "Financial Adversity, Internal Competition, and Curricular Change in a University." *Administrative Science Quarterly,* 23, 541–52.

Mansfield, Roger (1973). "Bureaucracy and Centralization: An Examination of Organizational Structure." *Administrative Science Quarterly,* 18, 77–88.

March, James G. (1981). "Footnotes to Organizational Change." *Administrative Science Quarterly,* 26, 563–77.

March, James G., and Herbert A. Simon (1958). *Organizations.* New York: John Wiley.

March, James G., and Lee S. Sproul (1990). "Technology, Management, and Cooptative Advantage," in *Technology and Organizations,* ed. Paul S. Goodman, Lee Sproul, and Edwin Amenta, 144–73. San Francisco: Jossey-Bass.

Marcus, Alfred A., and Robert S. Goodman (1991). "Victims and Shareholders: The Dilemmas of Presenting Corporate Policy during a Crisis." *Academy of Management Journal,* 34, 281–305.

Marglin, Stephen A. (1974). "What Do Bosses Do? The Origins and Functions of Hierarchy in Capitalist Production." *Review of Radical Political Economics,* 6, 60–112.

Mariolis, Peter, and Maria H. Jones (1982). "Centrality in Corporate Interlock Networks: Reliability and Stability." *Administrative Science Quarterly,* 27, 571–84.

Marple, David (1982). "Technological Innovation and Organizational Survival: A Population Ecology Study of Nineteenth Century American Railroads." *Sociological Quarterly,* 23, 107–16.

Marrett, Cora Bagley (1971). "On the Specification of Interorganizational Dimensions." *Sociology and Social Research,* 56, 83–99.

——— (1980). "Influences on the Rise of New Organizations: The Formation of Women's Medical Societies." *Administrative Science Quarterly,* 25, 185–99.

Marsden, Peter V. Cynthia R. Cook, and David Knoke (1996). "American Organizations and Their Environments: A Descriptive Overview," in Organizations in America: Analyzing Their Structures and Human Resource Practices, ed. Arne L. Kalleberg, David Knoke, Peter Marsden, and Joe L. Spaeth. Thousand Oaks, CA: Sage.

Marsh, Robert M., and Hiroshi Mannari (1980). "Technological Implications Theory: A Japanese Test." *Organization Studies,* 1, 161–83.

——— (1981). "Technology and Size as Determinants of the Organizational Structure of Japanese Factories." *Administrative Science Quarterly,* 26, 32–57.

Masuch, Michael, and Perry LaPotin (1989). "Beyond Garbage Cans: An AI Model of Organizational Choice." *Administrative Science Quarterly,* 34, 38–67.

Maurice, Marc, Francoise Sellier, and Jean-Jacques Silvestre (1980). "The Search of a Societal Effect in the Production of Company Hierarchy: A Comparison between France and Germany." Paper translated from Revue Françoise de Sociologie (June 1979).

Maurice, Marc, Arndt Sorge, and Malcolm Warner (1980). "Societal Differences in Organizing Manufacturing Units: A Comparison of France, West Germany and Great Britain." *Organization Studies,* 1, 59–86.

McCaffrey, David P. (1982). *OSHA and the Politics of Health Regulation.* New York: Plenum.

McGuire, Jean B., Alison Sundgren, and Thomas Schneeweis (1988). "Corporate Social Responsibility and Firm Financial Performance." *Academy of Management Journal,* 31, 854–72.

McKelvey, Bill (1975). "Guidelines for the Empirical Classification of Organizations." *Administrative Science Quarterly,* 20, 509–25.

——— (1978). "Organizational Systematics: Taxonomic Lessons from Biology." *Management Science,* 24, 1428–40.

——— (1982). *Organizational Systematics: Taxonomy, Evolution, Classification.* Berkeley and Los Angeles: University of California Press.

McKelvey, Bill, and Howard Aldrich (1983). "Populations, Natural Selection, and Applied Organizational Science." *Administrative Science Quarterly,* 28, 101–28.

McKinley, William (1987). "Complexity and Administrative Intensity: The Case of Declining Organizations." *Administrative Science Quarterly,* 32, 81–105.

McMillan, Charles J. (1973). "Corporations without Citizenship: The Emergence of Multinational Enterprise," in *People and Organizations,* ed. Graeme Soloman and Kenneth Thompsons. London: Longman Group Limited.

McMillan, Charles J., David J. Hickson, C. R. Hinings, and R. E. Schneck (1973). "The Structure of Work Organizations across Societies." *Academy of Management Journal,* 16, 555–69.

McNeil, Kenneth (1978). "Understanding Organizational Power: Building on the Weberian Legacy." *Administrative Science Quarterly,* 23, 65–90.

McNeil, Kenneth, and Edmond Minihan (1977). "Regulation of Medical Devices and Organizational Behavior in Hospitals." *Administrative Science Quarterly,* 22, 475–90.

Mechanic, David (1962). "Sources of Power of Lower Participants in Complex Organizations." *Administrative Science Quarterly,* 7, 349–64.

Meindl, James R., Sanford B. Ehrlich, and Janet M. Dukerich (1985). "The Romance of Leadership." *Administrative Science Quarterly,* 30, 78–102.

Mentzer, Marc S., and Janet P. Near (1992). "Administrative Cuts amidst Decline in American Railroads." *Organization Studies,* 13, 353–73.

Merton, Robert K. (1957). *Social Theory and Social Structure.* Glencoe, IL: Free Press.

Metcalf, J. L. (1976). "Organizational Strategies and Interorganizational Networks." *Human Relations,* 29, 327–43.

Meyer, Alan D. (1982). "Adapting to Environmental Jolts." *Administrative Science Quarterly,* 27, 515–37.

Meyer, Alan D., Anne S. Tsui, and C. R. Hinings (1993). "Configurational Approaches to Organizational Analysis." *Academy of Management Journal,* 36, 1175–95.

Meyer, John W., and Brian Rowan (1977). "Institutionalized Organizations: Formal Structure as Myth and Ceremony." *American Journal of Sociology,* 83, 340–63.

Meyer, John W., and W. Richard Scott (1983). *Organizational Environments: Ritual and Rationality.* Beverly Hills, CA: Sage.

Meyer, John W., Richard Scott, and David Strang (1987). "Centralization, Fragmentation, and School District Complexity." *Administrative Science Quarterly,* 32, 186–201.

Meyer, Marshall W. (1968a). "Automation and Bureaucratic Structure." *American Journal of Sociology,* 74, 256–64.

—— (1968b). "Two Authority Structures of Bureaucratic Organization." *Administrative Science Quarterly,* 13, 211–18.

—— (1971). "Some Constraints in Analyzing Data on Organizational Structures." *American Sociological Review,* 36, 294–97.

—— (1975). "Leadership and Organizational Structure." *American Journal of Sociology,* 81, no. 3 (November), 514–42.

—— (1994). "Measuring Performance in Economic Organizations," in The Handbook of Economic Sociology. ed. Neil Smelser and Richard Swedberg. Princeton, NJ: Princeton University Press.

Meyer, Marshall W., and Associates (1978). *Environments and Organizations.* San Francisco: Jossey-Bass.

Meyer, Marshall W., and M. Craig Brown (1977). "The Process of Bureaucratization." *American Journal of Sociology,* 83, 364–85.

Meyer, Marshall W., and Lynn G. Zucker (1989). *Permanently Failing Organizations.* Newbury Park, CA: Sage.

Mezias, Stephen J. (1990). "An Institutional Model of Organizational Practice: Financial Reporting at the Fortune 200." *Administrative Science Quarterly,* 35, 431–57.

Michels, Robert (1949). *Political Parties.* New York: Free Press.

Miles, Raymond E., Charles C. Snow, and Jeffrey Pfeffer (1974). "Organization Environment: Concepts and Issues." *Industrial Relations,* 13, 244–64.

Milgrom, Paul, and John Roberts (1988). "An Economic Approach to Influence Activities in Organizations." *American Journal of Sociology,* 94, Supplement, S154–S179.

Miller, C. Chet, William H. Glick, Yau-de Wang, and George P. Huber (1991). "Understanding Technology-Structure Relationships: Theory Developing and Meta-Analytic Theory Testing." *Academy of Management Journal,* 34, 370–99.

Miller, Danny (1987). "Strategy Making on Structure: Analysis and Implications for Performance." *Academy of Management Journal,* 30, 7–32.

Miller, Danny, and Ming-Jer Chen (1994). "Sources and Consequences of Competitive Inertia: A Study of the U.S. Airline Industry." *Administrative Science Quarterly,* 39, 1–23.

Miller, Danny, and Cornelia Droge (1986). "Psychological and Traditional Determinants of Structure." *Administrative Science Quarterly,* 31, 539–60.

Miller, Danny, and Peter H. Friesen (1984). *Organizations: A Quantum View.* Englewood Cliffs, NJ: Prentice Hall.

Miller, George A. (1967). "Professionals in Bureaucracy, Alienation among Industrial Scientists and Engineers." *American Sociological Review, 32,* 755–68.

Milliken, Frances J. (1990). "Perceiving and Interpreting Environmental Change: An Examination of College Administrators' Interpretation of Changing Demographics." *Academy of Management Journal, 33,* 42–63.

Milner, Murray, Jr. (1980). *Unequal Care: A Case Study of Interorganizational Relations in Health Care.* New York: Columbia University Press.

Miner, Anne S. (1987). "Idiosyncratic Jobs in Formalized Organizations." *Administrative Science Quarterly, 32,* 327–51.

Miner, Anne S., Terry L. Amburgey, and Timothy M. Steams (1990). "Interorganizational Linkages and Population Dynamics: Buffering and Transformational Skills." *Administrative Science Quarterly, 35,* 689–713.

Mintz, Beth, and Michael Schwartz (1981). "Interlocking Directorates and Interest Group Formation." *American Sociological Review, 46,* 951–69.

Mintzberg, Henry (1979). *The Structuring of Organizations.* Englewood Cliffs, NJ: Prentice Hall.

———— (1983). *Power In and Around Organizations.* Englewood Cliffs, NJ: Prentice Hall.

Mintzberg, Henry, and Jim Waters (1990). "Does Decision Get In the Way?" *Organizational Studies, 11,* 1–6.

Mitroff, Ian I., and Ralph H. Kilmann (1984). *Corporate Tragedies: Product Tampering, Sabotage, and Other Catastrophes.* New York: Praeger.

Mizruchi, Mark S. (1989). "Similarity of Political Behavior among Large American Corporations." *American Journal of Sociology, 95,* 401–24.

———— (1992). *The Structure of Corporate Political Action: Interfirm Relations and Their Consequences.* Cambridge: Harvard University Press.

Mizruchi, Mark S., and David Bunting (1981). "Influence in Corporate Networks: An Examination of Four Measures." *Administrative Science Quarterly, 26,* 475–89.

Mizruchi, Mark S., and Linda Brewster Stearns (1988). "A Longitudinal Study of the Formation of Interlocking Directorates." *Administrative Science Quarterly, 33,* 194–210.

Moch, Michael K. (1976). "Structure and Organizational Resource Allocation." *Administrative Science Quarterly, 21,* 661–74.

Moch, Michael K., and Edward V. Morse (1977). "Size, Centralization, and Organizational Adoption of Innovation." *American Sociological Review, 43,* 716–25.

Mohan, Mary Leslie (1993). *Organizational Communication and Cultural Vision: Approaches for Analysis.* Albany: State University of New York Press.

Mohr, Lawrence B. (1971). "Organizational Technology and Organizational Structure." *Administrative Science Quarterly, 16,* 444–51.

———— (1973). "The Concept of Organizational Goal." *American Political Science Review, 67,* 470–81.

Molnar, Joseph J. (1978). "Comparative Organizational Properties and Interorganizational Interdependence." *Sociology and Social Research, 63,* 24–48.

Molnar, Joseph J., and David L. Rogers (1979). "A Comparative Model of Interorganizational Conflict." *Administrative Science Quarterly, 24,* 405–24.

Molotch, Harvey, and Marilyn Lester (1975). "Accidental News: The Great Oil Spill as Local Occurrence and National Event." *American Journal of Sociology, 81,* 235–60.

Moore, Gwen (1979). "The Structure of a National Elite Network." *American Sociological Review, 44,* 673–92.

Morgan, Gareth (1986). *Images of Organizations.* Beverly Hills, CA: Sage.

Morrill, Calvin (1991). "Conflict Management, Honor, and Organizational Change." *American Journal of Sociology, 97,* 585–621.

Morrissey, Joseph P., Richard H. Hall, and Michael L. Lindsey (1981). *Interorganizational Relations: A Sourcebook of Measures for Mental Health Programs.* Albany: Special Projects Research Unit, New York State Office of Mental Health.

Mott, Basil J. F. (1968). *Anatomy of a Coordinating Council.* Pittsburgh: University of Pittsburgh Press.

Mouzelis, Nicos P. (1967). *Organization and Bureaucracy: An Analysis of Modern Theories.* Chicago: Aldine.

Mulford, Charles L. (1980). "Dyadic Properties as Correlates of Exchange and Conflict between Organizations." Unpublished paper, Department of Sociology, Iowa State University.

——— (1984). *Interorganizational Relations: Implications for Community Development.* New York: Human Sciences Press.

Mulford, Charles L., and Mary Ann Mulford (1980). "Interdependence and Intraorganizational Structure for Voluntary Organizations." *Journal of Voluntary Action Research,* 9, 20–34.

Nagi, Saad Z. (1974). "Gate-Keeping Decisions in Service Organizations: When Validity Fails." *Human Organization,* 33, 47–58.

Nee, Victor (1992). "Organizational Dynamics of Market Transition: Hybrid Forms, Property Rights, and Mixed Economy in China." *Administrative Science Quarterly,* 37, 1–27.

Needleman, Martin L., and Carolyn Needleman (1979). "Organizational Crime: Two Models of Criminogenesis." *Sociological Quarterly,* 20, 517–28.

Negandhi, Anant R., and Bernard C. Reimann (1972). "A Contingency Theory of Organization Re-examined in the Context of a Developing Country." *Academy of Management Journal,* 15, 137–46.

——— (1973a). "Correlates of Decentralization: Closed and Open System Perspectives." *Academy of Management Journal,* 16, 570–82.

——— (1973b). "Task Environment, Decentralization and Organizational Effectiveness." *Human Relations,* 26, 203–14.

Nelson, Joel I. (1966). "Clique Contacts and Family Orientations." *American Sociological Review,* 31, 663–72.

New York Times (1981). April 27, sec. A.

Noon, Mike, and Rick Delbridge (1993). "News from Behind My Head." *Organization Studies,* 14, 23–36.

Oliver, Christine (1990). "Determinants of Interorganizational Relationships: Integration and Future Directions." *Academy of Management Review,* 15, 241–65.

——— (1992). "The Antecedents of Deinstitutionalization." *Organization Studies,* 13, 563–88.

Olsen, Johan P. (1981). "Integrated Organizational Participation in Government," in *Handbook of Organizational Design,* Vol. 2, ed. Paul C. Nystrom and William H. Starbuck. New York: Oxford University Press.

Organ, Dennis W., and Charles N. Greene (1981). "The Effects of Formalization on Professional Involvement: A Compensatory Process." *Administrative Science Quarterly,* 26, 237–52.

Ornstein, Michael (1984). "Interlocking Directorates in Canada: Intercorporate or Class Alliance?" *Administrative Science Quarterly,* 29, 210–37.

Orton, J. Douglas, and Karl E. Weick (1990). "Loosely Coupled System: A Reconceptualization." *Academy of Management Review,* 15, 203–23.

Ott, J. Steven (1989). *The Organizational Culture Perspective.* Chicago: Dorsey.

Ouchi, William G. (1977). "The Relationship between Organizational Structure and Organizational Control." *Administrative Science Quarterly,* 22, 95–113.

Ouchi, William G., and Alfred M. Jaeger (1978). "Social Structure and Organizational Type," in *Environments and Organizations,* ed. Marshall W. Meyer and Associates. San Francisco: Jossey-Bass.

Ouchi, William G., and Jerry B. Johnson (1978). "Types of Organizational Control and Their Relation to Emotional Well-Being." *Administrative Science Quarterly,* 23, 293–317.

Ouchi, William G., and Mary Ann Maguire (1975). "Organizational Control: Two Functions." *Administrative Science Quarterly,* 20, 559–69.

Palmer, Donald, Brad M. Barber, and Xuequang Zhou (1995). "The Finance Conception of Control: The Theory That Ate New York?" *American Sociological Review,* 60, 504–508.

Palmer, Donald, Brad M. Barber, Xuequang Zhou, and Yasemin Soysal (1995). "The Friendly and Predatory Acquisition of Large U.S. Corporations in the 1960s: The Other Contested Terrain." *American Sociological Review,* 60, 469–499.

Palmer, Donald A., Roger Friedland, P. Devereaux Jennings, and Melanie E. Powers (1987). "The Economics and Politics of Structure: The Multidivisional Form and the Large U.S. Corporation." *Administrative Science Quarterly*, 32, 25–48.

Palmer, Donald, Roger Friedland, and Jitendra V. Singh (1986). "The Ties That Bind: Organizational and Class Bases of Stability in a Corporate Interlock Network." *American Sociological Review*, 51, 781–96.

Palmer, Donald A., P. Devereaux Jennings, and Xueguang Zhou (1993). "Late Adoption of the Multidivision Form by Large U.S. Corporations: Institutional, Political, and Economic Accounts." *Administrative Science Quarterly*, 38, 100–131.

Parsons, Talcott (1960). *Structure and Process in Modern Society*. New York: Free Press.

Pascale, Richard (1985). "The Paradox of 'Corporate Culture': Reconciling Ourselves to Socialization." *California Management Review*, 27, 26–41.

Pennings, Johannes M. (1973). "Measures of Organizational Structure: A Methodological Note." *American Journal of Sociology*, 79, 686–704.

———— (1980a). "Environmental Influences on the Creation Process," in *The Organizational Life Cycle*, ed. John R. Kimberly and Robert H. Miles and Associates. San Francisco: Jossey-Bass.

———— (1980b). *Interlocking Directorates*. San Francisco: Jossey-Bass.

———— (1982). "Organizational Birth Frequencies: An Empirical Investigation." *Administrative Science Quarterly*, 27, 120–44.

———— (1987). "On the Nature of New Technology as Organizational Innovation," in *New Technology in Organizational Innovation: The Development and Diffusion of Microelectronics*, ed. Johannes M. Pennings and Arend Buitendam, 3–12. Cambridge, MA: Ballinger.

Pennings, Johannes M., and Paul S. Goodman (1977). "Toward a Workable Framework," in *New Perspectives on Organizational Effectiveness*, ed. S. Goodman and Johannes M. Pennings. San Francisco: Jossey-Bass.

Perrow, Charles (1961). "The Analysis of Goals in Complex Organizations." *American Sociological Review*, 26, 688–99.

———— (1967). "A Framework for the Comparative Analysis of Organizations." *American Sociological Review* 32, 194–208.

———— (1970a). "Departmental Power and Perspective in Industrial Firms," in *Power in Organizations*, ed. Mayer N. Zald. Nashville: Vanderbilt University Press.

———— (1970b). *Organizational Analysis*. Belmont, CA: Wadsworth.

———— (1977). "Three Types of Effectiveness Studies," in *New Perspectives on Organizational Effectiveness*, ed. Paul S. Goodman and Johannes M. Pennings. San Francisco: Jossey-Bass.

———— (1979). *Complex Organizations: A Critical Essay*, 2nd ed. Glenview, IL: Scott, Foresman.

———— (1983). "The Organizational Context of Human Factors Engineering." *Administrative Science Quarterly*, 28, 521–41.

———— (1984). *Normal Accidents: Living with High-Risk Technologies*. New York: Basic Books.

Perrow, Charles, and Mauro F. Guillen (1990). *The AIDS Disaster: The Failure of Organizations in New York and the Nation*. New Haven: Yale University Press.

Perrucci, Robert, and Marc Pilisuk (1970). "Leaders and Ruling Elites: The Interorganizational Bases of Community Power." *American Sociological Review*, 35, 1040–57.

Peter, Laurence J., and Raymond Hull (1969). *The Peter Principle*. New York: William Brown.

Peters, Thomas J., and Robert H. Waterman, Jr. (1982). *In Search of Excellence: Lessons from America's Best-Run Companies*. New York: Harper and Row.

Peterson, Richard A. (1970). "Some Consequences of Differentiation," in *Power in Organizations*, ed. Mayer N. Zald. Nashville: Vanderbilt University Press.

———— (1981). "Entrepreneurship and Organization," in *Handbook of Organizational Design*, Vol. 1, ed. Paul C. Nystrom and William H. Starbuck. New York: Oxford University Press.

Pfeffer, Jeffrey (1972a). "Merger as a Response to Organizational Interdependence." *Administrative Science Quarterly*, 17, 328–94.

———— (1972b). "Size and Composition of Corporate Boards of Directors." *Administrative Science Quarterly*, 17, 218–28.

——— (1977). "Power and Resource Allocation in Organizations," in *New Directions in Organizational Behavior,* ed. Barry Staw and Gerald Salancik. Chicago: St. Clair Press.

——— (1978). "The Micropolitics of Organizations," in *Environments and Organizations,* ed. Marshall W. Meyer and Associates. San Francisco: Jossey-Bass.

——— (1981). *Power in Organizations.* Marshfield, MA: Pitman.

——— (1982). *Organizations and Organization Theory.* Boston: Pitman.

——— (1983). "Organizational Demography," in *Research in Organizational Behavior,* Vol. 5, ed. L. L. Cummings and Barry M. Staw. Greenwich, CT: JAI Press.

——— (1992). *Managing with Power: Politics and Influence in Organizations.* Cambridge: Harvard Business School Press.

Pfeffer, Jeffrey, and Yinon Cohen (1984). "Determinants of Internal Labor Markets in Organizations." *Administrative Science Quarterly,* 29, 550–72.

Pfeffer, Jeffrey, and Alison Davis-Blake (1987). "The Effect of the Proportion of Women on Salaries: The Case of College Administrators." *Administrative Science Quarterly,* 32, 1–24.

Pfeffer, Jeffrey, and Huseyin Leblebici (1973). "The Effect of Competition on Some Dimensions of Organizational Structure." *Social Forces,* 52, 268–79.

Pfeffer, Jeffrey, and Anthony Long (1977). "Resource Allocation in United Funds: Examination of Power and Dependence." *Social Forces,* 55, 776–90.

Pfeffer, Jeffrey, and William L. Moore (1980). "Average Tenure of Academic Department Heads: The Effects of Paradigm, Size, and Departmental Demography." *Administrative Science Quarterly,* 25, 387–406.

Pfeffer, Jeffrey, and Phillip Nowak (1976). "Joint Ventures and Interorganizational Dependence." *Administrative Science Quarterly,* 21, 398–418.

Pfeffer, Jeffrey, and Gerald R. Salancik (1974). "Organizational Decision Making as a Political Process: The Case of a University Budget." *Administrative Science Quarterly,* 19, 135–51.

——— (1978). *The External Control of Organizations: A Resource Dependence Perspective.* New York: Harper and Row.

Pfeffer, Jeffrey, Gerald R. Salancik, and Huseyin Leblebici (1978). "Uncertainty and Social Influence in Organizational Decision Making," in *Environments and Organizations,* ed. Marshall W. Meyer and Associates. San Francisco: Jossey-Bass.

Pheysey, Diana C. (1993) *Organization Culture: Types and Transformations.* London: Routledge & Kegan Paul.

Pinder, Craig C., and Larry F. Moore (1979). "The Resurrection of Taxonomy to Aid the Development of Middle Range Theories of Organizational Behavior." *Administrative Science Quarterly,* 24, 99–118.

Pinfield, Lawrence T. (1986). "A Field Evaluation of Perspectives on Organizational Decision Making." *Administrative Science Quarterly,* 33, 365–88.

Pondy, Louis R. (1967). "Organizational Conflict: Concepts and Models." *Administrative Science Quarterly,* 12, 296–320.

——— (1969). "Varieties of Organizational Conflict." *Administrative Science Quarterly,* 14, 499–505.

——— (1970). "Toward a Theory of Internal Resource Allocation," in *Power in Organizations,* ed. Mayer N. Zald. Nashville: Vanderbilt University Press.

Portugal, Ed (1993). "Boards of Directors: Links, Breaks, and Reconstitutions." Ph.D. diss., State University of New York at Albany.

Powell, Walter W. (1985). *Getting Into Print.* Chicago: University of Chicago Press.

———, ed. (1987). *The Nonprofit Sector: A Research Handbook.* New Haven: Yale University Press.

Powell, Walter W., and Paul DiMaggio (1991). *The New Institutionalism in Organizational Analysis.* Chicago: University of Chicago Press.

Powell, Walter W., Kenneth W. Koput, and Laurel Smith-Doerr (1996). "Interorganizational Collaboration and the Locus of Innovation: Networks of Learning in Biotechnology." *Administrative Science Quarterly,* 41, 116–45.

Price, James L. (1968). *Organizational Effectiveness: An Inventory of Propositions.* Homewood, IL: Richard D. Irwin.

———— (1972). *Handbook of Organizational Measurement.* Lexington, MA: D. C. Heath.

Price, James L., and Charles W. Mueller (1986). *Handbook of Organizational Measurement.* Marshfield, MA: Pitman.

Priest, T. B., and Robert A. Rothman (1985). "Lawyers in Corporate Chief Executive Positions: A Historical Analysis of Careers." *Work and Occupations,* 12, 131–46.

Prokesh, Steven E. (1985). *New York Times,* October 28, sec. D.

Provan, Keith G., Janice M. Beyer, and Carlos Kruytbosch (1980). "Environmental Linkages and Power in Resource-Dependence Relations between Organizations." *Administrative Science Quarterly,* 25, 200–225.

Provan, Keith G., and H. Brinton Milward (1995). "A Preliminary Theory of Interorganizational Network Effectiveness: A Comparative Study of Four Community Mental Health Systems." *Administrative Science Quarterly,* 40, 1–33.

Pugh, Derek S. (1966). "Modern Organization Theory: A Psychological and Sociological Study." *Psychological Bulletin,* 66, 235–51.

———— (1969). "The Context of Organizational Structures." *Administrative Science Quarterly,* 14, 91–114.

Pugh, Derek S., David J. Hickson, and C. R. Hinings (1969). "An Empirical Taxonomy of Work Organizations." *Administrative Science Quarterly,* 14, 115–26.

————, eds. (1985). *Writers on Organizations.* Beverly Hills, CA: Sage.

Pugh, Derek S., David J. Hickson, C. R. Hinings, K. M. Lupton, K. M. McDonald, C. Turner, and T. Lupton (1963). "A Conceptual Scheme for Organizational Analysis." *Administrative Science Quarterly,* 8, 289–315.

Pugh, Derek S., D. J. Hickson, C. R. Hinings, and C. Turner (1968). "Dimensions of Organizational Structure." *Administrative Science Quarterly,* 13, 65–105.

Quinn, Robert E. (1977). "Coping with Cupid: The Formation, Impact, and Management of Romantic Relationships in Organizations." *Administrative Science Quarterly,* 22, 30–45.

Quinn, Robert E., and John Rohrbaugh (1983). "A Spatial Model of Effectiveness Criteria: Towards a Competing Values Approach to Organizational Analysis." *Management Science,* 29, 363–77.

Raelin, Joseph A. (1982). "A Policy Output Model of Interorganizational Relations." *Organization Studies,* 3, 243–67.

Rahim, M. Afzahur (1986). *Managing Conflict in Organizations.* New York: Praeger.

———— (1989). *Managing Conflict: An Interdisciplinary Approach.* New York: Praeger.

Rakowski, Cathy A. (1994). *Contrapunto: The Informal Sector Debate in Latin America.* Albany: State University of New York Press.

Ranson, Stewart, Bob Hinings, and Royster Greenwood (1980). "The Structuring of Organizational Structures." *Administrative Science Quarterly,* 25, 1–17.

Rao, Hayagreeva, and Eric H. Neilsen (1992). "An Ecology of Agency Arrangement: Mortality of Savings and Loan Associations." *Administrative Science Quarterly,* 37, 448–470.

Raphael, Edna (1967). "The Andersen-Warton Hypothesis in Local Unions: A Comparative Study." *American Sociological Review,* 32, 768–76.

Rawls, J. (1971). *A Theory of Justice.* Cambridge: Harvard University Press.

Reid, William J. (1969). "Inter-organizational Coordination in Social Welfare: A Theoretical Approach to Analysis and Intervention," in *Readings in Community Organization Practice,* ed. Ralph M. Kramer and Henry Spect. Englewood Cliffs, NJ: Prentice Hall.

Reimann, Bernard C. (1975). "Organizational Effectiveness and Management's Public Values: A Canonical Analysis." *Academy of Management Journal,* 18, 224–41.

Reinganum, Marc R. (1985). "The Effect of Executive Succession on Stockholder Wealth." *Administrative Science Quarterly,* 30, 46–60.

Reskin, Barbara, and Irene Padevic (1994). *Women and Men at Work.* Thousand Oaks, CA: Pine Forge.

Revkin, Andrew C. (1997) "Babbitt Assails G.E. Over Ridding Hudson of Chemicals." *New York Times,* September 26, sec. B.

Rich, Phillip (1992). "The Organizational Taxonomy: Definition and Design." *Academy of Management Review,* 17, 758–81.

Richardson, R. Jack (1987). "Directorship Interlocks and Corporate Profitability." *Administrative Science Quarterly,* 32, 367–86.

Rifkin, Jeremy (1995). *The End of Work: The Decline of the Global Labor Force and the Dawn of the Post-Market Era.* New York: Putnam.

Ritzer, George (1989). "The Permanently New Economy: The Case for Reviving Economic Sociology." *Work and Occupations,* 16, 243–72.

Ritzer, George, and David Walczak (1986). *Working: Conflict and Change.* Englewood Cliffs, NJ: Prentice Hall.

Robbins, Stephen P. (1974). *Managing Organizational Conflict: A Nontraditional Approach.* Englewood Cliffs, NJ: Prentice Hall.

Roberts, Karlene H., Charles L. Hulin, and Denise M. Rousseau (1978). *Developing an Interdisciplinary Science of Organizations.* San Francisco: Jossey-Bass.

Robins, James A. (1987). "Organizational Economics: Notes on the Transaction Cost Theory in the Study of Organizations." *Administrative Science Quarterly,* 32, 68–86.

Romanelli, Elaine (1989). "Environments and Strategies of Organization Startup: Effects on Early Survival." *Administrative Science Quarterly,* 34, 369–87.

Romanelli, Elaine, and Michael Tushman (1994). Organizational Transformation as Punctuated Equilibrium: An Empirical Test. *Academy of Management Journal,* 37, 1141–66.

Romo, Frank P., and Michael Schwartz (1995). "The Structural Embeddedness of Business Decisions: The Migration of Manufacturing Plants in New York State, 1960 to 1985." *American Sociological Review,* 60, 874–907.

Rosenbaum, James E. (1979). "Organizational Career Mobility: Promotion Chances in a Corporation during Periods of Growth and Contraction." *American Journal of Sociology,* 85, 21–48.

Rosenweig, Philip M., and Jitendra V. Singh (1991). "Organizational Environments and the Multinational Enterprise." *Academy of Management Review,* 16, no. 2, 340–61.

Rosner, M., B. Kovacic, A. S. Tannenbaum, M. Vianello, and G. Weiser (1973). "Worker Participation and Influence in Five Countries." *Industrial Relations,* 12, 200–212.

Rosow, Jerome M., ed. (1974). *The Worker and the Job: Coping with Change.* Englewood Cliffs, NJ: Prentice Hall.

Ross, Jerry, and Barry M. Staw (1993). "Organizational Escalation and Exit: Lessons from the Shoreham Nuclear Power Plant." *Academy of Management Journal,* 36, 701–32.

Rothschild, Joyce, and J. Allen Whitt (1986). *The Cooperative Workplace: Potentials and Dilemmas of Organizational Democracy and Participation.* New York: Cambridge University Press.

Rothschild-Whitt, Joyce (1979). "The Collectivist Organization: An Alternative to Rational Bureaucratic Models." *American Sociological Review,* 44, 519.

Rowan, Brian (1982). "Organizational Structure and the Institutional Environment: The Case of Public Schools." *Administrative Science Quarterly,* 27, 259–79.

Roy, William G. (1981). "The Process of Bureaucratization of the U.S. State Department and the Vesting of Economic Interests, 1886–1905." *Administrative Science Quarterly,* 26, 419–33.

——— (1983a). "Toward Clearer Thinking: A Reply." *Administrative Science Quarterly,* 28, 61–64.

——— (1983b). "The Unfolding of the Interlocking Directorate Structure of the United States." *American Sociological Review,* 48, 248–57.

Rubin, I. (1979). "Loose Structure, Retrenchment and Adaptability in the University." Paper presented at the Midwest Sociological Society meetings, Minneapolis.

Rus, Veljko (1972). "The Limits of Organized Participation," in *Proceedings of the First International Conference on Participation and Self-Management,* Vol. 2. Zagreb, Yugoslavia.

——— (1980). "Positive and Negative Power: Thoughts on the Dialectic of Power." *Organization Studies,* 1, 3–19.

Rushing, William A. (1968). "Hardness of Material as Related to Division of Labor in Manufacturing Industries." *Administrative Science Quarterly,* 13, 224–45.

Sabel, Charles F. (1982). *Work and Politics.* New York: Cambridge University Press.

Salancik, Gerald R., and Jeffrey Pfeffer (1974). "The Bases and Use of Power in Organizational Decision Making: The Case of a University." *Administrative Science Quarterly,* 19, 453–73.

——— (1977). "Constraints on Administrator Discretion: The Limited Influence of Mayors on City Budgets." *Urban Affairs Quarterly*, 12, 475–98.

Salancik, Gerald R., and James R. Mindl (1984). "Corporate Attributions as Strategic Illusions of Management Control." *Administrative Science Quarterly*, 29, 238–54.

Samuel, Yitzhak (1979). "An Exchange and Power Approach to the Concept of Organizational Effectiveness." Department of Sociology and Anthropology, Tel Aviv University, Israel.

Sanchez, Julio C. (1993). "The Long and Thorny Way to an Organizational Taxonomy." *Organizational Studies*, 14, 73–92.

Sanford, R. Nevitt (1964). "Individual Conflict and Organizational Interaction," in *Power and Conflict in Organizations*, ed. Robert L. Kahn and Elise Boulding. New York: Basic Books.

Schermerhorn, John R., Jr. (1975). "Determinants of Interorganizational Cooperation." *Academy of Management Journal*, 18, 846–56.

Schmidt, Stuart M., and Thomas A. Kochan (1972). "Conflict: Toward Conceptual Clarity." *Administrative Science Quarterly*, 17, 371–81.

Schmidt, Stuart M., and Thomas A. Kochan (1977). "Interorganizational Relationships: Patterns and Motivations." *Administrative Science Quarterly*, 22, 220–34.

Schneider, Susan C. (1989). "Strategy Formulation: The Impact of National Culture." *Organization Studies*, 10, 149–68.

Schollhammer, Hans (1971). "Organization Structures of Multinational Corporations." *Academy of Management Journal*, 14, 345–65.

Schoonhoven, Claudia Bird (1981). "Problems with Contingency Theory: Testing Assumptions Hidden within the Language of Contingency 'Theory.' " *Administrative Science Quarterly*, 26, 349–77.

Schreyogg, Georg (1980). "Contingency and Choice in Organization Theory." *Organization Studies*, 1, 305–26.

Schwochan, Susan, Peter Fenilee, and John Thomas Delaney (1988). "The Resource Allocation Effects of Mandated Relationships." *Administrative Science Quarterly*, 33, 418–37.

Scott, W. Richard (1964). "Theory of Organizations," in *Handbook of Modern Sociology*, ed. Robert E. L. Farris. Chicago: Rand McNally.

——— (1977). "Effectiveness of Organizational Effectiveness Studies," in *New Perspectives on Organizational Effectiveness,* ed. Paul S. Goodman and Johannes M. Pennings. San Francisco: Jossey-Bass.

——— (1981). *Organizations: Rational, Natural, and Open Systems*. Englewood Cliffs, NJ: Prentice Hall.

——— (1983). "Introduction: From Technology to Environment," in *Organizational Environments: Ritual and Rationality*, ed. John W. Meyer and W. Richard Scott. Beverly Hills, CA: Sage.

——— (1987a). *Organizations: Rational, Natural, and Open Systems*, 2nd ed. Englewood Cliffs, NJ: Prentice Hall.

——— (1987b). "The Adolescence of Institutional Theory." *Administrative Science Quarterly*, 32, 493–511.

——— (1990). "Technology and Structure: An Organizational-Level Perspective," in *Technology and Organizations*, ed. Paul S. Goodman, Lee Sproul, and Edwin Amenta, 109–43. San Francisco: Jossey-Bass.

——— (1991). *Organizations: Rational, Natural, and Open Systems*, 3rd ed. Englewood Cliffs, NJ: Prentice Hall.

——— (1996). "The Mandate Is Still Being Honored: In Defense of Weber's Disciples." *Administrative Science Quarterly*, 41, 163–71.

Scott, W. Richard, and Bruce L. Black, eds. (1986). The Organization of Mental Health Services: Societal and Community Systems. Beverly Hills, CA: Sage.

Seabright, Mark A., Daniel A. Levinthal, and Mark Fichman (1992). "Role of Individual Attachments in the Dissolution of Interorganizational Relationships." *Academy of Management Journal*, 35, 122–60.

Seashore, Stanley E. (1977). "An Elastic and Expandable Viewpoint," in *New Perspectives on Organizational Effectiveness*, ed. Paul S. Goodman and J. M. Pennings. San Francisco: Jossey-Bass.

Seashore, Stanley E., and Ephraim Yuchtman (1967). "Factorial Analysis of Organizational Performance." *Administrative Science Quarterly,* 12, 377–95.

Sebring, Robert H. (1977). "Health Councils as a Strategy for Community Change." *Journal of the Community Development Society,* 18, 74–85.

Seiler, Lauren H., and Gene F. Summers (1979). "Corporate Involvement in Community Affairs." *Sociological Quarterly,* 20, 375–86.

Selznick, Philip (1957). *Leadership in Administration.* New York: Harper and Row.

————— (1960). *The Organizational Weapon.* New York: Free Press.

————— (1966). *TVA and the Grass Roots,* Harper Torchbook ed. New York: Harper and Row.

Sewell, William H. (1992). "A Theory of Structure: Duality, Agency, and Transformation." *American Journal of Sociology,* 98, 1–29.

Shenkar, Oded (1984). "Is Bureaucracy Inevitable: The Chinese Experience." *Organizational Studies,* 5, 289–308.

Shrum, Wesley, and Robert Wuthnow (1988). "Reputational Status of Organizations in Technical Systems." *American Journal of Sociology,* 93, 882–912.

————— (1990). "Status Incongruence among Boundary Spanners: Structure, Exchange, and Conflict." *American Sociological Review,* 55, 496–511.

Sills, David L. (1957). *The Volunteers.* New York: Free Press.

Silverman, David (1971). *The Theory of Organizations: A Sociological Framework.* New York: Basic Books.

————— (1957). *Models of Men, Social and Rational.* New York: John Wiley.

Simmel, George (1902). "The Number of Members as Determining the Sociological Form of the Group II." *American Journal of Sociology,* 8, 158–96.

Simon, Herbert A. (1957). *Administrative Behavior.* New York: Free Press.

————— (1964). "On the Concept of Organizational Goal." *Administrative Science Quarterly,* 9, 1–22.

Simpson, Richard L. (1969). "Vertical and Horizontal Communication in Formal Organizations." *Administrative Science Quarterly,* 14, 188–96.

Singh, Jitendra V., David J. Tucker, and Robert J. House (1986). "Organizational Legitimacy and the Liability of Newness." *Administrative Science Quarterly,* 31, 171–93.

Smircich, Linda (1985). "Is the Concept of Culture a Paradigm for Understanding Organizations and Ourselves?" in *Organizational Culture,* ed. Peter J. Frost, Larry F. Moore, Meryl Reis Louis, Craig C. Lundberg, and Joanne Martin, 55–72. Beverly Hills, CA: Sage.

Smith, Kenwyn (1989). "The Movement of Conflict in Organizations: The Joint Dynamics of Splitting and Triangulation." *Administrative Science Quarterly,* 34, 1–20.

Smith, Mark, and Michael C. White (1987). "Strategy, CEO Specialization and Succession." *Administrative Science Quarterly,* 32, 263–80.

Smith, Vicki (1993). "Approaching Organizational Culture versus Cultural Approaches to Organizations: Let's Close the Gap." *Contemporary Sociology,* 22, 417–21.

Snow, Charles C., and Lawrence G. Hrebiniak (1980). "Strategy, Distinctive Competence and Organizational Performance." *Administrative Science Quarterly,* 25, 317–36.

Sorge, Arndt (1991). "Strategic Fit and the Societal Effect: Interpreting Cross-National Comparisons of Technology, Organization, and Human Resources." *Organization Studies,* 12, 161–90.

Spenner, Kenneth (1979). "Temporal Changes in Work Content." *American Sociological Review,* 44, 965–75.

————— (1983). "Deciphering Prometheus: Temporal Changes in the Skill Level of Work." *American Sociological Review,* 48, 824–37.

————— (1990). Skill: Meaning, Methods, and Measures. *Work and Occupations,* 17, 399–421.

Staber, Udo, and Howard Aldrich (1983). "Trade Association Stability and Public Policy," in *Organizational Theory and Public Policy,* ed. Richard H. Hall and Robert E. Quinn. Beverly Hills, CA: Sage.

Starbuck, William H. (1976). "Organizations and Their Environments," in *Handbook of Industrial and Organizational Psychology,* ed. Marvin D. Dunnette. Chicago: Rand McNally.

———— (1983). "Organizations as Action Generators." *American Sociological Review*, 48, 91–102.

Starbuck, William H., and Paul C. Nystrom (1981). "Designing and Understanding Organizations," in *Handbook of Organizational Design*, Vol. 1, ed. Paul C. Nystrom and William H. Starbuck. New York: Oxford University Press.

Staw, Barry M. (1982). "Counterforces to Change," in *Change in Organizations: New Perspectives on Theory, Research, and Practice*, ed. Paul S. Goodman and Associates. San Francisco: Jossey-Bass.

Staw, Barry M., Pamela McKechnie and Sheila M. Puffer (1983). "The Justification of Organizational Performance." *Administrative Science Quarterly*, 28, 582–600.

Staw, Barry M., and Jerry Ross (1989). "Understanding Behavior in Escalation Situations." *Science*, 246, 216–20.

Stearns, Linda Brewster and Kenneth D. Allan (1996). "Economic Behavior in Institutional Environments: The Corporate Merger Wave of the 1980s." *American Sociological Review*, 61, 699– 718.

Stearns, Linda Brewster, and Mark S. Mizruchi (1986). "Broken-Tie Reconstitution and the Functions of Interorganizational Interlocks: A Reexamination." *Administrative Science Quarterly*, 31, 522–38.

Steckmest, Francis W. (1982). *Corporate Performance: The Key to Public Trust*. New York: McGraw-Hill.

Steers, R. M. (1977). *Organizational Effectiveness: A Behavioral View*. Pacific Palisades, CA: Goodyear.

Stern, Robert, and Stephen Barley (1996). "Organizations and Social Systems: Organizational Theory's Neglected Mandate." *Administrative Science Quarterly*, 41, 146–62.

Stevenson, William B. (1990). "Formal Structure and Networks of Interaction within Organizations." *Social Science Research*, 19, 112–31.

Stinchcombe, Arthur L. (1959). "Bureaucratic and Craft Administration of Productions." *Administrative Science Quarterly*, 4, 168–87.

———— (1965). "Organizations and Social Structure," in *Handbook of Organizations*, ed. James G. March. Chicago: Rand McNally.

———— (1990). *Information and Organizations*. Berkeley and Los Angeles: University of California Press.

Stolzenberg, Ross M. (1978). "Bringing the Boss Back In: Employer Size, Employee Schooling and Socioeconomic Achievement." *American Sociological Review*, 43, 813–28.

Stone, Katherine (1973). "The Origins of Job Structures in the Steel Industry." *Radical America*, 7, 17–66.

Strang, David, and James N. Baron (1990). "Categorical Imperative: The Structure of Job Titles in California State Agencies." *American Sociological Review*, 55, 479–95.

Sutherland, Edwin H. (1940). "White-collar Criminality." *American Sociological Review*, 5, 1–12.

———— (1949). *White Collar Crime*. New York: Holt, Rinehart & Winston.

Sutton, John R. and Frank Dobbin (1996). "The Two Faces of Governance: Responses to Legal Uncertainty in U.S. Firms 1955–1985." *American Sociological Review*, 61, 794–811.

Sutton, John R., Frank Dobbin, John Meyer, and W. Richard Scott (1994). "The Legalization of the Workplace." *American Journal of Sociology*, 99, 944–71.

Sutton, Robert I. (1987). "The Process of Organizational Death: Disbanding and Reconnecting." *Administrative Science Quarterly*, 32, 542–69.

Swigert, Victoria Lynn, and Ronald A. Farrell (1980–81). "Corporate Homicide: Definitional Processes in the Creation of Deviance." *Law and Society Review*, 15, 163–82.

Tannenbaum, Arnold S. (1968). *Control in Organizations*. New York: McGraw-Hill.

Tannenbaum, Arnold S., Bogdan Kovacic, Menochen Rosner, Mino Vianello, and George Wieser (1974). *Hierarchy in Organizations*. San Francisco: Jossey-Bass.

Tannenbaum, Arnold S., and Tamas Rozgonyi (1986). *Authority and Reward in Organizations: An International Research*. Ann Arbor, MI: Survey Research Center.

Tausky, Curt (1984). *Work and Society: An Introduction to Industrial Sociology*. Itasca, IL: F. E. Peacock.

Tayeb, Monir (1987). "Contingency Theory and Culture: A Study of Matched English and Indian Manufacturing Firms." *Organization Studies*, 8, 241–61.

Taylor, Frederick W. (1911). *The Principles of Scientific Management*. New York: Harper and Row.

Taylor, James C. (1971). "Some Effects of Technology in Organizational Change." *Human Relations,* 24, 105–23.

Terkel, Studs (1974). *Working.* New York: Pantheon Books.

Terreberry, Shirley (1968). "The Evolution of Organizational Environments." *Administrative Science Quarterly,* 12, 590–613.

Thach, Liz, and Richard Woodman (1994). "Organizational Change and Information Technology: Managing on the Edge of Cyberspace." *Organizational Dynamics,* 23, 30–46.

Thomas, Alan Berkeley (1988). "Does Leadership Make a Difference to Organizational Performance?" *Administrative Science Quarterly,* 33, 388–400.

Thompson, James D. (1967). *Organizations in Action.* New York: McGraw-Hill.

Thompson, James D., and William McEwen (1958). "Organizational Goals and Environment: Goalsetting as an Interaction Process." *American Sociological Review,* 23, 23–31.

Thompson, Victor (1961). *Modern Organizations.* New York: Knopf.

Tolbert, Pamela S. (1985). "Institutional Environments and Resource Dependence: Sources of Administrative Structure in Institutions of Higher Education." *Administrative Science Quarterly,* 30, 1–13.

Tolbert, Pamela S., and Lynne G. Zucker (1983). "Institutional Sources of Change in the Formal Structure of Organizations: The Diffusion of Civil Service Reforms, 1880–1935." *Administrative Science Quarterly,* 28, 22–39.

——— (1996). "The Institutionalization of Institutional Theory." in *Handbook of Organization Studies,* ed. Stewart R. Clegg, Cynthia Hardy, and Walter R. Nord. Thousand Oaks, CA: Sage.

Tonry, Michael, and Albert J. Reiss, Jr., eds. (1994). *Beyond the Law: Crime in Complex Organizations.* Chicago: University of Chicago Press.

Tosi, Henry L., Jr., and John W. Slocum, Jr. (1984). "Contingency Theory: Some Suggested Directions." *Journal of Management,* 10, 9–26.

Toynbee, Arnold (1974). "As I See It." *Forbes,* 113, 68.

Tracy, Phelps, and Koya Azumi (1976). "Determinants of Administrative Control: A Test of a Theory with Japanese Factories." *American Sociological Review,* 41, 80–94.

Trice, Harrison M., and Janice M. Beyer (1993). *The Cultures of Work Organizations.* Englewood Cliffs, NJ: Prentice Hall.

Tsui, Anne S. (1990). "A Multiple-Constituency Model of Effectiveness: An Empirical Examination at the Human Resources Subunit Level." *Administrative Science Quarterly,* 35, 458–83.

Turk, Herman (1973). "Comparative Urban Structure from an Interorganizational Perspective." *Administrative Science Quarterly,* 18, 37–55.

Turner, Jonathan H. (1979). *The Structure of Social Theory,* rev. ed. Homewood, IL: Dorsey.

Turner, Jonathan H., and Alexandra Maryanski (1979). *Functionalism.* Menlo Park, CA: Benjamin/Cumming.

Tushman, Michael L., and Phillip Anderson (1986). "Technological Discontinuities and Organizational Environments." *Administrative Science Quarterly,* 31, 439–65.

Tushman, Michael L., and Richard B. Nelson (1990). "Introduction: Technology, Organizations, and Innovation." *Administrative Science Quarterly,* 35, 1–8.

Useem, Michael (1979). "The Social Organization of the American Business Elite and Participation of Corporate Directors in the Governance of American Institutions." *American Sociological Review,* 44, 553–72.

——— (1982). "Classwide Rationality in the Politics of Managers and Directors of Large Corporations in the United States and Great Britain." *Administrative Science Quarterly,* 27, 199–226.

——— (1984). *The Inner Circle.* New York: Oxford University Press.

Uzzi, Brian (1996). "The Sources and Consequences of Embeddedness for the Economic Performance of Organizations: The Network Effect." *American Sociological Review,* 60, 674–98.

——— (1997). "Social Structure and Competition in Interfirm Networks: The Paradox of Embeddedness." *Administrative Science Quarterly,* 42, 35–67.

Vallas, Steven P. (1990). "The Concept of Skill: A Critical Review." *Work and Occupations,* 17, 379–98.

Van Buren, Mark E. (1992). "Organizational Size and the Use of Firm Internal Markets in High Growth Establishments." *Social Science Research,* 21, 311–27.

Van de Ven, Andrew H. (1979). "Howard E. Aldrich: Organizations and Environments." *Administrative Science Quarterly,* 24, 320–26.

——— (1983). Review of Thomas B. Peters and Robert H. Waterman, Jr., *In Search of Excellence: Lessons from America's Best-Run Companies* (New York: Harper and Row, 1982), in *Administrative Science Quarterly,* 28, no. 4, 621–22.

Van de Ven, Andrew H., Andre L. Delbecq, and Richard Koenig, Jr. (1976). "Determinants of Coordination Modes within Organizations." *American Sociological Review,* 41, 322–38.

Van de Ven, Andrew H., and Diane L. Ferry (1980). *Measuring and Assessing Organizations.* New York: John Wiley.

Van de Ven, Andrew H., and Gordon Walker (1984). "The Dynamics of Interorganizational Coordination." *Administrative Science Quarterly,* 29, 598–621.

Van Houten, Donald R. (1987). "The Political Economy and Technical Control of Work Humanization in Sweden during the 1970s and 1980s." *Work and Occupations,* 14, 483–513.

Vaughan, Diane (1983). *Controlling Unlawful Organizational Behavior: Social Structure and Corporate Misconduct.* Chicago: University of Chicago Press.

——— (1990). "Autonomy, Interdependence, and Social Control: NASA and the Space Shuttle Challenger." *Administrative Science Quarterly,* 35, 225–57.

——— (1992). "Regulating Risk: Implications of the Challenger Accident," in *Organizations, Uncertainties, and Risk,* ed. James F. Short, Jr., and Lee Clark, 235–54. Boulder, CO: Westview Press.

——— (1996). *The Challenger Launch Decision: Risky Technology, Culture, and Deviance at NASA.* Chicago: University of Chicago Press.

Verhovek, Sam Howe (1993). "A Texas County Snubs Apple Over Unwed-Partner Policy." *New York Times,* December 2, A1, BII.

Waegel, William B., M. David Ermann, and Alan M. Horowitz (1981). "Organizational Responses to Imputations of Deviance." *Sociological Quarterly,* 22, 43–55.

Wager, L. Wesley (1972). "Organizational 'Linking-Pins': Hierarchical Status and Communicative Roles in Interlevel Conferences." *Human Relations,* 25, 307–26.

Walsh, Kieron, Bob Hinings, Roystor Greenwood, and Stewart Ransom (1981). "Power and Advantage in Organizations." *Organization Studies,* 2, 131–52.

Wamsley, Garry L. (1970). "Power and the Crisis of the Universities," in *Power in Organizations,* ed. Mayer N. Zald. Nashville: University of Tennessee Press.

Wamsley, Garry L., and Mayer N. Zald (1973). *The Political Economy of Public Organizations.* Lexington, MA: D. C. Heath.

Warren, Roland (1967). "The Interorganizational Field as a Focus for Investigation." *Administrative Science Quarterly,* 12, 396–419.

Warriner, Charles K. (1956). "Groups Are Real: A Reaffirmation." *American Sociological Review,* 21, 549–54.

——— (1979). "Empirical Taxonomics of Organizations: Problematics in Their Development." Unpublished paper. Lawrence: University of Kansas.

——— (1980). "Organizational Types: Notes on the 'Organizational Species' Concept." Lawrence: Department of Sociology, University of Kansas.

Warriner, Charles K., Richard H. Hall, and Bill McKelvey (1981). "The Comparative Description of Organizations: A Research Note and Invitation." *Organizational Studies,* 2, no. 2 (April), 387–88.

Weber, Max (1947). *The Theory of Social and Economic Organization,* trans. A. M. Parsons and T. Parsons. New York: Free Press.

——— (1952). *The Protestant Ethic and the Spirit of Capitalism.* New York: Scribner.

——— (1968). *Economy and Society: An Outline of Interpretive Sociology.* New York: Bedminster.

Weick, Karl E. (1976). "Educational Organizations as Loosely Coupled Systems." *Administrative Science Quarterly,* 21, 1–19.

——— (1979). *The Social Psychology of Organizing,* 2nd ed. Reading, MA: Addison-Wesley.

———— (1990). "Technology as Equivoque: Sensemaking in New Technologies," in *Technology and Organizations*, ed. Paul S. Goodman, Lee Sproul, and Edwin Amenta, 1–44. San Francisco: Jossey-Bass.

Weick, Karl E., and Karlene H. Roberts (1993). "Collective Mind in Organizations: Heedful Interrelations on Flight Decks." *Administrative Science Quarterly*, 38, 357–81.

Weiner, Nan (1977). "Situational and Leadership Influence on Organizational Performance." Columbus: College of Administrative Science, Ohio State University.

Weisbrod, Burton A. (1989). "Rewarding Performance That Is Hard to Measure: The Private Nonprofit Sector." *Science*, 244, 541–46.

Weitzel, William, and Ellen Jonsson (1989). "Decline in Organizations: A Literature Integration and Extension." *Administrative Science Quarterly*, 34, 91–109.

Whetten, David A. (1980). "Sources, Responses and Effects of Organizational Decline," in *The Organizational Life Cycle*, ed. John R. Kimberly and Robert H. Miles and Associates. San Francisco: Jossey-Bass.

White, Harrison (1971). *System Models of Mobility in Organizations*. Cambridge: Harvard University Press.

Whitley, Richard D. (1991). "The Social Construction of Business Systems in East Asia." *Organizational Studies*, 12, 1–28.

Wholey, Douglas R., Jon B. Christianson, and Susan M. Sanchez (1992). "Organizational Size and Failure among Health Maintenance Organizations." *American Sociological Review*, 57, 829–42.

Wiewel, Wim, and Albert Hunter (1985). "The Interorganizational Network as a Resource: A Comparative Case Study on Organizational Genesis." *Administrative Science Quarterly*, 30, 482–96.

Wildavsky, Aaron (1964). *The Politics of the Budgetary Process*. Boston: Little, Brown.

Wilensky, Harold (1967). *Organizational Intelligence: Knowledge and Policy in Government and Industry*. New York: Basic Books.

Williamson, Oliver E. (1975). Markets and Hierarchies: *Analysis and Antitrust Implications*. New York: Free Press.

———— (1981). "The Economics of Organizations: The Transaction Cost Approach." *American Journal of Sociology*, 87, 548–77.

———— (1985). *The Economic Institutions of Capitalism*. New York: Free Press.

Williamson, Oliver E., and William G. Ouchi (1981). "The Markets and Hierarchies Program of Research: Origins, Implications, Prospects," in *Perspectives on Organizational Design and Behavior*, ed. Andrew H. Van de Ven and William E. Joyce. New York: Wiley Interscience.

Withey, Michael, and William H. Cooper (1989). "Predicting Exit, Voice, Loyalty, and Neglect." *Administrative Science Quarterly*, 34, 521–39.

Wood, James R. (1975). "Legitimate Control and Organizational Transcendance." *Social Forces*, 54, 199–211.

———— (1981). *Leadership in Voluntary Organizations: The Controversy over Social Action in Protestant Churches*. New Brunswick, NJ: Rutgers University Press.

Woodward, Joan (1958). Management and Technology. London: Her Majesty's Stationery Office.

———— (1965). *Industrial Organizations: Theory and Practice*. London: Oxford University Press.

Work in America (1973). Prepared under auspices of W. E. Upjohn Institute. Cambridge: MIT Press.

Yarmolinsky, Adam (1975). "Institutional Paralysis." *Daedalus*, 104, 61–67.

Yeager, Peter C. (1982). Review of Francis W. Steckmest, *Corporate Performance: The Key to Public Trust* (New York: McGraw-Hill), in *Contemporary Sociology*, 11, 747–48.

Young, Ruth C. (1988). "Is Population Ecology a Useful Paradigm for the Study of Organizations?" *American Journal of Sociology*, 94, 1–24.

———— (1989). "Reply to Freeman and Hannan and Brittain and Wholey." *American Journal of Sociology*, 95, 445–46.

Yuchtman, Ephraim, and Stanley Seashore (1967). "A System Resource Approach to Organizational Effectiveness." *American Sociological Review*, 32, 891–903.

Yukl, Gary A. (1981). *Leadership in Organizations*. Englewood Cliffs, NJ: Prentice Hall.

—————— (1989). *Leadership in Organizations,* 2nd ed. Englewood Cliffs, NJ: Prentice Hall.

Zajac, Edward J., and James D. Westphal (1996). "Director Reputation, CEO-Board Power, and the Dynamics of Board Interlocks." *Administrative Science Quarterly,* 41, 507–29.

Zald, Mayer N. (1969). "The Structure of Society and Social Service Integration." *Social Science Quarterly,* 50, 577–67.

——————, ed. (1970). *Organizational Change: The Political Economy of the YMCA.* Chicago: University of Chicago Press.

Zalkind, Sheldon, and Timothy W. Costello (1962). "Perceptions: Some Recent Research and Implications for Administration." *Administrative Science Quarterly,* 7, 218–35.

Zaltman, Gerald, Robert Duncan, and Jonny Holbek (1973). *Innovations and Organizations.* New York: Wiley Interscience.

Zammuto, Raymond F. (1982). *Assessing Organizational Effectiveness.* Albany: State University of New York Press.

Zeitlin, Maurice (1974). "Corporate Ownership and Control: The Large Corporation and the Capitalist Class." *American Journal of Sociology,* 79, 1073–1119.

—————— (1976). "In Class Theory of the Large Corporation: Response to Others." *American Journal of Sociology,* 81, 894–903.

Zeitz, Gerald (1980). "Interorganizational Dialectics." *Administrative Science Quarterly,* 25, 72–78.

—————— (1983). "Structural and Individual Determinants of Organizational Morale and Satisfaction." *Social Forces,* 61, 1088–1108.

—————— (1984). "Bureaucratic Role Characteristics and Member Affective Response in Organizations." *Sociological Quarterly,* 25, 301–18.

Zenger, Todd R., and Barbara S. Lawrence (1989). "Organizational Demography: The Differential Effects of Age and Tenure Distributions on Technical Communication." *Academy of Management Journal,* 32, 353–76.

Zey, Mary (1992). "Criticisms of Rational Choice Models," in *Decision Making: Alternatives to Rational Choice Models,* ed. Mary Zey, 9–31. Newbury Park, CA: Sage.

Zhou, Xueguant (1993). "The Dynamics of Organizational Rules." *American Journal of Sociology,* 98, 1134–66.

Zucker, Lynne G. (1977). "The Role of Institutionalization in Cultural Persistence." *American Sociological Review,* 42, 726–43.

——————, ed. (1988). *Institutional Patterns and Organizations: Culture and Environment.* Cambridge, MA: Ballinger.

Name Index

Subject Index

336